DECATUR-DeKALB LI
REGIONAL SERVIC
ROCKDALE COUN
NEWTON COUNT

D1172867

WITHDRAWN

ELGAR O.M.

ELGAR

O.M.

A Study of a Musician

By
PERCY M. YOUNG
M.A., MUS.D.

WITHDRAWN

DECATUR-DeKALB LIBRARY.
REGIONAL SERVICE
ROCKDALE COUNTY
NEWTON COUNTY
109044

COLLINS
ST JAMES'S PLACE, LONDON
1955

B
Elgar
Yo

PRINTED IN GREAT BRITAIN
COLLINS CLEAR-TYPE PRESS : LONDON AND GLASGOW

Ga 420(600)
56

To * * *
semper fidelis

And thou art wrapp'd and swathed around in dreams,
Dreams that are true, yet enigmatical;
For the belongings of thy present state,
Save through such symbols, come not home to thee.

Cardinal J. H. Newman's DREAM OF GERONTIUS

CONTENTS

CONTENTS
Part Two

ILLUSTRATIONS

With the exception of the engraving, all illustrations
which are not acknowledged above are from the
Elgar papers at Broadheath, and are reproduced by
permission of Mrs. C. Elgar Blake.
On some of the sketches shown the letter 'K' is
written, in abbreviation of 'Koppied.' When Elgar
transferred his ideas to a fair copy he invariably
made this mark. The more orthodox 'copied'
was reserved for music which had been
professionally transcribed.

PREFACE

In the roll of great composers stand the names of three or four Englishmen. Native scholars and critics will continue to argue the relative merits of those few of our race who have by their genius enriched the music of the world; but Elgar, beyond the reach of critics and scholiasts, will remain firm in universal respect. He it was who, in the depressed days of English music, conquered a tyranny, and released us from the ignominy of being a mere colony of German pedants. To the glory of Germany, however, let it be said that there Elgar's greatness was recognised before we ourselves were quite alive to it.

Elgar wrote great works. He also wrote works which, though outside the range of accepted greatness, have compelled the attention and affection of a nation. It must not be overlooked that it requires rather more than talent to achieve what Chesterton described as " tremendous trifles."

A man and his music are inseparable. Elgar's music is as it is because of his upbringing, his environment, his inherited traits of character, his acquired opinions and prejudices. This study is an endeavour to show both the man and the musician.

In the chapters which deal with the music I have not occupied space with detailed technical analysis, which, to my mind, too often makes for very dull reading, and has, in any case, been zealously done by other hands. I have, however, tried to show the progress of the composer as revealed in his manuscripts, and the relationship between the ideas expressed in the music and those which were shown otherwise. On the other hand it has not been forgotten that music (which may be inspired by external events or ideas) has its own life and rules of conduct. In order to maintain the continuity of the text the music examples are placed together at the end of the book (pages 383 to 401). There, it is felt, they will not impede those who do not easily read musical notation, and, at the same time, be more convenient for reference at the keyboard for those who do. Reference to these examples in chapters 16-23 are shown thus : Ex. 1, Ex. 2, etc.

For economy of words occasional references have been made to the numbers which act as landmarks in published scores. Apart from this and a handful of inescapable technicalities (far fewer, I believe, than are taken for granted in works for the amateur of, say, architecture or painting) I have attempted to make my story clear for all those who would appreciate the significance of the works of Elgar, but are ill at ease among the thickets of contemporary musicology. I have, perhaps, gone more fully into the subject of the unfinished opera than the music in itself deserves ; but the way in which the composer left his workroom open to inspection therein holds a particular fascination, and the incomplete work informs us in respect of those which are complete.

When Mrs. C. Elgar Blake encouraged me to undertake this work I was aware both of a great honour and a high responsibility. Let it be said at once that the load of responsibility has been greatly lightened by Mrs. Blake's appreciation of the judicial requirements both of the biographer and of posterity : she must be esteemed not only for her devotion to the great reputation of her father but also for her outstanding honesty. It has long been understood between us that the biographical part of this work should be a record of unassailable fact and not an essay in piety.

I have had access to many private family papers, and I have engaged in discussions which have been conducted with frankness and detachment. I have been a guest at Broadheath on many occasions and have been taken to the places in Worcestershire and Herefordshire which are associated with Elgar's career. For all this, and for her consistent sympathy I owe to Mrs. Blake a debt of gratitude, which I hope these pages may repay, if only in part.

The wealth of material which has come into my hands has suggested that a fully adequate memorial to Elgar cannot be confined to a single volume. He has some claim to be ranked with the great letter writers. There is, therefore, in preparation a volume of his letters and writings on various subjects to supplement the few quoted herein. Beyond this an examination of his writings on music and his sketch books (as full of interest in their way as those of Beethoven) suggest a third work, which will complete this writer's intentions and signalise, in 1957, the centenary of Elgar's birth.

It is more than twenty years since I, as an undergraduate, first sat in Worcester Cathedral to hear the oratorios (and orchestral works), conducted by Elgar himself. I was at that time tutored by those whose attitude to Elgar lacked enthusiasm—to say the least of it. When I admitted to one that *Gerontius* had overwhelmed me he said, " Ah ! yes—the *first time*. But wait, it won't happen again." Yet here I am, still within the memory of being similarly affected by a recent and superb performance of the same work, conducted by Barbirolli. Or, still more recent, there was an illuminating presentation of *The Apostles* at the Three Choirs Festival. The authority of the music was absolute. " For God's sake," said one of our great singers to me, " don't let them say it is disconnected. I know it is. But it is *so beautiful*."

Midway between these recollections lies another, of Willie Reed. His memories of Elgar, his interpretation of Elgar's music, his sensibility, and his generosity of spirit have remained in mind as another spur to the present task.

October 1954   P. M. Y.

PART ONE

PART ONE

CHAPTER I

GREENINGS AND ELGARS

My head like a bulrush it hangs very low
And yet it is white as the driven snow.
My body is green as a greengage plum
Tell me the riddle, I'll give you my thumb.

Anne Greening, at the age of nine (1831)

THERE WERE not many inhabitants of the village of Elmore, in Gloucestershire, in the eighteenth century, and of what there were the majority belonged in some way or other to the Greening family. Greenings had been prominent in the life of that little community throughout the eighteenth century. The most prosperous of them were comfortably established as yeoman farmers. At the end of the century, however, it was this class that was most affected by the rapid increase in the practice of land enclosure. Thus the surviving sons, of a family of seven children, of William and Martha Greening of Elmore were compelled to look for their livelihood away from home.

One son, William, born in 1782, joined the Royal Navy. Possibly he was a victim of the press-gang which practised efficiently in the western counties. But he made for himself a not undistinguished career. He took part in the battle of Alexandria, in the sack of Washington, and—on the *Fairy* under Sir Charles Durham— in the capture of Guadeloupe. At the end of his service he retired to Newnham, in Gloucestershire, where in 1881, he was recorded as the oldest Pensioner of the Royal Navy. He died in the next year. His record was prized by his relatives and, in a roundabout way, his story inspired one of the grandsons of his brother Joseph.

Joseph Greening, three years older than William, either lacked the adventurous spirit or was able to escape the recruiting officers in time. In 1806 he married Esther Apperl[e]y,[1] of Newnham, and left Gloucestershire for the neighbouring county of Herefordshire. He settled at Handley Farm at Weston-under-Penyard. Esther Greening, who in old age was said closely to resemble Hannah More, has her principal memorial in a sampler—worked, when she was a child of seven, in 1796—which she gave to her daughter Anne. Anne, born in 1822, was taught the same craft—one of her samplers of 1833 still being extant; but she also had early literary aspirations. An enigmatic quatrain composed at the age of nine points to a sound tradition of scholarship in the parish school of Weston-under-Penyard and also to some support for letters at home. Longing for artistic fulfilment led her in the course of time to marry a musician. Native obstinacy encouraged her never to neglect her own little talent and so she continued to write verses throughout a long life. It was well that she did for they were the starting point of the creative career of the greatest English musician of his age.

Just as Joseph Greening had left home so too his children went away from Weston-under-Penyard. One son migrated to the neighbourhood of Worcester and it was to his house, in idyllic surroundings near Claines, that Anne came. Besides helping her brother and sister-in-law, Anne was employed in the city, in the Shades Tavern (still there, but its antiquity gracelessly disguised by latter-day restoration) in Mealcheapen Street.

The Shades Tavern is nicely situated close by the Cross and therefore in the centre of affairs. The excitement caused by stirring events in the life of the city was good for trade and if, as frequently happened, the weather was bad no one was better pleased than Mr. Francis Simmonds, landlord of the Shades.

In 1843 the Queen Dowager—Adelaide, widow of William IV—decided to take up residence at Witley Court in Worcestershire, which had been put at her disposal by the Earl of Dudley. Having arrived at Witley, on August 8, the Queen took a week to settle and then arranged to make her first visit to Worcester, to attend divine service in the Cathedral. Constant to ancient loyalty—*semper*

---

[1] Esther's wedding present from her father, now in the possession of her great-great-granddaughter Miss May Grafton is inscribed: " This table was made by WILLIAM APPERLY of Elton by Newnham, Wheelwright, and given to his second daughter, ESTHER, on her marriage to JOSEPH GREENING, May 26th, 1806, at Westbury on Severn, Gloucestershire, from a tree grown on his own land at Pope's Hill. ANNE ELGAR his granddaughter July 22, 1882."

fidelis—the citizens were prepared for a reception suitable to the occasion : " but the torrents of rain which descended spoilt the whole affair ; so that all the civic dignitaries could do was to rush down the Guildhall steps in their scarlet robes, just as Her Majesty passed, and bow their acknowledgements at the carriage door." For this abridged display of esteem the Queen Dowager showed her goodwill to the citizens by a gift of £100 to the Worcester Infirmary.

The arrival of royalty at Witley gave various opportunities of employment. Regarding the office of piano-tuner the Comptroller of the Household, Sir Andrew Barnard, conscientiously approached the London firm of Coventry and Hollier, of Dean Street, Soho, for their nominee. Coventry and Hollier selected a young man from Dover who had served his apprenticeship with them and had settled in Worcester by 1841.[1] He was William Henry Elgar. As a musician W. H. Elgar may be said to have worked his way up from the bottom, for his abiding memory of Coventry and Hollier was of hearing on their premises the great Dragonetti, practising the pedal parts of Bach's organ fugues on the double bass.

Just as the Greenings in Gloucestershire so may the Elgars be noticed in Kentish parochial affairs as far back as the early eighteenth century. There are, to this day, Elgars among the farming community of East Kent.

William Henry, son of Henry and Susan (*née* Hogbin) Elgar, had three brothers and two sisters. The family was musical—being friendly with Mr. Sutton,[2] organist of St. Mary's Church—but also interested in drama, in drawing and in literature. They possessed an impish quality, a capacity to comment on people and affairs allusively, which, through William Henry, infected another generation. Some programmes remain of family concerts—" Kitchen Concerts." In these we find Tom Elgar, the eldest son, adopting the occasional names of " T. Edgar " or " T. Serago " to perform " Teddy the Tiler " or an " Irish Wake "; Anne, the elder daughter, taking a hint from Mozart in masquerading as " Aliss Seraglio " or " A. Elgarino "; Henry *père*, who was a builder by trade, singing, " in character," as " Mons. H. Kino," the comic ballad " I'm 95."

---

[1] The notepaper of Elgar Bros. records 1841 as the year in which the business was established.

[2] Partner in the music-selling firm of Sutton & Potter, New Bridge, Dover. Sutton had been a pupil of Ferdinand Ries, who had been a pupil of Beethoven. Another Dover acquaintance of the Elgars was William Salter (b. 1793), a former pupil of Mozart's friend, Michael Kelly.

An overture by Mozart, known neither before nor since, except to Elgars, was a *Karactisum in C sharp*. It may be that " P. Satea " [*sic*] disguises the uncle who was a Trinity House pilot at Dover, for he sang " The Cabin Boy." These " kitchen concerts," held in what is now the " Silver Grill " fried-fish shop, were in aid of various charities.

When William Henry had settled in Worcester he found himself drawn into the general musical activity of the neighbourhood. In 1842 he was chosen to succeed Mr. C. Baldwin as organist of St. George's Roman Catholic Chapel. Various engagements, either to tune or to play, took him into the county. The accounts of his excursions made good reading for the family in Dover. On June 11, 1843, for instance, he wrote to his parents and, after referring to the wet weather and the flooding of the Severn, gives this lively and breathless account of his engagements at that time :

" Tomorrow Monday I am going to Mr. d'Egville's [1] to practise some Quartetts, some of Correlli's [*sic*] music, good *stuff*. On Monday June 19 *Braham* is going to give a second Concert. I off [*sic*] course tune the Piano and in a short time our next Harmonic Concert takes Place—in about 3 weeks.

We started for Kidder [Kidderminster] at about 10 o'clock on Tuesday about 18 in number and a fine swell we cut I assure you. We started from the *Punch Bowl Inn* [2] a Stage coach for the occasion with four horses and two postillions, in the Top of the Coach were most of the Instruments. Double Basses, Violoncellos Fiddles and the Devil knows what—I was stuck on the Boot with that old Monkey-Coat that I used to wear in Dover with my Cap—and some with Great Coats Mackintoshes and a pretty lot we was. We sang all the way their and all the way Back—and a good spree we had—we reached our journey end at ½ past 12 and returned home at 11 and got to bed at 2 o'clock=bye the bye we had a good dinner at ½ past 2— *rehearsal* at 4 Tea at ½ past 5 Concert at 7=Supper at ½ past 10. The Concert went off pretty well. It was led by Mr. d'Egville and conducted by *Mr. E. Rogers*. I almost forgot to say that it was second fiddled by Mr. W. H. Elgar. Total Number of Performers 50."

[1] The d'Egville family, of 32 Britannia Square, Worcester, kept a dancing academy.
[2] In College Street.

William Henry was lodging with the Greenings beyond Claines and in 1845 he sent home a " sketch map of The Environs of Worcester—From Worcester Cross to Mrs. Greenings—Published at the Shades Tavern, Mealcheapen Street, Worcester. Entered at Stationers' Hall." Thus he showed where much of his interest lay. The first to make use of this map was Tom who came up to Worcester in the same year and made some entertaining caricatures of the staff and management of the Shades Tavern. At, or about, the same time Tom's sister Susannah also made the journey from Dover. She formed an attachment for Simmonds, the innkeeper, and lived with him for some years in sinful contentment.

Tuning was a tiring occupation. As a result of too much of it William Henry used to find his head " very queer indeed, though it soon goes off again." As a relief, however, there were the upper reaches of music as explored by the Worcester Instrumental Society. A programme of June 9, 1845, is more enterprising than some of later date. It comprised :

Concerto grosso—Handel
2 Movements Mozart Symphony in C (Adagio and Allegro), followed by " Flora gave me fairest flowers " (Wilbye), followed by the rest of the Mozart Symphony
" Witches Scene " (*Dido*) Purcell
Overture " Fra Diavolo "—Auber
       „   " Egmont "—Beethoven
" Down in a flowery vale." Festa
Sinfonia in D—Romberg
[This was split half-way by Benet's " All Creatures now."]
" Come if you dare " (*King Arthur*) Purcell.

Wilbye with Mozart reads like the proper choice of wine for a main course.

II

" Elgar–Greening : 19th January 1848, at St. Mary's, Islington, by the Rev. R. P. Hutchinson, William Henry Elgar, of Dover, to Anne, daughter of the late Joseph Greening, of Handley, Herefordshire."

At the time of their marriage both Anne and William Henry were 26. Although the Queen Dowager had left Witley Court in 1846 the tuning connection had grown considerably over five years and William was now engaged by the best families of the county. Additional remuneration came from numerous fiddle-playing engagements and from his connections with St. George's. This post brought him a salary of £40 a year [1] with an honorarium of £25 at Christmas and Easter. St. George's, in Sansome Street on the edge of the city and by the old Town Ditch, had been opened in the year 1829 by Dr. Walsh, Bishop of the Midland District. James II, in 1687, had attended Mass at an earlier chapel, first mentioned in any record in 1595, on the same site. It was on this occasion that the Protestant Mayor and Corporation, with loyalty tested, waited outside the chapel door while His Majesty prayed within.

Although much occupied in domestic affairs Anne, whose eldest son Harry was born in 1850, devoted her leisure to improving pursuits. Lucy was born in 1852 and was greeted by her mother in these exhortatory lines :

TO MR. W. H. ELGAR ON THE BIRTH OF HIS DAUGHTER

Another child is born, another guest,
Elgar, to thy domestic hearth is given;
Receive her as a precious boon from heaven,
And while thine eyes with a father's fondness rest
On thy fair babe, reposing on the breast
Of her, thy lov'd wife, whose smile
Can all the cares of busy life beguile
Be in her love and in thy children blest—
Yet, ah, be mindful that 'tis Heaven's behest
With added blessings duty's claims increase :
Train up thy children in the paths of peace,
Be Christian precepts on their minds impress'd,
Then shall their upright walk, o'er life's rough stage
Solace thine anxious heart in thy declining age.

August 25, 1852. ANNE

---

[1] Edward Elgar (see p. 52) said that his father was organist of St. George's for thirty-seven years. This does not agree with Alderman Hubert Leicester's dates as given in his *Notes on Catholic Worcester* (p. 33). He states that W. H. Elgar succeeded C. Baldwin in 1842 and gave way to Mr. Foster in 1880. The latter date seems wrong; the former may well be correct.

William and Anne corresponded fully and regularly with the
Dover Elgars and some of their correspondence took the form of
an ambitious series of *Worcester Papers*, each 16 pages long. These
were modelled on the *Dover News* which came from Tom with
news and gossip from Kent. In addition to family affairs matters
engaging public attention were discussed in thoughtful essays,
which displayed both a zeal for general improvement and wide
reading. Matters of topical concern, to which the joint wisdom of
the Elgars was brought, included " The Necessity of the Study of
Religion," " The Deluge of 1852," [1] " Sanitation " and " Capital
Punishment."

By 1852 Anne was a Catholic convert and her devotion
to the Faith was strict and fervent. Anne followed ecclesiastical
developments closely and William—who became a Catholic at a
later date—sometimes composed religious verses. Both put the
thesis expressed in the *Worcester Papers* of 1852 into practice
and inculcated into their children a sense of religious duty.
" Sanitation " (lying properly in the neighbourhood of godliness)
brought to Dover echoes of a long controversy which had raged
in Worcester. In 1848 the Public Health Act was given the
Royal Assent. Despite the fact that " scarcely a street in the
whole city is supplied with a sufficient drain, and that it contains
more open cesspits, prolific of noisome smells and active disease,
than any other town of equal size in the kingdom " there was a
vigorous, obstructive, and vociferous " anti-sanitation " party in
the city. Anne Elgar spoke her mind :

" Let the full operation of the Sanitary Measures be adopted to
the good city of Worcester." In respect of the opponents of the
proposed schemes she was equally forthright :

". . . but we have a vague notion : probably it is a natural feeling
of indignation at the monstrous idea of a poor labouring class of
people wishing to live somewhat in a wholesome state ! but more
likely because the introduction of such a system of Sanitary reform
in this city would entail upon them an extra demand from their
purse a little further expenditure of their income."

Anne was moved to record her opinions on capital punishment
by reason of the condemnation to death, at the Worcester Assizes
in 1852, of one Mary Robins—found guilty of child murder, but

[1] In February of that year the river was 13 ft. 6 in. above normal, in November
15 ft. : the worst record for eighty years.

reprieved by the intervention and " generosity of a few persevering individuals." It was during the year after the Elgars' marriage that the last public execution—of Robert Pulley—took place in Worcester—" on the roof of the County Gaol, in the presence of a large crowd of spectators, who behaved with much propriety." As a result of this spectacle a debate was held in the Guildhall on the expediency of capital punishment. Among those who spoke in favour of the retention of the death penalty was the Rev. W. H. Havergal, who is more generally remembered for his composition of numerous hymns. Mrs. Elgar, not among the important people who were entitled to discuss such matters, expressed herself in her private papers with a commendable charity.

On music we may read William. He noted the musical habits of German workmen, and heartily wished " that if a History of Music were to be published the same account might be recorded of the labourers of England, for I consider that the English stand rather in the background as far as regards Musical affairs. . . . Comparatively speaking how very few English composers are there when we look at the superior number of foreign . . . before I conclude allow me to say that I hope the time is not very far distant when England in all her glory will stand pre-eminent, at least in Musical Affairs." He himself was to do something towards this end.

Among the *Worcester Papers* may be noted enthusiastic mention of the Great Exhibition of 1851 ; entertaining " answers to correspondents "—the distant Elgars—on points of history, geography, animal and human welfare ; references to such authors as Addison —who was at times a guest of Sir Roger de Coverley at Abberley in Worcestershire, Steele, Isaac Watts, and George Hogarth. The authors signified their contributions thus ** (Anne Elgar), and +++ (William Henry Elgar). On one occasion the latter transcribed himself as " W. H. Elgie "—a fanciful allusion to a sometime Mayor of Worcester—F. T. Elgie who was in office in the year 1846–47.

In the middle years of the century Worcester had its diversions. Public meetings such as those concerned with sanitation and the establishment of railways—on this subject an even greater acrimony was aroused—were one sort. Theatrical entertainments were another. For the more serious there were the meetings of the Natural History Society, the lectures given at the Literary and

Scientific Society's Athenæum in Foregate Street, and literary amenities at the City Library, the City and County Library and the Mechanics' Institution. Music was provided in the cathedral; by the Madrigal Society; by the Glee Club; by the Harmonic Society; and by the Instrumental Society. On account of its industries —china and glove manufacture, and some engineering—and the distinguished families of the neighbourhood, visitors came to Worcester in large numbers and among the cathedral cities of the west it was the virtual capital. We may note that Constable once lectured in the city on landscape painting, that Paganini played there, and that Jenny Lind lived in nearby Malvern.

In 1848 Jenny Lind had been unable to take part in the Three Choirs Festival. On February 3 of the next year she partially compensated for the disappointment caused by giving a concert in the College Hall (assisted by the Band of the 5th Dragoon Guards and the Worcester Harmonic Society) in aid of the Infirmary. The amount raised thereby was £850.

The Elgars lived in the middle of all these activities and, for Worcester at that time had a population of only 27,000, were doubtless content to believe that theirs was a remarkable cultural environment. William must also have appreciated the tangible rewards that came to him in the shape of fees for piano-tuning and fiddling.

Meanwhile the family grew and when Lucy (1852), and Susannah Mary—or Polly—(1855) were added to Harry it was decided to go from the city to the quieter atmosphere of Broadheath. In 1856 it was announced in the local press that Mr. W. H. Elgar was leaving his residence in the College Precincts.

Broadheath Common, by which stands the cottage (then known as " The Firs ") taken by the Elgars is an enchanting place. Three miles below and to the south-east stands the city, dominated by the tall grey tower of the cathedral, and the slender spire of St. Andrew's, which the Elgars could see from their upstairs windows. To the west, a little farther away, are the Malvern Hills, home of Caractacus at one time and of William Langland at another. Across this country the British were pursued by the Romans, the Saxons by the Danes, the Cavaliers by the Roundheads. It was at Powick on the Malvern road that the first engagement of the Civil War took place. In this neighbourhood wild flowers abound and fantasies of folk-lore used to fascinate and frighten the superstitious.

Anne Elgar loved the countryside. She collected the wild
flowers and put them into her scrap books, side by side with
gleanings from local history and tradition. She was indefatigable,
cheerfully controlling a large and lively family on slender means,
and pursuing her private interests at the same time. Thus in 1878
she could write two poems which catch the awareness of beauty,
the affections, the humour of a remarkable woman, and the gracious-
ness of the Worcestershire scene.

The first commemorates a visit to the Wold Hills [1] in June :

> *Only a sprig of heather*
> *But it grew upon the wild*
> *When you and I together*
> *The summer day beguiled.*
> *When the skylark high was singing*
> *Above the yellow broom*
> *And the cool hill-breeze was bringing*
> *The sweet scent of its bloom.*

The second, more ambitious and with echoes of Cowper,
remembers a visit to the same place a month later :

> *Is it a tuft of bright thistle downe*
> *That came in the window and settled down?*
> *Or is it the perfume of new-mown hay?*
> *Something has roused my mother today.*
> *She talks of a picnic of only three,*
> *Gilda our guest, herself, and me.*
> *Spiers [2] must drive us, and Tip of course*
> *Will run with Billy the old black horse,*
> *The air is lovely, sunny and bright*
> *Pa says there'll be a full moon tonight.*
> *There's nothing to hinder a little spree*
> *We're to go to Wold Hills and get our tea,*
> *And being Thursday we close [3] at four.*
> *The carriage will come and wait at the door.*

---

[1] Now known as the Old Hills.
[2] For many years the Elgars' servant : a Worcestershire man who had been a
travelling actor. He was compelled to give up acting because of a leg injury.
[3] The shop.

It will not be more than a six mile drive,
We shall be there all right by five.
This was no sooner arranged than done,
Our faces all beaming over with fun.
We mounted and packed away our store
Of provisions, cloaks and wraps galore.

The second son of the Elgars—Edward William, and the only child of theirs to be born at Broadheath, was born on June 2, 1857. He, more than any of his brothers and sisters, inherited his mother's poetic perceptivity. He, however, acquired a capacity for expression which she never knew, but which she was able to admire in wonderment in its maturity. So was she rewarded.

CHAPTER II

EDWARD

. . . at our backs " the unthrift sun shot vital gold,"
filling Payne's Meadows with glory and illuminating for two
small boys a world to conquer and to love.

Elgar's Foreword to Forgotten Worcester,
H. A. Leicester (1930)

It is improbable that Edward was very much aware of the Three Choirs Festival that was held in Worcester three months after he was born. But it was appropriate that a Festival, to which he was in due course to contribute so much, should have taken place in his native city in 1857.

For William Elgar festival time was busy. He tuned pianos and he played in the orchestra, whose extra rehearsals made additional demands on his scant leisure. But for one whose vocation was so strongly marked—Elgar senior held music as a high mystery and himself as one of its modest celebrants—the effort was worthwhile. It was an opportunity to see, to hear, and, perhaps, to meet the high priests and priestesses of the mystery. In his time William had heard, in Worcester, Lockey and Staudigl who had sung in the first performance of Mendelssohn's *Elijah* in 1847. In 1857 Clara Novello, to appear at Worcester for the last time three years later, was singing, as well as the immortal Sims Reeves. The music in 1857 was unadventurous—even though Mendelssohn, who then supplied much of the programme, was almost a modern composer. But one occurrence was memorable. The Duke of Cambridge announced his intention of attending at the second of the evening concerts in the College Hall. But he mistimed his approach. " The interruption caused by the entrance of the Duke during the singing of the air ' Tho' clouds by tempests driven,' by Mrs. Weiss, greatly marred its effect."

During Edward's childhood the Festival performances at Worcester continued steadily, except that in 1875 some disturbance was threatened when the Earl of Dudley—representing a powerful minority opinion—offered £10,000 to the Cathedral on condition that musical festivals therein were discontinued. In fact a reduced festival was given that year, for the pietists temporarily got the upper hand. But so ancient a tradition was unbreakable and after one attempt to attack it had failed no more were seriously attempted. To the standard works of Handel and Mendelssohn were added Mozart's *Requiem* in 1863 and Beethoven's *Mass in C* in 1866. In 1869, by which time Edward was old enough to take a lively interest in the comings and goings of the great, Sullivan came to conduct his *Prodigal Son*. Among the distinguished singers was Santley, and the great Dr. S. S. Wesley of Gloucester (something of a law to himself as the festival organisers discovered) was at the organ. It was Wesley who undertook Bach's *St. Matthew Passion* at Gloucester in 1871. So impressive was this that its performance was repeated at Worcester in 1872.

But before Bach arrived at the Festival he had been upheld as the supreme model for the Elgar household. So Edward, aged 9, was impelled to make an act of anagrammatic reverence. This scrap of paper (reproduced opposite p. 49) is the earliest extant example of his manuscript. It will be noticed that the substance, except to the initiated, is enigmatic. The professional will also notice that acquaintance with the less usual clefs was made at a preternaturally early age.

At the same time Edward was also aware of certain other solemnities. Father Waterworth and Father Meagher, who were the priests at St. George's, supplemented the family instruction in the Faith of the Catholic Church. Reverence for royalty—a lifelong characteristic—was engendered by daily sight of the royal coat of arms which, by reason of his Warrant, William Elgar proudly set at the head of his advertisements, by the effigies of King John in the cathedral and those of the two Kings Charles and Queen Anne set outside the Guildhall.

On December 11, 1859, William proposed extending his business by taking into partnership his youngest brother Henry. His letter of that date offers to Henry an interesting career and a firm wage of two guineas a week. It also describes the winding-up of the Correlli [*sic*] Society and William's fortunate acquisition of the parts of the Mozart quintets. Mozart was, perhaps, William's greatest passion. This enthusiasm also was passed on to Edward. In his way William was a composer. He had the habit, which Edward also had, of carrying sketch books about with him on his country excursions. In later years Edward recalled how once when he and his father were forced to shelter from the rain under a tree the latter brought out his manuscript book to note some passing inspiration. But William found too many cares to advance his creative career. " I must," he concluded to Henry, " leave off now it is near teatime and I want to try to compose an introduction to a Litany of Mr. Waterworth, he expects me to do these things —but I don't at present feel inspired, my mind wanders [wandering ?] too much in my business."

In daily affairs, however, William was conscientious. Advertising, in 1860, his removal to 1 Edgar Street, he

" Respectfully informs his Patrons that in consequence of his Business he has obtained the assistance of his Brother

Mr. Henry Elgar

(from Messrs. Kirkman's, London, and Messrs. Hime & Addison's, Manchester), and as numerous mistakes have lately occurred he begs to state that the TUNING will be attended to SOLELY by THEMSELVES."

When Henry came to Worcester in 1860 he was 27. He remained in the business until his death in 1917. Like his brother he was a competent musician. He was for many years organist at Blackmore Park Roman Catholic Church and at Emmanuel Church, Malvern. He had tuned for Sir Charles Hallé in Manchester and in that city had learned a great deal about the technique of orchestration. His knowledge of this craft was indispensable in Worcester, for " on instrumental nights (at the Glee Club) he presided at the harmonium with rare skill and judgment, " filling in " the missing orchestral parts, and playing the many solos which would fall to him with great beauty and expression." Edward learned a good deal in this respect from Uncle Henry. He also derived from him a love of the theatre. Uncle Henry was an inveterate theatre goer. He had, however, a fine sense of dignity, never appearing in public without frock-coat—a flower in the button-hole—and top hat. Of regular habits he put in a nightly appearance in the Private Saloon Bar of the Crown.

Sometimes the Theatre in Angel Place went beyond its normal

entertainment of hack touring companies (from one of which Ned Spiers, the Elgars' manservant, had graduated to domestic employment), local amateurs, Italian marionettes and nigger minstrels. Edward was eight or nine when he was taken into the orchestra pit—which had room for only a handful of players—to hear his first operas. He was grateful for the rest of his life to those who arranged his introduction to *Norma*, *Il Trovatore*, *La Traviata* and, above all, *Don Giovanni* as presented by the Haigh-Dyer company.

From Edgar Street the Elgars moved house to 10 High Street, where business accommodation had been taken in 1860. In addition to the tuning connection they now had a music shop. On the street level the houses at the cathedral end of the High Street are now, more or less blatantly, refurbished. Above the crude gestures of contemporary commerce, however, the late eighteenth century stands in silent dignity and reproach. The tall buildings—the Elgars' house had four stories—come nearer and nearer together at the neck of the street. It is a jostling, neighbourly place, which must, when lived in, have encouraged sociable habits.

Within, the Elgars' establishment consisted of a shop on the ground-floor with a small living-room behind. On the first floor most of the space was taken by a show-room, in which customers inspected a variety of instruments and William and Henry also gave lessons. Above the show-room the family and its retainers—Spiers and an occasional maid-of-all-work—slept. There was not much room and not much tranquillity for a boy of scholarly habits. Thus Edward was practically compelled to cultivate the habit of out-of-door study.

But in boyhood High Street was a magical place. During the long days when his father and uncle were abroad, touring the county by horse-and-trap in search of pianos that were out of tune, and his mother was ceaselessly engaged in the family chores, Edward explored the city. A radius of half a mile from the front door allowed him as much acquaintance with English history as many would be glad to obtain in a lifetime of reading.

In late years Elgar admitted the fascination of the names of which he was first aware—names, he said, " That would have made Quintilian stare and gasp." Round the corner and behind the house was Newdix Court, where were the stables, and the Leicesters'

E.   C printing premises, and some gardens with trees that still relieve the hot surround of red brick. Across the road, and beyond the parish church of St. Helen, was the district known prettily as Birdport. From there, on the other bank of the river, was Bedwardine, ruled by another ancient church. Some of the gracious names in which Edward revelled—Dolday, for instance—are now lost to all but motorists in search of parking places. Some—and " above all " Pope Iron—have disappeared with the separate hundreds " with which our forefathers, prodigal in this matter if in nothing else, have handsomely dowered us."

It was a stone's throw for Edward to the Commandery—remembered in his *Severn Suite*—which had been founded by St. Wulstan himself and in 1651 was the headquarters of the Royalist forces defending the city. In another direction there were other noble remains of medieval charity and learning in the surviving buildings of the Greyfriars. Behind the High Street, in the direction of the Foregate, there was the clean, white church of St. Swithun, its plain Georgian interior relieved by the most handsome three-decker pulpit in the country. As he stood at the front of his house Edward saw the majesty of the place summarised in the cathedral tower.

It was a fine place in which to live, even if, like W. H. Elgar, poor and overworked. The dignity of the house was always maintained, however, and sometimes occasional commitments came to enhance that dignity. William served on the Grand Jury at the Epiphany Quarter Sessions in 1869 and was accordingly qualified to draw the attention of his sons to the advantages of a career in law. This, very nearly, became Edward's destiny.

His schooling was thorough and not without its inspiration. He went at first to a dame school in Britannia Place, where a Miss Tyler began his formal piano instruction. For some years he was a pupil at Littleton House. This academy on the Powick Road nurtured about thirty " young gentlemen " and was directed by Mr. Francis Reeve who lived on for many years to appreciate the fame of his distinguished, and always grateful, pupil. Mr. Reeve's portrait was preserved by Mrs. Elgar and Edward was especially impressed by his religious instruction [1]; in after years he frequently

---

[1] For a short time Edward was sent to a Catholic school at Spetchley, maintained by the lord of the manor, Robert Berkeley. But this experience left no strong impression, although in later years he was always glad to return to Spetchley as a guest of the Berkeleys.

repeated Reeve's striking presentation of the Apostles as simple men. " The Apostles," began Reeve, " were poor men at the time of their calling ; perhaps before the descent of the Holy Ghost not cleverer than some of you here." This lesson was to be expanded into an oratorio.

Edward learned the rudiments of education thoroughly and if there is no direct evidence of early mathematical distinction his reading was wide and his competence in writing assured. His promise as a scholar was marked in 1868 by a school prize. (Not only do we know that one great man did win a prize but also we may still refer to it at Broadheath.) This was John Ormsby's *Autumn Rambles in Africa* (1864).

There were many books at home. Of Edward's earliest reading there still survives a catholic selection : J. Erskine E. Clarke's *Chatterbox* ; the *Boys' Own Magazine* (1861) ; Frank Smedley's *Frank Fairleigh* (1863) ; Cuthbert Bede's *The Rook's Garden* (1865) ; Gautier's *Wanderings in Spain* (1853) ; *The Pilgrim's Progress* ; the Rev. Byrnes's *Lyra Angelicana* (1864) ; *Popular Errors Explained* (1841) ; *Waverley Anecdotes* (1851) ; and Ramsay's *Reminiscences of Scottish Character* (1864). Edward later recorded how one day he was engrossed in a heap of second-hand volumes which somehow found their way to High Street. From among them he took Baker's and Holinshed's *Chronicles*, Drayton's *Polyolbion*, Sidney's *Arcadia*, a wide selection from the older poets, Voltaire in translation, and numerous works of theology. He was an early riser and was often engrossed in his literary explorations an hour or two before the rest of the family were astir. This habit of early rising persisted throughout his composing life. Anything of a historical nature especially caught his fancy and, later, people told him " that he knew more of life up to the eighteenth century than he did of his own time." [1] It was encouraging to have sympathy in these studies. We have knowledge of Anne Elgar's reading during Edward's schooldays and of impressions which he, sometimes unconsciously, received.

Anne was a keen student of Longfellow. Many of her choice extracts are from *Hyperion*,[2] and it may be that some inner fear in

---

[1] *Strand Magazine*, May 1904.
[2] Edward recalled having read *Hyperion* with his mother in a letter to her written from Heidelberg on Aug. 12, 1892.

1876 urged her to write down two quotations which may at some time or other have seemed apt.

" Beware of dreams ! Beware of fancy ! Beware of the solemn deceivings of thy vast desires."

and

" And thus do the world and society corrupt the scholar." From her large acquaintance with this author it is to be assumed that Edward derived his first knowledge of *The Black Knight* and *The Saga of King Olaf.* There was another early source of knowledge of the Danes, for Anne also made excerpts from the more or less formidable Warsac's *Danes and Norwegians in England, Scotland, etc.* History of any sort was a passion with her, whether related to the establishment of needle manufacture in Buckinghamshire in the sixteenth century (by a Greening she was pleased to note) or to the proposed taxation of funerals in the reign of George III. Archæ-ological discoveries caught her eye, especially in Kent and the western counties. She collected any periodical contributions on ecclesiastics or royalty. She ranged the magazines from Cassell's *Illustrated Paper* to the *Live Stock Journal and Fancier's Gazette.* She collected comic pictures and popular anecdotes. She could not resist pictures of famous places so that she could travel in her arm-chair. She read Emerson and Washington Irving ; Ouida and Mrs. Henry Wood—a native of Worcester ; Byron and Spenser. A poem by Thomas Hood—*Singing for the Million*—she had specially printed for her by Uncle Thomas in Dover. That General Gordon —admired for his saintly qualities—had his place in his mother's miscellany may well account for Edward's admitted desire later in life to compose a commemorative symphony. That, however, was a *sinfonia eroica* that was not written, although indirectly *Gerontius* has a curious connection with Gordon.

It is clear that general knowledge was not neglected by the Elgars, for William passed on to his children essays on Berlioz, on Mozart, on Oratorio. He, or Uncle Henry, or both, saw to it that Polly learned to sing, Edward to play the piano, the organ and the violin, and, in due course, Francis Thomas (Frank) to play the oboe. Harry and Jo had shown signs of musical promise, but they both died of scarlet fever in 1866. Lucy, the eldest sister and the most volatile member of the family, had certain literary and histrionic gifts that were invaluable in childhood but something of a handicap in later life. There was, to complete the family, Helen, seven years younger than Edward and three than Frank. She possessed exceptional talents which became apparent when, after living at home for many years to look after her parents, she became a Dominican nun and finally the Superior of her Order.

It may be said that all the Elgar children had talent, while Edward had genius. They all, as they say, did well for themselves, having been brought up on sound, if austere, principles. They were sent out to explore the country and Edward often went to stay at Broadheath. They were encouraged to appreciate nonsense. So it was that in 1869 (or 1871 [1]) they worked off a grievance against authority by composing a play (in the best Barrie style) to represent a perfect world—across the stream at the bottom of the garden—from which ill-tempered grown-ups were barred. (There is a good deal to be said for the general principle.) Apart from the Elgar children the only candidates for election to this paradise were Fairies and Giants, Moths and Butterflies . . . but perhaps, after all, repentant old people might be admitted to be shown the error of their ways ! Edward sketched some tunes for this fancy and also knocked together an effective, if limited, bass viol for their better support. In due course these tunes became the basis of the two *Wand of Youth* suites.

When, at the age of 15, Edward left school there was no intention that he should become a professional musician. He was, it is true, a good all round musician for his age. He played his first Mass at St. George's on July 14, 1872, and he was rather more than an average fiddler. He had taken lessons in violin from a local teacher of considerable ability—Fred Spray, and played with an *élan* that was surprising in a boy who otherwise was commendable for his sobriety. The quiet, studious habits marked him, in his parents' eyes, for some slight distinction in a profession where quiet and studious habits might be thought desirable.

Edward was shown to a friendly lawyer—Mr. William Allen, treasurer of the local Law Society, whose office was at 3 Sansome Place. Mr. Allen, a member of the congregation of St. George's, agreed to take him into apprenticeship. Edward did his best. But his legal career terminated within a few months. He was, so he afterwards said, grateful to have learned something about method and to have been compelled into clear penmanship.

[1] Edward later quoted both dates. To add to this confusion the tune of " Fairies & Giants " is in a sketch book of *c.* 1902 as " Humoreske, Broadheath, 1867."

At the end of January 1873 there was a concert at the Union Workhouse. The performers were Masters Newth and Elgar, and Messrs. Price, Brookes, Smith, Tyers, Quaterman, Spray, W. H. Elgar and H. Elgar. The programme included the overtures *Preciosa* by Weber and *Semiramide* by Rossini.

Edward had commenced his career.

CHAPTER III

"PASSED WITH HONOURS"

Self-taught I sing; 'tis Heaven and Heaven alone
Inspires my song with music all its own.

From Homer's Odyssey

WHEN THE Public Orator of the University of Cambridge thus apostrophised Edward Elgar in 1900 he intended generosity, but the term "self-taught" has more generally been applied in a derogatory sense. If Elgar was self-taught then so was Bach and so was Mozart. I suspect that those who adjudge Elgar to have been self-taught have been guilty of inaccurate definition. It is true that Elgar did not go to Oxford or to Cambridge. Nor —except for one fortnight—did he go to Leipzig to study, although that was his early ambition. He depended, almost entirely, on the resources of Worcester and on his own inflexible determination. We shall, I hope, conclude finally that this was his salvation.

Mr. Cardus, whose devotion to Elgar is above suspicion, gives voice to a further misconception. "I can think of no greater composer who took his rise from an environment as unpromising to his art as Elgar's when he was a young man. England, in those years, was solemnly and surely 'Das Land ohne Musik.' Elgar lived for long in his formative years in the narrowest of holes and corners of culture—Worcester and the West Country, not amongst the yokels thereof but in the presence day by day of the dull middle classes." [1] This kind of comment Elgar eventually answered himself. In 1930 he wrote a foreword to Hubert Leicester's *Forgotten Worcester*. In it he protested—"I am said to have 'left the humdrum atmosphere of Worcester for' etc. I object to this. I deny that my atmosphere could be exactly humdrum while

[1] *Elgar* in *Ten Composers*, p. 125 (London, 1945).

Hubert Leicester and myself were of it and in it ; it might well have
been disagreeable but that is another matter."

By 1873 Edward had crystallised ambition. He was going to be
a composer. Behind him lay some tunes invented for a family
charade, a whimsical little piano piece—*Chantant*, a song—" The
Language of Flowers " [1]—in honour of Lucy's birthday, and sundry
scribblings. He had begun to relieve his father in the organ loft
at St. George's. He had established himself among the peripatetic
music-makers who were the bread and butter of Worcestershire
music. He set out to learn his trade, and at the same time to earn
his living.

Beyond his father's instruction in composition Edward relied
on books. But before attempting to master the intricacies of the
academicians he set about learning how to learn. He armed himself with John Pillery's *Student's Aids, How to excel in Study*,
and A. Smyth Palmer's *The Ideal of a Gentleman*. Thus fortified he
picked up the more formidable works on music which his father
stocked : Crotch's *Elements of Musical Composition*, Mozart's *Thoro'
Bass School* (pub. by Novello, 1854), Reicha's *Orchestral Primer*. In
the next year or two he acquired Stainer's *Composition* and *Harmony*,
Berlioz's *Instrumentation, Grove's Dictionary*, J. Hiles's *Dictionary of
Musical Terms* (1882), Catel's *Treatise of Harmony*, Cherubini's
Counterpoint and works by Ouseley—whom Edward knew from
visits to Tenbury—and Macfarren. Two other books of this
period gave further instruction and pleasure : *Hymns Ancient and
Modern* (1877) and, well-loved and often read, Jessie Fothergill's
romance entitled *First Violin* (1882).

Edward found Parry's essays in *Grove* substantial and helpful.
To Mozart he turned with relief, for it was " something human."

On Sunday mornings he attended Mass, more often than not
playing the organ. When service was finished he used to run the
quarter-mile along the High Street in time to hear the end of the
cathedral service. On Sunday afternoons he took part in a wind
ensemble—privately known as the " Waits." The other members
were Frank Elgar (oboe), Hubert Leicester (flute), William Leicester
(clarinet) and Frank Exton (flute). They met in the Leicesters'
house, which was next door but one to the Elgars', at 6 High Street.
Edward played the bassoon, which later he gave up in favour of
the 'cello. (There was an occasion when on a moonlit night

[1] Dated Mar. 29, 1872.

outside the Leicesters' house Edward took out his bassoon to assemble it in the street. " Hi ! " said a voice, " if you shoot that here it'll cost you five shillings ".) Since a suitable supply of music was limited Edward took the opportunity to compose and arrange what the team wanted. Sometimes he used the morning sermon-time profitably to this end.

At St. Helen's Church, at the end of Fish Street, the curfew was rung nightly. In the middle 1870's the ringer, not averse from a night's respite now and then, allowed Edward to stand in as his deputy. " We were," said Elgar in 1932 when he spoke in Worcester at the conferring of the Freedom of the City on Hubert Leicester, " supposed to ring the day of the month, but in my exuberance I rang the 35th of September. The parishioners interfered, and I was asked to resign my position as a bell-ringer." At this time he became aware of Beethoven for he was given the scores of the symphonies. The " Pastoral " gave him the greatest pleasure—as might perhaps have been expected—and he used, on summer days, to take it and other works to Broadheath Common or to the churchyard at Claines. A year or two later he added a full score of the *Midsummer Night's Dream* to his treasures.

His violin teacher Spray gave him opportunities for quartet playing and an incident recorded as in 1877 is informative. In that year Edward, having saved up[1] for the purpose, went to London for the first time to have some lessons from Adolphe Pollitzer.

Pollitzer was a Hungarian Jew and as a boy he had played Mendelssohn's *Violin Concerto* before its composer. He was one of the best players in London. Edward found him a stimulating teacher. One day they were working at the first violin part of a Haydn Quartet. There was a lull. Edward played some of the 'cello part on his fiddle. " You know the whole thing ? " asked Pollitzer. " Of course." " Do you compose yourself ? " " I try." Pollitzer thereafter saw whatever Edward had with him and in due course gave him an introduction to August Manns, director of the orchestra at the Crystal Palace. Pollitzer gave his early impressions of his pupil. " I always thought him a most earnest musician. . . . Mr. Elgar, although leaning towards the modern German school, does not lose either his love or respect for the composers of the past."

[1] He spent £7 15s. 9d. on his twelve-day visit, of which £3 12s. 6d. went on his rail fare and Pollitzer's five lessons.

Progress on the violin continued until 1881 when the Royal Academy of Music published the results of its local examinations[1] held in Worcester :

Passed with honours :

Mr. Edward Elgar, Worcester, violin and general musical knowledge.

Master W. Wolstenholme, Blind College, organ and general knowledge.

Passed :

Miss Frances Ellen Gedge, Malvern Wells, piano.

Examiners : { Brinley Richards, Prof. R.A.M.
{ Alfred J. Caldicott, Mus.Bac. (Cantab.)

William Wolstenholme became one of Edward's most notable pupils at the Worcester College for the Blind [2] and when in due course he went to Oxford to sit for his Mus.B. degree Edward went with him to act as his amanuensis. The Gedge family were also to be closely associated with Edward.

In the month in which he had celebrated his twenty-first birthday an advertisement had appeared in the *Tablet*, probably through the good offices of the Leicesters (who were Catholics) or Father Waterworth.

" To Musical Catholic Noblemen, Gentlemen, Priests, Heads of Colleges, etc., or Professors of Music—a friend of a young man, possessed of great musical talent, is anxious to obtain partial employment for him as Organist or Teacher of Piano, Organ, or Violin, to young boys, sons of gentlemen, or as Musical Amanuensis to Composers or Professors of Music, being a quick and ready copyist. Could combine Organist and Teacher of Choir, with Musical Tutor to sons of noblemen, etc. Has had several years experience as Organist. The advertiser's object is to obtain musical employment for him, with proportionate time for study. Age 21,

[1] Examination pieces—*Cavatina* (Raff) and *Concerto in D mi.* (Kreutzer). Elgar took the examination to oblige Caldicott, so that there should be sufficient candidates to establish a local centre : see *Musical Times*, Oct. 1907.

[2] " In 1881, Miss Eliza Warrington of Malvern . . . (made) a gift of £1000 for the foundation of a musical scholarship, whose first holder was William Wolstenholme. . . During his schooldays he was a pupil of Edward Elgar, to whose kindness he owed much : in later years Wolstenholme brought honour to his old school as Oxford's first blind Mus. Bac., and as an organist and composer, famed both here and in America." *The First Seventy Years : history of Worcester College for the Blind*, Mary G. Thomas. (Nat. Inst. for the Blind [1937].)

of quiet, studious habits, and gentlemanly bearing. Been used to good society. Would have unexceptional references. Neighbourhood of London preferred ; the Continent not objected to. Disengaged in September." That is to say, after the conclusion of the Three Choirs Festival. In this year Edward played, for the first time, among the second violins of the Festival orchestra.

There was, however, no satisfactory response from the possible patrons addressed through the medium of the *Tablet* and Edward was compelled to possess himself in patience and to continue the ceaseless round of casual engagements which furnished a modest livelihood. The pertinacity of his ideals can be appreciated when the substance on which they were obliged to depend is examined.

The competent instrumentalist in a provincial town is, even now, likely to find his evenings well occupied with exhausting and not very remunerative activity. The Elgars were obliged to accept every engagement that was offered for thus pupils were attracted and, in respect of Elgar Bros., business was increased. By such occupation, however, a sense of camaraderie is engendered and some of Edward's most appreciative friends and supporters were accumulated in the fulfilment of his obligations.

The application of music to good causes is well illustrated by some of Edward's performances in his formative years. On April 28, 1876, he took part in a concert in aid of the enlargement of the organ in St. Michael's Church, in the Natural History Society's Room ; on February 13, 1878, he appeared at Callow End as solo violinist so that the vicar might be enabled to " light the School Room for the Evening Service "; a year later he was at Stourport " for the benefit of the Stourport Cricket Club "; on June 18, 1880, the Worcester Amateur Instrumental and Musical Societies united for the " Royal Albert Orphan Asylum Saturday Fund." It was during this concert that he spent some time in practising a variety of signatures—Edward Wm. Elgar, E. W. Elgar, Edward Elgar, Elgar Bros., and finally EEEE. . . .—in order to assess the most impressive final effect for future use. It was, I suspect, while Mr. Hadley was singing Carafa's *Bolero*, or the Misses Reader Glover's *Sister Fay*, that he took his mind away from the matter in hand.

There were concerts arranged by particular bodies for the diversion of their members. On June 12, 1878, certain military gentlemen arranged a concert in consonance with their tastes. and

advertised the 1st Worcestershire Artillery Volunteers' Amateur
Christy Minstrels. The *Introductory Overture* (" written expressly
for this occasion ") was by E. W. Elgar. There followed :

" Keep one little kiss for me "—Pratt
" Take this message to my Mother "—Westrop
" Sally Smart "—E. Bullen
" Napolitaine "—Alexander Lea
" Silver Moonlight "—Ordway
" The Mulligan Guards "—Braham
" Come where my love lies dreaming "—S. C. Foster
" The Anvil Chorus " (by desire)—Verdi

After this superior part of the programme followed a " Fiddle
Extravaganza " which, Edward notes, was played by " E. Cleve-
land." Then

Banjo Song
Clog Dance
Part Song—" The Image of the Rose "
Comic Trio—" Awkward Squad "
Farce—" The Ticket Taker "
Plantation Walk Round.

On January 22, 1879, Edward appeared as a composer under the
auspices of the Worcester Early Closing Association, his minuet,
" Grazioso," being played at the Natural History Museum. On
August 16, 1882, the British Medical Association held a Soirée at
the Shirehall and the Instrumental Society's Orchestra gave the
first performance of Edward's *Air de Ballet*. This was no
ordinary meeting of the B.M.A., but the Jubilee of its inauguration
by the great Worcester physician Sir Charles Hastings.

Among those at this Conference was Dr. C. W. Buck (1851–
1932) of Giggleswick, Yorkshire. Dr. Buck was an ardent amateur
musician—'cellist and conductor—and he immediately made
friends with Edward Elgar. The friendship lasted for a lifetime
and Elgar's letters—perhaps the most delightful he ever wrote—
extend from 1882 to 1932. Until his marriage he went regularly to
Yorkshire to stay with the Bucks and there enjoyed some of the
happiest experiences of his life. It was a fortnight after the B.M.A.

Soirée (at which Dr. Buck played in the orchestra) that Edward replied to his first invitation to visit Yorkshire:

> *Loretto Villa* [1] *Chestnut Walk,*
> *Worcester, August 25,* 1882.

MY DEAR SIR,

How about next week? If you are still in the same mind about my visit, I shall be most pleased to spend a few days with you. Monday next would suit me best. Will you let me know how this will suit you?

I see there is a train to Leeds arriving there at 3.40. I could then go on to Settle by the next. Is this the correct way? I was sorry I did not see you on Wedy. last. I called at Beare's, [2] but you were still at the Rehearsal, I suppose.

I hope you arrived home quite safely after your labours.

> And from,
> Yours very truly,
> EDWARD ELGAR

There were regular invitations to assist in the more or less informal performances of the Glee Club held in a large room in the Crown Hotel, in Broad Street; in the orchestras for the concerts of the Worcester Musical Society, conducted by A. J. Caldicott, the Philharmonic Society, conducted by William Done the Cathedral organist, the St. John's Choral Society (a modest body which Edward helped until 1888 and which held its performances in the Infants' Schoolroom), and choral societies at Hereford,[3] Pershore, Malvern, Alcester, Bromsgrove, and Droitwich. Edward normally played the violin, but sometimes the pianoforte. On some occasions four Elgars appeared in the same programmes, for, by 1877, Polly had made her début as a soprano soloist. (In the following year she was among the sopranos in the Three Choirs Festival Chorus. Her father and Edward were among the second violins.) The music which comprised these affairs was astonishingly diversified. Worcestershire taste knew no arbitrary divisions and

---

[1] Polly Grafton's house.

[2] John Beare, of Rathbone Place, London, was one of Elgar's early publishers. His sister, Emma Foote Beare married Dr. Buck at St. Leonard's Church, Streatham, in 1884.

[3] *Vide* letter from Elgar to N. Heins, Hon. Sec., Hereford Choral Society, dated Feb. 18, 1883: "My terms have always been £2 2. 0. I went for £1 11. 6 last Concert to oblige you but do not see my way to do the same again as the expenses are so much."

enjoyed Scotson Clarke (" Marche aux Flambeaux ") side by side with Haydn—at the Union Workhouse. Edward learned the standard oratorios of Handel, Haydn, Mendelssohn, and Spohr, as well as the newer choral works of Gade, Cowen and Bennett ; he became intimately acquainted with the stock overtures of Boieldieu, Hérold, Auber, Weber, Bellini, Balfe, Rossini, Gounod, Flotow, and symphonies and concertos by Mozart, Haydn, and Beethoven. The orchestra sometimes depended rather largely on Uncle Henry's capacity for simulating woodwind detail on the harmonium ; but to those to whom authentic presentations were denied visions of enchantment were revealed.

Edward's local prestige was enhanced by two regular appointments. In old age he liked to deflate affectation on the part of sycophantic visitors by commencing a conversation—" When I was at the Lunatic Asylum. . . ." In fact he visited the County and City of Worcester Pauper Lunatic Asylum at Powick from 1877 until October 1884, when other and more lucrative work caused his retirement. Under the enlightened superintendence first of Dr. Sherlock and then of the celebrated Dr. Marriott Cooke, and with the goodwill of George Jenkins, the Clerk, orchestral concerts were given at regular intervals for the benefit of patients and staff. On each Friday there was a dance for the inmates, for which polkas, quadrilles and lancers were written by the Band Instructor. On January 1879, Edward succeeded Fred S. May in this post and, as he put it, as " Composer in Ordinary to the W.C. & C.L.A." On the change of appointment the Visitors economised a little by paying the new functionary £4 a year less ; taking into account, no doubt, inexperience. Into his programmes Elgar inserted numerous works of his own composition and he grew bold as a conductor, for he frequently astonished the audience by dispensing with the score and conducting from memory. His work was appreciated and the local newspapers kept an eye on the response of the less fortunate section of the audience :

" However much," one reporter wrote, " their mental powers might be damaged in other respects it was apparent that those of the unfortunate inmates of the institution who were able to be present had not lost the faculty of enjoyment, and they were not the least hearty with their applause."

Edward was paid about £32 a year with additional emoluments at the rate of 5s. for quadrille or polka, and 1s. 6d. for any accom-

paniment added to the " burnt-cork ditties " then the fashion. The
Asylum band, formed from among the staff, had piccolo, flute,
clarinet, 2 cornets, euphonium, three or four 1st and a similar
number of 2nd violins, occasional viola, 'cello, double bass and
pianoforte. Edward had one chief assistant—John Roberts, a
carpenter-attendant, who for an extra £10 a year put out music-
stands, and gave some instruction to the wind players. The establishment also maintained a choirmaster and a pianist and organist.
This latter was Miss J. Holloway, to whom Edward dedicated two
works.

Edward was also engaged, in 1877, as " Leader and Instructor
of the Worcester Amateur Instrumental Society." The *Advertiser*
duly gave this association its blessing : " To young men learning
instrumental music the society affords great advantages, as it enables
them to participate at once in real orchestral work, and gives them
extraordinary facilities for acquiring that technical knowledge and
experience which are so essential to a successful instrumentalist.
The object of the society, we should say, is to form an orchestra
which will be capable of taking part in the concerts of the Musical,
Philharmonic and other societies, and so save those societies the
great outlay they have at present to bear in engaging instrumentalists, and judging by the results already achieved, we are sanguine
of their being able very soon to afford valuable aid to our local
vocal societies to whom it should prove an important auxiliary."
Among the members were eager representatives of the " dull
middle classes "—undertakers, grocers, hop factors, millers and
" gentlemen ", and several families provided more than one
player. There were two Binns, two d'Egvilles, two Griffiths, two
Hadleys, two Joneses, two Quartermans, three Hopkinses and four
Elgars. Frank had taken his place as oboist. Among the violinists
was a local grocer—Oswin Grainger—whose name enjoys a little
posthumous fame, for it is inscribed at the head of Edward's
Op. 1 *Romance in E Minor* for violin and piano.

The Instrumental Society gave to Edward—and to others, for
George d'Egville's name appears as composer as well as 'cellist—
his best opportunities for performing his own music. A concert
of March 14, 1882, shows the quality of the programmes of that
date. The conductor was Caldicott and Edward led the orchestra.
The works performed included an *Air de Ballet*—" Pastorale " and
a new march " Pas Redouble " by Ed. Elgar, the overtures to

Flotow's *Martha*, Weber's *Abu Hassan* and Gounod's *Mirella*, Handel's " Hymn for Orchestra "—*Largo in G* and the " Hungarian National War March *Rakoczy*, arr. Liszt."

It gives rare satisfaction to a composer when it is requested that a work of his shall be repeated. The *Air de Ballet* came up again in 1883 : " It assuredly does not lose by repetition. One, though perhaps not the highest, mark of good music is that it fixes itself on the memory ; and there is so much character and sparkling life in Mr. Elgar's *Air de Ballet* that it cannot easily be forgotten."

This range of instrumental experience shows the background to one side of Edward's later fame. His progress towards another objective is indicated by the record of an occasion at St. George's on June 6, 1880. On that day the new chancel was opened by Bishop Ullathorne, O.S.B. ; William Elgar was at the organ and Edward led the orchestra. Motets by Pergolesi and Haydn were given and Hummel's *Mass in B Flat*. But the most significant music was written for the occasion : *Domine Salvam fac*, *Salve regina*, and *Tantum ergo* by E. W. Elgar. *Domine Salvam fac* and *Tantum ergo* had been performed a year earlier on the Feast of SS. Peter and Paul when also the fiftieth anniversary of the opening of the church was commemorated.

Although his interests were confined to Worcestershire Edward's experience was widening in many ways. In this process his sisters were helpful. In 1879 Polly married William Grafton and Lucy married Charles Pipe in 1881. In each cáse husband and wife were well suited, but the pairs afforded a strong contrast.

The Pipes were temperamental and had more imagination than application, the Graftons level-headed and industrious. Lucy Pipe was generous, impetuous, and given to expressing herself in high flown and sometimes melancholic language. Charlie cut a considerable figure in the town for many years but his various interests adversely affected his prosperity. He was a merchant and for some time a Governor of the Hop Market. He was a member of the Glee Club—in 1922 he was, to his relief and delight, presented with a cheque in honour of his long membership—and the treasurer of the Worcestershire Naturalists' Club. He enjoyed the theatre and the company of actors and actresses—especially actresses. In the summer of 1880 he had persuaded Edward to go to Paris with him for a short holiday. On the official side, so to speak, they

Anne Greening at the Shades Tavern ; from a painting by Tom Elgar

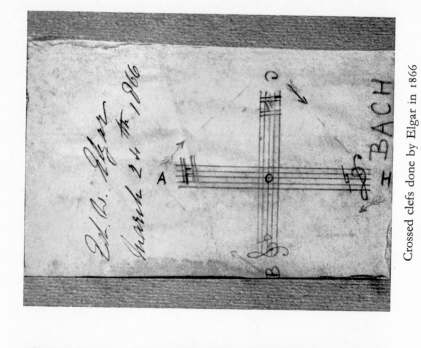

Crossed clefs done by Elgar in 1866

Title page of a song for Lucy

heard Saint-Saëns play the organ at the Madeleine and saw Molière's *Malade imaginaire*. This visit prompted a set of five quadrilles —*Paris*—which were dedicated to Miss Holloway, the organist at Powick Hospital.

In 1883 Edward went to live with the Pipes at 4 Field Terrace, Bath Road. He had previously been living with his sister Polly at Loretto Villa; but the Graftons moved from Worcester in 1883. Will was a manager in the Salt Works at Stoke, by Bromsgrove and had the opportunity of an official residence. "The Elms" was a good, spacious house, with some farmland attached. Whenever he wished to escape the rigours of professional life for a day or two Edward went to this congenial household where he could relax as he liked, and be, as they still remember, as a child with the children. He was, however, never averse from helping Polly at a Works Concert and through his fiddle he conferred many benefits on local charities.

When out of Worcester Edward seized opportunities for relaxation. In 1879 he spent four days in London, ostensibly for lessons with Pollitzer. One night he went to the Vaudeville Theatre, in the Strand, to see Henry J. Byrom's *The Girls*: the next day he went to Alexandra Palace to hear the Military Band; the third day he explored the Royal Aquarium Summer and Winter Gardens, where Blondin, the acrobat, was to be seen and—at a different time—Dubois, the conductor, to be heard in the Grand Hall; and when *She stoops to conquer* was acted in the Theatre; on the last night he went to the 373rd performance of *Les Cloches de Corneville* at the Globe Theatre. Between January 1 and 18, 1883, Edward paid his first visit to Germany. He went to Leipzig. "I heard no end of stuff. Schumann principally and Wagner no end. They have a good opera in Leipzig and we went many times." [1] "We," no doubt, indicates a fräulein who, much taken with the young Englishman, came to visit him in Worcester in the summer. [2]

Schumann and Wagner were rare delights, for their compositions were, at that time, frowned on in the English West Midlands. But there was music played in the Gewandhaus concerts which also might be heard in Worcester. "We used to attend the rehearsals at the Gewandhaus; 9 a.m.! Most of our pros. are not up by that time. There the violinists play 3 over one desk, except

---

[1] Letter to Dr. Buck, May 13, 1883.
[2] Letter to Dr. Buck, July 1, 1883.

the principals ! The first thing I heard was Haydn Sym. in G—the Surprise. Fancy ! ! I was so astounded. I thought it strange to go so far to hear so little. After that I got pretty well dosed with Schumann (my ideal !), Brahms, Rubinstein and Wagner, so had no cause to complain." [1]

None of the more ambitious compositions of Edward's apprentice days are now contained within the Elgarian canon, but his sketches show feverish energy and all the evidence of too little time for their adequate fulfilment : polkas, quadrilles, minuets, waltzes, motets, masses, fugal expositions, tentative symphonic suggestions, impressionist scenes, serenades and intermezzi, studies for violin and even a fantasia on Irish airs jostle one another. If, in 1882 or 1883, the competent professor had seen these he would have noted promise but recommended their author to some other career than that of composer. But, just as Edward fulfilled his desire to go to Germany, so he intended to fulfil his larger ambition. In his lonely confidence lay a large part of his genius : he went forward on an independent way.

[1] *Ibid.*

CHAPTER IV

MR. ELGAR

Mr. Elgar's modesty . . . was of the kind that so often accompanies great talent.

W. C. Stockley

IN 1881 Mr. Elgar junior was promoted to the first violins in the Festival Orchestra. The works for 1881 included Beethoven's *Engedi* (*Mount of Olives*) and fifth symphony, Cherubini's *Mass in D Minor*, (which was included in the Three Choirs repertoire on W. H. Elgar's suggestion), some parts of Handel's *Jephtha* and three new works. These were Caldicott's *Widow of Nain* (composed expressly for the Festival), Mackenzie's *The Bride* and J. F. Barnett's *The Building of the Ship*. It was not, perhaps, an extravagantly adventurous programme, but it raised £972 13s. 9d. for the charity and it gave an opportunity to a local composer—Caldicott.

Elgar's elevation to a first fiddle desk assisted his creative career indirectly. For in 1882 he joined the first fiddles in W. C. Stockley's orchestra in Birmingham. He was obliged to Dr. Herbert Wareing [1] for his introduction to Stockley as a composer. One day Stockley, as impressed as Wareing with what he saw, offered to include a work in one of his concerts. The red-letter day was December 13, 1883. The piece which had its first performance was the *Intermezzo Moresque* (*Mauresque*). Stockley gives this account. [2]

" Mr. Elgar's modesty . . . was of the kind that so often accompanies great talent, for I could not persuade him to conduct his ' Intermezzo,' or even listen to its performance from the auditorium but he insisted on playing in his place in the orchestra, from whence

[1] Herbert Wareing (Mus.D., Cantab.), who lived in Birmingham was a prominent exponent of " correspondence courses " in musical theory, and a minor composer.
[2] In *Fifty Years of Music in Birmingham* (1850-1900) (pub. Birmingham, 1913), pp. 41-2 : Stockley mistakenly puts this performance as in 1880 in his book.

he came to the front in response to a most cordial demand from the audience."

One newspaper gave this judgment: "We hasten to give Mr. Elgar every credit for a musicianly work. A unanimous recall served to discover quite a young composer to the audience, and as Mr. Elgar is not deficient in scholarship, has plenty of fancy, and orchestrates with facility, we may hope that he will not ' rest and be thankful,' but go on in a path for which he possesses singular qualifications." Others were less helpful and Elgar resented one critic who had a personal axe to grind. Thus he wrote to Buck :

4, *Field Terrace, Worcester.*
Jany. 14, 1884

MY DEAR DOCTOR,

If not too late—a happy new year and many of them. I have been loth to write before, for I have had nothing worth telling you. I had a good success at Birm. despite what the papers say ; the man who wrote the slighting article is a Mus. Bac. who had sent in two pieces and they were advertised and withdrawn because the orchestration wanted so much revision as to be unplayable ! Enough of this—I had a characteristic letter from Pollitzer—he asked for the parts and is trying to introduce the sketch in London—I don't anticipate a performance tho' I will let you know if it comes off.

I was sorely disappointed at not going to town—but 'tis no use going there to sit in the house all day—well—I have no *money*—not a cent. And I am sorry to say have no prospects of getting any.

We have had a very quiet time ; my father was ill just before Xmas which made it dismal ; the younger generation at the Catholic Ch : have taken an objection to him and have got him turned out of the Organist's place ; this he had held for 37 years ! ! He thinks a great deal of this and I fear 'twill break him up. Frank gets on : was playing 2nd to Horton at Birmingham on Dec. 26. and it seems to me that the only person who is an utter failure in this miserable world is myself.

I have heard from Arthur and was glad he is going to Leipzig. I fancy he will get good lessons, there are few, comparatively, for the 'cello.

What have you gone and done ? He says " the Doctor is in great glee over this last business ! " Surely 'tis not matrimony : I am more than anxious to know all about it. I suppose I begin regular work next week, but I don't look forward to it. I am disappointed, disheartened and sick of this world altogether.

I hope you had a good time in town, did you get any music ? I thought much about you and wondered how the trios went. What a business about Barrett ! I saw he was garotted but have heard nothing since. Well—'tis time I was retiring—I am afraid I have sent you a dismal epistle—sorry for it—better next time.

Will you please give my kind regards to Mrs. Buck and all I know

> & with best wishes, I am, my dear doctor,
> Always sincerely yours,
> EDWARD ELGAR

P.S. Miss Weaver is remaining in Worcester and the little Music *etc.* that we get together is the only enjoyment I get and more than I deserve no doubt.

It is one thing to write music and another to persuade people to play it. With his feet firmly set on the ground Elgar, despite larger ambitions, considered the immediate possibilities of performance and judiciously contented himself with slender pieces. One day in the autumn of 1885 there was a concert at the Deanery in Worcester. The programme, no doubt, was contrived to suit the Dean's tastes. It included Haydn's *Toy Symphony* as the *pièce de résistance* and the Reverend E. Capel-Cure, a 'cellist of some capability, played a sonata by Handel. But there was also a *Romance* for violin by Ed. Elgar which was entrusted to Master W. H. Dyson. This was the work which was dedicated to Oswin Grainger, the grocer, and it was published as Op. 1 by Schotts. It is a very good *Romance* to be played in a Deanery—competent, tuneful, yet poetic. At a soirée in the following year Fred Pedley sang Elgar's *A Soldier's Song*. This was also published, but at a later date.

The published works which date from this period contain much intimate interest. There is a *Gavotte* in A Major for violin and pianoforte (which sounds like an arrangement of a classical piece by Kreisler) which was also issued by Schotts. This was dedicated to Dr. C. W. Buck, " in memory of the old days." Another work

for the same medium is an *Allegretto* on a theme of five notes
—GEDGE—which spelt the name of a Malvern family to whose
daughters (one of whom has appeared in the R.A.M. examination
successes of 1878) Elgar was tutor. The Misses Gedge were surely
enchanted with this clever, yet affectionate, addition to their store
of drawing-room music.

On the other hand Elgar was not neglecting his larger ambitions.
This is shown in a programme of the Amateur Instrumental Society
which he conducted at the Public Hall on April 9, 1885.

> Symphony in B Minor—Schubert
> Fest Marsch—Raff
> Entr'acte " Manfred "—Reinecke
> Overture " Haydée "—Auber
> Overture Alfonso and Estrella—Schubert
> Adagio from Scotch Symphony—Mendelssohn
> Sevillana—Ed. Elgar
> Gavotte " Stephanie "—Czibulka

There were also songs by Hon. Mrs. Robert Lyttleton and Lord
William Compton and 'cello solos by Mr. W. F. Roden of the
Hallé Orchestra.

The Amateur Instrumental Society was fulfilling its promise to
provide a competent orchestra for the city and the conductor was
vigorously enlarging its repertoire. At the same time he was
educating the public by canalising his literary talents into instructive
programme notes. That which he wrote about *Sevillana* is of special
interest.

" This sketch is an attempt to portray, in the compass of a
few bars, the humours of a Spanish fête. It consists of three
principal themes, which may be briefly characterised thus—1st
an imitation of a Spanish folk-song, played by the Violins on
the fourth string ; 2nd, a softer strain in the major which may
(or may not) be taken to represent ' un passage d'amour,' for
which, as in England, such gatherings are supposed to lend
opportunity ; and 3rd, a brisk Valse measure in D major.
Something very like an *émeute* takes place during the progress
of this, missiles are freely thrown, and at least one stiletto is
drawn—but these are only modern Spaniards, and no tragic

result follows. ' Cela était autrefois ainsi, mais nous avons changé tout cela.' Quiet is restored—the itinerant resumes his song—the Valse continues, and somehow or other all ends happily.

It is not assumed that this little piece embodies an accurate representation of all the above ; suffice it to say that amidst some such scene, and as a souvenir thereof, was it written."

The people of Worcester found *Sevillana* " pretty and tuneful, dashing and spirited," and they asked to have it played a second time. The piece had been performed once previously in Worcester, but its value was more fully recognised in 1885, for in the previous year Manns—through Pollitzer's interest—had included it in a Crystal Palace concert during the London International and Universal Exhibition of Arts.

Mendelssohn was one of Elgar's earliest heroes. That the slow movement from the *"Scotch" Symphony* should appear in a programme of the Amateur Instrumental Society was, therefore, not surprising ; particularly since Elgar himself had spent holidays in Scotland in 1883 and 1884. A relic of a transient intimacy lies in the dedication of *Une Idylle* (Op. 4, No. 1)—to " E. E. [of] Inverness." But there was another, Mendelssohnian, sequel. Edward sketched a *Scotch Overture*, which failed to gain a hearing. So—to Dr. Buck on January 8, 1886 :

" We had festive night at the Glee Club last Tuesday. Haydn's retiring Symphony—candles and all—it went very well. Cast an eye over the Clef Club Scheme. I shall not go—can't afford it. Oh ! about the Scotch overture—I have turned it up. I don't know if I told you about it before—I showed it old Stockley and he candidly said he could not read the Score and it sounded to him disconnected. So I have retired into my shell and live in hopes of writing a polka someday—failing that a single chant is probably my fate."

In November 1885 Elgar succeeded Mr. Foster as organist of St. George's, and thus had more opportunity to write occasional pieces for its services. There were complications about this appointment, for W. H. Elgar still smarted under a sense of grievance. " The old man," wrote Edward to Buck,[1] " does not take

[1] Letter of Oct. 29, 1885.

kindly to the organ biz : but I hope 'twill be all right before I commence my ' labours.' " On October 9, 1888,[1] for instance, there was an important event in the life of the church when the Apostleship of Prayer and the League of the Sacred Heart were inaugurated. Bishop Illsley, Bishop of Birmingham, came to preach and in his honour Elgar set as a motet the appropriate text : *Ecce Sacerdos Magnus*. This was published together with other liturgical pieces by Cary. It may be inferred from the nature of this music and knowledge of the limited capabilities of Catholic Church choirs at that time (reinforced by Elgar's " the choir is awful and no good is to be done with them ") that Elgar worked as conscientiously with his singers as with his instrumentalists.

The most exciting event during these years was the visit of Dvořák to Worcester. He came to the 1884 Festival to conduct his *Stabat Mater* and *Symphony in D Major*. Elgar, as usual, was in the orchestra. The immediate effect of this was that he began playing *Slavonic Dances* at local concerts. But the warmth of this new Bohemian music infused his whole nature and his creative genius saw more clearly in what direction its objective lay. Dvořák was a musician for whom Elgar always retained a great affection. Under the immediate experience of having met Dvořák's music for the first time he wrote to Dr. Buck : " I wish you could hear Dvořák's music. It is simply ravishing, so tuneful and clever and the orchestration is wonderful : no matter how few instruments he uses it never sounds thin. I cannot describe it ; it must be heard." [2] It was at this time that someone showed to Dvořák Newman's *Dream of Gerontius* and suggested it for his consideration as an oratorio. But that project never went further.

Despite his increasing reputation Elgar still had to endure the old routine, for, practically, composition was a profitless occupation. " My prospects " he had written to Dr. Buck on April 21, 1884, " are about as hopeless as ever. I am not wanting in energy I think ; so, sometimes, I conclude that 'tis want of ability and get in a mouldy desponding state which is really horrible." There was

[1] " . . . some special things had to be sung for which we had no music ; then I had to set to work and compose it all and copy out the parts ! ! Had to get it in anyhow and broke my neck doing. Anyway the leading paper says the new composition was " exquisite " so I suppose it was good enough." Letter to Dr. C. W. Buck, Oct. 13, 1888.

[2] Sept. 28, 1884. Elgar also played under Dvořák when the Symphony was played in Birmingham in Oct. 1886.

no change since January and these moods were recurrent throughout life.

As a solo violinist Elgar was still much in demand in most of the towns in the county, and at concerts in support of such opposite ends as the Girls' Friendly Society and the Worcester Vagrants' Relief Society. He played ostentatious pieces by Wieniaski, Godard, de Bériot and Vieuxtemps, as well as sonatas by Brahms for the more polite atmosphere of Malvern. He took some interest in the biography of Vieuxtemps, indicating in one of his programme notes an analogy for those who cared to notice it. Vieuxtemps was the son of a music dealer and learned most of his craft from the shelves of his father's shop.

II

Elgar was spending a good deal of time in Malvern, a town inhabited exclusively by " nice people." This distinguished it from Worcester, which had a mixed population and was, in Elgar's views at Election time, a " radical hole." Indian civil servants, prosperous manufacturers, generals, and a few clergy of rank not lower than Archdeacon retired to Malvern. They went there in hope, for its reputation for longevity was unequalled in the British Isles. Attracted by this and by the waters many neurotics, hypochondriacs and valetudinarians went to live there in the eighties. They had, however, not been unmusical. A curious publication of the mid-nineteenth century—*Three Weeks in Wet Sheets; Being the Diary and Doings of a Moist Visitor to Malvern*—testifies to this, for:

" Here, too, a German band, supported by subscription, plays every morning at eight, when invalids slowly imbibe the pure elements to an andante of Haydn's, or toss off tumblers from the ' sacred rill ' to a Pot-Pourri of Donizetti, or the measured time of the Presburgh Polka."

A feature of Malvern in the eighties was the number of daughters produced by the residents. For their benefit a number of high-class schools were established. The prestige which the young ladies acquired simply through living in Malvern was enhanced when and if they could also gain some practical skill in the polite art of music. Elgar was the fashionable teacher. He had two recommendations : a considerable reputation that was not entirely local and " a gentlemanly bearing." (It was, nevertheless, some time before he lived down the solecism of arriving at Miss Fletcher's school clad in tweeds and knickerbockers more suitable to a countryman than a professor of music.) He was also able to maintain the polka tradition. His sketch books are full of works in this form written for the Malvernians.

Among some of his pupils and their families Elgar found congenial company. The Gedges, the Acworths and the Fittons were both hospitable and encouraging. In response to an advertisement announcing his Malvern teaching Caroline Alice Roberts became Edward's pupil on October 6, 1886. Alice, in her thirty-sixth year (her birthday was on October 9), was a lonely, somewhat frustrated woman, looking for fulfilment in art and in good works. She is the perfect example of the Victorian lady of, sometimes unwelcome, leisure whose destiny it had been to serve the family. Her family had been of service to the state. Her father, Major-General Sir Henry Gee Roberts, had spent a lifetime in India. In consequence of his devoted service his health was impaired and the K.C.B. which was conferred on him in 1859 and the official thanks of both Houses of Parliament were small reward. Roberts had entered the service of the East India House as a cadet in 1818. As Charles Lamb was a clerk there at that time it is possible that the composer of *Dream Children* derived some part of his enthusiasm for the essayist through the Roberts connection. Roberts served through the Sikh wars and the Indian Mutiny and was commended by Sir Charles Napier as " the best officer in the Bombay Army and perhaps in India, capable of commanding any army in the field."

At the age of twenty Roberts—himself a Gloucester man—married into a celebrated Gloucestershire family. His wife was Julia Maria Raikes, granddaughter of Robert Raikes who promoted the Sunday School scheme. Four children were born to the Robertses in India ; Albert, who died young, Frederick, who died in 1882, Stanley Napier and Caroline Alice. Against his return home Roberts purchased a Georgian house at Redmarley d'Abitot in the extreme south-west of Worcestershire. It was here that Alice was brought up. When she was ten her father died. Her two surviving brothers entered the army and went their several ways. Thus Alice was left with her mother. She devoted much time to animal welfare, with a special affection for Persian cats, and to country pursuits. She was, however, something of a scholar and the index to Rev. W. S. Symonds' *Records of the Rocks* was her work. (Symonds, a considerable geologist, was rector of Pendock in Worcestershire.) On her own account Alice published a story or two in *Home Chimes*; a narrative poem, bearing many marks of Tennyson's influence, *Isabel Trevithoe* (1879); and a 2 volume novel, *Marchcroft Manor* (1882).

Two reviews of Alice's writings give some accurate definition of her personality. The *Scotsman* on *Isabel Trevithoe* commented on " some graceful and poetic thoughts . . . but as a rule the writer seldom rises above it, if she does not sink below, the dead level of mediocrity." Of the novel the *Glasgow Herald* said " We feel it very difficult to do justice to the singular charm of ' Marchcroft Manor.' The story is very slight, the characters few, there are no startling incidents, and yet there is a quiet brightness and sunniness which are very attractive."

Alice and her mother, living at Hazeldine House, were expected to occupy some part of their time in good works. They were generous in their efforts. Alice arranged readings from Shakespeare, taking good care that any lack of propriety in the text was adequately, and often drastically, removed. She also sang in Pearsall's glees and played duet arrangements of Rossini's overtures at village concerts.

There were neighbours at Redmarley who collaborated in musical entertainment. Among them were the Baker family of Hasfield Court. Without the Bakers the " *Enigma* " *Variations* would have had a different complexion. The owner of Hasfield, William Meath Baker, figures therein as W. M. B. One of his sisters, Minnie, married the father of " Dorabella "[1] and the other —Dora—married Richard Baxter Townshend—R. B. T.

In 1887 Lady Roberts died and Alice, unwilling to shoulder the burden of a large house and estate alone, let Hazeldine. But by this time her interest in her music teacher was so considerable that a change to a furnished room in Malvern was not so undesirable as it might have been. She had, during the previous year, taken Elgar over to Redmarley and he had met various members of the family. When, however, an engagement was announced on September 22,

---

[1] Rev. Alfred Penny, Rector of Wolverhampton from 1895-1919. He had one daughter, by a previous marriage, and married Miss Baker in 1897.

1888, cousins and aunts naturally scented a *mésalliance*. One aunt charitably showed her disapproval by withholding a considerable sum of money which, in other circumstances, she would have settled on Alice. Such money as the family did allow was on no account to pass to any issue of the marriage.

Alice, however, realised that she had found a purpose and she fulfilled it. With determination and affection, tact and reassurance, and a simple faith she made Edward into a great composer.[1] The most recent milestone on this road had been erected by Stockley who had performed a *Suite* on March 1, 1888, the second movement being the familiar *Sérénade mauresque*.

Although he was very busy in the early part of 1889 Elgar found time to go to London—to see Pollitzer again, an exhibition of old masters at Burlington House, and the *Merry Wives of Windsor* at the Haymarket; and to buy Alice's engagement ring with " 6 little pearls." Back in Worcestershire he spent his time rehearsing Cowen's *Sleeping Beauty* for the Festival chorus, and an ode by the acting cathedral organist Hugh Blair, a Ladies' Class organised by Mrs. Fitton in Malvern, and the choir at St. George's; in teaching his pupils ; in playing each Thursday in Birmingham ; and in taking part in chamber music in Malvern with the Fittons and the Rev. E. Capel-Cure. It was with some relief that Elgar noted in his diary for May 1 :

"Ladies Class *last*. Ch. rehearsal *very last*."

He was in process of burning his boats. He was going to London where, it might have been thought, fame and fortune awaited.

As is the way with local newspapers some of the facts got misplaced. Thus we read :

" It is rumoured that a well-known and distinguished member of the musical profession in Worcester has gained the hand of a wealthy patroness living in a neighbouring town. This has caused a considerable flutter in musical circles, and the interest

---

[1] cf. " And now (after all our talks about the mystery of living) I must tell you how happy I am in my new life and what a dear, loving companion I have and how sweet everything seems and how *understandable* existence seems to have grown : but you may forget the long discussions we used to have in your carriage when driving about but I think all the difficult problems are now solved and—well I don't worry myself about 'em now." Letter to Dr. Buck, Oct. 6, 1889.

of it is enhanced by the further rumour that the lady, thinking an uninterrupted experience of the happiness of home is better than the rewards of professional fame, ordains that there shall be no further professional engagements."

More accurate was the subsequent note of the presentation by local music-lovers " of a handsome travelling-bag, with silver mountings ; each of the fittings engraved with the recipient's initials " and from " the ladies' recreative class . . . an elegant Canterbury for books." Father Knight of St. George's gave to Elgar, as wedding present, a copy of Newman's *Dream of Gerontius*, into which he had copied the markings made by General Gordon on his copy.[1] The teaching practice in Worcester was passed into the hands of Herr Heinrich Sück, formerly of the Cologne Conservatorium. Sück made his own small mark both as fiddler and conductor. On November 16, 1900, he conducted *Froissart* at St. James's Hall—its first London performance.

III

The marriage took place before the Lady Altar of Brompton Oratory on May 8, 1889, Father Fawkes being the celebrant. Edward was delighted that Dr. Buck came all the way from Yorkshire for the wedding. The honeymoon was spent in the Isle of Wight first at Shanklin and then at Ventnor—where Edward bought Alice a copy of Moritz's *Travels in England in* 1782. In Elgar's diary is a moving gloss made in his later days on an early entry. On May 14 he noted " Had to wade. *Kissed her wet foot* ": forty years or so later he scribbled " she remembered this the week she died." Three days later a newspaper cutting was sent to Worcester, where it gave much pleasure, for it was a " Fashionable list of Visitors and Residents for Ventnor and its environs corrected up to May 16." Among the fashionable were Mr. and Mrs. Edward Elgar.

At the end of the month the Elgars returned to London to set up house temporarily at 3 Marloes Road, Kensington. Alice wrote to her former neighbours :

[1] Fr. Knight must have had access to the copy which Gordon gave to Frank Power, *The Times* correspondent in Khartoum, in 1884.

DEAR FRIENDS AT REDMARLEY,

I have received your present and send you many, many thanks for your most kind thought of me. I shall value the beautiful water-colour picture deeply as a remembrance of many friends of the days and years I spent in my old home, and although I am away from Redmarley, I am sure you know that I take a great interest in the place, and wish earnestly for all good to you all there. I hope I may see many of the contributors, whose names are in the frame, which I shall keep with the picture, some day, and be able to introduce my husband to you, and give you many warm thanks in person, and tell you how your present is always before our eyes in our new home, reminding us of the kind thoughts of so many old friends, although you may be sure I am not likely to forget Redmarley. You will see that these few lines are meant to convey my thanks to you all.

Believe me,

Yours sincerely,

C. ALICE ELGAR

On August 15, the Eastnor Flower Show was held and Mrs. Elgar remembered her former obligations in sending 2 prizes of 6s. and 4s. for the best flower borders. In August the Elgars spent a brief holiday in Malvern, being there for Ethel Fitton's wedding and Isobel's twenty-first birthday. At Alice's instigation they called on the Hon. Mrs. Roper-Curzon—later Lady Teynham. " Gosh ! " wrote Edward in his diary.

This first year of marriage had its disappointments. There were days when Edward found it difficult to settle and he was much troubled with his eyes, his throat and with headaches. But there were new and valuable experiences. He was able, living in London, to go to the opera—for 2s. 6d. a performance—and he became deeply interested in Wagner. That year at Covent Garden he saw *Die Meistersinger* twice, Verdi's *Otello* (for some reason he left the theatre after two acts) *Carmen* and *Don Giovanni*. There were the Richter concerts, with programmes which included Wagner, Schubert's " great " Symphony in C Major and Parry's fourth symphony. There was a concert at which Albéniz played, and there were the Crystal Palace performances under Manns. Edward and Alice went frequently to the London Library and read voraciously. They called in at the Dog Show at the Crystal Palace in October as

it was enticingly, if embarrassingly, near to Manns's field of operations. They explored the City churches, the Art Galleries, and
most of the famous and ancient buildings. They went unfailingly
to church—usually to the church of the Carmelites or sometimes to
Farm Street—and on one occasion heard Cardinal Manning, then
at the height of his popularity, preach at the Pro-Cathedral.

Alice did her best to preserve the traditions, never forgetting
that her family's coat of arms was granted in the sixteenth century.
She entertained frequently. Sometimes there were visitors from
Gloucestershire and Worcestershire, sometimes relatives like the
Dowager Lady Thompson, or friends of the Robertses like the
Kingdon Andersons.

But Edward's progress towards his goal was slow. He called
on Schotts, Beares, Orsborn and Tuckwood, and Hawkes, to all of
whom he submitted manuscripts. On September 8 he revised his
first copy of *Liebesgrüss* from Schotts. He had sold it for, perhaps,
£5. It was the best-selling *salon* piece of the century. On November
11 *Liebesgrüss* was played at the Crystal Palace. A song—*Queen
Mary's Song*—was accepted by Orsborn and Tuckwood and a letter
from Lord Tennyson came with permission for use of the poem.
Sevillana was revised and left with Hawkes ; but without any positive result. The difficulty of those days is underlined by a brief
note recording the sale of some pearls of Alice.

The Elgars left Marloes Road during the year to live for a time
at Oaklands, Fountain Road, Upper Norwood, whence they moved
to 51 Avonmore Road, West Kensington, on March 24, 1890.
They took the house in Kensington for three years after extensive
house-hunting in Bromley, Notting Hill, Hampstead and Highgate.

The only London musician who took any interest in Elgar was
Manns. He played the Suite at a Crystal Palace midday concert on
February 24, 1890, and was good enough to give tickets of admission to rehearsals to both Edward and Alice. But Manns could
not work miracles, nor could he include works by Elgar in his
programmes more than occasionally. So Elgar went from publisher
to publisher : to Orsborn and Tuckwood about his Organ Voluntaries and a song, to Novellos with part songs, to Goodwin and
Tabb with an overture to be copied. Sometimes dispirited he
noted laconically " no business." Once he left a score in the
Underground—but recovered it. Some days were enlivened by
meeting new and interesting acquaintances—like Edward Lloyd—

or old friends. The Fittons, the Townshends and William Wolstenholme and Lady Montgomery[1] came during the year. Edward went
to as many concerts and operas as he could manage and Alice went
to lectures. On May 15 she heard Andrew Lang lecture on
" Criticism " at Kensington Town Hall. Three days later she
noted " E commenced a tale."

Faraway memories had stirred and the chivalries of *Froissart*
pushed Elgar into what was for him a new form—an overture of
romantic exploration. On August 7 Elgar heard that Novellos
wished to see him about the overture. The next day they promised
to publish it. Before the end of the month the final proofs had been
corrected. In the meantime the work had been put down for the
Worcester Festival, for which Elgar was engaged to play.

There were two events to write home about, for on August 14,
a daughter had been born to Alice. Elgar wrote to his youngest
sister, Dot, on August 26 :

" All is going on smoothly but very dull being all alone.

" I *did* wish mother and dad had been coming (to the christening)
but I did not say much to mother in the way of regret as I thought
it might make her more sorry she did not come.

" I hope you won't get too hard worked during the Festival
and feel it so awkward that Frank's wife will not be able to do her
share : but we must hope for the future. I suppose Polly will be
coming over. I am very proud that the parts of the overture are
to be done and by Novello : shall you hear the row ? I trow not.

" Are you going to do anything special at Church for the
edification of the visitors ? "

Preliminary orchestral rehearsals for the Three Choirs Festivals
were held in London and a day or two before he set off for home
Elgar was pleased to hear a run-through of *Froissart* in St. George's
Hall. In Worcester he found time to call on the Leicesters and to
play the organ at St. George's for Benediction.

There were two modern works at the Festival by established
composers. One was Parry's *Ode to St. Cecilia,* hot from Leeds :
the other Dr. Frederick Bridge's *Repentance of Nineveh.* Bridge's
work drew two columns of detailed criticism from the correspondent of the *Musical Times.*[2] On *Froissart* he said :

---

[1] Widow of Sir Robert Montgomery, Governor of the Punjab and saviour of Lahore
in the Indian Mutiny; she was the grandmother of Field-Marshal Lord Montgomery.
[2] Oct. 1890.

" Mr. Elgar, formerly of Worcester, is now, we believe, a resident in London, where, it may be hoped, and, given opportunity, even expected that he will make his mark. The Overture is of course chivalric in style, and, perhaps, more commendable for what it tries to say than for the manner of its expression. There is upon it, what surprises no one—the mark of youth and inexperience ; but it shows that with further thought and study, Mr. Elgar will do good work. He must acquire greater coherence of ideas, and conciseness of utterance—those inevitable signs of a master, only to be attained by extended and arduous effort. For such effort, no doubt, Mr. Elgar may be trusted. *Froissart* was much applauded—the Prophet had honour even in his own country." It cannot be said that the Prophet's own country deserved this cut.

Elgar suffered inevitable reaction after this excitement. His eyes gave him trouble again and he suffered much pain from a septic wisdom tooth. In London as the year ended hope ebbed. For a time, in November, the ambition to write on a grand scale set Elgar to a violin concerto which, however, he destroyed. He saw *Orfeo* at Covent Garden. He went up to Worcester to give lessons. He "practised the violin very much." He advertised in the November issue of the *Musical Times* for pupils in "violin, accompaniment, orchestration, etc."; but none came. Alice's last two entries in the diary for the year are eloquent of disillusionment and prepare the way for a return to Worcestershire—to the old teaching round in order to make ends meet.

Dec. 30. " A. thought this the coldest day she ever felt (I cried with the cold.)

   31. E. wrote for permission to give as references to several."

CHAPTER V

"SPLENDID SAGA-ING"

. . . that lively heartfelt music . . .
Sir George Grove to Alice Elgar,
Oct. 24th, 1897

By THE age of thirty-four or -five the model composer has successfully emerged from his " first period " and is, beyond doubt, well
established. Elgar was no model composer. He was, however,
a composer. But in 1891 there were very few to believe this. The
man from the west had failed in his frontal attack on the metropolis
and began, with some bitterness and much disappointment, to
plan a strategic withdrawal to a safe defensive position. At the end
of January he engaged in a last minute tour of the publishing
houses—Schotts, Metzlers and Beares—before going down to
Birmingham for Stockley's concert at Birmingham on February 5.
Stockley put *Froissart* into his programme and Chivalry's uplifted
lance struck a response from the Midlanders. " E. called and
applauded on to platform. A. very proud." In London prospective tenants were being shown round 51 Avonmore Road, and in
April a *House to Let* notice was put up. In the following month
the Elgars were house-hunting in Malvern, where Edward had been
visiting regularly to extend his teaching connection.

On June 20 they entered into possession of Forli, their
Malvern home for the next few years. Throughout this year
anxiety and the wear and tear caused by much travelling brought
Edward into a debilitated state of health. The record, in the diaries,
of minor and major bouts of ill-health is an index to the nervous
condition of an excessively sensitive individual. He had not been
well in April. On August 26 he was ill enough for Alice to send
for the doctor. Four days later " quinsy " was pencilled in the

66

diary. At the end of a week Dr. Weir lanced Edward's throat. On September 14 Alice was woken in the night by Edward agonising in a nightmare.

> *O ghosts of a forgotten past*
> *And many a well fought field.*

Alice found consolation in an apt quotation and attended to practical affairs, especially to the planning of the garden. At the end of September W. H. Elgar was seriously ill and for the rest of the year Edward's throat gave considerable trouble. Once or twice he went to London to see *Lohengrin*, *Orfeo* and *Cavalleria Rusticana*. For the most part, however, he had to devote himself to the musical affairs of high school girls, and the only work completed was a trifling fiddle piece, *Capricieuse*. This was finished on Christmas Eve, Elgar the Catholic being aroused to a greater optimism by the joyful festival of the Church's year. The depth of his general pessimism, however, is indicated by a not infrequent observation in these three years of disappointment : " E. very mouldy all day."

This was the time when friends could help. There were many who did. The Fittons and Bakers on the social side were indispensable. Mrs. Fitton frequently entertained the Elgars (Alice was punctilious in returning hospitality and indefatigable in making new social contacts) and Edward was plunged into the chamber music of Schumann, Brahms and Grieg. Miss Frances Baker, meanwhile, was intent on arranging a holiday for the Elgars and in the early part of 1892 was instructing them in her plans for a joint summer expedition to Germany.

Edward had influenza in January and entertained himself with the nonsense poetry of Edward Lear. He was further excited by the arrival of furniture and trophies, which had belonged to General Roberts, from Hazeldine. Many of the effects were sold, but Alice kept what she wanted and sent Edward off to Worcester, in high excitement, to have some swords cleaned. By March his spirits were improved. He was writing some string pieces, to become the *Serenade*. By May inspiration was in flood. One day he met Isobel Fitton, took her in to tea, and played to her some of his sketches for *The Black Knight*. On June 1 some music arrived from Schotts, and three days later his *Very easy exercises* for violin and his *Etudes caractéristiques*, which were inscribed to Pollitzer, from Chanot.

A frequent visitor to Forli was Hugh Blair, Done's successor at the cathedral, a lively composer and an imaginative critic who, alas! was to drown his talents too deep to retain the goodwill of the Dean and Chapter who employed him. Elgar wrote to Dr. Buck on December 20 : " Blair (of the Cathedral) and I are pulling together and making things lively here, that is to say in Worcester ; we have an orchestral service in the Cathedral on Sunday evening 27th . . ." Blair's present renown is that when it was most needed he gave sympathy and encouragement to Elgar. Blair heard *The Black Knight* on June 11. " If you will finish it," he said, " I will produce it at Worcester." When, in later life, Elgar had the opportunity to help his old friend he did so.

Meanwhile the *Serenade* neared completion and before the holidays it was accepted by Novellos. At the end of July some of *The Black Knight* was also left at Novellos for an opinion.

In August the Elgars went, by way of Dover, Ostend, Malines, Cologne, Bonn—where they visited Beethoven's birthplace, and Mainz to Bayreuth. There they saw *Parsifal* (twice), *Tristan*, and *Die Meistersinger*. In Nuremberg they saw *Cavalleria Rusticana*. But most of the holiday was spent in the quieter parts of Bavaria. Edward and Alice took pleasure in the country life, noting the beauty of the fresh snow on the hills, the charm of wild life in the woods, the flickering fires lit by the haymakers at night, the cows ringing their way home, the oxen drawing their wagons, the swallows flying in and out of the houses, and the native dresses. They were entertained one day when tea, brewed in a coffee-pot—for there were no teapots in the whole of Hammersbach—was served to them as a black concoction and when the daughter of the house, in honour of visitors, felt obliged to put on stockings, but not shoes. As a storm broke when they were in this cottage they stayed to shelter and were thrilled when, as the men came home from the fields, the little community spontaneously broke into four part harmony. Edward noted every detail of Bavarian folk-lore that he could discover, compared the details of domestic architecture with what he knew so well in England, and examined every church and wayside shrine. Oberammagau was something of a disappointment. It was expensive and the people were spoiled by " enthusiasts " and a visit to the theatre was somewhat marred by the eccentric behaviour of the local trombonist who "made most awful inflation every note."

Thus recreated the Elgars returned home with added determination. Edward was "fired with songs," for some of which Alice wrote the words, and, with Novellos' interest aroused, worked hard at the completion of *The Black Knight*. At the end of September he undertook a new teaching appointment at Cambridge House, Malvern, and early in October was asked to go to London to discuss the publication of *The Black Knight*. This was finally accepted by the publishers on November 11. At the end of a more propitious year Elgar had started to score *The Black Knight*. The worst calamity of the year was the death of the collie dog Scap, which had come from Dr. Buck in 1885 and had been a loyal and amusing companion until, in 1889, he had to be entrusted to the care of Lucy Pipe.

The fairer course on which his music appeared set sent Elgar to the golf links or the billiard-table for relaxation, and he enjoyed chamber music at home with Basil Nevinson, who played the 'cello and H. D. Steuart-Powell, a pianist. On April 18, 1893, the Worcester Festival Choral Society, under Blair, gave the first performance of *The Black Knight*. Alice was thrilled by the press notices, which more than compensated for the destruction of the breakfast service two days previously through the incompetence of a domestic. It was also on April 16 that Alice saw her first swallow of the year. Three days later she noted the first cuckoo.

It was, outwardly, a happy summer. Edward learned to speak German and went to see a Covent Garden performance of *Tristan and Isolde* in preparation for another continental holiday, in which Miss Rosa Burley, a Malvern schoolmistress who frequently helped out with the infant Carice, was to accompany the Elgars. Malvern put out its flags and sent up fireworks on July 6 in honour of the wedding of the Duke of York. In August the Elgar party, which also included Dora Penny, went to Munich. They heard *Die Meistersinger*, the whole of the *Ring*, *Tannhäuser*, *Tristan and Isolde* —" the great opera " wrote Alice obedient to Edward's opinions— and *Die Feen*. They went back to Worcester in time for the Three Choirs Festival, wherein Edward, as usual, was to play.

Hugh Blair conducted the Festival and the *Mass in B Minor*, the *German Requiem* of Brahms, and Parry's *Job* were performed as the main works. Perhaps it was the greatness of the chosen music that emphasised for Elgar the broad chasm lying between thought

and deed, between the projection of the masterpiece and its acceptance. He was profoundly depressed and scribbled a pencil note
for posterity on his programme :

" I played 1st violin for the sake of the fee as I cd. obtain no
recognition as a composer. E. E."

He went off to golf with Townshend and Acland and other
enthusiasts. He took part in " fearsomes " (golf à 4), lost six balls
in one day, and gladly noted on another that he had played with
Sir Capel Wolseley and Mr. Strickland and had beaten them. He
wrote a few songs in January.[1] But at the end of the month throat
trouble recurred. At the end of February the doctor recommended
a holiday at Bournemouth.

Immediately, however, it was not easy to leave Worcestershire,
because of his commitments. On February 23 Novellos wrote
their acceptance of a part song *Happy eyes* (to Alice's words).
Edward added one of his brief annotations to the effect that Novellos
would also pay for the song. This heralded a period of significant
activity.

On March 30 Elgar went over to Hereford for a performance of
Sullivan's *Prodigal Son*. He returned and immediately set about a
short ceremonial work—*Sursum Corda*. On April 2 he tried it over
on the organ of Holy Trinity Church. A day later Worcester was
en fête for the visit of the Duke of York. Elgar's solemnity—for
brass, strings and organ—was played in the cathedral on April 4.
He was forbidden by the doctor to conduct it in the evening,
although he had done so at the afternoon rehearsal. The *Sursum
Corda* made an impressive interlude in the service. It is, perhaps,
to be doubted whether it made quite such a stirring effect as the
Dean's sermon, in which he reminded them " that they all entered
into the enthusiasm of Tuesday when the future heir to the Crown
passed in triumphal procession through the streets. When they
mingled with the singing crowd, when they saw the banners
waving, and when they heard the boom of the guns, some of them
perhaps sent forth their thoughts to the great future when the
Royalty of the Lord should be revealed."

Such was the spirit of the age.

The Elgars left Worcestershire at the end of April for a holiday
in Sussex. They went to Littlehampton and then on to Chichester.
One day they visited Arundel " saw the Keep, then lunched at the

---

[1] *The Wave, Muleteer's Song, Rondel* (from *Froissart*), Jan. 4.

Norfolk Arms, bewahre : and then saw the Cathedral [church of
S. Philip Neri] and then walked into the Park. . . ." The great
church built by the Norfolks at Arundel is the very place to set
mystical impulses abroad. When he went home Elgar turned to
Parsifal and contrived an arrangement of the Good Friday music
for a concert at the High School.

The concert took place on June 13. One of the Misses Gedge
(there were seven !) played Mendelssohn's second pianoforte
concerto. Miss Averil Woodward played Elgar's *Bizarrerie*. But
the *pièce de résistance* was the *Parsifal* arrangement—for 3 fiddles,
'cello, "organ" and 2 pianos. "He has," reported a local newspaper,
"found a congenial theme, and has approached it with a poetic
perception of its reverential character. Although two of the most
important elements of a string band were necessarily absent on
Wednesday—the viola and double bass—the result was admirable,
and gave some idea of the grandeur which a full orchestral setting
would display." During an interval Miss Ottley, the headmistress,
expressed her pleasure at the fact that the programme consisted of
performances by past and present pupils and members of the staff ;
and then explained that the concert was given owing to the fact
that they wished to add to the beautiful art room—supplied by the
munificence of the Council—a very much needed science room, at
present entirely unfitted, and the cost of which would far exceed
the amount realised by the concert. Miss Ottley then expressed
her indebtedness to Mr. Elgar who, she said, had raised the tone
of the music in the school.

II

In July 1894 Elgar was busy on a new work. " E. wrote sagas all
day " noted Alice on July 15. *King Olaf* was in sight. But the
frequent presence at Forli of Father Knight suggests that
Gerontius was also in gestation. A summer holiday, however, not
only interrupted these projects but also stimulated another. It was
a long carefree holiday through August and three weeks of September, mostly spent in Garmisch in the Bavarian Highlands, at the
Villa Bader, a pension kept by Mr. Slingsby Bethell (sometimes
credited as Captain and sometimes as Colonel). Elgar entered the
spirit of the party, played at musical chairs and charades and even,

with the smaller male guests of the pension, at football. Out of this came the evocative suite of *Bavarian Highland* songs. There were welcome excursions to Munich to hear Wagner's *Götter-dämmerung* and *Die Meistersinger*. On the way home the Elgars stayed in Bruges, where they enjoyed the picture collections and the carillon.

In the winter of 1894 *The Black Knight* was performed in Hereford and Walsall. Alice was exhilarated. She wrote how at one re-hearsal at Hereford the music was " triumphant over feeble or scanty performers "—the beginning of a long battle with choral singers whose resistance to " modern music " was obdurate—and how, in the concert, with all the extra players present, the orches-tration was " quite blazing and splendid "; and royalties on the work began to come in. Elgar's gratitude to Blair is in the dedica-tion of *The Black Knight* but it also took a practical form, for he orchestrated Blair's *Advent Cantata* " Blessed are they who watch " for a performance in St. John's Church, Worcester, on December 4, and he led the orchestra.

In between superintending performances, teaching, and com-posing, Elgar continued to take part in a good deal of chamber music. George Sinclair, since 1889 organist of Hereford Cathedral, came over to play Bruch and Spohr ; there were frequent visits to Severn Grange where Mr. Whinfield delighted in musical ensembles and was glad of Elgar's advice on the hanging of pictures ; and, of course, there were the ever-ready Fittons ten minutes' walk away from Forli.

Novellos accepted *Snow* and *Fly Singing Bird*. Edward immersed himself in his " Bairisch part songs." For all of these works Alice had written pretty texts. In February 1895 the tide of fortune began to flow. Edward was acclaimed as a genius. It was in the draughty discomfort of the Agricultural Hall in Wolverhampton, and the appreciation of the local choral society was unmistakable. " Directly we entered," wrote Alice, " such a warm welcome and enthusiasm and such a reception of E. Mr. Adams introduced him, saying the B. K. was the work of a genius. Tremendous enthusiasm of chorus. Most stirring . . . Wonderful evening. Chorus insisted on going through the cantata again and sang from their hearts. . . ." Alice too had her personal triumph, for in the May issue of *London Society, a Monthly Magazine* there appeared her translation of Hoff-man's *Ritter Glück*.

In July Blair played the *Organ Sonata*, which had been composed mostly in June, to a congress of American organists, with whom Elgar had lunch at the Star Hotel in Worcester, and Swinnerton Heap telegraphed to say that *The Black Knight* was to be given in Birmingham in December. Alice, also was busy on her own account, in preparing the notice of her father's career for the *Dictionary of National Biography*. It was, so far, the happiest year of the Elgars' life. They went up to London to a Wagner concert and to see *Hänsel and Gretel*. They amused themselves at the circus which was held in honour of the Duchess of Teck, who came to Worcester to open the Waterworks. They played bowls in the garden with Basil Nevinson, when he came from London to stay with his brother Edward, and Isobel Fitton. Edward took Alice over to Broadheath to show her the house in which he was born and the country in which he played as a little boy. And the Conservatives won the General Election in July. " E. . . . so excited about Election that he left his great-coat and part of suits in the train. Saw the red light for Conservative majority about 10.30."

In August there was the usual holiday in Bavaria, where in the woods at Garmisch Edward one day played cricket in an " Elgar benefit." In Salzburg they paid a pilgrimage to Mozart's house and, with some acquaintance with the industry in Droitwich, to the salt works. They stayed in Berchtesgaden one night but complained of a horrid room.

For the rest of the year Edward was furiously busy. *Sevillana* and the *Organ Sonata* provided proofs to be corrected. There were rehearsals to attend in Birmingham. *Snow* was in preparation for Hereford and Shrewsbury. Above all *King Olaf* claimed attention : Nov. 3. " Wrote his Sagas," 4. " Sagas progressing," 5. " Splendid Saga-ing," 6. " Wrote all day "—and so on until December 11, " furiously writing Saga." On December 12, " Heard from J. Williams, Bavarian pt. songs finally settled—Joy— and also that E was to write *Lux Christi* for Worcester Festival as far as sub committee cd. say."

Meanwhile *The Black Knight* had been performed in Birmingham. It was not a good performance. Birmingham was long in mastering the idiom but one of the newspapers was candid in explanation— the work was " too little rehearsed."

" The vocal parts are doubtless exacting, and hardly grateful to singers, but this does not explain the numerous faults of attack, the worst instance of which was the premature lead of the soprano in the dance scene, when for several bars a complete fiasco was threatened." But, short of a complete stoppage, an audience faced with a new work tends to miss such accidents or to consider them as part of the novelty of style : so it was that on this occasion the composer was recalled with acclamation.

On the way home the Elgars stayed in Wolverhampton, where they were met at the station by Miss Penny. From now on the Pennys figure prominently in the Elgars' life. Alfred Penny had been instituted as Rector of St. Peter's Collegiate Church on April 24, and on August 28 had married May Frances Baker of Hasfield Court. Mrs. Penny, an old friend of Alice's family, was delighted to be able to entertain her and Edward. Mrs. Penny's stepdaughter—Dora—twenty-one and impressionable—was also delighted. She was musical and lively. She was more congenial company for Edward when he stayed in the Rectory than her father, whose musical sense was confined to half a dozen hymns and whose principal enthusiasm was for the Melanesian Mission in which he had served. Dora Penny (Dorabella) has told her own story. Here it may be recorded that for many years she was always ready to assist the Elgars and that they were grateful for her assistance.

The first half of 1896 was devoted mostly to the completion of *King Olaf*. The orchestration was done in the summer ready for a promised performance in the Potteries in December. This was due to the active interest in Elgar's music of Dr. Swinnerton Heap, to whom the *Organ Sonata* had been dedicated. But there was also *Lux Christi* for which a libretto was prepared by Edward Capel-Cure. Once or twice Elgar was able to go up to London—to dine with Basil Nevinson at his club, to hear *Die Meistersinger* and to call on Novellos, who printed *O happy eyes* in the March issue of the *Musical Times* (as a free supplement). Among those who came to Forli while *King Olaf* was in progress was R. P. Arnold, who is commemorated in the " *Enigma* " *Variations*. On April 21 the " dear Bavarians first time. Immense enthusiasm. E. conducting most of the concert." A week later, and also in Worcester, the Musical Union—in which Mrs. Fitton was the accompanist and the Rev. E. Vine Hall, of Anglican chant fame, the conductor —gave *Fly Singing Bird*.

There was no holiday abroad in 1896. There was no time.

Edward found the going heavy and was unwell in August. But he was less unwell this year than formerly : growing appreciation was settling his nervous disorders. On September 3 he was in London for the orchestral rehearsal of *Lux Christi* at Queen's Hall. Sir Walter Parratt, at that time Master of the Queen's Music, Lloyd and Randegger were " quite carried away with enthusiasm for E.'s great music. Also soloists."

Lux Christi, Elgar's first extended work, impressed the Festival audience. " His masterful orchestration and originality of thought and idiom convinced all who heard Mr. Elgar's music that a great musician was arising of whom much would be heard later on." The programme otherwise included Beethoven's " Pastoral," Schumann's " Rhenish " symphonies and Verdi's *Requiem*. It may be suspected that their selection was influenced by Elgar.

On September 15 Dr. Heap came to lunch at Forli. There also came Dr. and Mrs. Stanford, the former to play his new *Requiem*, which Heap was to conduct at the forthcoming Birmingham Festival. This visit of the Stanfords was at their request, for as they were staying at Tintern House in Abbey Road, Stanford thought it a good opportunity to meet Heap. And so he wrote to Elgar on September 7. Stanford called once or twice during that holiday and heard parts of *King Olaf*. In one of his inevitable postscripts Stanford gave Elgar the first evidence of his generous attitude to a brother composer. " Good luck to yr. Norseman " he wrote on October 21.

Nine days previously the Elgars had gone to Wolverhampton to stay at the Rectory. It being Saturday Edward followed the habits of the natives by stepping across the road from the Rectory to the football ground. It was a good period in that respect, for two years previously Wolverhampton Wanderers had won the F.A. Cup and heroes of that engagement were still active. In one of them—the redoubtable half-back Malpas—Edward took the greatest interest. In the evening of this match day there was a rehearsal at Hanley and Edward was sent off with a packet of sandwiches.

On October 30 the Graftons came up with other friends to hear the first performance of *King Olaf*. " Glorious King Olaf a magnificent triumph. D. G." Alice was ecstatic.

The Victoria Hall [1] in Hanley, is perhaps the ugliest concert hall in England. Acoustically, however, it is among the best. At

[1] See *Music in the Five Towns*, R. Nettel (London, 1944).

the end of the nineteenth century and for a few years at the beginning
of the present century it housed choirs which were among the most
notable in the history of English music. Potters, and miners, and
their families dedicated themselves to music with a fervour that
has never been surpassed. Together with this fervour went a
remarkable integrity of taste and judgment, and also an adventurousness which particularly benefited Elgar, Coleridge-Taylor,
Bantock and Delius. An association with Elgar remained to the
end of his life. The works in which the Potteries' musicians had
an especial interest—*King Olaf* and *Gerontius*—have their record in
native art. Two commemorative cups were designed in 1903 by
Mr. Nokes of Hanley, the one inscribed from the former work :

> *The ale was strong,*
> *King Olaf feasted late and long,*

the other from the latter :

> *Learn that the flame of the everlasting love*
> *Doth burn ere it transform.*

The *Gerontius* cup also carried portraits of Newman and Elgar.

The credit for this reception of Elgar goes to Swinnerton Heap.
Now Heap was no mere provincial. He had been a Mendelssohn
Scholarship winner and had thus been enabled to study in Leipzig,
where he was taught by Moscheles, E. F. Richter, Reinecke and
Hauptmann. He had played in the Gewandhaus Concerts and had
accompanied on tour Ferdinand David, the celebrated violinist and
friend of Mendelssohn. Before the first performance of *King Olaf*
Heap had worked in the Midlands (of which he was a native) for
thirty years, sometimes conducting as many as seven choral societies
a week. It was, perhaps, his cosmopolitan interests that drew him
to Elgar. However that may be it was primarily to Swinnerton
Heap that Elgar was indebted for his first prominence. But there
was another champion, who had previously encouraged smaller
works.

In November 1896 Elgar took *King Olaf* to Manns at the Crystal
Palace. At the end of the month he received a telegram to say that
the work would be given in 1897 at the Crystal Palace. This
performance was on April 3. " Most magnificent. Deo gratias."

wrote Alice. Within the same month *King Olaf* was given at
Bishop Auckland, where the choral society conductor was Nicholas
Kilburn, an amateur and a pump manufacturer by profession.
Thereafter Kilburn became one of Elgar's greatest friends. There
was also a second performance at Hanley on April 29. This was
followed by a first performance in Worcester on May 4, and on
May 19 Elgar heard from Cowen that it was down for Liverpool
(Nov. 9. " The most glorious ' K. Olaf ' we had heard ") and
Bradford (Nov. 5). In the meanwhile Novellos were deciding on
an appropriate binding for a presentation copy for the King of
Norway. A further copy was presented to, and duly acknowledged
by, the King of Sweden.

Not only *King Olaf* but also the *Songs from the Bavarian Highlands*
were enhancing the composer's reputation and it was becoming
clear to the general that there was a new voice in English music.
Sir George Grove, at the age of 77, showed his interest. In the
autumn of 1897 he wrote to Alice, who had sent him the words
of the " Bavarians," of " that lively heartfelt music " and to Elgar
himself [1] " I hope you were pleased [Crystal Palace concert in Oct.
conducted by Elgar] and will do some more dances at once—so
pert and spirited and tuneful. I confess (though I hope I don't
hurt you) I liked them better than ' King Olaf.' I find it very hard
to bring my mind to Siegfried and Olaf and hoc genus omne. . . ."

Life was beginning to become extremely energetic. We left
Elgar in Hanley. From there he went up to London, where he
lunched at his club, saw Novellos and left on an evening train for
Cheltenham. There he rehearsed *Sevillana* the next morning, went
on to Hereford in the afternoon to " see Sinclair about '97 festival
—cool reception," and back to Cheltenham for an evening concert.
Sinclair's coolness was noted by Elgar himself in Alice's diary :
but it passed and may be put down to the varying moods of an
Irish temperament. Two days later the Elgars were in London
again to see Manns and Novellos. But Alice took the opportunity
to slip off on her own to the London library, of which she had
been a member for many years, to see her father's memoir in the
Dictionary of National Biography.

[1] Oct. 24.

CHAPTER VI

DR. ELGAR

*. . . we stood at the door looking along the back of the Hills
—the Beacon was in full view—I said Oh! Ed. look at the
lovely old Hill. Can't we write some tale about it. I quite
long to have something worked up about it, so full of interest
and so much historical interest . . . in less than a month he
told me Caractacus was all cut and dried.*

Anne Elgar to Mrs. M. W. Grafton,
Dec. 11, 1898

THERE WAS a time when it was taken for granted that illustrious,
or up-and-coming, composers would celebrate national occasions.
The quality of such occasional music not unnaturally varied, but
no discredit was attached to Purcell, Handel, Bach, Haydn, Mozart,
Beethoven or Brahms because they attempted to symbolise events
and moods of national importance. Elgar, on the other hand, has
suffered some posthumous victimisation on account of his following
their example. There is, however, no valid reason why his ceremonial music—*qua* music—should be chased out of town by
political students with obsessions. Elgar's nominal political ideas
were straightforward. He was a Conservative. He did, in fact,
take a modest part in more than one General Election on
behalf of Tory candidates. But he was not above expressing
radical opinions on a occasion, and rebelling against the
politics of some of the words he had to set on others.

It was, I think, a friend of Leigh Hunt whose devotion to the
Crown was such that he was considered capable in any future life
of encouraging his soul to take off its hat on some chance recognition of the tune of " God save the Queen." That was the kind of
the soul of Elgar. His character in some respects was astonishingly
simple and his simplicity is one of his endearing qualities. He was

78

firmly convinced that the Monarchy and the Empire were both admirable and necessary. Thus 1897 was an *annus mirabilus*. On Jubilee Day, June 22, the Elgars went out to the common to see the bonfires. They entered into the spirit of that light-hearted summer in other ways, welcoming relaxation. For a couple of months they amused themselves in flying kites and in playing bowls on the lawn. The former occupation was attended with hazards for there was an embarrassing evening when one of the kites— " Isobel " (as of the *Variations*)—got entangled with a neighbour's chimney. With them on this occasion was the playful, faithful Troyte Griffith.

In the earlier part of the year, however, Elgar had been industrious. On February 1 he had sent the final score of the *Imperial March* to Novellos. Six weeks later *The Banner of St. George* followed. At the same time there was a work to be composed for the Hereford Festival. On June 5 Elgar played through his *Te Deum* to Sinclair in Hereford. By the end of July both the *Te Deum* and the *Benedictus* were completed. On August 4 Elgar heard from Jaeger [1] of Novellos. He was, wrote Alice, " quite as enthusiastic as he shd. be over E's music for Hereford."

In 1897 Elgar was beginning to succeed where seven years earlier he had failed. *King Olaf* went well at the Crystal Palace, and at the St. James's Hall Charles Phillips had sung *Through the long days* and *Like to the damask rose*. The latter was repeated at a " Monday Pop." on March 8. The *Imperial March* made a greater impression than either the cantata or the songs. It was the popular music for the popular mood, broad, simple, and richly garnished. It was played by massed bands at the Crystal Palace on April 25, at a Royal Garden Party on June 28—the anniversary of the Queen's coronation, at a State Concert on July 15, and at the Albert Hall, by the Royal Artillery band, on October 24. This was not the most satisfactory performance the Elgars complained, for the tempo was sluggish. Meanwhile a choral society in London—St. Cuthbert's—had given the first performance of *The Banner of St. George*. Whenever he could find time when in London Elgar lunched at the Conservative Club with Nevinson and went to the Richter and Lamoureux concerts.

With events crowding in one on the other there was not a great deal of time for a summer holiday, but Alice insisted on going

---

[1] The first time that Jaeger's name appears in the diaries.

to Garmisch. They saw *Tristan, Don Giovanni* and *Der fliegende Holländer* at the Residency Theatre in Munich. More memorable were two encounters with Richard Strauss on August 22 and September 1.

At Hereford the *Imperial March* as well as the *Te Deum and Benedictus* was performed and Elgar was pleased to hear Canon Donaldson, in his Festival Sermon, " claiming for orchestral music a place in religious service " and urging that " it moved the soul to thought and feeling attainable by no other means." This accorded with Elgar's own convictions.

He held pertinaciously to another conviction : that composers should be adequately rewarded. The triumphs of 1897 were not markedly profitable and Elgar felt obliged to pursue opportunity. He was determined to conquer London. He wrote to Stanford in regard to a possible performance of a choral work by the Bach Choir. It was, wrote Stanford [1] " a very inopportune moment financially . . . [but] I will with pleasure recommend a work of yours at the right moment. . . . You need not worry yourself over the slowness of societies in London to take up your works. You're better off in the way of performance than many others. Even my Requiem (not per se but as the principal novelty at Birmingham) will not I believe be given by a single society in London this winter, and that has never been the lot of the principal Birmingham novelty before. Composers' names to attract entrepreneurs must now end in ' vitch ' or ' offski ' . . . When I see a chance of doing an English work which is worth its salt I shall do it."

At this time another work was taking shape. The ghost of Caractacus, the great British chieftain, haunted the Malvern hills and Elgar, living, as he did so often, in the glories of the past seized the subject to state his loyalty to his own countryside. But his inspiration was spurred. His mother's influence was still powerful.

She wrote to her daughter Mrs. Grafton on Sunday night, December 11, 1898 :

DR. POLLY,

    It has just occurred to me I never told you about Caractacus —when I was at Colwall E and Alice came to see me—on going

[1] Nov. 5.

out we stood at the door looking along the back of the Hills—
the Beacon was in full view—I said Oh ! Ed. Look at the lovely
old Hill. Can't we write some *tale* about it. I quite long to
have something worked up about it ; so full of interest and so
much historical interest.

I said to write some *tale*, and you *can* " do it yourself Mother "
He held my hand with a firm grip " do " he said—no I can't
my day is gone by if I ever could and so we parted—and in less
than a month he told me Caractacus was all cut and dried—and
he had begun to work at it—that's the story—So I feel a sort of
Godmother to it—I never meant music. I meant a *tale*—and
asked Alice if she could get me any books of old Welsh history,
or anything leading to it.

Tuesday Night

DR. POLLY,
    All have gone to the concert but me—and I didn't feel up to
it, and had no-one to go with without parting Loo [Lucy] and
Dott [Helen] so I got busy with my papers after all had gone
—feeling I would be very busy and then I shouldn't mind—in
a very little while *Ed* came in he was not conducting and they
had been dining at *Arnolds*. The ladies went to the concert
and he came here—and we had a jolly time—all to ourselves—
he played and sang a lot of choice bits from Caractacus—oh
lovely, for ever so long—and then a lot of the Banner. I was
so glad to be at home—now he's gone to Arnold's to wait for
the rest and supper before they go home. Now Dott will not
fret about my being at *home* poor kid how hard she tried to
get me to go—oh I am glad—the dear old boy—then we had
some talk of course—and he is very well and seems so happy
and bright he has not decided what to write for Birmingham
yet.

Goodnight

Elgar wrote *Caractacus* in the spring of 1898. He worked
rapidly as ever. He began the full score on June 21 and finished
it on August 21. During this spring he had taken a cottage in the
woods below Malvern—at Birchwood. It was there that his great
works of this period were mostly written. *Caractacus* had been

E.   F composed, as Alice noted, with enthusiasm. For its first performance had been promised for the Leeds Festival in the autumn of 1898. The terms were that the composer should be paid £100, but that he should himself provide the chorus and orchestral parts. Alice lent a hand in copying orchestral parts and so did Winifred Norbury (W. N. of the *Variations*). After an impressive rehearsal of the orchestra in London all was set fair for the first performance. The importance of the work had been enhanced by a communication on August 4 from Sir Walter Parratt, Master of the Queen's Music, to the effect that the Queen had accepted its dedication. In Leeds all went well, except that Frederick Spark, the Festival Secretary, had interfered in rehearsal.

Caractacus was given on October 5. The occasion was greeted with quiet satisfaction by the aged William.

Worcester Oct. 4/98

DEAR TED AND ALICE,

I hope you are well and enjoying yourselves and getting the steam up for tomorrow. I have not the least doubt your works will go well and give great satisfaction and also astonish the good people I have looked through it [i.e. *Caractacus*] well and am much pleased. I only wish I was there to hear it. I shall think of you and shall look in the papers wishing you every success.

From
Your old
wornout
DAD

The next day the Elgars heard some music of Palestrina and a *Te Deum* by Stanford, and had lunch with the Lord Mayor. Some supporters of Elgar travelled to Leeds for the Festival. Among them were the Kilburns, Miss Burley and her pupil Miss Lees, Cowen, Sinclair and Lady Mary Lygon, of Madresfield Court. Gabriel Fauré, whom Elgar had met in London at the Schusters, was also present and Elgar introduced him to Lady Mary. Parry was present for the *Blest Pair of Sirens* and he met the Elgars at lunch at the Sparks' house. The final celebrity was Sir Arthur Sullivan, who had, as Elgar reminded him, once inadvertently stolen Elgar's rehearsal time at the Crystal Palace. Years afterwards

Elgar related—in a letter to Herbert Sullivan [1]—how helpful
Sullivan had been at the rehearsals in London. " I had urged him,"
he wrote, " to rest while I went through *Caractacus*; but he remained and made notes of anything which struck him in that most
charming self-sacrificing way which was always his." As well as
Caractacus the organ sonata was played during the Festival by
Herbert Fricker, the City Organist.

The Leeds Festival made Elgar a prominent public figure. He
wrote, in the best of spirits, to Griffith from the Queen's Hotel.

DEAR TROYTE;
 All goeth well : it would be japey to see you here but it's a
long unprofitable way up.
 I will send you a M[usical] standard which is the first to give
me the place I've fought for.

Yrs. ever

ED. ELGAR

II

Caractacus, in one sense, is a public work—if one is unaware of its
place in the family history. But private circumstances were beginning to create works of a different order; for those whose faith in
Elgar was unshakeable and unaffected by outside circumstances
were around him at home.

Harry Acworth, who had spent his working life in the Civil
Service of India, and retired as Municipal Commissioner to the
City of Bombay, had had some part in preparing the libretto of
Caractacus. (This was not his first literary work. He had published
an English translation of the *Ballads of the Marathas* in 1894.) H. D.
Acland, a member of the Worcestershire Philharmonic Society and
a bank manager, was a constant companion on the golf-links. The
Pennys in Wolverhampton were ever-ready hosts, and the Elgars
were entertained by them either in exploring the Staffordshire
countryside (one excursion was to the historic house of Boscobel,
with its associations with Charles II) and the industries of the
Black Country, or in visiting the football ground. The Fittons

[1] Dec. 29, 1926.

listened to most of the new works as they came, in sketch form, from the composer's pen. Mr. and Mrs. R. P. Arnold (Arnold was a son[1] of Matthew and inherited some of his father's poetic sensitivity) of Eastbourne Lodge, Worcester, were also sympathetic companions. There were competent amateur musicians who helped Elgar by reading through his music as it came in proof. Miss Capel-Smith, of Fairfield, Malvern, for instance came in one day early in 1897 to sing parts of *St. George.* Father Bellasis, of the Oratory in Birmingham, was himself a musician and a friend of the Fittons ; and Elgar used to discuss *Gerontius* with him on country walks. Father Bellasis was a son of the saintly Sergeant Bellasis, who had been intimate with Newman.

Lady Mary Lygon[2] was the sister of Lord Beauchamp, of Madresfield Court near Malvern. She was a handsome, cultured woman—since 1895 a Woman of the Bedchamber to the Princess of Wales—with a zest for starting musical festivals. One of her inaugurations was the Madresfield Festival, at which works by Elgar were performed and at which he conducted. When she went with her brother to Australia, where he was Governor-General of New South Wales from 1899 to 1901, she also spread the gospel of musical uplift there. Lady Mary visited the Elgars often and they in turn enjoyed visiting Madresfield Court. W. H. Elgar, as piano tuner, formerly entered Madresfield by the back door. Edward had the satisfaction of being greeted at the front. His acceptance by people of culture and charm—as well as of importance—gave him some pleasure and more pride.

Troyte Griffith was the staunchest and most unvarying of friends. He was an architect—with rooms above the Priory Gatehouse in Malvern—and an artist, with an irrepressible humour which harmonised with Elgar's own impishness. Thus he wrote to Leeds on the eve of the first performance of *Caractacus* :

" Caractacus will be immense. C'est moi qui vous le dit. French. And I ought to know as I have heard more of it than anyone else except Mrs. Elgar and your cook.

" Which reminds me that I didn't buy Mrs. Lynn Linton's cooking stove because it fetched more than the published price ; such is the power of Literature. I don't think Art is quite such

---

[1] Presumably ' Dick ' mentioned in Matthew Arnold's letters, who was at school at Harrow and musical. He showed early promise in composition and was a friend of John Farmer, music master at Harrow.

[2] Married in 1905 Major the Honourable H. W. Hepburn-Stuart-Forbes-Trefusis.

a draw, but what should you say to a cheap line of Elgar's Musical Cooking Stoves, Caractacus pattern, plays airs out of this celebrated composer's works while the kettle boils. Each stove tested under the special supervision of the composer, tunes changed at frequent intervals, on a small subscription to the central foundry.

"Aren't you fearfully excited about Caractacus, supposing it doesn't sound right or you have made a mistake somewhere. . . ."

Such were the people who stood faithfully by Elgar during the crisis of his career. But it was not only words. Between them they formed the Worcestershire Philharmonic Society, which Elgar conducted from its first concert on May 7, 1898, until he was succeeded by Granville Bantock in 1904. Then Elgar served the Society as a Vice-President.

Among the founder members of the Philharmonic was Ivor Atkins who succeeded Blair as cathedral organist in 1897, Sinclair from Hereford who used to come over to play the drums and Sück the violinist who had taken over Elgar's Worcester practice in 1889. In the course of the next year or two Atkins and Sinclair became honorary members of the Society : among other honorary members were Cowen, Mackenzie, Richter, Stanford and Granville Bantock. In addition to showing his gratitude in this way Elgar went out of his way to include works by his honorary members in his programmes. So Bantock was represented by a scene—"The Funeral"—from *Kehama* and by his *Russian Suite*, Stanford by his *Last Post*, Mackenzie by his *Dream of Jubal*, and Cowen by his symphony, "The Idyllic." Other composers indebted to Elgar for performances were Parry, Percy Pitt and Walford Davies. The composers otherwise represented by major works afford an index to Elgar's tastes : Berlioz (*L'Enfance du Christ*), Beethoven (*The Ruins of Athens*), Brahms (*Schicksalslied* and Op. 44 part songs), Grieg (*Landerkennung*), Wolf (*Prometheus*), Wilhelm Berger (*Der Totentanz*), Max Bruch (*The Lay of the Bell*). There were overtures and suites by Beethoven, Tchaikovsky, Berlioz, Wagner, Mozart, Chabrier, Sterndale Bennett, Delibes and Weber. Symphonies and concertos were infrequent but Beethoven's fourth piano concerto and Schubert's fifth symphony held honourable places. Twice there were first English performances of continental works. One was Humperdinck's cantata *Die Wallfahrt nach Kevlaar* (May 7, 1898), the other Philipp Wolfrum's *Ein Weichnachts-Mysterium* (December 12, 1901).

Elgar's programme notes on these two works illuminate his own style and illustrate the working of his mind.

On Humperdinck :

" In Hänsel and Gretel, the Opera which made his name famous over all the world, HUMPERDINCK employed the ' representative theme ' in quite as elaborate a way as WAGNER, illustrating every character and idea in as marked a manner. In the present work, the same intricacy is displayed ; not, be it noted, the intricacy of the mere contrapuntist, but elaboration abounding in poetic and suggestive touches. In the orchestral accompaniment phrases of the well-known hymn tune ' O Sanctissima ' (Sicilian Mariners) are introduced.

" The listener should note the theme in the orchestra, accompanying the soprano solo, follow as it weaves into the procession music, and knitting the whole together, until it forms an ethereal adjunct to the vision of the mother in the high register of the violins.

" The work offers again and again lovely phrases of melody, occasionally homely (keeping in view the quasi-antique style of the ballad), and sometimes reaching a great depth of pathos and impressiveness."

On Wolfrum :

" The technique is beyond criticism, and one must admire the daring with which the musician has completed the task he set himself ; it is a bold thing in a sacred work, which most hearers will probably persist in calling ' an oratorio ' to throw over the whole convention of the Oratorio maker, fugues, canons, etc., and to give us a piece of pure and expressive music. The chorales naturally have not the striking effect on English ears that they possess for the German people : tunes inseparably connected with certain ecclesiastical seasons and with certain sets of words (hymns) have a sort of practical as well as poetical significance to the people who have all their lives been accustomed to sing them in their proper place. But if this aspect of the work does not appeal to our deepest feeling, we can all feel the beauty of the simple melodies of the folk songs, and the almost infantine tenderness of the music, woven (always with consummate art) around the gentle and gracious Christmas scenes.

" The members of the Philharmonic Society will not treat this performance as an ordinary, conventional concert, which in England is supposed to begin ' loud ' and end ' louder,' whereupon the audience is dismissed with a feeling of satisfaction that they have not met altogether in vain. In listening to this work, one's feelings become elevated and purified, and one's thoughts are taken with more than superficial understanding to those words recorded by the Evangelist, ' Except ye . . . become as little children.' "

Fuller Maitland, music critic of *The Times*, regretted, on January 17, 1898, that he could not devote space to the society but he took the opportunity to record his admiration for Elgar's own music. " It is," he wrote, " but another proof that in England, even more than in any other country, there are the real signs of musical life, i.e. men who have something of their own to say and a way of their own of saying it." He concluded with an apology for a misprint in a notice of Elgar's music at the 1889 (" I think ") Three Choirs Festival. One sentence of the notice referred to the fact that " the depth of his double bassoon was remarkable." It should have read—but for an inattentive telegraph operator—" the depth of his affection for the double bassoon. . . ."

III

We begin now to see clearly the Elgar dichotomy : the Worcestershire Elgar and the London Elgar, the private Elgar and the public Elgar. The division is apparent in the music. The great works of 1899 and 1900 belong to Worcestershire and to the private Elgar, accordingly they have an authentic ring of truth. On January 24, 1899, Elgar completed his *Characteristic Pieces* and his *Lute Song*. The following day he was busy with some variations, sketches for which had been prepared over the past few months.[1] The beginning of February brought snow followed by rain. Elgar was indoors from February 6 to February 9, orchestrating. On the 11th his work was interrupted by *King Olaf* at the People's Palace. Two days later *Caractacus* was given at Cheltenham. Elgar continued with the variations until February 21. On that day Lady Mary Lygon and Winifred Norbury came to tea and the variations were sent to Richter's manager, Nathaniel Vert, for Richter's scrutiny.

[1] See quotation of " Troyte " variation sent to Griffith, Nov. 25, 1898. According to a letter of Alice Elgar a copy of the variations (short score) had been sent to Vienna —but without result.

In March Novellos received the pianoforte arrangement. During this busy period—on March 21—the Elgars moved house from Forli to Craeg Lea, at Malvern Wells. From this house there was a fine view across to Gloucestershire, and immediately behind was the great mass of the Herefordshire Beacon. On June 3 Richter, having accepted the work, rehearsed the variations at St. James's Hall and was much pleased. A fortnight later he had the composer in town to go through the score with him. On June 17 the "*Enigma*" *Variations* were first performed. "Great success," recorded Alice—with her accustomed D.G. Edward went on to supper with Richter.

A month later the *Sea Pictures* were commenced. The second song had, in fact, been written in 1898 and published separately. The words were by Alice. *Sea Pictures* were rehearsed by Clara Butt on August 11. They were then orchestrated. By September 18 the final proofs were in hand and *Sea Pictures* were down for performance for the Norwich Festival—together with *Lux Christi*—on October 5. During the composition of *Sea Pictures* Elgar quarrelled with Novellos and prepared to transfer his business to Booseys, but at a conference with Alfred Littleton, of Novellos, on September 8, a reconciliation was effected—to Alice's relief.

It was on September 14 that " E. walked with Father Bellasis." *Gerontius*, the supreme expression of Elgar's deep Catholic convictions, was shaping. The diary record of *Gerontius* is as follows :

" 1900. Jan. 1. Mr.[1] & Mrs. Johnstone came to church and arranged for E's work Birm. Fest. Deo gratias."

Jan. 2. E. sent telegram accepting terms. Began again at former libretto.

Jan. 12. E. & A to Birmingham at 8.30. E. to Oratory.

Mar. 2. Sent 1st part of Dream of Gerontius to Novello.

Mar. 20. Sent 2nd set of M.S. Gerontius to Messrs. Novello.

Ap. 3. Had proofs of 1st part of Gerontius.

Ap. 6. With Fr. Blakelock to go through Dream of Gerontius.

May 4. Jaeger to lunch.

[1] Chairman Birmingham Festival.

May 21, 22, 23. E. writing hard.
 25. E. very engrossed last chorus Gerontius.
 29. Very hard at last chorus.
 30. Nearly finished great chorus. A. not out. Jaeger *delighted*.
June 6. E. finished the Dream of Gerontius. Deo gratias. Rather poorly."

Meanwhile Alice noted the Relief of Ladysmith, and Mafeking, and went to inspect the flags put out in Worcester. In July Edward began to bicycle, in which recreation he found relaxation from the tedium of writing his full score. One day (June 22) he took an afternoon off to see some cricket at Worcester, the county being involved in a thrilling tussle with Leicestershire. On July 27:

"E. finished setting out score of Dream of Gerontius.
August 3. E. finished orchestrating Dream of Gerontius.
 24. Heard chorus were delighted with Dream of Gerontius.
Sept. 12. Rehearsal of Gerontius in Birmingham."

Then the tone of the record changes:

"Sept. 20. E. worried with part correcting.
 21. Queen's Hall. Rehearsed Gerontius.
 27. E. to Queen's Hall. Found harpists playing Gerontius.
 29. (Birmingham) Rehearsal not so good as London & chorus dull and wretched."

During the rehearsals of *Gerontius* Swinnerton Heap, who was chorus master, died, and the aged Stockley who took over was past such work—even if he could have grasped the implications of this style of music. Elgar himself could have conducted the first performance (he conducted *Sea Pictures* during the Festival) but preferred to entrust its direction to Richter. The chorus justly came in for hard words from the critics, but the critics themselves were not disposed to sympathy with the subject of the oratorio. Thus circumstances conspired to make October 3, 1900, less pleasantly memorable than it should have been. Among those

present, however, were Julius Büths, of Düsseldorf, and Otto
Lessman, editor of the *Allgemeine Musik-Zeitung*. They saw more
of the true quality of *Gerontius* than any of the other critics.

While he was living inwardly as a composer Elgar was also
being compelled to become a public figure. He was noticed at the
Festivals and entertained in London. His contacts widened.
Rodewald in Liverpool, Cowen in Manchester and Liverpool,
Granville Bantock in New Brighton saw to it that the provincial
fame of Elgar increased. Cowen, in particular, was prepared to
back his judgment against that of the public. He performed *King
Olaf* in Manchester on December 1, 1898, and wrote " The public
—well, they treated the work as they treat everything over here,
with a sort of critical apathy which is put on and *not* genuine, for
they are not better (if as good) judges than in many other towns,
despite their unmerited reputation." But he immediately proposed
Caractacus for the following year in Liverpool. Besides the Norwich
and Birmingham Festivals of 1899 Elgar was present also at New
Brighton (July 14), where a new and charming *Minuet* had a first
hearing, and at Sheffield (October 11). At the Worcester Festival
Lux Christi and the *Variations* were performed. By the time the
Sheffield performance of *King Olaf* took place Alice's nerves were
also on edge. She complained that there was no one to meet
them at the station, that the hotel room was horrid, and—to crown
all—they were at first refused admission to the hall. However the
performance was excellent and the chorus superb. But Edward,
not at all well, was unable to attend the civic banquet.

What Elgar thought of the Sheffield chorus, directed by Coward,
he expressed in a letter to Jaeger :

" I say : I went over to Sheffield to conduct a Festival rehearsal.
Do you know that the chorus is absolutely the finest in the world !
Not so large as Leeds, but for fire, intelligence, dramatic force, they
are electrical. *Do* go to the Festival. For the first time in my life
I've heard *my* choral effects (*Olaf*) and very terrifying they are.
Laus Deo (and Cowardus)."

On December 12, 1898, the Queen, through Sir Arthur Bigge,
expressed her thanks for " the specially bound copy of your cantata
' Caractacus.' " During 1899 further recognition came from the
same source. On May 23 " heard by 12 post that Sir W. Parratt
wanted E. at Windsor. Started at 4.45 train and went to G. W.
Hotel Paddington. . . . (May 24) went to Sir. W. Parratt's. All

very interesting and Part Song [1] lovely." On October 18 Edward was again at Windsor Castle for a concert, at which ten of his pieces were performed. Two days later *Sea Pictures* were sung, by royal command, by Clara Butt at Balmoral.

IV

When in London Elgar divided his time between pleasure and duty. Sometimes the two overlapped. He went to the opera when he could—he had Sir Arthur Sullivan's box at the Savoy on April 22, 1899—and to the theatre, particularly enjoying Tree's *Julius Cæsar*. He took Alice one day to see an exhibition of Rembrandts at Burlington House. Alice, remembering the Chart of Painters they had once designed, also went off to a Burne Jones exhibition on her own. Fairly often Elgar enjoyed lunching at the Conservative Club or at Paganis. He attended the Inaugural Meeting of the Folk Song Society, having on a previous occasion entertained Lucy Broadwood to dinner. Among musicians Elgar saw, from time to time, Mackenzie, Randegger, Kalisch, Stanford, Percy Pitt and Dr. McNaught—who came sometimes to take part in the Madresfield Festival. He went to Richter's concerts when he could and on one occasion in Manchester made the acquaintance of Adolf Brodsky. He attended Charles Phillip's wedding and that of Edward Lloyd's daughter. And he went to Frank Schuster's house at 22 Old Queen Street.

The first mention of Schuster is on May 11, 1899,[2] when Edward went to an " at home." Schuster, who was to become one of Elgar's closest friends and most generous supporters, was a wealthy dilettante who invested much of his substance (he belonged to a famous banking family) in the entertainment of composers and artists. Among those who had been at Schuster's a good deal during the previous year was Gabriel Fauré. A letter (undated) from Fauré to Schuster is extant, in which Fauré recommends that if Elgar wishes his choral music to be performed in France he would be well advised to communicate with the Euterpe Society.

---

[1] *To her beneath whose steadfast star*, written in honour of the Queen's eightieth birthday.
[2] It is clear, however, that they had met previously.

In 1900 the acknowledged leader among English musicians was Stanford. Parry, appointed Professor at Oxford in that year, was, perhaps, *proxime accessit*. Parry, however, lacked Stanford's colourful personality—the source of both affection and misunderstanding. Stanford was impulsive to a degree, ready to quick gestures and words. So, in 1900, he could say of *Gerontius* to an acquaintance (who was so lacking in tact as to report it to Elgar) " My boy, it stinks of incense." At the same time having locked himself with a pupil in his room at the Royal College of Music he played through the score, growing more and more excited. It was entirely due to Stanford, who was Professor of Music, that the University of Cambridge conferred on Elgar the honorary degree of Doctor of Music.

Stanford's letters to Elgar throughout 1900 to 1901 throw much light on his opinion of and his deepening respect for Elgar. They also answer a passage in Plunket Greene's *Stanford*,[1] which suggests that at this time there was friction between the two composers. There was not.

On March 7 Stanford wrote asking Elgar to take him through the score of *Sea Pictures*, which were to be performed a week later at the Royal College. Muriel Foster was the singer. " She has not got," commented Stanford, " the whopping voice of C. B. [Clara Butt] but she has more poetry, and is musical to her finger tips." But Stanford could not, after all, conduct—

" The divvle was in it. After rehearsing the things to the point of perfection on Sunday, on Tuesday night I go and get influenza and am still locked up at home, better but miserable." It was, thanks to Parry who deputised, an excellent performance. Stanford signed himself " very sincerely (tho' d——d cross) " and added a diverting and characteristic postscript—" Maitland tells me that in the proof of his Times critiques . . . the compositor called the songs *Sea-Shrimps* ! " This worthy the day before called Bach's Thirty Variations " Batch of Tricky Variations." True, of course, in a sense.

On May 8 Stanford accepted honorary membership of Elgar's " go ahead society " in Worcester and much appreciated that Elgar had asked him to suggest a work of his own for performance. In the event it was *The Last Post* that was chosen, though Stanford's first proposals were the *Te Deum*, or *The Voyage of Maeldune*, or

The Elegiac Ode, or "lastly, *Mass in G*, which I wrote for the Oratory."

On October 17 Alice, now convinced of her success in creating a great artist out of the one-time shy, studious, music teacher of Malvern (though still he was obliged to live by teaching and to rush back from here and there to attend to the modest needs of the ardent young ladies of Malvern) entered, triumphantly:

"E. received letter from Cambridge begging him to accept Mus. Doc. Degree—as a tribute."

Edward notified his acceptance on the next day and, on October 24, heard from Stanford that he had tried for the degree in May, but that there were then too many LL.D.s for election. Stanford warned Elgar that he himself would probably be absent from the ceremony because of his rehearsals, at the Royal College, of *Euryanthe*, which was to be played at Daly's Theatre at the end of November. Actually it was a visit to Leeds, in regard to the 1901 Festival of which Stanford was conductor-in-chief, that prevented his attendance. The train, he wrote on November 19, would only reach Cambridge by 2.20 "and you wd. be all doctored and done by 2.15. So take the will for the deed please." Cowen was made a Doctor at the same time—happily on St. Cecilia's Day.

It is one thing to recommend the conferment of an honour. It is another to demonstrate by personal effort that the honour is more than honorific. In 1901 Stanford's attitude changes slightly. He is less a sympathetic friend than a disciple. The height of his generosity is reached in his implied recognition of Elgar as a greater composer than himself.

On January 30 he wrote the "Enigma Variations were down for the Leeds Festival, but the information is to be regarded as confidential"—"as the Comte may play all sorts of variations on my theme yet. If they cast you out, there'll be H-L." On April 11 he was able to announce the date—Friday evening 25 October. "I hope you'll be able to come & conduct them." The next letter of April 15, detailed the new regulations for the Mus.D. examinations at Cambridge. A month later Stanford had managed to get Elgar's advice regarding the Leeds performance accepted by the committee—"by a coup de main at the last moment" *Leonora No.* 2 and the Schumann Symphony in D Minor were incorporated in the programme. On July 3 Stanford wanted Elgar's markings of the *Enigma* and apologised for not having been able to hear the new

overture *Cockaigne*. In November, however, he heard a performance
by Richter who " I thought, played Cockaigne excellently. Were
you there ? and were you at Queen's Hall when they did the
Marches [*Pomp and Circumstance* Nos. 1 and 2]. . . . I found myself
in a minority in liking No. 1 better than No. 2—for which you may
curse me or not as you like. Anyhow the public liked the other
best : so it is their affair, and you have translated Master Rudyard
Kipling into Music in No. 2 certainly, and said ' blooming beggar '
in quite his style. (He always reads (but does not print) those two
words in a less polite fashion !). Anyhow they both came off like
blazes, and an uncommon fine stuff."

In this métier Elgar achieved what Stanford would have liked
to have achieved. On December 15 he wrote concerning a performance of *Enigma* he had conducted at the Royal College. " As
I got to know them I liked them better every time." He continued
about his own arrangement of " a splendid Petrie tune for Irish
Guards "—" It is a kind of Irish British Grenadiers. It will make
your blood get up a little if they put the swing into it." In his
customary postscript—of which the tail refers to the writing of the
letter in red ink—Stanford put what was foremost in his mind.

" Will you do me a great kindness ? Give us the première of
an orchestral thing someday. There's cheek. I only ask it because
I could give such a thing a dozen rehearsals : and that tells. And
I'd like a big thing, a Symphony please. I'll pledge my conscience
to make them play it right for you.

" Xcuse my writing in blood. I have been correcting proofs
in it."

When Mr. Elgar became Dr. Elgar, Alice was delighted to
find how magnificently the change enabled him to dress. The
sum of £45 which Halls of Trinity Street, Cambridge, quoted for
appropriate robes was a problem, but fortunately there were friends
who took charge of the situation. Granville Bantock sent round a
subscription list. In it were the names of H. D. Prendergast, a close
friend of Garmisch days, Slingsby Bethell, the pension keeper and
the dedicatee of the " Bavarians," Nicholas Kilburn of Bishop
Auckland ; Hew Steuart-Powell, Nevinson and the Bakers of Hasfield as representing the *Enigma* fraternity ; West Country musicians
in Brewer and Lee Williams ; London admirers and colleagues
in Kalisch, Stanford, Randegger, Percy Pitt, Jaeger, Henry Wood
(who sent three guineas in contrast to the more general guinea),

Plunket Greene, and Parry.   Parry offered to send Granville Bantock another guinea if enough should not be subscribed.   All, however, was well and Elgar received his gift [1] without any further call on Parry.

The robes arrived on December 3, 1901.   The next day Edward took them to Worcester and showed them to his parents.

[1] Elgar's Cambridge robes were presented subsequently to Dr. F. W. Wadely, organist of Carlisle Cathedral.   His father, W. E. Wadely (1855–1943), a well-known Kidderminster musician and organist of the Parish Church for 66 years, had been a fellow-pupil of Spray with Elgar.

CHAPTER VII

SIR EDWARD

Buckingham Palace, July 5, 1904: " The King smiled charmingly and said ' Very pleased to see you here Sir Edward.' "

From Lady Elgar's Diary

THE YEARS which lay between the first performance—both at Birmingham—of the *Dream of Gerontius* and *The Apostles* were years of justification, of faith and by works.

The composer's record of those years, as regards his major works, was as follows. On February 6, 1901, he was busy with the sketches of *Cockaigne*, which on March 24 was completed and had its first performance at a Royal Philharmonic Society Concert on June 20. While in the mood for pageantry—being alive to the joyous circumstances of the year of King Edward's accession—he went on to his marches. At the same time he was characteristically helping an old friend by orchestrating Brewer's festival cantata *Emmaus*. *Emmaus* was finished on July 7. Five weeks later the second of the *Pomp and Circumstance Marches* was ready for Alice to take to the Post Office.

During the summer George Moore wrote, asking if Elgar would write a horn tune to be played during *Grania and Diarmid*, a joint work with W. B. Yeats, which was to be performed under Benson's direction at the Gaiety Theatre in Dublin. Moore, having heard and liked Elgar's music at Leeds, wrote out of the blue. In the end, as the result of a cordial correspondence, Elgar composed not only the requested horn motiv but some incidental music, a song and a Funeral March. When Elgar sought permission from Yeats to publish a song from the play he received this letter—one of Yeats's rare utterances on the subject of music.

Monday, March 23 [1903]   18, *Woburn Buildings, Euston Road*
DEAR SIR :

Yes certainly. With great pleasure. I must give myself the
pleasure of letting you [know how] wonderful, in its heroic
melancholy, I thought your Grania music. I wish you could
set other words of mine and better work than those verses,
written in twenty minutes but you are welcome to them.

Yrs. sincerely,

W. B. YEATS

Excuse this scrawl I am very busy as I am off to Dublin to look
after the rehearsal of a play of mine.

The *Pomp and Circumstance Marches*, played at Liverpool, under
Rodewald on October 19, were immediately successful and there
were enthusiastic scenes at the Queen's Hall a few days later when
Henry Wood conducted them. The *March in D*, indeed, had to be
repeated on the day following. Among the little pieces of this
year was a pianoforte solo—a rare essay, for Elgar disliked the pianoforte—written for Fanny Davies to play at a recital on December 2.

In the early months of 1902 Elgar completed *Dream Children* and
had the *Coronation Ode* under way. This was completed in short
score on April 1, despite the interruption of an endless flow of
proofs, and at the end of the month the orchestral score was ready.
Because of the king's illness the Coronation ceremony was postponed
and the *Ode* had to wait for its London performance, but it was sung
at Sheffield on October 3, and at Bristol on October 7. One
grateful recipient of a score comes up as a voice from the past.
Thus wrote the old schoolmaster of Littleton House.

Sept. 23/02

DEAR DR. ELGAR,

Accept my warmest thanks for the Coronation Ode which
I shall treasure much. It was very kind of you to think of the
poor old master who is now become very shaky.

I was sorry to hear of the death of your maternal parent, but
I trust she is better off than remaining in this valley of tears.

With kindest regards believe me,

Yours very sincerely,

FRAS. REEVE

E.   G

At Sheffield the Elgars lunched one day with Lady Alice Fitz-william—but " E. not pleased with the company or food & excused himself & went off." In mitigation of this apparent brusqueness it should be said that Elgar was suffering acute toothache. He put up with it for two days but eventually had to have the tooth extracted on Sunday. " E. conducted ' Gerontius ' all the time he was under gas." Elgar, however, enjoyed Sheffield and was well looked after by the Member of Parliament for the Hallam division, Charles Stuart-Wortley, whose wife, a daughter of Millais, and a keen pianist, adored Elgar's music. Through the Stuart-Wortleys the Elgars first met the Duke of Norfolk, himself a keen amateur musician. The *Ode* was performed in London for the first time on the afternoon of October 26. The last chorus had to be repeated and the whole *Ode* was done again in the evening—it being Sunday— by the Sunday League. On October 31 Elgar conducted the *Ode* at a Promenade Concert. " Immense audience. Overwhelming enthusiasm. [Robert] Newman had to make a speech and say E. wd. conduct Ode again next Sunday. Yells of delight and then came Choral Symphony." Perhaps Alice found the last work something of an anticlimax. There was a further performance of the *Ode* on November 9. The powerful effect of the work on Empire builders is well represented by a letter from John Nisbet, lately retired from the India Forest Service :

Royal Societies Club, St. James's Street, S.W.
11 *Novr.* 1902.

Dear Sir,

Permit me to congratulate you very heartily on the great successes which your Coronation Ode has achieved twice recently at the Queen's Hall.

It seems to me that the last song and chorus is one particularly well adapted for a *national song*, and no doubt at the present moment there exists a splendid opportunity for trying to make it (or some modification of it) into a new, great national song. Of course the words wd. require slight alteration, such as the final

      . . . " we have crowned our King "
which wd. have to run more like

      . . . " trusting in our King."
Whether the music wd. require any alteration is a matter I am

not competent to say anything about : but I take the liberty of writing and making the above suggestion, because it struck me at the first time of hearing it that the song was preeminently suited for becoming a national anthem—and this feeling was even stronger when I heard it sung again last Sunday.

Again, congratulating you on the success achieved.

Yours faithfully,

J. NISBET

And so it was to be ! The words added by A. C. Benson to the trio melody and thus giving " Land of Hope and Glory " came in fact by way of a royal suggestion. Many years afterwards—on November 21, 1927—Elgar wrote to Clara Butt :

Battenhall Manor, Worcester

DEAR CLARA :

I have just returned home and found your letter here.

I have not seen the Daily Sketch and do not know how my remarks were reported. King Edward was the first to suggest that the air from the Pomp and Circumstance March should be sung and eventually the song as now known was evolved, *via* the Coronation Ode in which you were to have sung.

There is nothing to contradict in this

Believe me to be

Yours very truly,

EDWARD ELGAR

Elgar finished the fair copy of his *Greek Anthology* part songs on November 11. These were dedicated to Sir Walter Parratt. Since one of these songs is to a translation by Andrew Lang it is presumed that Lang relented from his attitude of 1900.

June 24 [1900]   *Alleyne House, St. Andrews, Scotland*

DEAR SIR,

I regret that the lines are not such as I want to be set to music. No musician has ever given me a penny for my lines.

Faithfully yours,

A. LANG [1]

[1] Elgar made a second application and received an even snortier reply : " It is a pity that you did not begin by asking permission. I have already expressed my regret hat I cannot give it, and trust that you will accept this as final."

Edmund Gosse, with whom Elgar had dined at Madresfield, was more generous and in giving authority for the use of his words wrote his appreciation of Elgar's music.

The year 1903 was almost entirely devoted to *The Apostles*, but *Weary Wind of the West* was composed for the Morecambe Festival. Elgar did not like Morecambe when he arrived there in the evening of April 30, but the kindliness and culture of Canon Gorton, who as chairman of the festival looked after the Elgars, the zest of the working-class singers who came to compete (Elgar's old friends from Hanley won the chief competition by 1 point) and the affection showed by them to him personally, made his stay entirely agreeable.

Canon Gorton and Howson the conductor were two remarkable men. Howson was a bank manager in Morecambe, but his interests were wide. Considering that Morecambe should " be made a place not only to trip to but to live in " [1] he was active in the establishment of the cricket club, the three golf clubs, and the art and technical institutions of the town. He directed the music at St. Lawrence's Church and was the musical genius of the Morecambe Madrigal Society and the Musical Festival, which, being born out of a church bazaar in 1891, took its place at the turn of the century as one of the principal festivals in the country. " He was," wrote Canon Gorton, " supremely catholic in his taste. The Old English Madrigalists were his first love, but Palestrina, Bach, Beethoven, Wagner, Brahms, Schubert, and Elgar would occupy their due place." Elgar's interest in Morecambe and his composition of a part song for the Festival of 1903 gave the greatest pleasure to Howson. He died in 1905 and is commemorated in another part song—a setting of Coventry Patmore's " Evening Scene " (from *The River*).

Canon Gorton, son of Archdeacon Gorton of Madras, was Rector of Morecambe from 1889 until 1908. He was prodigal of energy. He renovated his own church and opened mission churches ; he served on the School Board and was Secretary to the Morecambe Technical Instruction Committee, as well as on many diocesan bodies. His sympathies were immense, so that on his retirement the fishermen recalled his assistance to them in times of need and the nonconformists his generosity towards their causes. The administration of the Musical Festival he held as one of his principal duties : not merely as a useful secular duty which he

[1] Quoted from Canon Gorton's obituary notice of Howson, June 30, 1905.

DECATUR-DeKALB LIBRARY
REGIONAL SERVICE
ROCKDALE COUNTY
NEWTON COUNTY

could competently perform, but as a spiritual commission. He used to preach a Festival Sermon in his parish church and to write in his parish magazine [1] in this manner of " the gathering together of members of a village choir in a winter's night, the patience and skill of the conductor, the discipline of those taught, and the added purpose to life. But still greater the blessing where the need is greatest. Was there not a man and dog fight in Hanley? Contrast the power and shame of such a sight with the marvellously sweet tone of the Hanley Choir. Contrast the common plan of Nelson and Colne, the straggling, huddled houses, the stinted groups of tree and grass, with the employing of Mozart's overture.[2] We cannot but feel that it is a good gift of God, a vast compensation for the toilers. We are not afraid to ask God's blessing on the workers for their work."

Canon Gorton became one of Elgar's closest friends and on his retirement he and his family moved to Hereford, to a house found for them by Elgar and Sinclair.

It was fortunate that Elgar came upon him when he was fully occupied in shaping his long desire to compose an oratorio on the subject of the apostles, for the Canon's advice on theological detail was invaluable. On January 1, 1903, Edward, having been ill, was feeling better and was reported keen on his work. The next day *The Apostles* is mentioned by name in the diary. Alice was much involved also. One day she went into town and " tried to get Pinnel's Analysis of Old Testament for E. was first offered a game and then a scripture puzzle ! " Within a week the Johnstones were over from Birmingham to discuss Novello's terms in respect of production at the autumn Birmingham Festival. Richter came on January 12. " After lunch (he first came into drawing room and looked round with evident satisfaction and with a gesture ' Ach wie gemüth lied ') E. and he went through the ' Ode ' and some of the ' Apostles.' He was much impressed and said to me ' Ach, grossartig, eine so heilige Stimmung, aber er ist ein ganz famoser Mann, und es ist so wunderbar (or something like that) ein so leebenvoller Mensch.' "

A particular friend of Elgar—since the Leeds Festival of 1901 —was Edward Speyer, a wealthy banker with intimate knowledge of music and musicians. Although born in Frankfürt, Speyer was

---

[1] May 1904.
[2] *Magic Flute* " played by the Nelson band with excellent precision."

a naturalised British subject and lived in the style of an English country gentleman at " Ridgehurst," Shenley, Hertfordshire, where the Elgars were frequently to be guests and where they were to meet many people of distinction.[1] Edward Speyer's cousin Edgar was a benefactor to and chairman of the Queen's Hall Orchestra. The Speyers were the next to hear parts of *The Apostles*. On January 21 Alice " posted first music of the Apostles to Novello." Edward went doggedly on, although pained with rheumatism and Alice typed some of the libretto. Next Capel Cure, who had arranged the text of *Lux Christi* came to lend a hand. Moments of depression such as afflict every great artist (and also financial anxieties) slowed down the rate of work but by February 10 the first score was complete. On February 17 everybody was thrilled to see the first proofs. After a Philharmonic Society practice in Worcester that day Edward, less tired than usual, rushed home and nearly finished his " Wayside Scene." This, said Alice, was " quite new and different from anything else."

No friends called who were not shown *The Apostles*. Littleton Wheeler, a cultured county magnate and also a Catholic, was thrilled. So on February 25 was Rodewald. On March 3, Edward's sister Dot fulfilled an ambition, impossible while her mother was alive, and became a nun at St. Rose's Convent, Stroud. Her investiture met Edward at an appropriate time and he was much moved. Three weeks later the " Mary Magdalene " scene was finished. On Easter Day Sinclair played some of *The Apostles* music in Hereford Cathedral on the organ and on April 19 the composer Pedro Morales came to meet Elgar and was obliged to hear some of it. Two days later Nicholas Kilburn said to Alice that this work " was cosmic, Gerontius personal." After that, and before going to Morecambe again, Edward worked at the " Judas Scene." By June he was tired and worried. But he went on and was able to play most of the score to Ivor Atkins on June 13. At the end of June he set about the great task of orchestration. By August 17, after a holiday in Wales, he had finished the entire score.

There were still, however, corrections and emendations to be made to the libretto, and notes to be written. Elgar continued at this happily, deriving, as always, great pleasure from literary activity. During these late summer months, in which preparations

---

[1] See *My Life and Friends*, Edward Speyer (pub. London, 1937).

for the Hereford Festival [1] occupied some time, he lived in a mood
of tranquillity.

Hereford was, in some ways, a welcome change from Malvern
and the Catholic Church of the monastery at Belmont, which the
Elgars attended sometimes when they wished to go farther afield
than the town church, afforded great contentment. Rodewald and
Schuster came up for the Festival. On September 3 " E. Rode &
Frank S. walked through fields, bright sunny morning to Belmont.
Heard the *Missa Est* to the tune of the Angel in Gerontius. Both
men [i.e. Rodewald and Schuster] much impressed by all they saw
& heard. This beautiful church out in the country. . . ." Ten days
later " E. & A. & C.[arice] drove to Belmont. The Litany was
being chanted as we arrived, the same as in ' Gerontius ' then we
went in, lovely sunny day. After Mass, the Preacher came across
to E. & asked to take him over the Monastery. We waited and
the monks filed out. The grounds looked lovely. E. asked if he
might go & stay there a week sometime. A glad consent . . ."

On October 6 the first orchestral rehearsal of *The Apostles* took
place. Alice remembered Richter's comment : " ich dachte dass er
den Gerontius nicht ubetreffen würde, aber, doch, etc." The
performance took place at Birmingham Town Hall on October 14.
Nothing, perhaps, illustrates the many sides of Elgar's character
more than that on this day he could note the winner of the Cesare-
wich—" Grey Tick " at 20 to 1.

For various reasons there was little or no composition that
autumn. At the end of November the Elgars went to Italy.
There, at Alassio, *Fly*, *Singing Bird* and *Snow* were orchestrated and
the overture *In the South* was born. The score was completed on
February 21. The only other composition of this year was the
third of the *Pomp and Circumstance* Marches.

II

From the time of the *Variations* to the production of *The Apostles*
Elgar's popularity was greater with the public than with the critics.
The attitude of many of the critics rankled. It may be said that the

---

[1] Gerontius was performed, after opposition from the Dean had been overcome
(at Worcester it was the Bishop who had scruples in 1902) : also, but without much
success, Wolfrum's *Weichnachts-mysterium*.

situation frequently arises as between an artist and his professional assessors and it has been suggested that Elgar's reactions were unwarrantable. But there was a great contrast in the German musical press. Indeed it is surprising that a composer so apparently " English " as Elgar should first have been most fully appreciated by the Germans. Among those present at the first inadequate performance of *Gerontius* were Professor Julius Büths, director of music in Düsseldorf, and Otto Lessman, editor of the *Allgemeine Musik-Zeitung*. That both were immensely impressed with the originality and power of the music had almost immediate repercussions. Elgar wrote, on October 30, to his friend Henry Ettling :

... *Very many* thanks for sending the ' A.M.-Zeitungen ': my wife has translated the articles to me and I am—I need not say—intensely gratified at being taken seriously & being understood. I wish my own countrymen could do this—but alas ! in England this can never be—& I know it.

If you see Dr. Richter give our love to him & with very kind regards

Believe me
Yrs. sincerely,
EDWARD ELGAR

In February 1901 the *Variations* were played, with great success, at Düsseldorf. It was in respect of this that Stanford wrote his congratulations, adding " However your plucky success will bear fruit probably beyond yourself for England generally." Büths, by this time, enthusiasm unabated, had started to translate *Gerontius* into German. In the summer accompanied by his wife and daughter, he came to see the Elgars at Malvern to discuss a production of the oratorio at the forthcoming Lower Rhine Festival. In the middle of December the Elgars set out for Germany to attend rehearsals. They were met at Düsseldorf by the attentive—if, at close quarters, fussy—Büths, and were entertained generously by the principal musicians of that part of Germany. Among their hosts was another conductor, Fritz Volbach, who also was an ardent Elgarian. In May 1902 after Edward's ill-health had delayed their start, the Elgars were again in Düsseldorf for the Festival. On May 20 Alice recorded the great day :

" E. rehearsal. A. later sat in Balcony with Mr. Rodewald,

H. Wood, Kalisch, Johnston, Cooper. Same in evening. . . . Gt.
enthusiasm at end. Phœbus & Pan [an odd follow-up to Gerontius]
delightful. Great Fest Essen followed & Strauss made beautiful
speech about Meister Elgar. No end of toasts. In bed at 3."

Alice wrote to Anne Elgar and received from her a last, proud
letter.

High St. June 23rd

MY DEAREST ALICE,

Thank you so much for sending me a nice [?] account of the
reception & what can I say to him the dear one—I feel that
he is some great historic person—I cannot claim a little bit of
him now he belongs to the big world. I hope dear Carice is
better & that you are all well. Dad is only poorly . . . I am
very well now. How useless my hand is, cannot guide the pen.
With my dearest love,
to you all—yours affecty.

A. ELGAR

Elgar saw a good deal of Strauss during these years both in Germany
and London, but he found Strauss's music perplexing. *Ein Heldenleben* was "very astonishing." *Don Quixote* he did not like at all.
Strauss, for his part, was overwhelmed with Elgar's genius. The
gist of his "beautiful speech" was contained in the *Allgemeine
Musik-Zeitung*: "An Englishman, Edward Elgar, came to the
Lower Rhine Festival & gained a hearing for his oratorio the
Dream of Gerontius. With that work England for the first time
became one of the modern musical states."

Later in the same year the Meiningen Orchestra—the last great
private orchestra in Europe—visited London. This orchestra—
famous for its associations with Wagner (the bulk of its members
were in the Bayreuth orchestra), von Bülow (who was its conductor),
and Brahms—was at that time probably the finest to be heard.
It was conducted by Fritz Steinbach, von Bülow's successor.
Edward Speyer arranged with the Duke of Meiningen that the
visit should take place, and with Steinbach that Elgar's *Variations*
should be played. Steinbach's comment on Elgar's work was
exceedingly gratifying. "Here," he said, "is an unexpected
genius & pathbreaker in the field of orchestration. Nowadays
nearly every composer is content merely to adapt Wagner's inno-

vations, but Elgar, as this work shows, is a real pioneer with a new technique in orchestration, combining entirely original effects with almost unique virtuosity." [1]

In 1903 news came of other performances of *Gerontius*, at Dantzig (March 11), at Darmstadt (October 19), at Chicago (March 26), and at New York three days later. American interest in Elgar was stimulated by Professor Sanford, of Yale, who was at Three Choirs Festivals in 1900 and 1901. It was Professor Sanford who in 1904 presented Elgar with a new Steinway pianoforte as a token of the great pleasure he had received from his music. It was through Sanford's pioneering that Theodore Thomas and Walter Damrosch became deeply appreciative of Elgar's music. In the same year Weingartner was added to the list of conductors including Elgar in their repertoire. In May *The Apostles* was given in Cologne and in November both in Mainz, under Volbach ("It was said there had never been such a triumph in Mainz") and Rotterdam.

Henry Ettling (whose intimate acquaintance with Elgar would appear to have begun at a dinner party given by Rodewald in Liverpool towards the end of 1900) was a useful liaison officer between Elgar and the leading Germans. Ettling himself was a native of Mainz, a wealthy amateur who pursued Richter—to him "the King"—with a set of timpani which he played whenever the opportunity presented itself. Ettling was affectionately known to the Elgars as "Uncle Klingsor." His magical powers extended in two directions. He could fascinate the household at Craeglea with his feats of conjuring, but also persuade his fellow countrymen to promote the music of his English friend. His letters furnish evidence of the success achieved in the second direction.

On July 3, 1901, he wrote from Mainz, asking Elgar to have the score of *Cockaigne* sent to Weingartner (who had promised a performance of the *Variations* for the next season) and the score of the *Variations* to Steinbach in Mainz and Gustav Kogel in Frankfürt. "I arrived home on Monday after spending all Sunday *with Paderewski*. He was delighted with your Overture and was so pleased to have met you." In token of friendship Elgar gave to Ettling the MS. score of *Cockaigne*. On September 7, 1902, Richter wrote of a new friend in Mainz: "I have young Backhaus staying here for a few days, he is a grand player and he plays your March in D, some Gerontius etc., by heart, wonderfully well." Ettling

[1] See *My Life and Friends*, Edward Speyer, p. 176 *et seq.*

frequently quotes Richter's tremendous devotion, which reached a climax early in 1903 when Richter told Ettling that he preferred Elgar's " noble music " to that of either Brahms or Tchaikovsky.

On June 23, 1904, he wrote, " Today I paid a visit to Fritz Kreisler & found him at the Piano, deep in the ' Dream of Gerontius,' he told me full of Enthusiasm for you, whether it is true that you once wrote a Violin Concerto [1] & if so, he would feel happy if you would trust it to him, he would play it with great pleasure & would hope to do honour to it. Please let me know, if there is such a work existing ? "

Finally Ettling gives a hint of Weingartner's pioneer vigour. He refers, on June 11, 1905, to Geris who was singing the part of Beckmesser at Covent Garden. He said, one day, to Richter : " There is in Munich etc. Weingartner who pushes (poussirt) an English composer, I never heard of him nor have I heard any of his compositions but Weingartner pushes him fearful. I think his name is Elgar ! Now you should have seen Richter's face and his lecture to Geris ! You can imagine ! Geris did not think before that it was possible & is now longing to hear something of you."

The solemnity and richness of the oratorios made them especially congenial to the Germans. The *Variations*, however, carried further, for they were unconfined by theological tenets. They went across Europe reaching Russia, via Budapest, in the autumn of 1904.

" I have," wrote Alexander Siloti of St. Petersburg on November 2, " great pleasure in informing you that your variations, which I conducted (the 1st time in Russia) have had a very great success, both with the public & with the ' musical world '; so great a success that I shall play them again next season. Mr. N. Rimsky Korsakoff & Mr. A. Glazounoff were particularly pleased with them. I studied them very carefully (because I am quite in love with them), & the rendering was very good. I should be very much obliged if you would let me know whether you have already written, or will write a great *orchestral work*."

Elgar, undaunted by the Leeds misadventures discussed on p. 122, promised a great orchestral work ; for Siloti wrote again on January 11, 1905 :

" I send you many thanks for your kind letter. I am writing to know if the symphony you speak of is in print, or if not how

[1] See p. 65.

soon it will be. The parts I shall not want until the early Autumn
the score as soon as possible. It would be a good thing to have a
greater work follow ' the Variations ' shortly ; having given them
I will take anything of yours without seeing it. I ask you to give
me the sole permission of giving the symphony next winter ; as
my concerts take the *first place* here in the general opinion. In
consequence of their having been given here ' the Variations ' will
be given this season in Moscow. . . ."

III

At the beginning of this century English musical standards were
powerfully influenced by German. It is often stated that this was
wholly disadvantageous. This is not so, least of all in so far as
appreciation of Elgar was concerned. His keenest supporters,
both in amateur and professional circles, were those who, of
European origin themselves, felt that his place was among the
most honoured European composers and not merely with the
small group of Englishmen at that time grudgingly recognised.
Richter's opinions, of course, were influential. But he was well
supported by Brodsky ; Randegger, the singing professor and
conductor of the Norwich Festival ; Rodewald ; Jaeger of Novellos;
Kalisch, the critic ; the Speyers ; Frank Schuster ; Henri Ver-
brugghen the violinist ; Marie Brema and Ludwig Wüllner, who
as singers were distinguished in their interpretation of Elgar.

Brodsky, born in Russia and trained in Austria, was one of the
great violinists of his generation. On several occasions his quartet
visited Worcester and Malvern—when Elgar virtually directed the
Concert Club—at Elgar's invitation. Brodsky whose experience of
practical music was nearly unparalleled was not loth to express his
opinions, which are characterised by sincerity and simplicity.
Thus, after hearing *Gerontius* in Manchester he could write :[1]

" My wife Anna & I pray to God that you may long live &
write many more of such great works as your ' Dream of Gerontius.' We just came home from the concert. It was an idial [sic]
and overwhelming performance. The impression we have from
this work is : greatness and sincerity ; and then only you begin to
realise that it is also a great master work from the technical point of

[1] Mar. 12, 1902.

view.—Only a genius & a pure practical soul could have created such a work." The regard in which Brodsky held Elgar found also practical expression. It was well understood among his friends that while Elgar might be a great composer he was perpetually finding it difficult to make ends meet. So, sometime in 1903, Brodsky saw Elgar at the Grand Hotel in Manchester and proposed the creation of a special appointment at the Royal Manchester College of Music, of which Brodsky was Principal. On April 15, Brodsky, having had no answer, wrote again and recapitulated the conditions :

" 1st the Royal Manchester College of Music offers you the post of Professor of Instrumentation & Composition.

" 2nd The Victoria University offers you the same post at the Musical Faculty.

" 3rd The teaching for both . . . will take place in the Building of the R.M.C.M.

" 4th As little as we would expect Franz Liszt to be a piano teacher, as little are we expecting you to be a ' teacher ' in the common sense of the word. It is your personality we want to secure. Your name would give glory to the Institutions & attract, I am sure, all the talent of the country."

The routine teaching would be done by Dr. Walter Carroll, to whose capacity Brodsky pays a deserved tribute. " You," he continues, " would only admit them to the mysteries of modern instrumentation & you would criticize their compositions & develop their taste by which to be guided when composing."

Elgar was to have £400 a year and " all personal freedom " for his own work. He disliked teaching so intensely, however, that he turned down this generous and attractive proposal. Had he accepted it he would have been spared the inconvenience and misfortune that attended his tenure of office at Birmingham University.

If Richter and Brodsky largely built the great musical reputation (*pace* Cowen) of Manchester it was Alfred Rodewald who was responsible for the betterment of that of Liverpool. Rodewald, although of German descent, was born in Liverpool and educated at Charterhouse. He was an amateur musician, for otherwise he was a member of the Cotton Exchange. But his knowledge and practical ability were great : his enthusiasms greater. He first met Richter at Bayreuth and Richter reckoned him among the most discriminating Wagnerians. Rodewald sometimes played the double bass for Richter, but his achievement was to build the largely amateur Liverpool Orchestral Society into an ensemble efficient enough to play, as well as the classics, the great modern works of Wagner, Tchaikovsky, Elgar and Strauss. At the time of his death in 1903—which was said to have been hastened by the extent to which he wore himself out in the service of music—he was preparing for a performance of *Ein Heldenleben.* So far as Elgar was concerned he showed all of his " open-hearted, kindly & loyal nature." [1] He entertained him at 66 Huskisson Street, in Liverpool, at his house at Saughall, near Chester, or his holiday cottage, near Bettws-y-Coed; he essayed every work as it came from Elgar's pen ; he defended his actions and proclaimed his virtues.

It was after *The Apostles* when Elgar was dispirited and worried with financial matters that news of Rodewald being gravely ill reached Malvern.

He wrote to Schuster on November 10.

My dear Frank,

I am just home from Liverpool & can *only* send you thanks for your letter.

It is all too dreadful about my dear friend Rodewald : he passed away peacefully yesterday. O my God ; it it too awful.

I had a card from him last Wednesday quite cheerful saying he was " over the influenza "—he became unconscious on Thursday & has never recovered. I could not rest & fled to Liverpool yesterday only to be told all was over.

I will write again soon but this is all too cruel & horrible.

Forgive an incoherent note. I can only weep over the awfulness of it.

Much love to you

Yr. ever

Edward

For days afterwards Elgar was in the deepest depression and went alone into the country for " long, long walks."

It was through Schuster that Elgar came to know Beerbohm Tree and Sargent the painter, and such cultured members of high society as Lord Northampton, Lord and Lady Charles Beresford and Lady Maud Warrender. At the time of the Elgar Festival at

[1] See obituary by Arthur Johnstone in *Musical Times,* Dec. 1903.

Covent Garden, in March 1904 Schuster gave a dinner party in honour of his friend. Reference has been made to the occasion elsewhere [1] and Elgar's apparent indifference to the proceedings construed as boorishness. The truth is that he went to the party with great difficulty. At times of stress he was liable to severe headaches. So it was on March 13, 1904. He had been unable to get up that morning and Alice spent the time in sending out for such remedies as the doctor prescribed. In the afternoon he struggled up, and in the evening he pulled himself together sufficiently to attend the function. It was, said Alice, a beautiful party and she recorded how Frank " proposed E's health in the most touching way with his heart in his voice." Among those who were fellow guests at the Speyers' at this period were Laurence Binyon, Richard Strauss (Frau Strauss was there too and told Alice how much she liked Edward), Francis Oppenheimer, a discriminating judge of the arts and of painting in particular and the Consul-General at Frankfürt, William Shakespeare, a celebrated singing teacher, young Donald Tovey, Colonel Collins, one of the King's Gentlemen Ushers, Lady Sybil Smith, the Stanfords and Henry Wood and his wife Olga, the singer. Between them Schuster and the Speyers knew practically everybody.

Alice Elgar, who by birth at least was " upper class," had a respect for the " nobility " that was not at all uncommon in the Edwardian era. Edward's entry into society—on his merits as an artist (which were vouched for by the cognoscenti) and his personal qualities—was greeted by her with naïve delight : this spectacular advance in social prestige with ecstasy. It was wonderful to attend Lord Mayoral banquets in Sheffield, and Leeds, and Birmingham ; for Alice to be taken in to dinner by the Right Honourable Stuart-Wortley while Edward supported Lady Alice Fitzwilliam, and to hold conversation with the Duke of Norfolk and his sister ; to be asked to join Lord Howe's party ; to be introduced at a private reception to the Prime Minister ; to sit beside the Duchess of Bedford ; to go to Lady Howe's and to find among the company the Portuguese Ambassador, the Warrenders, the Duchess of Marlborough, Lord Vane Tempest and the Prince Francis of Teck. The Edwardian period has not, in general, received credit for culture ; but Elgar's aristocratic friends were often both knowledgeable and effective in promoting his interests. Lady Warrender,

---

[1] *My Life of Music*, Henry J. Wood, p. 179.

for instance, wrote[1] proposing the Union Jack Concert—at which the *Coronation Ode* was given—on the same day as Mrs. Stuart-Wortley, who suggested a scheme whereby *Gerontius* might be performed in Westminster Cathedral.

The performance of *Gerontius*—the first in London—took place on June 6. Among those who were present were some of distinction who were also keen enough to listen to the rehearsal. They included Lord Northampton, Lord Shaftesbury, Lady Edward Talbot, Gervase Cary Elwes and Lady Winifred Elwes, as well as the Stuart-Wortleys. The choristers, to whom this performance was entrusted, represented a different section of the community. They were the North Staffordshire Choral Society, whose presentation of the oratorio in the Potteries, on March 13, had moved Elgar very deeply. The soloists were Muriel Foster, David Ffrangcon-Davies, and Ludwig Wüllner—who, as Gerontius, was finer than anyone in Alice's opinion.

In assessing Elgar's place in music it must never be forgotten that his great achievement was to express, perhaps as no English composer either before or since,[2] the mood of the nation. One may, of course, deplore the mood ; one may criticise the style of its expression : but one may not deny the fact. Elgar won the affection of countless modest music lovers, but also that of the Royal Family.

Elgar's special genius for producing occasional music had been appreciated by Sir Walter Parratt and noticed with gratification by Queen Victoria.[3] With the accession of King Edward VII Elgar was honoured by the personal attention of the monarch, and of Queen Alexandra also. On November 24, 1902, the Queen wrote to Lady Mary Lygon asking her to thank Dr. Elgar—" the great master "—for the compliment to her in the *Coronation Ode*. Some weeks afterwards Elgar was requested to go to Kensington Palace to see Princess Henry (Princess Beatrice, widow of Prince Henry of Battenberg) and, in the company of Sir Walter Parratt, he enjoyed pleasant and informal conversation. In the interval of the Union

---

[1] Mar. 15, 1903.
[2] Unless we except Handel.
[3] Parratt, with the *Triumphs of Oriana* in mind, arranged for a choral anthology for Queen Victoria's eightieth birthday. The composers whom he invited to contribute were Elgar, Stainer, Parry, Stanford, Mackenzie, Frederick Bridge, Martin, Wood, Somervell, Walford Davies, C. H. Lloyd and A. M. Goodhart.
[1]No. 1 ?

Sketch of Minuet (1879) for the *Wand of Youth*

The 'Enigma' theme in draft

Jack Concert, which was given in the Albert Hall on June 25, 1903, Elgar was presented to the King " who spoke to him quite a long time & very touchingly told him how he liked his music & in his illness used to have some of his favourite pieces played to him once & sometimes more than once a day, & how it soothed him very much, then the Prince of Wales came up & introduced himself & sd. how disappointed they were not to hear the Ode last year & how looking forward to it now." On the following day the Elgars used tickets which had been given to them by Lady Margaret Levett to see the Trooping of the Colour, after which they walked down to Buckingham Palace to hear Edward's *Marches* played— alas ! badly.

In December and January 1904 the Elgars were at Alassio. They had been gratified to see some press notices of the Elgar Festival which it was proposed should take place at Covent Garden in March. On January 21 a letter was received from Sir William Carrington, Comptroller of the Prince of Wales's Household, requesting that Dr. Elgar should dine at Marlborough House on February 3 to meet the King. Further it was requested that he should afterwards attend the smoking concert of the Royal Amateur Orchestral Society and conduct his *Pomp and Circumstance March*.[1] Alice " told people must return & that E. had command to meet the King." So the Elgars took leave of their Alassio friends, among whom were the Archbishop of York, the Dean of West-minster, Professor Lewis Campbell, an Emeritus Professor of Greek of the University of St. Andrews who earned his Italian holiday by giving lectures, and Lady Acland-Hood.

February 3 was the day after the opening of Parliament, the procession for which the Elgars were glad to see. Edward sat at dinner between Lord Howe, a keen Elgarian, and Lord Suffield, a Lord of Waiting in Ordinary and a prominent sportsman. Howe talked music and Suffield horses : Edward was at home with both. He met Prince Christian of Denmark and Prince Louis of Battenberg and, having conducted his March was gratified that the King asked for it to be repeated. The next day he drove with Frank Schuster to Buckingham Palace and to Marlborough House to write his name in the Visitors' Books. So he was invigorated for the com-pletion of *In the South*. He wrote, noted Alice cryptically, on February 8, " splendid ' Romans ' in his Overture."

On March 14 Elgar attended a levée at Buckingham Palace.

E. H

The Festival at Covent Garden, patronised by the King and Queen, took place on March 14, 15 and 16. On the last night the Queen sent for Elgar and offered her congratulations. In June an honorary Mus.D. was conferred by the University of Durham. Elgar took the opportunity, when in the North, to stay with the Kilburns at Bishop Auckland. He left Bishop Auckland on June 22. By the morning post a letter came from A. J. Balfour : Alice put it in the safe for his return : " A. told E. of letter, he sd. with such a light in his face ' has it come ? ' but then thought it wd. only be about copyright. Then he opened the letter & found H.M. was going to make him a Knight. D. G. Both very pleased."

The next day Edward went over to Stoke Works, to the Graftons, to tell his father.

" How good of you," wrote Dot [1]—now Sister Mary Reginald—from her Convent at Stroud, " to go & tell Dad—if only dear old Mother could have heard this her joy & pride in ' her boy ' would have been complete. I do with all my heart congratulate you both. . . .

" *Each* of the other members of the family wrote & told me. I can plainly see their hearts are full of joy—Dad was most anxious that I should be told at once—bless him—I *know* he is delighted."

On July 4 Edward went to London and tried on his court suit. He also went to Queen's Hall and spoke on the subject of musical copyright, on which prominent musicians were endeavouring to have satisfactory legislation introduced through a parliamentary bill. On July 5 Edward was at Buckingham Palace to receive his knighthood. " The King smiled charmingly and said ' Very pleased to see you here Sir Edward.' " A little while afterwards Monica Buck, in Settle, asked ' Uncle Teddy ' what the King had said to him on this occasion. The answer she got was " Good sport to your fishing ! "

Sir Edward was now well suited for fishing. On July 1 the family had moved to Plas Gwyn, a miniature mansion after the style of Potsdam, on the edge of Hereford. The advantage of this expensively rented property was its proximity to the Wye. Mordiford village was near at hand—ten minutes by bicycle—and Elgar spent many summer hours thereabout in the next few years.

[1] Undated, Saturday.

IV

Elgar's progress towards celebrity was marked in other ways. The Cambridge degree had given great pleasure, for it was taken, according to its intention, as a spontaneous tribute to a composer on account of his compositions. Stanford continued in his enthusiasm for conducting Elgar, on one occasion taking the R.C.M orchestra to Cambridge to play the *Variations* and on another promising to " play Cockaigne like Billy-oh at the next College Concert." On April 20, 1902, Stanford asked permission to have Elgar nominated for the Athenæum, where the principal attraction might be thought " the best private library in London." Since Parry was on the committee and would probably act as Elgar's proposer, Stanford seconding, it was considered likely that his election would take place. Elgar, who enjoyed clubs, was pleased; but uncertain as to how the entrance fee, of thirty guineas, might be afforded. Could one get out of it under Rule 2 ? Stanford cheerfully replied that at the time of his election he, too, had been hard-up, but had written a couple of songs and with the royalties collected in advance paid the fee. He advised Elgar to do the same.

It was two years later that Elgar was elected to the Athenæum, *honoris causa*, according to Rule 2, and on April 14, 1904, he was able to accept an invitation from Stanford to lunch then to be shown round and to be introduced to " one or two nice inhabitants."

Besides the Cambridge and Durham degrees other academic honours accrued. In March 1899 the Royal Academy of Music had put the seal on the " passed with honours " of 1881 by making Elgar an honorary member and in 1902 the Birmingham and Midland Institute appointed him their " Visitor." Other local honours included Vice-Presidency of the Worcester Festival Choral Society (1903) and Patronage of the Birmingham Festival Choral Society. During the Leeds Festival of 1904 the University conferred on him the honorary degree of LL.D.—an honorific sublimation in law which the one-time solicitor's clerk in Sansome Place could hardly have envisaged among his ambitions.

The public figure inevitably attracted writers. The *Musical Times* was early in the field with an excellent article (unsigned, but by F. G. Edwards the then editor) in its issue of October 1900.

The *Allgemeine Musik-Zeitung* was next, early in 1901—thanks to Lessman—and the German periodicals were generous through the next few years. Sometimes would-be essayists were nursing private aspirations. The editor of *La Vie Musicale* proposed a special Elgar article at the end of 1902 and furnished details of an Elgar Festival which might advantageously be held in Paris in the following year. Events were proceeding smoothly until he informed Elgar that he would be expected to pay the expenses of the Festival, although no doubt in the end he would make a handsome profit.

" I regret," replied Elgar, " you did not mention in your first communication that there would be any risk or expense attached to the proposed undertaking, as I would have at once said—& thereby saved you the trouble of making enquiries—that I never pay anything for the furtherance, performance, or publication of my music."

A number of publications of the years 1903 and 1904 show Elgar's own appreciation of his proper portraiture as a great man. An essentially modest and retiring man he did, nevertheless, see no reason why he should not be displayed to the best advantage. In fact this was due to a desire to fulfil family expectations—his father's delight in his achievements gave him great satisfaction, and in part to live up to Alice's aspirations. Thus, on September 16, 1903, he willingly submitted to being photographed fourteen times (both in the study and out-of-doors) by *The Sketch* and, a week later, to being interviewed by R. J. Buckley, a Birmingham journalist, who was intending a book on Elgar. This book, published in 1904, was authoritative to that date, the proofs having been read by Elgar himself. In May 1904 the *Strand Magazine*—a distinguished number with Sarah Bernhardt's Memoirs (part II), a Sherlock Holmes story —*The Adventures of the Six Napoleons*, and an instalment of W. W. Jacobs's *Dialstone Lane*—published an account of Elgar as given by him in an interview to Rudolph de Cordova. Here we begin to see the twin aspects of the great man—the composer reaching into the air for handfuls of inspiration and the country gentleman, walking, golfing and cycling—hardening into convenient myth. Valuable though this article is for information on early days it is infected by the strain of playing the expected role. Thus Elgar answered, too pompously, the detractors of his *Pomp and Circumstance* manner and embellished some of his juvenile experience. So he claimed to have written wind quintets during morning service at St. George's and to have played them at the Leicesters' during the afternoon. That life-sized busts and plaquettes (showing him " conducting his new overture *In the South* ") of the conductor were purchasable and that he supported the claims of Schiedmayer pianos and Metrostyle pianolas gave opportunities for acid comment to those whose thoughts rose above commerce.

If Elgar had received the conventional upper-class education of his time he would, in all probability, have been a less distinguished composer. He would, on the other hand, have been more diplomatic. His sensitivity, his pride, and his gratitude to those who befriended him were very near the surface and his honesty sometimes made valour the better part of discretion. The letter which he sent to Canon Gorton at the conclusion of the Morecambe Festival of 1903 (it was published in the *Musical Times* for July) was hardly likely to endear him to those London critics, whose dubiety regarding his music was one of his banes.

DEAR CANON GORTON,

I should like to thank you and the Committee for the very pleasant time I spent at the Morecambe Festival.

I was delighted, & will add surprised, at the general excellence of the choral & orchestral work ; the singing of the children especially was a revelation.

In all the advanced classes there was displayed a quite uncommon appreciation of the poetical possibilities of the music, & the words were pronounced and (apparently) understood by the singers in a refreshingly sure way. Soon—a good day for art when it arrives—we shall all know the difference between sentiment and romance, and between what is theatrical & what is dramatic : these distinctions are unknown to many critics and to more performers—all of whom might have listened to a considerable portion of the Morecambe Festival with advantage.

I cannot well express what I feel as to the immense influence your Festival must exert in spreading the love of music : it is rather a shock to find Brahms's part-songs appreciated & among the daily fare of a district apparently unknown to the sleepy London Press : people who talk of the spread of music in England & the increasing love of it rarely seem to know where the growth of the art is really strong and properly fostered. Some day the Press will awake to the fact, already known abroad and to some few of us in England, that the living centre of music in Great Britain is not London, but somewhere farther North.

. . . In conclusion I will say it was a unique pleasure to hear so much that was truly admirable, & I look forward to the next Morecambe Festival with keen pleasure ; I think it amply worth a long journey to be a listener, and as the enthusiasm is somewhat unusual to the eyes of a chorally-starved southerner, may I say a spectator also ?

I offer you a personal congratulation on the great organization you have called into being, & trust you may long be able to direct & advise your coadjutors.

> Believe me,
> Yours sincerely,
> EDWARD ELGAR

Elgar found that all musical controversy was not in the open like the familiar contest between artist and critic. Some of it arose from political machinations with which he was incompetent to deal. He was, for various reasons, unhappy about the preparations for the Leeds Festival of 1904. During the course of negotiations for a new work for that Festival he was surprised with a letter, marked *Strictly Private*, from F. J. Spark, dated October 27, 1902. It will be remembered that the Sheffield performance of *Gerontius* had taken place at the beginning of the month.

DEAR DR. ELGAR,

When you asked the Sheffield Festival Chorus to sing your Coronation Ode in London, it seemed to me to be the wise & natural course. That chorus was in full practice, & you were rehearsing with it for Gerontius. Whether there was a direct mandate from the King that you were to select the *best Chorus in existence* is not much to the point, as a matter of choice. But your selection has been exploited here by some of Stanford's people, as proof that you considered the Leeds Festival Chorus far inferior to the Sheffield Chorus. *Ergo*, Mr. Benton is not fit to be a Chorus Master.

This foisting upon you of opinions, to serve professional

jealousies by Leeds men, I have long intended to bring to your
notice.

Sincerely yours,

FRED R. SPARK

Stanford had his own complaints about the Leeds Committee,
finding them unco-operative and at all times likely to ignore his
suggestions. Elgar's drafted reply shows him in his diplomatic
incapacity. (He is also replying to an invitation contained in a
separate letter of October 27 to compose a work for the Festival.)

DEAR MR. SPARK :

Many thanks for your letter : it would give me very great
pleasure to write for the Leeds Festival if it is desired. I am
under no obligations except that I hold the chief place at the
Birmingham Festival next year : this is not announced yet but
I think it is generally talked about.

I can quite imagine that it is to the interest of some people,
whose position & popularity are not quite secure, to manufacture
ideas to suit the varying moods of their constituents ;—these
methods are not mine & I have yet to learn how to combat
them : it will be a new experience if I, an Englishman and I will
say, a straightforward one, have to apologise to English people,
in an English town in the English county which is the backbone
of England for having an honest opinion & for expressing it
honestly :—since *when* has it been necessary to impart into Leeds
—I cannot believe it to be an indigenous growth—intrigue &
all the other pettinesses now rife amongst a section of your
musical folk ?

I blush for your town, or city isn't it ?

Kindest regards,

Yours sincerely,

EDWARD ELGAR

This explains why, a few days later, Elgar was not willing to
commit himself to a laudable scheme of Stanford's to encourage the
Society of Authors to do for composers what they had succeeded
in doing for literary men. It was hoped that publishers could be
compelled to draw up proper contracts and so to reward adequately
their composers. Mackenzie, said Stanford, was afraid ; Parry was

careless and ready to give away what he wrote ; Cowen was playing
exclusively for his own hand. Stanford relied on Elgar. And
Elgar, in his view, let him down : " I am of course glad that your
experience leads you to think that the big publishers are often
everything that is considerate. I can tell you of many cases where
they are not. Some horrible cases. One e.g. of a man out of whom
a big firm made *circa* £1000 (out of one of the " small works to
take care of themselves ") & gave nothing, and who is now precious
near starvation.

"But if you & the other prominent men won't move, it makes
an amelioration all the more difficult. I shall do my best, but it will
be an uphill job. I think if by accident you saw the accounts of
Messrs. Novello concerning Hiawatha, it might open your eyes a
little as regards the ' considerate ' treatment of your composers."

Eventually, as has been stated, Elgar did so far support collec-
tive action as to speak on the subject of Musical Copyright. By
1904 his position was unassailable. In the course of his speech he
referred, obliquely, to Stanford's protest.

" I have sometimes been accused of having done little to help
the young men forward. Nothing would give me greater pleasure
than to be the means of helping them." He was, at least in one
instance, as good as his word. One evening at the Leeds Festival of
1904 he entertained Josef Holbrooke to dinner and stayed away
from the beginning of Walford Davies's *Everyman* to talk to him.
Holbrooke, like many composers, suffered from persecution mania.
He thought—and this in no way unusual—that he had been
neglected. This, in fact, in the early years of the century was not
true and his lambasting of Henry Wood in particular was unjust.
Elgar he regarded as a likely champion as one who had broken the
ring and upset the complacency of the " older men, the dry-as-
dusts." Holbrooke was a man of talent—but not of genius—and
he had a large capacity for affection. Elgar replied to his many
letters with his usual promptness and (even when Holbrooke's pen
ran out indiscretion and discourtesy) calm sympathy. He gave help
when he could and on one occasion sent the Holbrookes their
Christmas dinner ! So far as this young man was concerned we may
refer to a letter from Holbrooke's father, of September 29, 1906 :

DEAR SIR EDWARD ELGAR :
    I should like to thank you very much for your many favours

to my Son in his tussel (sic) to make headway. He feels this
I know, your kindness to him more than once leaves us both
indebted to you.

The letter is sent in confidence & I feel that you will understand the spirit it is written in.

I beg to remain,

Sincerely Yours,

CHAS. HOLBROOKE

V

The impression of prosperity given to the outside world by the
Elgars was illusory. Since their marriage—and Alice's forfeiture
of her inheritance—it had been a constant struggle to keep up
appearances. It was so still and for some time to come. Greater
composers than Elgar did not concern themselves overmuch with
appearances : but they did not live in Malvern or Hereford, nor
was it an article of faith to raise the social standing of the vocation
to a reputable middle-class level. To Elgar—and to his wife—
these things did matter. On the occasion of his address on the
Copyright Bill he shot at the hypocrites. " But our second-rate
painters may build themselves magnificent houses & indulge in all
sorts of eccentric luxuries & no-one has a word to say against
them." Behind this lay years of insecurity. It was not until February
3, 1903, that prospects began to brighten : " E. received his Royalty
cheque from Arthur Boosey. Gott sei dank. A true blessing after
such a long struggle. Also (to enhance the one pleasure) a nice letter
from Görlitz with invitation from Strauss & Mengelberg that one
of his works shd. be given at the Strauss Fest. in London." Two
days later Elgar's bank manager wrote " a nice letter about his
private a/c." Within a few months, however, Elgar was gloomy
at the prospect of meagre reward for *The Apostles*. Elgar's disposition was not naturally optimistic and royalty payments do not last
for ever.

Private cares and a more than normal share of ill-health are
calculated to stultify the best intentions. So it was that Elgar
ran into trouble in respect of the composition he promised for the
Leeds Festival of 1904.

Spark had written on October 27, 1902, asking that Elgar should write a work. It happened that this was not a propitious time, for Anne Elgar had died on September 1 and her death immediately removed a great source of inspiration. He asked the nature of the work, it having been suggested " that you will not write a Choral Work except for Sheffield." Elgar did not reply immediately as to the nature of the work. The matter rested until December 18 (Spark having, in the meantime, expressed a hope that *The Apostles* was not proving an impediment). On that date Spark commissioned a symphony. The terms were " fifty guineas as a douceur for the right of first performance . . . the composer to provide the necessary parts. . . ." Elgar considered the remuneration inadequate and substituted a choral work for contribution. By March 19, 1903, however, Elgar had said that a choral work was, after all, imprac-ticable and Spark returned to the possibility of a symphony, the suggested fee now being raised to £100. This offer was accepted. But by the end of October Elgar stated that the production of a symphony at Leeds would preclude his writing a large choral work for the Festival in the future.[1]

That Elgar was so hesitant at this time can only be ascribed to the debility from which he suffered, having produced *The Apostles*. During this crucial period of correspondence the diaries show Elgar to have been in a generally depressed state which, in a few days' time, drove him to walk the darkened streets of Liverpool when Rodewald died and from which Alice hoped to rescue him by taking him to Italy. By a " great choral work in the future " he meant *The Kingdom*, of which much was already sketched.

Spark and the Leeds Committee were not in a position to read behind the composer's correspondence and they began to feel that they had been let down. Nevertheless they persevered and asked for a short choral work. At this stage Stanford came in. On November 23 he wrote to say that he had been to Leeds for an Executive Committee " & I was very sorry to hear from them that you had withdrawn your symphony : I asked if it was irre-vocable & they said that it was, & that they had accepted another novelty." It was, he said, the first occasion since 1901 that he had

[1] To Griffith, however, he wrote as follows (Dec. 26, 1903, from Alassio) : " The history of the Leeds Symphony is this : I always promised the *dedication* to Richter : early this year (I think) I promised the first performance at Leeds : at the Birmingham festival time I learnt that R. was counting upon conducting the *first performance*—so I withdrew it from Leeds & gave it to him—*if it's ever ready* : That's all." No doubt, Elgar should have written precisely this to Leeds : but he didn't and the situation became more and more involved.

met the Committee and " I could say nothing beyond expressing my great regret : in fact it was evidently a sore subject with them (which I regret also) so there was nothing to be done."

In the end Leeds arranged the second performance of *In the South* [1] and Stanford was able on March 30, 1904, to write, " I am glad you have put yourself all right with the Leeds Committee. I have not heard anything from them but I suppose I may some time or other. If the journalists continue to credit me with sentiments & actions which I do not profess or perform, no doubt it will amuse them, & as the situation was none of my making it does not really concern me at all ; & the genial Hans (Richter) is in the position, always aspired to by Bismarck, of Tertius gaudens, I hope he will use it more wisely."

It is, perhaps, not surprising that all that Lady Elgar enjoyed at Leeds was seeing the Kilburns, and Edward arrayed in scarlet and green—with a white front showing—for his honorary degree, and hearing *In the South*.

The elusive symphony,[2] however, was not quite out of mind. On March 30 Holbrooke had written " America is the Sym. going ? I wish you luck. Not ' luck ' indeed but yr. deserts." There were rumours abroad that a symphony was to be performed at Essen, and that Weingartner was anxious to procure a first performance either for Munich or Berlin. And up to 1906 Siloti was still pressing for a symphony for St. Petersburg. The most patient, and prescient, of Elgar's acquaintances, however, was Richter, who wrote on February 15, 1905, " Re the Symphony we follow the advice of Psalm XXXVII, 1, 7 ' wait patiently for it.' I am completely sure that you *will* write your first Symphony which will be the herald of the following brothers (major) and sisters (minor)." But so far as Leeds was concerned years were to pass before any such a work was to be first produced at the Festival. When, in 1913, it came it was *Falstaff*. So in the end was honour satisfied.

---

[1] Although they would have cut out Elgar altogether, but for the energetic intervention of Stanford and possibly Parry (see *Charles Villiers Stanford*, Plunket Greene, pp. 154-5).

[2] See p. 336. The sketches for this work formed the basis of the Symphony in E Flat (No. 2).

CHAPTER VIII

THE PROFESSOR

*... there is at the present time a special opportunity of
offering an appointment to a Chair of Music in the University
to one of the most eminent of English musicians, whether of
the past or the present time; and the offer which I have the
honour & the pleasure to make is to contribute a sum of
£10,000 (ten thousand pounds) for the endowment of such a
Chair, the only condition being that it should in the first
instance be offered to & accepted by Sir Edward Elgar,
Mus. Doc., LL.D.*

> Extract from letter from Mr. Richard Peyton to Mr.
> Joseph Chamberlain, Chancellor of Birmingham University.[1]

WHEN, in 1904, Mr. Richard Peyton decided to endow a Chair of
Music in Birmingham University he intended to honour the
University and City on the one hand and Sir Edward Elgar on the
other. It would, however, have been better had Peyton not
expressed his conditions publicly. Sir Oliver Lodge, Principal of
the University, wrote [2] regarding this : " a wish of a Donor should
be only privately expressed ; otherwise you see—not in this case
of course, but in some cases—a man with wealth could flood the
Senate with Professors of extraordinary quality." In a sense Elgar
was part of Birmingham. His association with the musical community of the place was already of more than twenty years duration
and the fact that the second part of the oratorio trilogy would be
performed in 1906 ensured that then, once again, the musical
public of Europe would be aware of its great musical proclivities.
There was another point. It was well known locally that Elgar's

---

[1] Published in the Report of the Proceedings of the Council of Birmingham University of Feb. 6, 1905.
[2] Nov. 9, to Professor Fiedler.

material circumstances were a constant source of anxiety and it was considered that the emoluments of a professorship would effectively relieve these circumstances and thus secure conditions proper to the composing genius.

But genius is incalculable. Care and grief may attack the soul but resistance to them often creates the masterpiece. Certainly this was so in the present case. So it seems that by aggravating what it set out to alleviate Mr. Peyton's generosity achieved its purpose by a paradox. A wiser man than Elgar would have pocketed the salary, treated the duties more or less casually, and satisfied everybody. In fact by too much concern he reduced himself to a dangerously neurotic state, and succeeded in turning friends into enemies and accumulating ridicule and mistrust.

After the Leeds Festival of 1904 the Elgars went to Birmingham to hear Sir Oliver Lodge deliver an address in the Town Hall. Elgar efficiently seconded the vote of thanks. He was a good speaker—which convinced the authorities of his competence in lecturing—but at his best only when unhampered by notes. Sir Oliver Lodge and Professor Fiedler—Dean of the Faculty of Arts, Professor of German, and a keen musician [1]—assured him that the doubts which he expressed concerning his fitness for the Chair were without foundation. Nevertheless Elgar spent a month in restless indetermination, consulting Schuster, Granville Bantock, and Alfred Littleton of Novellos. When he met Richard Peyton and found that he liked him, and was fortified by Littleton's firm opinion that he should undertake it, he decided on acceptance of the Professorship. On November 18 he indicated this to Fiedler, suggesting that after the first year special lecturers should be engaged—" each on a modern subject & generally to direct the influence of Music into Modern & *practical* ways." Four days later misgivings returned.

DEAR PROFESSOR FIEDLER :

I am sorry to trouble you with another letter.

I wish to add that if I am appointed to the professorship I shall look forward to a long term of service on the lines I have already set forth ; but I should like it to be *clearly understood* by all concerned that if I find the increasing duties interfere with my composition I may resign the post, say after three years,

[1] He published *Tannhäuser in England* (1905).

without causing any disappointment or ill feeling—kind regards,
Yours sincerely,

ED. ELGAR

On this basis he wrote his acceptance of the post on November 26.
Two days later Mr. Peyton, satisfied with the negotiations, wrote
his formal offer to Mr. Chamberlain. On December 7 Sir John
Holder made a further offer of a donation of £1000 towards the
intended music department.

Having concluded his business with the University for the time
being Elgar set off for Mainz, for a performance of *The Apostles*.
One thing disturbed him. He had previously refused an appointment in Manchester. When, however, he mentioned the new
appointment to Brodsky the latter assured him that he had "*no*
feeling about Birm. except pleased for anything wh. wd. be good
for E." [1]

The year 1905 opened auspiciously. Elgar had his portrait
painted by Talbot Hughes and worked at the *Introduction and Allegro*
through January and the first fortnight of February. He was in
high spirits when it snowed and pulled Carice, in an old tin bath,
over the snow-covered lawn. He was equally in high spirits one
day when Alice came back from a meeting for the Prevention of
Cruelty to Animals with the information that she had made a speech.
She was much teased. Then, with the new work for strings almost
complete, the Elgars went to Oxford where they enjoyed the
hospitality of Dr. Spooner at New College. Elgar, on February 7,
was made an honorary Doctor of Music, Parry making a fine
oration. (Parry's appreciation at this juncture is important. On
December 27, 1904, Elgar had received " an odious letter from
Stanford," to which he is said to have replied with patience and
courtesy. What it was about is not known, but it would appear
to have been personal. Stanford barely spoke to Elgar again—to
Elgar's distress. Certainly there is no truth in a report that once
had currency that Elgar in some way resented and antagonised both
Stanford and Parry.[2]) A week later Elgar had an invitation from

[1] Diary, Dec. 3.

[2] See Plunket Greene, *op. cit.*, p. 150 *et seq.* Elgar gave ample evidence of his
loyalty to Parry in the autumn of 1905. It was proposed then that a memorial volume
of the writings of Arthur Johnstone should be issued. Elgar was asked to contribute
a preface. He agreed to do this, but felt obliged to withdraw it " when I saw that
among the collected critiques were some words or passages ' against ' Parry. I cd. not
give my name to this."

Professor Sanford, of Yale, to visit America. Provisionally he accepted. On February 5, helped by Mr. Austin of Worcester— " honest John " as he called him—Elgar went through the parts of *Pomp and Circumstance No. 3*. Alice took an active part in a domestic performance by playing the drum part " on brass tray with E's spectacle case. Much praised." Elgar was not too busy to help Ivor Atkins, by preparing the libretto for his *Hymn of Faith*—a congenial side-task to his theological studies for his own oratorios. The Elgars went up to London and were delighted with the charming new decorations of their room at the Schusters and everyone was excited at a private rehearsal of the *Introduction and Allegro* in Frank's music room. Elgar's apprehensions about the professorship were, however, increasing ; so that when he went to conduct at Queen's Hall on March 5 Alice had to take a " bag of restoratives " with her.

Notes for the inaugural lecture at Birmingham had been collected and on March 15 he called in his niece, May Grafton, to put them into final shape. Alas ! for the notes. On the day they were mislaid and Elgar had to rely on his memory. On March 16 the Elgars reached Birmingham from London and were met by Mr. Peyton. After tea they went to the University. There was a large crowd (including many reporters) and appropriate Elgar tunes were played on the organ by C. W. Pearce. " E. lectured most splendidly, held his audience breathless." His subject was *A Future for English Music*.

" Curious things," he said, " occur in our art in England." He proceeded to enumerate some of them. Song-writers or pianists were commissioned to compose cantatas or symphonies for Musical Festivals. Some of the works of the " New English School " since 1880, described by a friendly Press as " glorious " were dry. A few worthily held their places but mostly they had no hold on the affections of the people, nor were they respected abroad. " Our English composers too frequently write their works as if for an audience of musicians only," whereas Bach, Beethoven and Brahms " addressed a larger party, a responsive, human & artistic mass. . . ." If the old men were dry, their juniors too often adopted a pose. Some people deplore vulgarity. Elgar much more deplored the commonplace. " Vulgarity in the course of time may be refined. Vulgarity often goes with inventiveness, & it can take the place of initiative—in a rude & misguided way no doubt—but after all it does something, and can be and has been refined. But the commonplace mind can never be anything but commonplace, & no amount of education, no polish of a University, can eradicate the stain from the low type of mind which is the English commonplace. . . . English music is white, & evades everything." Elgar's own aspirations for the future of English music lay this way: ". . . What I want to see coming into being is something that shall grow out of our own soul, something broad, noble, chivalrous, healthy & above all, an out-of-door sort of spirit. To arrive at this it will be necessary to throw over all imitation. . . ." Certainly a stimulating lecture—with proper references to the Founder of the Chair, and from the classics of literature and philosophy—and not without humour : but it would have been better delivered by anyone but Elgar. His statements were true enough (and, in some ways, still are) but their secondary meaning revealed a tactlessness that, had he fully recognised it, would have surprised their author. In brief Elgar had separated himself as a composer from the " schoolmen " and neither they nor the musical journalists appreciated the situation. Whether vested interests are in effect healthy or not is beside the point : they resent disturbance. Elgar was aware that he had said more than he should have said—even if he had said what he wanted to say. Coming out from the first lecture he asked Professor Fiedler to find a chemist—" I must go and buy some strychnine. This is the end of me."

Further lectures followed: on *English Composers*; on *English Executants*; on *Critics*; on Brahms' third symphony; and on Mozart's fortieth; it was all very worrying. Elgar did his best to prepare his lectures. Alice and the indispensible May Grafton helped in calming him down and in putting his notes into order. Dr. East, the family doctor, came to administer nerve tonics and advice. But the total effect was catastrophic. Having stated a case in his first lecture he held firm to his tenets, reiterated and expanded them in the ancillary addresses. He complained that we had too many brainless singers ; too many conductors (organist-conductors, or composer-conductors) " who, if they must keep time at all, would do it more successfully in a factory yard "; too few excellent wood-wind players ; too many ponderous choruses—" duller & heavier than Handel desired "; and, in drama, no sense of acting. The wolves descended. Sir Frederick Bridge rampaged from his organ loft,

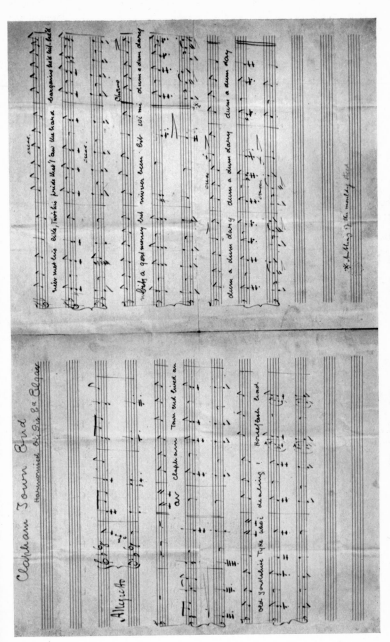

Yorkshire folk song as arranged for Dr. C. W. Buck

Worcester from the Quay c. 1840; from an engraving by B. Winkles

At the Morecambe
Festival of 1904

Mackenzie Rogan, on behalf of wind players, from his rostrum in the Household Brigade. Forbes-Robertson took up the cudgels from the stage. The leading newspapers had leading articles. It was overlooked that English pianists and organists and orchestral players as a whole were put in the front rank ; that Henry Wood was upheld as a shining example of conductorship ; that Bennett, Newman, Baughan, Kalisch and Johnstone were praised as critics. His views on "absolute" music as expressed in the lecture on Brahms appeared strongly to conflict with his own practice. This, of course, did not interest the popular press, but it did catch highly critical attention. "He still looked," he said, "upon music which existed without any poetic or literary basis as the true foundation of the art. . . . He held that the symphony without a programme was the highest development of the art. Views to the contrary, they would often find, were held by those to whom the joy of music came somewhat late in life, or by those who would deny to musicians that peculiar gift which was theirs—the musical ear, the love of music for its own sake." It was Ernest Newman [1] who principally questioned the integrity of this attitude, but at that time Newman was not to know that Elgar was, in fact, contemplating its justification in symphony and concerto. It must be concluded that in this respect Elgar meant what he said and that he implied his personal difficulties in attaining the ideal. Of the difficulties in verbal expression he based his own professional problems, as well as those of critics in general, on this epigram, which stands in his lecture on *Critics* : "Language is less than no language at all when used in reference to music."

Looking back, the storm raised by Elgar's utterances seem no more than a storm in a teacup. But the feelings aroused at the time engendered bitter attack and counter-attack, and many intemperate words were written and spoken by partisans of both sides. The Elgars were fortified by the loyalty of Troyte Griffith, who wrote abusively to the *Birmingham Post* (and wished he could have pitched it stronger), by R. J. Buckley who came over to Hereford to determine defensive action, by Joseph Bennett, of the *Daily Telegraph*, who telegraphed his disapproval of the journalistic practice of printing wrong or misleading quotations, and by Professor Fiedler who described the fourth lecture as an "intellectual treat," by Donald Tovey who was much interested in Elgar's

[1] See *Elgar*, Ernest Newman (pub. London, 1905), p. 177 *et seq.*

views on Brahms, and by Rosa Newmarch, who approved his contention that there should be more critical music journals.

Lady Elgar's final note on the year 1905 concluded in a mood of devoted optimism : " Much worry in some ways. E. oppressed with the Birmingham Prof. & quite unable to write music. *Very* unwell over Inaugural lecture, & again over Winter lectures, but did them splendidly & made a great mark, so can look back with clear content on his 1st year's work there."

Within this year, however, there were pleasures and compensations. There was a glorious performance of *Gerontius* at Hanley, in March, and the chairman, conductor and committee of the North Staffordshire Choral Society were, in every way, kind and hospitable. So it was, too, at Leeds in April when Embleton entertained the Elgars. *Gerontius* was performed there also and a couple of days were spent in York where the Elgars appreciated the hospitality of Tertius Noble, the Minster organist, and the sights of the city. Elgar was at the Royal Academy Private View, and Banquet, and was much pleased that the Prince of Wales insisted on his company through two or three rooms. Schuster, the Speyers, the Taylors of Carlow Abbey, Norwich,[1] and Canon Gorton (Elgar had thought it impossible to attend the Morecambe Festival this year but, in the end, arranged it so that he would not disappoint the Lancastrians) were constant in offering comfort and appreciation, and in September, after the Worcester Festival, Schuster took Elgar for a Mediterranean Cruise. At Smyrna, on October 1, Elgar bought a *Red Letter New Testament* to replace one which he had lost and this he annotated in preparation for the libretto of *The Kingdom* and the third oratorio of the sequence.

In June he had, at Professor Sanford's invitation, been to America and had received an honorary Mus.D. from the University of Yale. He also discussed an invitation to conduct at the Cincinnati Festival of 1906. But most of the time he was unwell, spending his time between bed and social commitments. He was glad to arrive home and to be able to speak his mind on the state of America, in which, at that time, he found much to criticise.

The robes of his American doctorate made a startling appearance in the streets of Worcester on September 12. During Elgar's absence his life-long friend Hubert Leicester had carried the City

[1] Oct. 23–28 for Norwich Festival (*Apostles* and *Introduction and Allegro*). Among those whom Elgar met at Norwich were R. H. Mottram and Fritz Kreisler.

Council with him in a determination to accord to this prophet fitting honour in his own country. It was resolved to make Elgar a Freeman of the City [1] and this was the subject which Leicester wished to discuss when he came to tea at Plas Gwyn on August 10. On the day of the ceremony Elgar, robed, passed in procession down the High Street: at number 10, at an upper window, sat W. H. Elgar, old and infirm, to witness his son's "apotheosis." As he went by Elgar gravely raised a hand to salute his parent. At Worcester that week *Gerontius*, *The Apostles*, and the *Introduction and Allegro* were given. Among other works were Ivor Atkins's *Hymn of Faith*, in which Elgar had assisted with the orchestration as well as the text, and Strauss's *Tod und Verklärung*. Elgar was " much touched by all the work and success of works & love shown him."

Although he was a native of Worcester, Elgar was now resident in Hereford and that city did not propose to be outdone by its sister. On October 31 a deputation, headed by the Mayor and the Town Clerk offered to Elgar the office of Mayor as " the highest honour in their power." As usual Elgar was in doubt as to what he should do and consulted most of his friends. Canon Gorton, who regarded it as one of his missions in life to superintend the welfare of this genius—by warning off autograph hunters who would " invade " Elgar, and the Secretary of the Oxford University Extension lectures who considered approaching him for a series of talks in November, and by arranging bicycle tours in the Lakes— helped to decide the issue. He was against accepting the Mayoralty or anything else that would interfere with " the gift for prophecy —in music."

So Elgar replied to the Mayor.

" I have carefully thought over the proposition so kindly made to me, but I find for many reasons I must decline the honour.

" I shall never forget the touching way in which the request that I should become mayor of the city of my adoption (was made) by the deputation headed by yourself and I thank you & the cor-

---

[1] Extract from *Minutes of City Council*, dated Sept. 5, 1905 : *Sir Edward Elgar, Mus. Doc., LL.D. Honorary Freedom.*

" It was moved by the Mayor, seconded by the High Sheriff, and resolved unanimously :—That pursuant to the Honorary Freedom of Boroughs Act, 1885, the Honorary Freedom of the City of Worcester, be conferred upon Sir Edward William Elgar, Mus.Doc., LL.D. ; in recognition of the eminent position which he, a Citizen of the Faithful City, has attained in the Musical World ; and that he be admitted as an Honorary Freeman accordingly."

poration of Hereford most heartily for the great honour they did me in making the request.

" It would have given me the greatest pleasure could I have seen my way to accept the invitation." [1]

It only remained to write a later letter of congratulation to the mayor elected in his stead—Edwyn Gurney, his land-lord.[2]

In 1906 the Birmingham lectures were disposed of summarily. That they were to be given at all hung like a blight over the early part of the year and Elgar's health grew worse and worse. However, he went to the University on November 1 and November 8 on the second occasion showing some displeasure at relegation to a small and ill-lit room—too small for the audience. His eyes were troubling him and he felt compelled to suspend his lecturing. Sir Oliver Lodge wrote and urged him not to worry but to get better. The Birmingham episode was virtually at an end.

Elgar was out of England in the spring of 1907 and, during his absence, Alice showed an unusual initiative—unusual, that is, in regard to her husband's professional activities. She went to the University [3] and saw Professor Fiedler, who expressed himself as distressed that Sir Edward had been so troubled by the Professor-ship. Alice proposed that the Professor of Music should not give any lectures at all but that others should deliver them—as had formerly been proposed—in his place, but subject to his jurisdiction. So it was that in November 1907 Elgar took the Chair at lectures given by a Mr. Surette (of Boston) and by Dr. Walford Davies. During the summer Elgar had attempted to inaugurate a series of 8 concerts, primarily for the benefit of young composers. They did not materialise as he had hoped. But his hopes were prophetic : " One day," he wrote to Miss Harding,[4] " Birmingham will neces-sarily possess a large and fully equipped municipal orchestra & I hope the public may be educated to wish for this possession by the

[1] Copy of Elgar's much revised draft.
[2] The week after Mayor-making on Nov. 9 the *Hereford Times* (through its " Man in the Street ") noted: " I am glad Sir Edward Elgar did not accept the Mayoralty. Hereford is justly proud of the world's greatest living composer, but Sir Edward showed excellent judgment in refusing to come down to the turmoil of municipal life."
[3] Mar. 21.
[4] July 8.

provision of a short series of concerts second to none in quality."

In the meantime the University had conferred the honorary degree of Master of Arts and Alice approved a " pretty new hood." There was a dinner party at the Peytons and among the guests was Neville Chamberlain, in due course to become Lord Mayor of Birmingham—in which office he began to implement Elgar's hopes regarding a city orchestra—and Prime Minister of England. Less than a year later [1] Elgar wrote his resignation of his University office and immediately felt a great weight lifted from his mind.

When asked why he had ever accepted this appointment Elgar replied that he had only done so until Granville Bantock should be ready to take it over. He was, indeed, succeeded by Bantock, but it is doubted that this was his first intention; although, as has been shown, he had at the outset taken only a provisional lease of office for three years.

II

During the whole of this period Elgar's health was at its worst. Physical and mental disturbances interacted on each other so that a whole cycle of ailments inordinately depressed Lady Elgar. It took much to upset her equilibrium and the index to her own depression and distress lies in the manner in which she allowed herself fully to express her grief in her diary. She did not expand, but deepened her text by the employment of words hitherto absent from her vocabulary : distress, dismay, very sad . . . She noted changes in Edward ; how, showing " distinct traces of trials gone through," he became " less vivacious & more self assertive in opinions etc." [2] She felt lack of confidence in herself, so that when hotel rooms turned out badly and Edward grumbled she accused herself of incompetence. Yet she remained content to minister to waywardness and greatness, to nurse sickness to health, and to idealise.

The Apostles had been performed in 1903 and its sequel (known for the time being as Part II) was expected for Birmingham for the autumn of 1906. Thus the year 1906 opened, with this obligation on the composer's mind. He turned to his numerous preliminary

[1] Aug. 30, 1908.
[2] Feb. 9, 1906.

sketches and by January 16 Novellos had received the Introduction
and Scene I. But Elgar was dispirited and losing faith in himself
and his work. One day Canon Dolman, the much loved parish
priest of Hereford, came and had a long talk. On that day Elgar
wrote a " beautiful new tune for Priests " (" O ye Priests "). Less
than a month later he was saying that he must give up his work and
wrote to Birmingham asking whether they would be satisfied with
half of the oratorio. He sought the advice of his own doctor—Dr.
Collens, who gave advice and encouragement so that work progressed favourably if in spasms. In the meantime Troyte Griffith,
Ivor Atkins, Embleton, Littleton, Jaeger, and R. H. Wilson, the
Birmingham chorus master, having heard and seen parts of the
score, were greatly impressed—so Elgar " wrote magnificently "
and by March 27 the " St. Peter Scene " had been sent to the
publisher. It was two days before this that Alfred Littleton had
been to Plas Gwyn. He suggested as a title for the whole work
His Kingdom, which Elgar liked.

In April Elgar was in America, but he continued, despite
numerous engagements, to go ahead with the orchestration. While
in America, on May 1, a telegram arrived announcing the death
of W. H. Elgar. This was a grave blow, even if not entirely unexpected,[1] and on reaching England at the end of the month further
severe depression set in. Lady Elgar wondered whether a London
doctor could help but, for the time being, she followed Dr. Collens's
advice, and took her husband to New Radnor. Slowly, although
the weather was miserable, he began to pick up. Just when he
felt able to work at the oratorio again he slipped on some wet
stones and hurt his knee. Although no bones were broken,
as was at first feared, he was sent home to bed and all the good of
the holiday was undone. In July, urged on by his American
friends Sanford and Mrs. Worthington, by the Stuart-Wortleys
and Schuster (whose guest he was at Maidenhead for the best part
of the month), he wrote furiously. At the beginning of August
the end was in sight and this encouraged prodigious effort. Further,
he had a call one day from an American photographer—Mr. Hewitt
of the *Outlook*, who wanted a portrait for his periodical. Hewitt,
whom the Elgars liked, told how he himself had begun life sweeping

---

[1] As early as 1899 (Dec. 29) Elgar had written to Dr. Buck " My poor old father
is just hovering 'twixt this world & the next. I saw him yesterday & he knew me
but the end cannot be far away."

snow from the streets of New York and how one day he met an old man who said to him " Hold on till you can hold on no longer, & then go on holding on."

Three days later 168 pages of full score were complete—68 having been accomplished in ten days. The rate was increased and by August 9 200 pages were done. The Three Choirs Festival was at Hereford and the Kilburns and Gortons came, but Elgar attended no part, staying at home to work. At the end of September orchestral rehearsals of *The Kingdom* took place in Manchester. The orchestral players were enraptured and when Lady Elgar asked Richter if he was " zufrieden " he answered " Zufrieden, aber es ist wieder ein grosses Werk, grossartig." On September 26 Elgar was in Aberdeen where his friend Professor Terry had procured for him another honorary degree : again that of LL.D. After this the final rehearsals took place in Birmingham. The performance was on October 3. A special train brought down hosts of well-wishers —among them Schuster, the Speyers, the d'Ozleys, Mrs. Worthington, Percy Pitt, Kalisch—from London. It was yet another great occasion but Elgar's reaction was severe and he relapsed into apathy and depression. " I don't," he wrote to Frank Schuster,[1] " seem to realise that I have written anything & am trying to forget all about it & *myself*."

The continual advice of doctors and friends was " change of surroundings." So the Elgars went to Italy after Christmas, but even on the ship to Marseilles a doctor had to be called in to deal with a cyst which Edward had developed. Returning from Italy in April there was a business trip to America. Edward went alone. At the end of 1907 the family returned again to Italy, but in January 1908 Edward was laid up with influenza and further depressed by the death of his brother-in-law Will Grafton. This was not only saddening but also inconvenient, for May Grafton had become a part of the household and was invaluable in many ways. Throughout this period Elgar was in a continual state of nervous and physical debility. He disguised his state in general, however, and it was only his intimates—Schuster, Griffith, Canon Gorton, Julia Worthington—who recognised it. At the end of 1908, after Dr. Collens had appeared impotent to effect any great change, Lady Elgar arranged for Edward to see Dr. Bertrand Dawson in London —a " nice seeming cultured man, understanding temperaments.

[1] Oct. 10, 1906.

Trust advice will do much good." The following year took a similar course. Edward was often too depressed for words, neither caring for music nor for his hobbies ; and more friends died during the year—Jaeger and Count Bodenham Lubiensky in the spring, Alice's aunt and uncle during March, Basil Nevinson and Olga Wood in December. Alice, while mourning them, thanked God for " all mercies and a truce from *some* anxieties."

III

Against this background two of the greatest works in English music were conceived : it may well appear that the *Symphony in A Flat* and the *Violin Concerto* mirror anxieties and perplexities and that these throw into relief a deeper certainty and faith. In the early part of 1907 composition was put on one side. In the spring some small works—two motets and a part song—*Love* (to C. A. E. " which made A. feel very unworthy & deeply deeply touched ")— prefaced the fourth of the *Pomp and Circumstance* Marches. In the middle of June Lord Northampton came to stay at Plas Gwyn. He was a delightful guest who sat at the piano and gossiped while Elgar corrected proofs, or else played the pedal parts of Bach fugues while Elgar did the rest. Elgar had on the piano his old manuscript books from his young days. From them he was reconsidering his children's music and indeed rewriting some of the pieces. At the same time a new tune was inescapable. On June 27 he was displaying to the family circle a " great beautiful tune "—the opening of the first symphony. At the end of July Dr. Brewer of Gloucester and a younger composer—John Pointer, who was also a reader at Novellos—brought manuscripts on which Elgar gave ready and helpful advice. He was in the mood for music—and also fishing. On July 29 he spent part of the day fishing, the other part working on symphony and suite. Early in August Alfred Littleton heard the children's music and was delighted. The next day Elgar worked the whole day at the " Sunbeam " dance. On August 8 he turned out Peter Rabbit's hutch for Carice, orchestrated his " Sunbeams " and the trio of the March. The children's music brought back memories and encouraged playfulness. The Elgars had a short holiday at Harlech and on the way back Edward and Carice played—in the most unknightly manner—in the corridor of the train. " E. fell full length. A. laughed so much sh. cd. not even urge him to rise before someone came down the corridor."

In September the *Wand of Youth Suite* (*No.* 1) was finished to the delight, among others, of Henry Wood. On September 22 Alfred Littleton was at Plas Gwyn and in the evening Elgar played his " gorgeous new tune " (of the symphony) and some suggestions for a violin concerto. In October Richter conducted a concert in Birmingham and took the opportunity to " appeal to E to finish the sinfonie." In the meantime another " abstract " work began to take form. On October 26 and 27 Elgar was busy with a string quartet : being much with Brodsky and desiring to show his appreciation of Brodsky—as he continuously displayed his affection for his friends—in a dedication, he felt a particular urge. He went on with the quartet in Rome, but it was the symphony which dominated his work. On November 24 he was with the *scherzo*. On the side, however, he worked at a Christmas piece for Sinclair of Hereford and his choristers, and a part song to words by Bret Harte.

For six months composition, apart from jottings in the sketch books, lay fallow. It was the middle of June 1908 before the symphony resumed its entries in the diaries. Two or three days before the Feast of Corpus Christi, which he celebrated by attending Mass with the family at Belmont Church, he was again immersed in it. That the music was beginning again to flow put Elgar into better spirits. He bicycled far into the country and immersed himself in the tranquil beauty of the country of the Marches. One night, after a hard day's work, he stayed out late and " thought he had never felt or seen such lovely atmosphere in country & sights." Early in July he had to go to London for a meeting of the newly formed Musical League : he hated leaving his symphony, his garden, Carice's pet rabbits and the baby swallows. But he was, after all, able as well to go on to Schuster's cottage at Maidenhead where Max Beerbohm was also staying ; and, as always, Schuster's violent enthusiasm spurred him on, so that a day or two later he was able to go on working at the symphony even though the King and Queen were passing through Hereford.

On July 5 he broke off to write an account of the origins of the *Wand of Youth* music. During the remainder of July he took little rest, often working all day at the symphony. The consequence was that by August 5, trying to finish the *scherzo*, he showed signs of overwork. On August 5 he was " very badly all p.m. distressingly so." Fortunately a visit to Ostend intervened and a magnificent reception there restored him to better form. On August 15 he was further elated by the rapture which greeted the *Wand of Youth* music and *Pomp & Circumstance* No. 4 at a Queen's Hall Concert. Three days later he was " feeling his way to his Symphony again." The Speyers came to stay and under their benign influence the slow movement was accomplished. He finished the orchestration of this movement on August 23. The next day was a *dies non*. He watched the swallows for hours and transformed part of an outhouse at Plas Gwyn into a chemistry laboratory. By August 27 the *Finale* was going ahead ; so fast that the sketch was practically complete on the next day.

Then came the interruption of the Three Choirs Festival, when *Gerontius* and *The Apostles* were performed. But by September 20 the *Finale* was mostly orchestrated. Finishing the *Finale* worried Elgar. Alice entertained him by reading aloud—*Reminiscences of an Irish R. M.* When, on September 25, the great work was completed Elgar practically collapsed and Dr. Collens was sent for. There was not much rest, for the Norwich Festival was in October and, as before, the Elgars went to stay at Carrow Abbey. Early in November Richter came to Plas Gwyn. He read the symphony —his symphony—and said " ' I think (it) will be *the* symphonie . . . it is a continuation of the great series . . .' or words to that effect."

The first orchestral rehearsal was at Queen's Hall on November 23. On December 3 the first performance took place in Manchester. Elgar was poorly in the morning and even doubtful about attending the concert, but he made himself go to the rehearsal and showed Richter and the orchestra how he wanted various sections played. It was after the third movement that the reserve of the Manchester audience broke down. They had listened to two movements with critical correctness. But the slow movement was too overpowering for neutrality. Elgar and the orchestra had to rise at that point to acknowledge the generosity of the applause. Four days later in London enthusiasm was more intense. " Wonderful playing " wrote Alice, ". . . orch. & large part of audience simply rose, people *wept*. E. looked very *apart* and beautiful being recalled again & again." Richter had spent December 6 rehearsing the symphony and among those in Queen's Hall for that rehearsal was Fauré, who was staying with Schuster. Schuster celebrated the

London *première* by a magnificent dinner party, at which the Elgars were with such devoted friends as Lord Plymouth and the Sidney Colvins. On December 19 the second London performance was given. Hundreds of people were unable to obtain tickets and such was the general feeling that Novello's had scores of the symphony specially bound as Christmas presents.

During 1909 the symphony was played on eighty-two occasions, including seventeen performances in London, ten in America, others in Vienna, Berlin, Leipzig, Bonn, St. Petersburg, Toronto and Sydney. The year was set on its way by Elgar himself who conducted it at Queen's Hall on New Year's Day. " E. conducted splendidly & looked nobilmente as if he were his music." Later in the year a new conductor, who was to become one of the foremost interpreters of Elgar, came into view—Landon Ronald : he gave a memorable interpretation in the Albert Hall, conducting from memory.

Some performances were less meritorious. On October 28 Beecham appeared with his orchestra at the Victoria Hall, Hanley, for the first time. He elected to play some of the Elgar *Symphony*. " The first movement was cut down one half : part of the ' exposition ' & the whole of the ' development ' were cut out, & some minutes were sacrificed in the succeeding movements. Those who know the Symphony will be astonished to hear that the actual time occupied in its performance was only thirty-eight minutes ! It was an insult to the composer & also those responsible for the concert. This is surely not the use to which so exceedingly fine an orchestra should be put, to say nothing of the misuse of the genius with which nature has endowed Mr. Thomas Beecham." [1]

For a time the fount of inspiration again ran dry. Elgar took rather little account of music—but was pleased to be given a seat of honour by the side of the Prince of Wales (Parry was on the other side) at a concert in February—and retired into his customary apprehension concerning his future prosperity. There was a domestic crisis which upset him at the beginning of March. Mrs. Sandals, the cook, came in intoxicated one night and when Elgar summoned her to the study and dismissed her she " became infuriated, insisting on wages, & when threatened with Police raved & shrieked and seized chairs & shook her fists at us." Eventually the police came and drove Mrs. Sandals away in a cab.

[1] Letter from Havergal Brian to *Musical Times*, Nov. 1909.

In April the Elgars went again to Italy and sketches for a new work began to take shape. But it was only at home that Edward was able to work at ease, so it was not until August 19 that the new work was defined and other considerations became secondary. On that day Lady Elgar noted " E. possessed with his music for the VI. Concerto." As always ideas came in profusion. Some passed into lesser works—" Go song of mine," the Eastern European folk-songs (words by Pietro d'Alba—alias Peter Rabbit !), a small *Elegy* for strings, a song—*The King's Way*, and a set of songs to words by Gilbert Parker. The more significant ideas, however, went into the *Violin Concerto*, until October 3. On that day the value of a set of older sketches became apparent and Elgar became " quite inspired with symphony No. 2."

The grouping of the works of this period shows again the division between the private and the public sides of the composer's character. Little things, of personal and often ephemeral interest, were designed as charming tokens of affection—to McNaught, a colleague of the Morecambe Festival, to Alfred Littleton, to Lady Maud Warrender, to Canon Gorton, to Alice Stuart-Wortley—and to " Pietro d'Alba " ! Even more intrinsic were the thoughts which went into the Violin Concerto. Herein lies the most secret Elgar.

On the other hand the projected second symphony was to be a national monument—to King and country. It was a time in national affairs which called forth such utterance. Those of knowledge recognised signs and portents. Germany already was threatening the Edwardian era of peace. In March 1909 Elgar had composed a gorgeous march tune, to which he himself had set patriotic words ; but Arthur Boosey advised against publication on the sensible grounds that patriotic words seldom outlive the occasion which had provoked them. Shortly afterwards the Elgars dined with the Stuart-Wortleys. Admiral Lord Charles Beresford, who had once shown Elgar something of the fleet, was there and held forth on the " terrible tale of naval unpreparedness." Strangely, Alice found this disturbing account " most thrilling." Edward brooded : but on the former splendours and glories of our blood and state. He had set out his principles in 1904.

" I like to look on the composer's vocation as the old troubadours or bards did. In those days it was no disgrace to a man to be turned on to step in front of an army & inspire the people with a song. For my own part, I know that there are a lot of people who like to celebrate events with music. To these people I have given tunes. Is that wrong? Why should I write a fugue or something which won't appeal to anyone, when the people yearn for things which can stir them." [1]

IV

Paradoxically this man whose imagination set him " to step in front of an army " wished for nothing more than freedom to compose, and to recreate himself in the quietness of a deeply loved countryside, or among friends at the dinner table, the theatre, the billiard-table, the bowling green. Public occasions were a menace —but inescapable. And some few were profitable. So we find Elgar turned conductor. He had, of course, long been concerned with the direction of concerts in Worcester and Malvern and, as has been shown, his initiative in provincial musical performances was outstanding. But in the eyes of the greater world this is not conducting. Nor is it when a composer directs his own works.

In the autumn of 1905 Elgar undertook his first touring engagement as a conductor. He went, at the invitation of Percy Harrison the Birmingham impresario, with the London Symphony Orchestra to the midland and northern cities. The tour was reasonably successful from all points of view. Elgar enjoyed the appreciative provinces and was glad to see old friends. His performances were approved—Brodsky after hearing Elgar's interpretation of Brahms's third symphony wished that Brahms himself had been alive to hear such a faithful performance—and his relations with his players were excellent. In 1909 there was a similar tour. In this period Elgar conducted his own works in almost every town of any size in the country : apart from the regular festivals—Norwich, Leeds (by 1907 the committee had forgiven or forgotten the misunderstandings and recriminations of 1904), Birmingham, and the Three Choirs, special Elgar Festivals were arranged. Of these the most ambitious was that organised by the Leeds Choral Union, at Embleton's instigation, on November 3 and 4, 1909.

The programme for this event comprised the *Wand of Youth* suite, some of the *Songs from the Bavarian Highlands*, the incidental

[1] *Strand Magazine*, May 1904.

music from *Grania & Diarmid, Go, Song of Mine* and the *Symphony* on the first day ; *The Apostles* on the second.

In smaller towns and at rural festivals go-ahead committees settled on the *Banner of St. George, Lux Christi, Fly, Singing Bird* (perhaps in the new arrangement for mixed voices made by the grateful Mr. Pointer), *Liebesgrüss* now firmly fixed as *Salut d'Amour*, and so on. Some places catch the eye more than others so it is that Aldeburgh stands out, for in the Jubilee Hall there the *Banner of St. George* was sung on December 15, 1904. In more recent years the Jubilee Hall has been under the patronage of St. Nicolas rather than St. George.

On occasion Elgar was in demand as a speaker. He was fluent, witty and provocative. He had, therefore, all the qualities desirable, but too rarely evident, in an after-dinner orator. Three speeches stand out : one delivered to the Leeds Association of Professional Musicians on October 8, 1907 ; another at a Lord Mayoral Banquet in Liverpool on September 25, 1909 ; a third a month later at Aberdeen, on the occasion of a complimentary dinner to Sanford Terry. The first was spoken when Elgar was still smarting from the too zealous attentions of those journalists who had given adverse opinions on his Birmingham lectures. " As they probably knew," he told an audience, which included as guests Somervell, Brewer, Rutland Boughton and Hadow, " he did not think much of critics—(laughter)—he had not read any criticisms since 1900— but he liked to talk over his thoughts with his fellow composers and musicians. Those were the critics whom they wanted. They wanted one another. If a man must do independent things he must work a good deal alone ; but when his thoughts had come to a head there was nothing like mixing with his fellow musicians . . ."

The Liverpool speech was the focal point of the first—three-day —meeting of the Musical League. It was important in that it epitomised the enthusiasm with which Elgar had pushed forward a scheme, the intention of which was to help " the younger man." Elgar was President of the League. His fellow-promoters were Delius, Mackenzie, Brodsky, McNaught, Henry Wood, Bantock, Philip Agnew, Percy Pitt, Norman O'Neill, and the indefatigable conductor of the Liverpool Welsh choral union, Harry Evans. The younger men who benefited from this first venture were Balfour Gardiner, J. B. McEwen, Holbrooke, Cyril Scott, Edward Agate, F. Nicholls, W. H. Bell, Frederic Austin, Frank Bridge, Joseph

Hathaway, Arnold Bax, Vaughan Williams, Ernest Bryson, Havergal Brian, Percy Grainger : there was one woman—Ethel Smyth. Of those, some—who survived the Great War—made little stir in subsequent years ; but the majority well justified their selectors. That the Musical League did not survive its infancy was not in the best interests of British music. But its ambitions were set too high.

It had been hoped that Debussy, Mahler and Vincent d'Indy would have been present at the Liverpool Festival to conduct works of their own. This, however, did not prove practicable. But the inclusion in the programme of works by Debussy, Rimsky-Korsakov and Bach suggested what Elgar had previously said, that English music should not be nurtured away from the main culture of Europe.

The Aberdeen speech,[1] in a sense, was an extension of the Liverpool function, for it concerned the future welfare of English music. It was, however, concerned with practical affairs and it called from Elgar some strangely radical ideas. He said : ". . . if we educate young people to be first-class players—and our English orchestral players are second to none—what is to become of them afterwards ? Are all these young people going to teach ? Has it ever struck you that we are giving the world, or at least these islands, hundreds of good orchestral players ? . . . I would like you to think seriously whether the humanising sphere of music could not be enlarged by municipal aid—by assisting choral societies and orchestras from the rates." He made other proposals, which also, in the fullness of time, reached at least partial fulfilment. The great cities of Britain, he remarked—especially noticing Newcastle as a fine town with a fine choir—were generally without proper concert halls. " At Düsseldorf on the Rhine there is a magnificent hall, unequalled in London, with all the requirements of cloak-rooms and a restaurant, and the whole thing belongs to the town. The orchestra is also a municipal one. Düsseldorf is not a very beautiful town, but many people go to reside there on account of the music ; the town looks upon that orchestra as a valuable asset, and the municipality takes the responsibility of any loss which may arise. . . . We ought to bring the best music to the people who are least able to pay for it. The choral movement of this country is not only educating choralists, but is doing a very great work which is often overlooked—it is educating listeners . . . The time is

[1] See *Musical Times*, Jan. 1910.

coming when all towns must be able to give the people the good
music they want . . . sooner or later municipal aid is bound to be
given." So, unconsciously, he repeated some of the lessons he
had first learned from his father and mother.

It was the greatest source of pride to Elgar himself that his
music was, on its merits, accepted outside of England. The international reputation of the composer declined, for obvious reasons,
during and after the First World War and later critics have tended
to suggest that it never existed. In the pre-war years of the century,
however, there was not a European city in which Elgar's music was
unknown. Interest varied. In Germany Elgar was held in high
esteem on account of the nobility of his music. So also in Sweden,
where, in 1906, the King had personally complimented the Stock-
holm Philharmonic Choir and the Opera Orchestra on a performance
of *Gerontius*.[1] In Russia it was the brilliance of the scoring which
was esteemed.

In America appreciation gathered slowly, but surely. Elgar
conducted in the United States in 1906 and 1907[2] and his receptions
in New York, Chicago, Pittsburgh, assured him that no visiting
composer since Dvořák had been so welcome. France moved
more cautiously, even though Edward VII had himself spoken to
a lady of his acquaintance about the possibility of French performances,[3] and even though Fauré, through Schuster's advances,
had for years attempted to see Elgar given his due place. By 1908,
however, the *Variations* were in the repertoire of the Lamoureux
orchestra.

Belgian musicians showed their respect for Elgar in a special
Festival-Concert at Ostend on August 14, 1908. The guiding light
of this tribute was Léon Rinskopf, Musical Director of the Kursaal.
He invited the most distinguished Belgian composers and also
Edgar Tinel and Vincent d'Indy to meet Elgar. When Elgar
appeared on the rostrum to conduct the concert the brass of the
orchestra greeted him with a ceremonial fanfare. At the end of the
performance the sight of 7000 people standing to acclaim Edward
and to honour the British National Anthem was one of Lady Elgar's
greatest moments : it made her, she wrote, " proud to be English."

[1] Letter from Kaptan J. O. af Sillen, Chairman of the Society to Elgar ; Apr. 19,
1906.
[2] The honorary degree of LL.D. (University of Pennsylvania) was conferred in
this year.
[3] Letter from Madame Greffuhlle (*c.* May 10, 1906) to Elgar.

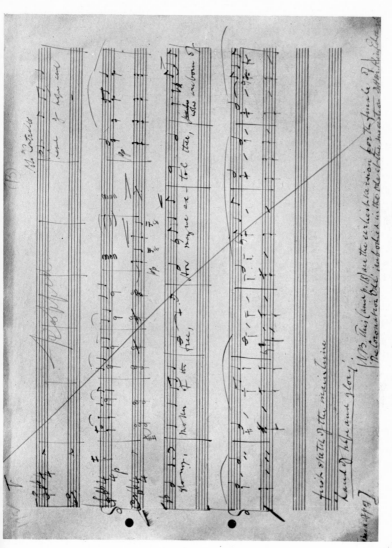

'At the suggestion of H.M. King Edward VII'

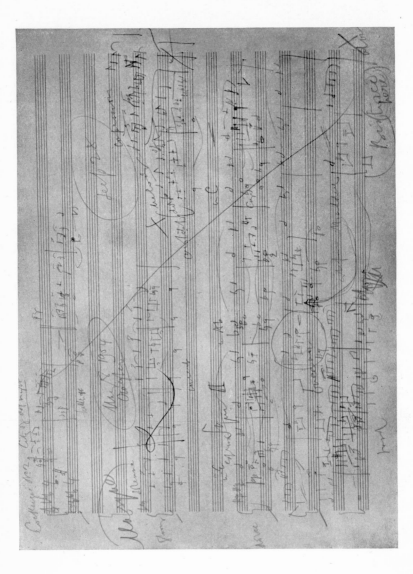

Sketches for *Cockaigne no. 2* and a symphony in E flat, 1904

V

" My dear Troyte," wrote Elgar to Griffith, on February 22, 1907, from Rome, " this is the place of all places : I cannot tell you how wonderful it all (nearly all) is . . ." Italy, more than any other place, convinced the Elgars of the integrity of European culture. They were " proud to be English "; they were often concerned with the little, as well as the large, issues of national life ; but they accepted it as axiomatic that national sentiment was valueless unless linked to the humane tradition of European thought. In the matter of musical style Elgar did not wish to be separated from the greatness of Germany : not, of course, that he regarded himself as subservient in any way, and he retained all rights in independent expression of opinion. In a philosophic appreciation of humane values Catholicism led to Rome. Thus it was that year after year the inclement English winter was avoided and an Italian pilgrimage was undertaken. It was not always easy.

The Elgars left England on January 1, 1907. They went with Canon Gorton—who was acting as British chaplain for a short time in Capri—and were joined by Frank Schuster on January 9. Elgar was much worried about the expense and was inclined—having been unwell with his throat—to go home. For a week he was in two minds. He was consistently ill and the weather was bad. He was glad, however, to visit Dr. Axel Munthe's villa on Capri and when he reached Rome desisted from planning for a hasty return. The musicians of Rome put themselves to some trouble on the Elgars' account and both Perosi, the priest musician of the Vatican, and Sgambati were especially attentive. In a postscript to a letter to Schuster, Sgambati had this to say, ". . . vous autres anglais vous avez grande raison d'être fiers de posséder un compositeur de la taille morale d'Elgar ! C'est une vraie gloire anglaise ! Est-ce qu'il y en a un autre dans ce moment de telle valeur dans d'autres pays d'Europe ? Et quel homme charmant ! " Perosi showed Elgar round St. Peter's and took him through the Vatican including, as Elgar wrote to Griffith, all the inner rooms not normally on view. Sgambati arranged a reception for the Elgars. This visit was cut short because Elgar was to sail for America at the beginning of March. At the end of the year, however, it was decided to take

E.   K up residence in Rome for a longer period. Plas Gwyn was let to Capt. and Mrs. Inglefield and a seven-room flat on the third floor of Via Gregoriana, 38, was rented from Mrs. Dawes Rose from November 7 to May 7.

This visit was extremely happy—after Alice had settled the engagement of an adequate domestic staff and Edward had, with Sgambati's help, hired a pianoforte. Edward took French lessons, solved the innumerable puzzles which he made his family—which at this time included May Grafton—buy for him, visited all the show places of the city, and worked hard at his symphony and quartet, as well as at smaller things. Sometimes there were untoward happenings which pleased Edward's love of the fantastic and embarrassed Alice. They went one day to visit the violinist A. Luthier : " we went up dark stairs & heard loud voices & found him very much in undress—Apologised & took us into his salon (with a great hole in the ceiling) & showed a Louis XV table & his arms embroidered in a frame & sd. his family was old & noble. Played on his Strad. violin for E. to hear." Among those who offered charming hospitality were the Egertons—Lord Egerton being the British Ambassador. Also in Rome were the Carpenters. John Alden Carpenter was an American composer to whom Elgar, as usual, gave such advice as he could.

In the New Year May Grafton had to go home because of her father's illness and death. But life became very full for the Elgars. It had been suggested by the Count di S. Martino that Edward should conduct a concert. Nothing came of this proposal ; principally on account of the bad performances which were experienced. One concert, conducted by Mertucci, was so indifferent that Elgar left at the interval. There were, however, operas which were worth hearing, notably La Tosca and Madame Butterfly. There was also Die Meistersinger, but " very curious in Italian dress." A constant companion of Edward's was Julia Worthington. She was wealthy enough to be able to devote herself to an easeful life—to mitigate the circumstances of an unhappy marriage. She loved the Elgars and was able to assist in their material needs. She was an ardent theatre-goer and often took Edward, who had a profound appreciation of drama, to the theatre.

The Elgars met members of the famous Gigliucci family—the children of Clara Novello—who superintended various excursions ; the Brodskys, who brought the quartet to play at the Embassy ; and the great scholar Abbot (later Cardinal) Gasquet, whom Elgar much admired and found a lively conversationalist. On March 13—such was the power of the dollar even then—there was a party, arranged by American friends, at the Hotel Bristol. The Sistine Chapel singers were engaged ; but, according to Elgar, their singing was disappointing. Holy Week was the climax of the visit—especially for Lady Elgar. On Good Friday she and Carice went to hear Monsignor Vaughan's sermon at St. Sylvester's, and on Easter Day to St. Peter's. The spectacle, however, disappointed them. They had " miserable places " and the ceremonial was devoid of " any beauty or impressiveness."

In the early summer of 1909, after the Symphony had safely been delivered, there was another Italian visit. Edward went on ahead and enjoyed ten days by himself in Paris. He wrote from the *Hôtel des deux mondes* to Canon Gorton.

[1909]   *Sunday*

MY DEAR CANON GORTON,

I hope you are enjoying such weather as we have been blessed with here : Paris *is* alive &, in a curious way, inspiring : all cities are built on seven somethings. Rome on seven hills, Hereford (!) on the cardinal virtues I suppose very much buried & Paris certainly on the seven deadly sins—which make life worth *looking* at if not worth living : this is nonsense & wd. " go " better in French than in English—or in Ovid's Latin. I send a rough proof of your chants.

Alice and Carice have arrived & send all messages. We travel to Florence on Tuesday. Send me a reprimand or anything else you think I deserve to

c/o Thos. Cook & Sons

Florence

which is a certain address in much travail and travel.

Love to you all

Yours ever

EDWARD

The Elgars stayed at Careggi with Julia Worthington and returned to England in mid-June by way of Garmisch, where they called on Richard Strauss.

In October Edward went again to Italy, having been invited to

Turin to conduct two concerts with Toscanini's orchestra during
the great International Exhibition.

The programmes of the concerts, on October 18 and 20,
comprised Weber's *Euryanthe* overture, Mozart's G minor Symphony, Mendelssohn's *Ruy Blas*, the " *Enigma* " *Variations*, the
March from *Caractacus*, the *Introduction & Allegro* (already in the
repertoire of the orchestra), the slow movement of the second
symphony, the Introduction to *Gerontius* and the Violin Concerto—
with M. Zacharewitsch as soloist.

When the family and Julia Worthington joined him they all set
out on tour. Apart from sketching ideas for the Violin Concerto
it was a carefree period. They went to Florence (and heard a
concert conducted by Mascagni), but were annoyed with a too
enthusiastic American acquaintance. " Mr. Welch came all the way
from U.S.A. to show E. his opera libretto, E. dragged out to see
him." From Florence they went to Pisa, Bologna, Venice and
Verona. In mid-June they started for home, but, coming via
Austria, stayed at Garmisch long enough to call again on the
Strauss family.

And so to England, in mid-June ; to stay with Schuster, to
rehearse the " Marching Song " at Kneller Hall, to dine with the
Dean of Westminster, to meet Lady Radnor—another great patron
of music, and to return to Plas Gwyn, for a visit from the Bach
scholar Sedley Taylor, and to prepare for the Three Choirs Festival.

It had been intended that a large party should be entertained at
Plas Gwyn during the Festival, but plans were disrupted by Carice,
who contracted scarlet fever. Undaunted, however, Elgar himself
took Harley House for the occasion, wherein there was much
merriment. The programme of a concert given (privately) at
Harley House shows the guests, the spirits of their host, and recalls
the gay nonsense of Elgar " Kitchen Concerts " of some sixty or
more years before.

HARLEYFORD MUSICAL FESTIVAL, 1909

Grand Culminating Cataclysmic
CONCERT & FIREWORK JERKATION
At
Harley House, Sept. 10th, 1909
At 8 p.m.

PROGRAMME (W.P.)

8.0 Tympanocrastic Detonation of a Brass Bombardon 'an
Delian [1] Heckelphone
Beware of Pick-pockets!

8.5 Overture " I Diavoli deliriosi " Sans-sens (Op. $2\frac{5}{8}$A)

ORCHESTRA

Strings	None
Wood Wind (the blooming lot)	Mr. L. F. Schuster
Trumpet	Sir E. J. Solomon Elgar
Precarious Horn	Mr. C. S. Terry
Percussion	Mrs. Worthington & Mr. N. Kilburn
Principal Solo Bagpipe	Mrs. N. Kilburn
At the Piano	A Chair

Conductor Herr Djetmann.

8.20 Rhapsodie Écossaise (unaccompanied) MacHavers
Mrs. Kilburn

8.30 Barley Water and Oat Cakes will be thrown to the crowd.

8.45 Lecture on " Tupsley Parish : or, Microbes I have met,
with some remarks on the Sewage Farm." By Plas Gwyn
of that ilk.

9.30 Grand Concluding Firework Display, including magnificent set-piece " Mrs. Worthington Discovering the
North Pole."

See Small Handbills and Perpend. Selah !
The Programme is liable to alteration or cancellation on any
and every (or thereby) ground. If the evening is wet, Aquatic
Sports will be wielded on the extensive sward. Costumes on
hire. Gents' medium at cut-throat prices.
By order of the Lord Chamberlain the Bomb-proof curtain will
make frequent descents.
Tickets from Concert-Direction Pietro Bunni and the usual
old gents.

[1] Delius' *Dance Rhapsody* was a " novelty " at the Shire Hall Concert on Wednesday
night.

CHAPTER IX

ORDER OF MERIT

Rarely, rarely, comest thou,
Spirit of Delight.

Shelley

THE EDWARDIAN era, despite the succession of George V to the throne in 1910, effectively ended in 1914. It was in the final years of this era that Elgar was at the height of his fame, and that he produced three incomparable works : the violin concerto—which Henry Wood considered to be the finest ever written, the eloquent and memorial second symphony, and *Falstaff*. The first was dedicated to Kreisler, who so many years before had hoped for such a work from Elgar. But this dedication was underwritten by another *Aquí está encerrada el alma de . . .* (Herein is enshrined the soul of . . .) : the soul of Julia Worthington, so it was said many years later.[1] The second was inscribed to the memory of King Edward VII, but remembered also [2] the beloved Rodewald. The third bore the name of Landon Ronald but, while dedicated to him in sincerity and gratitude, truthfully enshrined the character of Edward Elgar. Dedications, and " interpretations " based on them, should in all these cases be treated with reserve, and in conjunction with the development of the musical ideas over many years. These are discussed in detail in the second part of this work.

It is in the years of acknowledged greatness that Elgar's two-wordly character is most prominently displayed. The conflict between the two worlds is apparent. The *Violin Concerto* is a highly

---

[1] See Mrs. R. Powell, *op. cit.* p. 86, but see also the sketches " The Soul," inscribed to Miss Adela Schuster (p. 390), and the discussion on p. 335.
[2] Lady Elgar's Diary, see below, p. 156.

personal reflection of spiritual experience ; the symphony, more obviously extravert, is made to relate to temporal affairs ; *Falstaff* lies between the two. In 1912 Elgar became a Londoner, lived in becoming style at Severn House, Hampstead, and took part fully in the routine of Society. But his aggrandisement imprisoned him : his happiness lay in solitary ways. Thus he revealed himself to Schuster [1] from Porthgwidden in Cornwall, where Alice and he were the guests of Lady Mary Trefusis :

> MY DEAR FRANKIE,
>   It is heavenly etc. here ! but I would like to choose my company as you allow us (me ?) to do at the Hut. You remember we looked round the corner of the House on to the terrace. Lady M. is as of old and always very " nice " & dear & rather severe. Of the rest I will tell you. Alice is radiantly happy & sleeps always—the air is divinely reposeful.
>   You wd. love this garden of " nooks " & corners & the sea. I wish you and
>   ...! and
>   ...!! and
>   ...!!! were here.
>   I have a lovely letter from Lady Maud [Warrender] pressing me to go to Ober Ammergau but I cannot think of it.
>   I send this to Old Queen St. for I haven't a notion where you really are—you say you are living in boxes but even if I particularize & address the gentleman in Eton coloured boxes it wd. seem a little vague for the British Isles.
>   Now I am sleepy again—cream I suppose.
> > Love,
> > > Yrs. ever
> > > > EDWARD
>   That last movement is good stuff ! Kreisler saw it on Friday & is delighted.

When Alice was " radiantly happy " so too, for her sake, was Edward : but the patronage of the great sometimes pulled against his private desires, and stabbed a deep, inherited radicalism. He complimented himself, on occasion, that he did not look like an artist. But he thought as an artist.

[1] July 4, 1910.

It was his closest friends who were nearest to him when he wrote the concerto.

It had been conceived in Italy where the dynamic and generous influence of Julia Worthington was present to enliven and to encourage. In the early part of 1910 Elgar worked at the concerto a great deal at Schuster's and at Ridgehurst, as well as at home. Lady Speyer—wife of Sir Edgar—who as a professional violinist was known as Mme. von Stosch, was his first technical ally. But it was W. H. Reed, of the London Symphony Orchestra, who providentially came in to assist most in the detail of the work.[1] We may say providentially, for Reed had not only great talent, but a quippish and mercurial genius which could express the fitting mood in hilarious anecdote. Willie Reed was quick to humour, but not to triviality. His world was a joke ; on the whole a good joke and, accordingly, a serious place : Elgar thought the world a joke, but had many doubts as to how good it was. They were complementary personalities.

In April the concerto, after some early misgivings, was going well and Elgar invited his old friends Claude Phillips and Hugh Blair to the flat he had taken [2] in New Cavendish Street to hear it. He worked steadily through May, even though he was sad and unsettled by the death, on May 6, of King Edward. As usual he worked himself to a standstill. At the end of May the tenancy of the flat expired and the Elgars returned to the congenial surroundings of Hereford. On June 24 the last movement of the concerto —not yet orchestrated—was sent off to Novellos, who annoyed the composer by giving proofs a week later to Robert Newman to show to Kreisler. By the end of July the first two movements were orchestrated, and John Austin and Canon and Mrs. Gorton had been invited to hear Reed play through the work—and especially the slow movement. During this period the Elgars enjoyed a visit from Easthope Martin, whose recital of early misfortunes caught their sympathy and affection. By August 5 the whole work was complete. The next day the family went to Mass at Belmont and Edward relaxed for a day or two.

He went into Worcester and visited Mr. and Mrs. Whinfield (son and daughter-in-law of his old friend) at Severn House and told them of the old days, when old Mr. Whinfield had consulted

[1] See *Elgar as I knew him*, W. H. Reed, p. 22 *et seq.*
[2] Mar. 1.

him as to where the pictures should hang. Mrs. Fitton was there, too. The Elgars went for a walk, while in Worcester, to Claines Church. Edward showed where his grandparents [1] were buried and told Alice that he had, in youth, sat in that churchyard to read the first scores that he had possessed. There are few more beautiful churchyards in England. During this year a middle-aged nostalgia for former times set in. He had been in Worcester in April and had attended a Glee Club meeting, spending some time also with the Leicesters and the Pipes.

These informalities contrasted with the complexities of London life. The year 1910 was a critical year in public affairs. Home Rule for Ireland, relations between the Welsh Church and the State, the threatening trend of international affairs, growing unrest in industry : all these were ominous. But they were overshadowed by developments consequent on the House of Lords throwing out the Liberal Budget of 1909—a Budget which threatened aristocratic security by the imposition of taxes on the unearned increment of land. The Government went to the country in January to seek a mandate for the curtailment of the powers of the Lords.

The Elgars had no doubt as to what was best for the country. "Pray Heaven," wrote Lady Elgar, "for Conservative success." They were specially concerned for the electoral fate of John Arkwright and Sir John Rankin, two friends who were able to retain their seats at Hereford and Leominster respectively. Arkwright, who had conducted some of his electioneering from Plas Gwyn, in return entertained the Elgars to dinner at the House of Commons. After the accession of George V there was a second General Election in the same year, the Liberals again being returned in the largest number but only having an effective working majority in alliance with Labour and Irish votes. It was a sad state of affairs for those who believed in Conservative tradition, for the process of change threatened (or appeared to threaten) financial stability.

Elgar at this time was advised in many matters by Sir Edgar Speyer and was glad of his expert advice. But he had more probity than the financier. In April Speyer had successfully speculated on Elgar's behalf and, accordingly, sent him a cheque. Elgar felt that

[1] Joseph Greening: Lowersmoor, Oct. 29, 1848, aged 68.
Esther Greening: College Yard, Worcester [where she had lived with William and Anne Elgar], March 2, 1852, aged 63.
(from Claines burial registers)

he could not accept this cheque on moral grounds and returned it : Speyer ruefully reflected that it was the first occasion in his experience on which a refusal had been given to the fruits of speculation. Such adventures stimulated Elgar's portrayal of the speculator Meercraft in his late and unfinished opera. A year later there was further evidence of Elgar's principles in regard to money. Although (as a result of expert advice) he himself was experiencing disappointment in certain investments he offered to conduct the London Symphony Orchestra concerts—to which he had been appointed conductor and at the same fee as Richter had had—for nothing, because attendances were poor, and the funds of the orchestra were low.

In spite of political uncertainties and the change in the monarchy London society was easily able to dispense with apprehension. The usual round of elegance continued ; with elaborate dinner parties, balls, and with varied opportunities for other relaxation in the theatre, the art gallery and the concert hall. Elgar was, and had been since boyhood, devoted to the theatre and he had many friends in that profession. Being now more in London he was constant in attendance. He saw *The Importance of Being Earnest*, which amused him mightily ; Maeterlinck's *The Blue Bird* (" a beautiful idea," wrote Lady Elgar, " but made too material ") ; a play on the life of *Beethoven*—with Tree in the title role—which drew tears from the highly emotional Elgar ; Galsworthy's *Justice* —" gloomy "; *Trelawny of the Wells* ; *Elektra*,[1] to which he was taken by Lady Warrender ; and *Henry VIII*. In the latter Arthur Bourchier played Henry VIII. Elgar went backstage between the acts to see Tree and Bourchier, but found Bourchier so effectively in character that he was nervous to shake hands with him. In the following year the great event in the theatre was the Russian ballet, which both the Elgars adored. On the other hand they thought so poorly of *Fanny's first play* that they went home early, refusing to stay behind for a reception to the author. It was in 1912 that the Elgars began to change their opinion of the merit of Bernard Shaw as playwright. Previously Elgar had given considered judgments, not very favourable, on *The Devil's Disciple* and *Man and Superman* in letters to Troyte Griffith. When they saw *John Bull's Other Island*, however, they were full of admiration. Lady Elgar recorded

---

[1] " much impressed . . . but kept on saying ' The pity of it, the pity of it,' going back to murderous horrors." Diary, Mar. 15.

that it was " most delightful " and added " The noble & ideal left
in instead of the poison of other B. Shaw."

The great musical event of 1910 in Elgar's career was the
tremendous reception given to the *Violin Concerto* on November 10.
On the previous evening Schuster had given one of his princely
parties and had engaged the choirmen from St. Paul's to sing the
songs from the *Greek Anthology*. At the end of December the
concerto, again with Kreisler, was played in Liverpool. While he
was in Liverpool Elgar took the opportunity to see his favourite
picture—Millais's *Pot of Basil*. There had been other notable
musical occasions during the year so that Lady Elgar was able to
complete her diary on a note of the highest optimism : " End of
year of stirring event of concerto & greater recognition of E. in
every way."

At the beginning of the year there had been the Memorial
Concert for Jaeger. Elgar had prepared for this occasion three
songs, to indifferent words by Sir Gilbert Parker—a highly successful popular novelist of that time. It was not the songs that
made the occasion notable, however, so much as Richter's interpretation of " Nimrod," which thus came into its elegiac place in
English musical experience. At the end of April Elgar, having
again dined at Marlborough House, went to a concert with the
Prince of Wales, and about the same time he met Mancinelli and
Godowsky at Landon Ronald's. In July there was a tiresome episode
at Bournemouth. Parry, Mackenzie, Stanford and Elgar were all
there. Parry and Mackenzie spoke to Elgar, but Stanford—" who
fled when he saw E."—did not. Later in the month was a festival
at York—the first there since 1835—at which Elgar conducted
Cockaigne, the *Variations*, *Wand of Youth* (*No.* 2), *Sea Pictures* and
King Olaf. In November *The Kingdom* was given in Glasgow and,
a few weeks later, the Symphony in Krefeld. Elgar conducted on
both occasions.

II

Coronation Year—1911—was the climax of Elgar's career. It
saw him at the summit of achievement. It also saw him sensing a
fresh climate of opinion. The second symphony—looked forward
to, as every successive work is looked forward to by its creator, as

the *magnum opus*—failed to hit its mark.   On May 24 the first performance was received with such acclamation as would convince any contemporary that he is made for life.   Elgar was recalled several times.   But it was his reputation rather than his music that called the applause.   He recognised this.   " What is the matter with them, Billy ?   They sit there like a lot of stuffed pigs." [1]   And it was noticeable that the hall was by no means full, which was unusual for the première of an Elgar work.   Lady Elgar dismissed the audience as " dull & undiscriminating."   However, this was seen, at the time, merely as one of those episodes which unaccountably occur, for there was reward and recognition in other and more impressive ways.

For the time being Elgar himself was disconsolate.   He had worked at this symphony with even greater intensity than in the case of any other great work.   At the end of January he had completed the first movement, taking only a fortnight to score it from his sketches.   These in large part, dated from 1904, and the fact that the symphony in effect was an early work (in Elgar's symphonic history) does tend to show.   Unconsciously, and comparing it with the first symphony, the audience reacted to this.   Hence a relatively cool response.   By February 6 the slow movement, in which " A. hears lament for King Edward & dear Rody [2] and all human feeling," was ready.   By February 21, after seven or eight days of unremitting exertion, the third movement was scored :   a week later Lady Elgar wrote, " This is a day to be marked.   E. finished his Symphony.   It seems one of his very greatest works, vast in design & supremely beautiful."   Certainly it was the work over which she waxed most ecstatic.   Having heard the work played on the pianoforte—Elgar, so they said, made the pianoforte sound " like an orchestra "—she annotated it.   " It is really sublime . . . it resumes our human life, delight, regrets, farewell, the saddest word [mood ?] & then the strong man's triumph."

Between the completion of the symphony and its performance there were other engagements.   On March 12 there was a great Elgar concert in Brussels, for which Ysaÿe had been negotiating since the previous autumn.   What pleased Elgar most was the fact that for the playing of the first symphony under his conductorship

[1] *Elgar*, W. H. Reed, p. 105.
[2] It had always been Elgar's intention to write an elegy for Rodewald : it would seem, since Lady Elgar's thoughts on music are normally those of her husband, that this movement served a double purpose.

Ysaÿe sat down at the first desk to participate as an ordinary member of the orchestra. On March 25 Elgar sailed for America. Before leaving he sent an *Offertorium*, commissioned for the Coronation, to the organist of Westminster Abbey—Sir Frederick Bridge. He also wrote his *Coronation March*, using up a ballet tune of 1903. Elgar hated America—much as he liked Americans—and the recent death of Professor Sanford had removed one of its principal attractions. He was homesick and, in Canada especially, felt the cold very much. He was in Toronto, New York, Cincinnati, Chicago, Milwaukee for a day or two's rest at the end of April, and St. Paul's. He sailed home on the *Mauretania* on May 3, to find the miniature score of the new symphony awaiting him and Lady Elgar's news regarding the houses she had seen in London. For by now they were determined to live permanently in London : a sort of poetic justice, it may have seemed, to balance the depression of the first, lonely, disillusioning year that they had spent in London when they were first married.

On May 12 Elgar went on with his *March*. After the symphony had been performed Elgar was due to conduct some rehearsals of the London Symphony Orchestra. So he went to the Speyers' for a few days, where Laurence Binyon and Robert Hichens made congenial company and convenient opponents at billiards, and then on to Schuster at Maidenhead. On June 10 invitations to attend the Coronation were received. On June 11 the *Coronation Ode* was performed at the Palladium. Three days later there was a Paderewski concert and at dinner at the Goetzs' afterwards the Elgars met the Paderewskis.

On July 17—recovering from a conducting engagement with L.S.O.—Elgar was looking through his letters. " He suddenly looked up & said ' It is the O.M.' What a thrill of joy. A. cd. see the pleasure in his face—*The* thing he wished for so much. D. G. for such happy moments . . ." Lady Elgar at once wrote to the old and valued Troyte, from 75 Gloucester Place, which had been taken for a few months as a *pied à terre*.

18 *June* 1911

MY DEAR TROYTE,

You have shared our joys & worries for so long, you must be one of the very first to be told what I know will give you pleasure. It gives Edward the greatest pleasure, & you may suppose I am *delighted* & Carice. E. had a letter yesterday saying the King wished to confer the O.M. on him—you know that this is the one thing which really delights him, & is a splendid acknowledgment of all his work. I believe the List is to appear on Tuesday so it must not be mentioned till then, but we wanted you to know. E. is at the flat today or wd. send love. We are invited to the Abbey for the Coronation. I do hope you are well & wish you cd. be up here. We are still hesitating about Kelston but must settle something soon.

Yrs.

C. ALICE ELGAR

Kelston—eventually to be renamed Severn House—was a house at Hampstead that Alice liked very much. After many delays and the surmounting of legal difficulties the Elgars purchased the house, but they were not able to move in until the New Year.

After receiving news of his O.M., Elgar went on to Church House for a Coronation rehearsal and two days later he was able to rehearse the *March* in the Abbey. On June 20 there was a full-scale run-through of the whole ceremonial and as a number of friendly peers and peeresses processed up the nave they saw Elgar, having rehearsed his music, sitting at the front and so were able to shout their congratulations on his Order of Merit. Because he was elected to this Order (which had been instituted at his Coronation by Edward VII) Elgar was expected to have his portrait done. This operation he generally found disagreeable and in this case he had a poor view of William Strang's ability : the portrait, nevertheless, was executed and is in the collection of portraits of recipients of the O.M. at Windsor. On June 29 there was a great service of thanksgiving at St. Paul's and Elgar, robed as a Cambridge Doctor, sat with Parry in the Choir. His *Coronation March* sounded thrilling in that vastness. But it was an unhappy day, for earlier Elgar had written to Novellos giving notice to cancel his agreement with them as from 1912. He was also disturbed by news of Dot's illness at Stroud, which necessitated an operation.

On July 7 there was an Investiture at Buckingham Palace.

Royal Societies Club
St. James's Street, S.W.

July 11, 1911

MY DEAR TROYTE,

They have made me a life member of the club ! dependant on the O.M.

I hope to see you soon as our tenure of the house in Gloucester Place expires next Saty. week.

I wish you wd. write to the Worcester paper & say a little what the Order of M really is ! Some of the [locals ?] think it is a sort of degradation & quite unworthy of me. I see in the festival [1] list of (Honours ?) they have put it *after* Mus.D. etc. At the investiture Sir A. Trevelyan & I were marshalled next G. C. B. & *before* G. C. M. G. (which is Ld. Beauchamp's highest distinction !) & of course before G. C. S. I. etc. It was very nice.

My portrait is done : it is part of the plan, a rule laid down by Kg. Edward that all members of the order shd. have their portraits " drawn " at the King's expense & hang in Windsor Castle ! There.

I wish you cd. come up & see Kelston before the workmen wade in. Is there a Lodging near you vacant for a day or two next week ? Write to A. please.

Ever yrs.

ED. ELGAR

After all this excitement Elgar relaxed. First at Ridgehurst, where he met Cobden-Sanderson— " most weird old gentleman & in weird clothes "—and Percy Grainger, and whence he went up to London to see *Pelléas et Mélisande* ; next in Hereford where he and Ivor Atkins wrote a preface to their joint edition of the *St. Matthew Passion* and there were appropriate ceremonies for Carice's twenty-first birthday ; then in the Lakes where Elgar recalled old times with Dr. Buck by showing Lady Elgar the White Lion at Patterdale where they used to stay.

For the Three Choirs Festival the Elgars were joined by Julia Worthington, Terry (who had been at Plas Gwyn in January, staying at home one night when everybody else went to the Hunt

---

[1] Worcester. The Earl of Beauchamp was the owner of Madresfield. Elgar took a particular pride in overtaking him in the matter of honours. Beauchamp was also an Honorary Freeman of the City of Worcester (1899).

Ball), the Kilburns, and a new admirer in the Ranee of Sarawak. An innovation at the Festival was the playing of chorales, from the *St. Matthew Passion*, by brass from the tower of Worcester Cathedral, as a tribute to the patronage of Princess Henry. The other talking-point of the Festival was a performance, in the Cathedral, of the third act of *Parsifal*. The principal Elgar works were the concerto and the second symphony.

After the Festival Elgar returned to London to prepare for the Norwich Festival and a series of L.S.O. concerts. His programmes for the L.S.O. concerts were as interesting as those he had formerly performed with his orchestra in Worcester—and, as in Turin, echoes of his earliest studies in score-reading were evident. On October 23 he played Wagner's *Meistersinger* overture, his own concerto (with Kreisler), Brahms's *Symphony No. 3*, and Liszt's symphonic poem *Die Ideale* ; on November 6 he gave " distinctive readings " to Bach's *Brandenburg Concerto (No. 3) in G*, Beethoven's *Seventh Symphony*, and Brahms's *Pianoforte Concerto* (No. 2) in D Minor, in which Donald Tovey was the soloist ; on November 20 he had Casals as soloist in Saint-Saëns's *Concerto in A Minor*, and other works were Tchaikovsky's fourth symphony and Dvořák's *Huszitska* overture. In the New Year Elgar's programmes included Hamilton Harty's *With the Wild Geese* (conducted by the composer), Mozart's G Minor symphony, and Tchaikovsky's *Romeo and Juliet* on January 29 ; and Holbrooke's *The Raven* (also conducted by the composer), Schumann's second symphony and Saint-Saëns's G Minor piano concerto on February 12. The soloist in this last work was Jules Wertheim. He, noted Lady Elgar, was not impeccable : " Wertheim agitating as he left out 1/2 bars. required a genius to keep it right. Schumann symphony most noble & splendidly conducted."

III

By now Alice had successfully housed her genius in Severn House which, as Landon Ronald tactfully remarked in the middle of February, was " quite right for the residence of a great gentleman." Severn House—designed by Norman Shaw—with spacious music room, fine library—of which the shelves were designed by Troyte Griffith, oriental room, drawing-room and dining-room intended for generous entertainment, billiard-room, picture gallery, servants'

FREEMAN OF THE CITY; Sir Edward and the Mayor (Alderman Hubert Leicester)

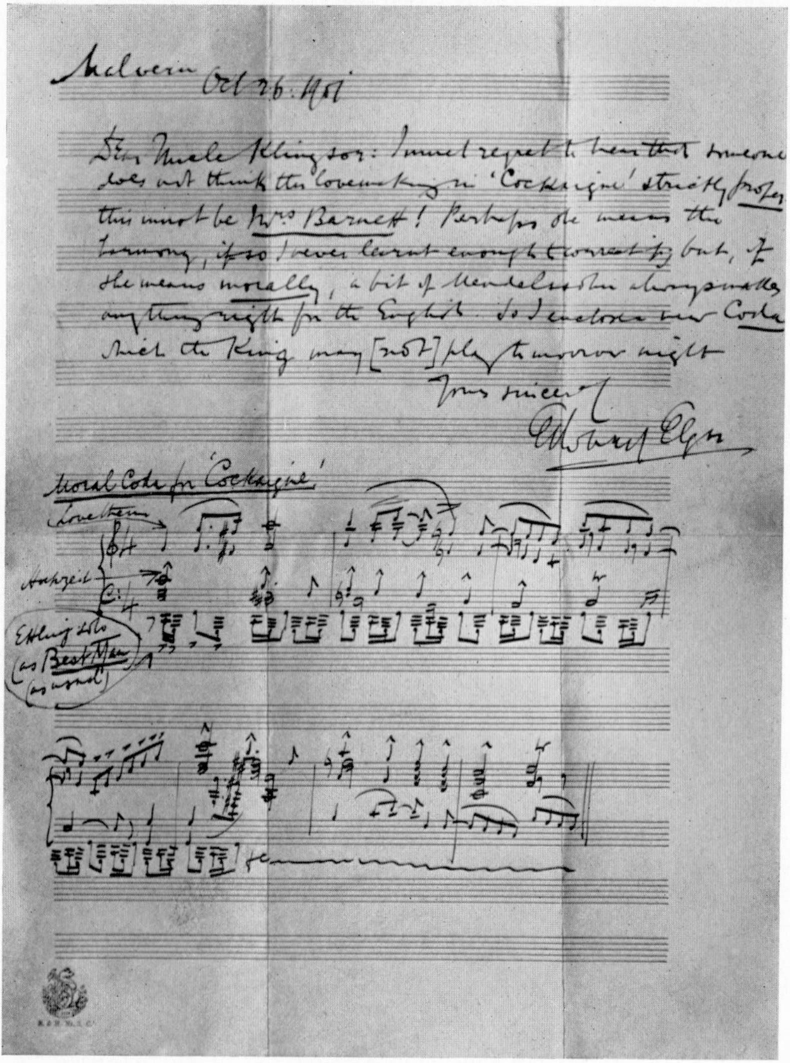

Malvern Oct 26: 1901

Dear Nicola Klingsor: I must regret to hear that someone does not think the lovemaking in 'Cockaigne' strictly proper; this must be Mrs Barnett! Perhaps she means the harmony, if so I never learnt enough to correct it; but, if she means morally, a bit of Mendelssohn always makes anything right for the English. So I enclose a new Coda which the King may [not] play tomorrow night

Yours sincerely

Edward Elgar

For 'Mrs. Barnett's' sake

quarters, and set in graceful grounds, was indeed a house for a Forsyte. But Elgar had missed his way to prosperity through a legal career and the hazards of his profession—increased within a short time by the outbreak of war—made the staffing and upkeep of such a mansion a continual source of anxiety. Lady Elgar, however, wrestled heroically with household problems and showed to the world an impressive façade of prosperity. More modest ambitions might have meant greater peace of mind; but Lady Elgar (with a lively memory of the former attitude of her "circle") considered that such success, in a worldly sense, as her husband had achieved deserved the comfort and dignity which similar success elsewhere would have brought. To live up to the standards of those in the next highest income group : that is to be (or to have been) middle-class English. Sir Edward, while generally preferring country to town life, was not without his pride. Thus the telegraphic address of Severn House summarised his honours—and his love of a palindrome—" Siromoris."

The Elgars took possession of Severn House, after spending Christmas at Brighton with Lord and Lady Charles Beresford, on New Year's Day. They spent most of January in getting the house straight. At the beginning of February Sir Edward went to conduct a concert in Cambridge (where Rootham had just conducted Dent's version of *The Magic Flute*—an epoch-making event). He found Cambridge " amusing," not least because he had to conduct a symphony [1] by Stanford. He claimed that the orchestra " played it splendidly." Then he went to Leeds, both to conduct and to interview the Festival Committee in regard to the 1913 Festival. Back in London he took the opportunity also to see *The Miracle*, which he attended with the Stuart-Wortleys and the Wilfrid Wards. It was " very, very beautiful." The next day he went to see Oswald Stoll about a patriotic masque—devised by Henry Hamilton— which it was proposed to put on at the Coliseum in honour of the King's visit to India. The music for *The Crown of India* was done quickly—the old sketch books again yielding a profusion of ideas—for the first performance on March 11. It should be noted that the Coliseum was a music-hall, that *The Crown of India* was but part of a music-hall entertainment, and that Elgar's genius for catholicity of utterance on this, and on other occasions, helped to eliminate distinctions between " light " and " serious " in music.

[1] No. 7.

E.

L

That the next work on which he was engaged was *Psalm XLVIII* —performed in Westminster Abbey on July 16—further illustrates his catholic capacity. As usual, however, with the public went the private work. *The Music Makers*, a project long thought of, was coming to maturity. On May 18 the Elgars went down to the Cotswolds—to stay with the de Navarros—and Sir Edward found composition difficult. He had, in fact, been ordered a rest cure in April, for he had been suffering from ear trouble, and " noises in his ear " had depressed as well as irritated. Sensitive as he was there were other disturbing factors. There was some anxiety, so far as Lady Elgar was concerned, as to who should present her at court—until Lady Trefusis offered her services. Carice had an operation on April 1 for the removal of her tonsils. The *Titanic* went down a fortnight later. There were still bills outstanding for Severn House. But in the sunny days of June work went on apace, at Severn House, at the Hut, at Ridgehurst. The *Ode* was finished on July 18, the day of the royal garden party at Windsor. The orchestration was done within the month and, as well, the orchestration of two of the songs [1] of 1909, and *The Wind at Dawn* from twenty years before.

Guests came and went at Severn House. Sidney and Francis Colvin were so frequent as to become almost members of the family. The Paderewskis came to tea, and on one occasion Hamilton Harty to lunch. He was then setting Whitman's *Mystic Trumpeter* and was grateful for the advice that Elgar was ready to give to any composer who, like himself, was working his way from the ranks. There were other interesting visitors to London : in particular Siloti—whom the Elgars enjoyed meeting—playing at a Chamber Music concert in March, and Siegfried Wagner who conducted some of his own works with the London Symphony Orchestra in May. In common with the majority of the audience the Elgars found this a dull affair—and left at the interval. To keep abreast of modern music Elgar looked in at one of Balfour Gardiner's rehearsals, the newest works then being undertaken coming from Delius, Bax, Grainger and John Ireland.

In the summer the family moved to Hereford for the Festival. Pleasure at seeing old friends and places—for Sir Edward motored over to Broadheath with Muriel Foster (Mrs. Goetz)—was lessened by the recent death [2] of Canon Gorton. Among newer acquaintances

---

[1] *The River; The Torch* (Hereford Festival, 1912).
[2] Aug. 20.

was Hugh Walpole, whom the Elgars had seen during the year at the Hut. The Birmingham Festival followed the Three Choirs, but as some of the orchestral rehearsals were in London the Elgars had to return there.

Lady Elgar for her own part was a quiet, peaceable person : on Sir Edward's behalf she could be fearsome. Any suggestion of disrespect or discourtesy sent her to her handiest weapon—her pen. *The Music Makers* was in rehearsal at Queen's Hall : " most annoying . . . people moving & going in & out & H. Wood quite unbearable even shutting door noisily." Besides *The Music Makers* the Birmingham programme included Sibelius's fourth Symphony —conducted by the composer—Bantock's *Fifine at the Fair*, Delius's *Sea Drift* and Walford Davies's *Song of St. Francis*—a generous allocation of unfamiliar works to set against *Elijah*, *The Apostles*, the *St. Matthew Passion* and the *Requiems* of Brahms and Verdi. There was other music besides so that for the *Musical Times* to speak of a " Gargantuan feast of music " was understating the case. It was the last of the great sequence of Birmingham Festivals.

When it was over, and the new work duly acclaimed, the Elgars had a short holiday in the Lakes and Sir Edward a few additional days with the Graftons at Stoke Works.

From Birmingham *The Music Makers* made its way to Worcester, to Brighton, to Sunderland, where it was produced by Kilburn, and to the Albert Hall on November 28 ; and Steinbach, with whom Elgar dined, talked of its production at the Lower Rhine Festival. In the meantime Elgar looked, as periodically he did, at his old sketch books and some of his pieces from the old days came out again. So on November 9 " Played his beautiful piece from former days rearranging it. Thinking about billiard table." This piece from former days went into the canon as *Cantique* (Op. 3) and was played at the Albert Hall on December 15.

In January 1913 an article in the *Musical Times* threw into prominence the meagre rewards generally to be won by creative musicians. Ysaÿe, who had been so generous to Elgar in Brussels, had lately announced, in New York, his inability to play the violin concerto on account of the high royalties demanded by Novellos. Novellos stated that their fees (in agreement with Elgar) for the usual orchestral material ranged from £4—if a number of performances were undertaken—to seven and a half guineas ; and that of the money received two-thirds went to the composer.

Ysaÿe was reluctant to pay for the use of the music at all and had, indeed, according to the statement of Novellos, pirated a number of continental performances with the aid of parts borrowed for rehearsal. The comment of *The Globe* (London), was : " When we consider how small is the possible money compensation for such an effort of the creative musician as the Violin Concerto of Sir E. Elgar, limited as it is by the comparatively few executants of capacity sufficient to give it effective performance, there is something churlish in the attitude of the world-famous executant as revealed in yesterday's correspondence. To contrast the fees of the man who composes with those of the man who plays is to realise one of the world's inequalities." So, even though Koussevitsky was enthusiastically introducing the concerto to Moscow and St. Petersburg, Elgar looked ruefully at his prospects for 1913.

The main consideration for this year was the Leeds Festival in the autumn, at which Elgar had contracted not only to share the conducting with Nikisch (an ardent Elgarian) and Hugh Allen but also to provide a new symphonic work. But in the early part of the year he was disinclined to compose. He was prepared to buy a new dog—an Aberdeen terrier which was lost almost as soon as it came to Severn House, to look at the Alma-Tadema picture exhibition, to dine at the Landon Ronalds (where he met Prince Albert), to sit for Philip Burne-Jones, who was preparing his portrait for the Summer Exhibition of the Royal Academy. But his moods were oppressing. The Elgars packed up at the end of January and went to Naples for a month. It was while they were preparing to come home that sudden, unexpected, tragic news came to them : Julia Worthington was dying of cancer.

Home from Naples Elgar still found London distasteful and went off alone to Llandrindod Wells. At the end of March he actually worked a little, at *Falstaff*, but without great keenness. He was sent by his doctor to see Morley Fletcher, one of the consultants of Bart's. Morley Fletcher pronounced him physically fit enough and prescribed more golf ! So to Stoke Works and the congenial household of the Graftons for another attempt at recuperation. It was during this absence that Lady Elgar met a Mrs. Crawshay who talked about the possible candidates for the Nobel Peace Prizes. " Pray it may be given to E.," noted Her Ladyship. There were no limits to her ambitions.

It was, however, not leisure but work which had the revivifying

effect on Elgar. He came back from his sister's in time to go
to the South Wales Musical Festival—concerts being held at
Swansea, Neath, Mountain Ash and Newport to replace the former
Triennial Festival at Cardiff. Elgar was invited to conduct *King
Olaf* at Mountain Ash on April 23. Lady Elgar was horror-struck
at the concert hall : a huge, gaunt, hangar-like erection leaning
precariously on the mountain side. But the singing was thrilling
and with such choristers as abounded in industrial places Elgar
was at his best. The Elgars were driven back to Cardiff, where the
new civic centre impressed them highly, by way of Bridgend and
Cowbridge through the fertile beauty of the Vale of Glamorgan.
So they returned to London well pleased and more ready for the
routine of London life. They met Lavery and Henry James, the
latter becoming rather more than an acquaintance if a little less than
a friend, and in the next year sending a presentation copy of *Notes
of a Son and Brother*. They went to the Private View of the Academy
and were pleased to see Philip Burne-Jones's portrait duly exhibited.
At the Banquet, however, Elgar disapproved of the place he was
given and left—dinner-less. Lindsay Macarthur was a faithful
companion at this time and he enlivened the household with wit
and fortified it with vigorous encouragement.

It was, perhaps, the theatre which finally brought Elgar into
the frame of mind for *Falstaff*. But it was no Shakespearian production. It was G. C. Hazelton's *The Yellow Jacket* which, like a
Punch cartoon in the case of Mendelssohn, made Elgar laugh for
days—if not weeks. He went four or five times to performances
and on May 25 again began to turn to *Falstaff*. On June 17 Lady
Elgar wrote to Troyte Griffith—" E. is just back from the Hut
and I *trust* better & has been flying on with his Falstaff." But the
same letter had tragic news : " Sunday week our dear dear Pippa
left this world—& now this last Sunday Lord Northampton died.
He had asked E. to go stay with him only a fortnight since. Such
blanks come into life." On the day that news of Julia Worthington's death came—June 9—there was a magnificent performance of
The Music Makers at Queen's Hall. The Leeds Choir had come up
to London for the occasion and also to take part in Beethoven's
Choral Symphony. This performance of *The Music Makers* to the
Elgars, was " Pippa's " *In memoriam*.

Throughout June, *Falstaff* proceeded intensively. Percy
Anderson rang up from the Hut one day, where Elgar did a good

deal of the work, to say how enchanting the music was and Lady Colvin and the Ranee expressed themselves as " radiantly happy " with it. One day Elgar went to see *Boris Godunov* at Covent Garden; on another *Pelléas et Mélisande* again. He enjoyed both, as also the acquaintance of Emil Cooper, the conductor of the Russian Opera. In July there was not much relaxation, though there was one entertaining afternoon at the Hut when Vernon Lee was also a guest. At the end of the month *Falstaff* was complete and the Elgars went off to Penmaenmawr for a family holiday. Sir Edward worked on his *Analytical Notes* and his proofs. It was not an altogether successful holiday—despite pleasant excursions to Conway, Caernarvon, and Anglesey. Penmaenmawr is not an ideal resort and the house they had taken was damp and gloomy.

The Gloucester Festival came almost immediately afterwards. Of Elgar there was the *Coronation March*, *Gerontius* and the second symphony. A notable visitor to the Festival was Saint-Saëns, whose new oratorio *The Promised Land* took pride of place among the new works. Elgar, resplendent in Court dress (or, perhaps, semi-Court dress) and wearing his Order, was duly photographed with the French composer.[1] On September 26 Elgar went to Leeds. On October 1 he conducted his first programme—Beethoven's *Leonora No. 3*, *The Dream of Gerontius*, Parry's *Ode to Music*, Brahms's *Alto Rhapsody* and third symphony. On the next evening his second programme : Bantock's *Dante and Beatrice* ("long & dreary," said Lady Elgar), Boito's *Prologue to Mefistofele*, a song by Verdi, *Falstaff*, Harty's *Mystic Trumpeter* (Harty himself conducted this), and unaccompanied choruses by Cornelius. This having taken three hours the Festival Committee, who had chosen the programme in the first place, decided to have no more. Thus Mozart's G Minor symphony, which should have concluded the evening, was cancelled. After *Falstaff* (of which the first London performance was on December 14 at the Albert Hall) Nicholas Kilburn spoke his admiration to Lady Elgar. Someone had remarked that " Falstaff was like turning over a new page in Hist. of Music, a page he sd., a whole book."

An autumn visit to Lord Beauchamp's at Madresfield Court gave much pleasure and excursions to the British Camp and the Old Hills also brought back old memories. Sir F. Macmillan, the publisher, was at Madresfield and pleased Lady Elgar by saying in

[1] See *Musical Times*, Oct. 1913.

how much respect he held Sir Edward and also by giving her a copy of one of Hardy's books. Another literary work came to the Elgars during this autumn. The Ranee of Sarawak published her *Life in Sarawak*. The copy she gave to Sir Edward was inscribed " To Edward Elgar—To one of the big Souls in the World, from a Savage who adores the Great Master's music." One day E. F. Benson came to submit his *The Friend in the Garden* to Elgar's literary judgment, which had lately approved Barrie's *Adored One* (" too clever for general comprehension ") and *The Will* (" most touching "). On Boxing Day, as in the previous year when they saw and enjoyed *John Bull's Other Island*, Shaw was the Elgars' diversion—*The Doctor's Dilemma*, " very interesting."

One Sunday in the May of 1913 the Elgars, out for a walk, had seen " an airship high, high up coming from Bremen to London." The significance of this flight escaped them : 1914 was but one more year to look forward to. Perhaps it might prove happier than the last, which was so summarised : " A year of loss of beloved friends & many trying things. Less financial good. So much worried. But the great blessing is E. being so much better & great artistic success."

CHAPTER X

"THE SPIRIT-STIRRING DRUM"

In England Elgar is still the one figure of impressive stature . . .

Ernest Newman " *The War and the Future of Music* "
(*Musical Times*, Sept. 1914)

Our divine art must unite what ugly politics will disunite.
Hans Richter, *in a letter to Elgar, Feb. 2, 1912*

SPRING WEATHER came early in 1914. Some January days, indeed, were summer-like. So it was, since Elgar could never bear the rigours of an English winter, that optimism seemed to prevail at Severn House. For the second year running Sir Edward was elected President of the Union of Graduates in Music—such re-election being unprecedented—and he was able to play the genial host to the committee of that body, with Hugh Blair and William McNaught as additional guests. After this luncheon party more congenial visitors followed : the Brodskys—Dr. Brodsky with welcome news of his success with the Violin Concerto in Vienna under Schalk ; Alice Stuart-Wortley, who came to play fragments of a Piano Concerto [1]; unexpectedly, Miss Griffiths, sister of the priest-in-charge at Broadheath ; Madge (Madeline) Grafton, to take her uncle to the pantomime ; Blair alone some evenings to play billiards ; Sinclair, outspoken as ever, who had " spoken plain truths to Walford Davies telling him he did not like his longer works " [2]; Embleton and two other Leeds men to ask Sir Edward to write the third part of his oratorio trilogy, and to discuss a projected performance of *The Apostles* in Canterbury. There

[1] See pp. 343-4.
[2] Diary, Feb. 23.

were novel delights in the gramophone which had been given by the H.M.V. Company, in visits to Thurston's, where Elgar was especially thrilled with the perfection of Tom Rees's play, and to the cinema. The Elgars went to the National Gallery and the National Portrait Gallery, and one evening Lady Elgar read aloud her old tale *The Two Summers*. She began to regret that her own literary career had ended but consoled herself with the dictum " the care of a genius is enough of a life work for any woman."

Some small works were written or sketched : *Carissima*, a re-arrangement of an old piece, a couple of part songs (from Ops. 72 and 73), a song—*Chariots of the Lord*, and a setting of *Psalm XXIX* for Sir George Martin and the choir of St. Paul's Cathedral.

On March 2 Elgar was called from these occupations and plunged into a national crisis. John Arkwright, an old friend and M.P. for Hereford until 1912, came with a copy of a letter which had been drawn up in protest against the intended grant of Home Rule to Ireland and the implied subordination of Ulster to an uncongenial government in Dublin. There should, it was pointed out, be a General Election or a Referendum on an issue for which the government had no specific mandate : otherwise there was grave risk of civil war. *The Times* printed this letter on March 3. Within the letter was this solemn Declaration :

" I . . . . . . of . . . . . . earnestly convinced that the claims of the Government to carry the Home Rule Bill into law, without submitting it to the judgment of the nation, is contrary to the spirit of our constitution,

Do Hereby Solemnly Declare

that, if that Bill is so passed, I shall hold myself justified in taking or supporting any action that may be effective to prevent it being put into operation, & more particularly to prevent the armed forces of the Crown being used to deprive the people of Ulster of their rights as citizens of the United Kingdom."

Arkwright had sought Elgar's signature to add to those of the Duke of Portland ; Lords Roberts, Aldenham, Balfour of Burleigh, Desborough, Halifax, Lovat, and Milner ; Admiral Sir Edward Seymour, Sir Alexander Henderson and Sir John Stirling-Maxwell ; Archdeacon Cunningham ; Dean Wace of Canterbury ; Sir George Chubb, the industrialist ; Goudy and Dicey, eminent professors of history and law ; the great Scottish humorist Sir William Ramsay ; Sir Herbert Warren, Professor of Poetry at Oxford, and Rudyard

Kipling. Elgar completed this list of " twenty distinguished men " but only after careful consideration. He was a Catholic and his position was clearly one of some delicacy. Arkwright went to consult Lord Lovat and discovered that he was prepared to answer for the Catholic side. Elgar still took a little longer but by the evening of March 2 he was able to answer Lord Milner, on the telephone, in the affirmative.

Within days this Declaration brought in more than a million supporters and, ultimately, its effect was to produce the civil war it sought to avoid, and to partition Ireland. But that lies beyond this narrative. That Elgar was invited to join the authors of the Declaration at the outset does, however, demonstrate his prestige in the country. As he was, in general, an unwilling signatory of public documents, and reluctant to serve on committees, it also shows the keenness with which he studied this issue.

The spring and summer passed happily by. The Elgars entertained and were entertained by the Ranee of Sarawak. They saw Albert Coates conduct *Die Meistersinger* at Covent Garden and found him deficient in dignity and poetry. Sir Edward conducted *Falstaff* and the *Variations* in Manchester and went, with Lady Elgar, to the Isle of Man, where they were entertained by Lord Raglan at Government House, while Elgar adjudicated at the island's musical festival. They were at Stratford for the Shakespeare birthday celebrations and at the de Navarros' home at Court Farm, Broadway. They celebrated their silver wedding anniversary at home, and enjoyed a wonderful performance of the violin concerto at Queen's Hall on May 14. On June 19 Elgar conducted the Leeds Musical Union, Henry Coward's choir, in a memorable performance of *The Apostles* in Canterbury Cathedral. The expenses of the performance were defrayed by Embleton so that the proceeds could be devoted to the restoration fund of the cathedral.[1] On June 30 Embleton came to Severn House on the matter most near to his heart. He " said beautiful things [to Lady Elgar, Sir Edward not yet being available] & made proposals about the 3rd Part of the Apostles in such a beautiful & delicate way like a friend who really loved E. & his work. E. had a talk when he came in & they clasped hands at parting, E. consenting. A feeling of great quiet joy settled down on us." In this frame of mind—and after Elgar had been down to Worcester to see his sister Lucy and to make

---

[1] See *Musical Times*, July 1914.

arrangements for the Three Choirs Festival (which never took place)—they went to Scotland for a holiday. On July 29 Lady Elgar wrote to Troyte Griffith from the Gairloch Hotel, Ross-shire :

My dear Troyte,

We are grieved to have missed you in London, we had so wanted you to come up & stay—Most interested to hear of your meeting Mr. Schuster & I am so glad you admire the Westminster Cathedral so much I always think it so wonderful. I sat next Lutyens at that amusing supper given by Granville Barker & Barrie at the Savoy Theatre—he was nice, & interesting to hear about Delhi & I always have a feeling of some affinity to the Cathedral in his Church in the Hampstead Garden City.

This is the most wonderfully beautiful place we have ever been in except Bavaria. We look straight across to Skye, an ever varying object, sometimes shimmering grey, sometimes magically blue, & the mountain views are gorgeous. I wish you were here to walk & talk & sketch. Edward & C. are out in a boat on the sea, fishing. I went with them yesterday afternoon but found it rather monotonous for 3 hours at a time. This morning they were enlivened by a sudden visit of those dear porpoises jumping & snorting quite close. This place is so mercifully untouched. There is only a scrambly bank down to the beach, no made path even, & the gulls fish & bathe & sleep close by ; from our window E. watched a stork like bird fish & swallow fish surround[ed] by an eager crowd of small gulls at 3 a.m. & the sheep wander down & lie on the sand at the water's edge, & this morning early a rabbit was quietly sitting out close by.

I hope we shall be able to stay some little time & there cd. hardly be a more inspiring place for E. & he loves it. He cannot stay in one minute ! So letters are nowhere. I am so thankful for it as of late nothing wd. induce him to go out. He has made a " workshop " in the long room over the stables [at Severn House] & paints heraldic shields [1] for the billiard room. He has done them so well. I heard Boris, but alas ! nothing else. Though as you say, I know I shd. hate La Légende

[1] Elgar's collection of crests and armorial bearings is now preserved at the College of Arms.

of Strauss—Chaliapine was wonderful, the greatest actor & singer I think I ever heard. E. was at Worcester for a Rehearsal, but I & C went to an afternoon party he [Chaliapine] gave. He sang & so did about 40 of the chorus. Very interesting to see the types of face etc. & they do sing well. Rather much for an ordinary room—Cooper was nicer than ever. Now I must finish & go out.

It is a wonderful drive here from the nearest station through ranges of mountains so awe-inspiring & desolate down to Loch Maree. I hope we shall go & see that again in sunshine some day, then it was wild & wet. The drive was a trial to Southern nerves. Now goodbye with our love.

Yrs. very sincerely,
C. ALICE ELGAR

I *should* like to come to Malvern very much.

II

On August 4 war broke out. " A glorious spirit," wrote Lady Elgar, " seemed to pervade all " as she watched the passage of troops through Inverness and Edinburgh. Ten days later the Elgars were at home and on the next day the special contribution which Sir Edward could make became clear. The first Promenade Concert of the season duly took place at Queen's Hall on Saturday, August 15. It was a tumultous evening. The principals of the orchestra and Henry Wood, their conductor, were rapturously received. There was one new work in the programme—Elgar's " sweet, melancholy " *Sospiri*, for strings, harp, and organ—but the main enthusiasm was for " patriotic " items. Among these " Land of Hope and Glory " took pride of place. The packed audience rose to it and shouted their approval. The effect, said Lady Elgar, was wonderful. At the first Ballad Concert, at the Albert Hall on October 10 (at which *Roll Call* and *King's Way* were sung) the audience applauded as soon as they recognised the onset of " Land of Hope and Glory " and joined in with the second verse. At St. James's, Spanish Place, on October 18, this was the out-voluntary. And so it continued throughout the war years. " Land of Hope and Glory " was the national song.

In fact Elgar was not happy with the words of 1902 and at the

beginning of the war had a new and more suitable set made by
Benson along these lines:

> Dear Land of Hope, our helm of pride
> Upon thy brow is set.
> Thy keen-eyed navies span the tide;
> Be strong, be patient yet!
> Then let thy thunders' rolling smoke
> O'er echoing seas be borne,
> To shatter with their lightning stroke
> The braggart sons of scorn
>
> Land of Hope and Glory, Mother of the free,
> How shall we uphold thee, who are born of thee!
> Gird thee well for battle, bid thy hosts increase
> Stand for faith and honour, strike for truth and peace.

But no one wanted to sing these lines in preference to those
they knew.

In August 1914, however, Elgar felt stirred to action. He had
often previously spoken with pride of his military connections (on
his wife's side) and now felt a call to emulate them insofar as he was
able.

On August 25 he wrote to Schuster from Severn House.

MY DEAR FRANK:

I don't know where you are so I send this home. I hope
you are well & getting some clean & clear air. Here we are
very hot but atmosphere quite bearable. London looks normal;
it seems incredible that things shd. go on so well. Alice is well
but worried. . . . I am a s. constable & am a " Staff Inspector."
I am sure others cd. do the work better but none with a better
will. I was equipping (serving out " weapons "), & taking
receipts & registering my men for hours last night: this
morning at six I inspected the whole district—so one does what
one can—its a pity I am too old to be a soldier. I am so active.

Everything is at a standstill & we have nothing left in the
world—absolute financial ruin—but we are cheerful & I will
die a man if not a musician.

That is all about us & now about you? do write. Con-

cerning the war I say nothing—the only thing that wrings my
heart & soul is the thought of the horses—oh! my beloved
animals—the men—and women can go to hell—but my horses ;
I walk round & round this room cursing God for allowing
dumb beasts to be tortured—let Him kill his human beings
but—how CAN HE ? Oh, my horses.

Bless you
Yrs. ever affcly.

EDWARD

Promotion had come rapidly, for Elgar had only joined the
Special Constabulary on August 17. He took his duties seriously :
when kept in for a day with a cold he "*fumed* and *raged* " to be back
at his post. On September 16 he wrote to Troyte Griffith announcing his appointment as *Staff Inspector* and requesting designs for a
" sort of certificate " for the members of his force. He did not,
however, take himself too seriously.

SPECIAL CONSTABULARY

Hampstead Station   *S. Division*
Staff Inspector   *Sept.* 13, 1914
SIR,

I have to acknowledge the receipt of your letter of the 9th
inst., in which you ask that a special constable shall be detailed
to visit The Hut for an indefinite period. I must point out that
it is necessary to receive fuller particulars than those contained
in your letter ; I shall therefore be obliged if you will give
replies to the following questions as soon as convenient.

(1) For how long is the presence of the Special Constable
desired ?

(2) For what emergency, if any, is a special guard required ?

(3) Failing the Constable asked for (Elgar, 0015014—who is
now Staff Inspector to the Division) would an ordinary policeman be equally welcome ???!!!???!!!

(4) State any circumstances known to you personally which
may lead the council to decide that the Hut is more important
than other private dwellings and should have the special guard
desired.

(5) State what feminine society The Hut will provide for
No. 0015014.

On receiving your reply the matter shall be proceeded with at once.

I have the honour to be,

Your obedient servant,

EDWARD ELGAR

Staff Inspector

Leo F. Schuster, Esq:
The Hut, Bray, Berks.

While Sir Edward was disporting himself at the Police Station, Lady Elgar was taking in hand the education of the Forces. She went enthusiastically down to Chelsea Barracks to teach French to a group of 50 privates, who were said to have been most disappointed when their commanding officers put an unexpected end to the course. Carice, for her part, undertook instruction in first aid until, in the course of the next year, she was appointed to the Censorship department. In 1915, her father resigned from the Special Constabulary and, at R. A. Streatfeild's suggestion, enrolled in the Hampstead Volunteer Reserve, exchanging a policeman's baton for a rifle. Lady Elgar, deprived of her teaching, threw herself into much committee work and participated in many worthy schemes. Sometimes Severn House was used as a philanthropic centre and on more than one occasion concerts were given in the Music Room in aid of one sort of charity or another.

It had been anticipated, at the outbreak of war, that music would cease for the duration. But, although the younger men almost immediately went, this was not so. There was (as during the Second World War) an abnormal normality. Concerts continued : but with German music, so far as was possible, excluded. " Of all arts," wrote Newman,[1] " music is the most cosmopolitan ; the regular interchange not only of compositions but of performers had made Europe virtually a single country so far as the practice of music is concerned. Musicians may well doubt the sanity of a world in which Kreisler is in arms against Ysaÿe and Thibaud, in which it is the business of those of us here who owe some of the finest moments of our life to the great living German composers to do all we can to prevent their pouring out any more of their genius upon us."

Elgar especially was in debt to the great Germans, whose

[1] *Musical Times*, Sept. 1914.

standards he wholeheartedly admired. His "true friend" had been Richter, who now was busy publicly renouncing his honorary English degrees. Yet Richter's private thoughts did not accord with his public utterances. He was able to write to his son-in-law in London, Sydney Loeb, on at least two occasions during the war. Thus in November 1915 [1]:

> "I notice that in the repertoire of the English opera season you sent me, there is not a single English opera. This made me think of my work. My endeavour was through the performance of well-translated Master-works to induce English talent to create national operas. A promising beginning had already been made: Mackenzie & Stanford caused one to hope for the best. I only know ' Colomba ' from the Piano Score. I conducted the ' Veiled Prophet.' I think ' Shamus O'Brien ' *most* successful, the score of which the composer himself played to me.
>
> The singers are there; what they lack is Routine, they more than make up with Talent & Enthusiasm. Even . . . Politics cannot lessen my gratitude, which fills me at the recollection of my artistic work in England.
>
> If you meet one of the good people, who helped me to further my endeavour to attain my artistic aim—greet him or her from me.
>
> Is ' Sir Elgar ' already writing an opera ? From him something great will be expected."

A year later :

> "Give my love to my friends & all the artists who worked with me, when you meet them. They are with me in my waking hours & in my dreams, & my thoughts of them are always good & pleasurable. With thankfulness I think of the hours I spent with them. They were the happiest of my artistic life."

Loeb's letter,[2] from which this is taken, continues :

> "I think I have told you that at Bayreuth at the beginning

[1] Quoted from Loeb's letter to Elgar, Dec. 15, 1915.
[2] Dec. 7, 1916.

of the war he (Richter) referred to ' Unser Elgar ' to an English
lady, who was still there, & you know he always had an especial
affection for you."

But nothing that Richter could say in private could alter the
fact that the outbreak of war brought to an end Elgar's greatness
in Germany.

Under conditions of war new opportunities arose, and mitigated
the financial hardship in which all musicians found themselves.
Since musical activities continued under the special conditions of
the time there was much for the older generation to do. There
were meetings at the Mansion House about Army bands, or " music
in wartime "; there were concerts to conduct ; there was music
to compose. The special characteristic of Elgar's war-time music
was not patriotism so much as pity. In 1916 a wounded officer
wrote to Schuster [1] who put his Hut at the disposal of the military
for the accommodation of the wounded, in memorable terms of
" all the people writing about war & soldiers when they haven't a
notion of either. Sensible people like Yeats keep quiet, or express
the feelings of non-combatants in the most touching & poignant
forms imaginable as Elgar & Binyon. How often the sad last
phrases of Elgar's *For the Fallen* echo despairingly & yet somehow
victoriously in my head."

Pomp and Circumstance was but one aspect of Elgar. He could
live up to the mood, but the critical spirit saw beyond. The
death of great friends, Rodewald and Jaeger, in particular, had once
shocked him terribly. The death of a civilisation wrung despair
from him. But moods coalesced and despair coupled with dignity :
thus there was pride and some hope of eventual triumph.

At the beginning of November 1914 Hall Caine wrote to Elgar
and asked him to contribute to *King Albert's Book*, an anthology of
which the proceeds were to be devoted to Belgian charities. As
usual Elgar was hesitant. He was, at the moment, not inclined to
composition ; nor could he discover an appropriate subject. He
felt obliged to decline the invitation. But Hall Caine (who had
ten years earlier persuaded Elgar into the *Queen's Xmas Carol Book*)
was persistent. If he was not to have Shaw as contributor (the
Daily Telegraph would not have him) he would have Elgar.

[1] Quoted by Schuster to Elgar in a letter of May 9, 1916.

E.

M

" My dear Sir Edward Elgar,

I do hope your decision is not absolutely final. I can hardly
imagine the book without you. At the same time I realise your
position. You would naturally want to do something worthy
of your great distinction to appear in a book of such importance,
containing the contributions of the most illustrious of your
living confrères.

It was I know a great thing I asked of you. I told the King
about the book on Friday & today there is a letter from Lord
Stamfordham saying that His Majesty is in warm sympathy
with it & recognises the great generosity of the illustrious artists
who are contributing.

It *is* great generosity & hence I feel myself to be greatly
daring in making, however, tentatively, a further approach. If
it had been possible for you to write any new piece of music
on this immense theme I am sure you would have done it
already. Or if any piece of verse by any of our poets, English
or French or Italian, were likely to stir you I should be eager
to send it . . ."

Within a week Elgar was busy, having, in the meantime, read
and been greatly moved by Emile Cammaerts's *Carillon*. Within
the month he completed a setting of this poem—to be recited
against an orchestral background. *Carillon* made a tremendous
impression when it was performed at Queen's Hall on December 7.
The recitation was delivered by Cammaerts's wife—Tita Brand,
who was a daughter of Marie Brema. Throughout the next year
there were many performances of *Carillon*. Constance Collier,
Lalla Vandervelde, Frank Schuster, Henry Ainley were all called
upon to declaim the poetry, sometimes in French, sometimes in
English. Lady Elgar was sometimes critical of the special audiences
solemnly assembled to serve charitable ends. At Lady Haliburton's,
where " Frank looked quite transfigured & did it wonderfully "
she was upset, but amused at the dullness of the congregation—
" like old county family people who knew *nothing* of music. Old
Lady Lurgan said occasionally that is pretty . . ." [1] At an Albert
Hall rehearsal at the end of the year Elgar gave a rare public exhibition of the boyishness known to his friends, and noted affectionately

---

[1] Diary, Jan. 7, 1915.

by Hugh Walpole. Being kept waiting by Tita Brand he seized a fiddle and played with the orchestra.

Elgar's love for Belgian art and architecture, his appreciation of past generosity on the part of Belgian musicians, and the gratitude specially shown to him by Lalla Vandervelde (Edward Speyer's daughter) and her husband (Belgian Minister of Justice), the Cammaertses, and other prominent refugees—Désiré Defauw, Arthur de Greef and Marcel de Vigneron—led him to other projects similar to *Carillon*. They were *Une Voix dans le désert*—an orchestral work with a setting for solo soprano interpolated—and another recitation with orchestra—*Le Drapeau belge*, both poems being also by Cammaerts. The former, composed in July 1915 brought Elgar into contact with Beecham. Beecham—an odd character (to Lady Elgar), who drank water at tea-time,[1] " very phantasmagoria, & not appealing to us *at all*," and wishing to be called " Thomas " [2] —conducted *Une Voix dans le désert* at the Shaftesbury Theatre on January 29, 1916. *Le Drapeau belge* was composed a year later.

In May 1915 the German general Mackensen swept back to their frontiers a menacing Russian army. Under this advance Poland was overrun and in London the cause of Polish refugees excited sympathy. On May 21 Elgar " contemplated his Polish piece " after a visit, a week previously, from Emil Mlynarski—the Polish conductor—who " longed for him to write something for Poland as he did for Belgium." As it happened there was already a latent interest in Poland through friendships, in Hereford days, with the Count Ludenham Bodiensky, and more recently the Paderewskis. *Polonia*, the resulting work and a fantasia on Polish airs, was complete at the beginning of June. It was while Elgar was correcting the parts that Embleton called—on June 14—to say that " he had just the same intentions about 3rd part of the ' Apostles ' when the war should be happily over."

When the war should be over! Then, said Elgar, would be time enough to consider oratorio. In the meantime he had other thoughts. Among his closest friends was Laurence Binyon—like Colvin and Streatfeild a member of the British Museum staff. One of Binyon's war poems—first published in *The Times* and then collected into *The Winnowing Fan*—" For the Fallen " had immediately fired his imagination. This, he felt, was the one work he

---

[1] Nov. 21, 1915.
[2] Mar. 18, 1916, at a luncheon party given by Lady Cunard.

could impressively furnish with worthy music. So early in 1915 he started sketches. At the end of March, after attending a Belgian Concert at Apsley House, he went up to Worcester for a few days. On March 26 he wrote home regarding an interview he had had at Queen's Hall with Cyril Rootham, of Cambridge. He discovered that Rootham was setting the same poem (and, in fairness to a composer of integrity, a fine setting it was to prove) which Novellos were to publish—but not if there were to be a setting by Elgar. Elgar decided to withdraw. Lady Elgar recorded his saying, " Wrotham's [*sic*] disappointed face comes between me & my work." Binyon was disappointed. Sidney Colvin was furiously distressed. On April 11 " Sidney (Colvin) overwhelming in his *attack* on E. to go on with L. Binyon's Poems [1] E. a little moved I thought." In the middle of writing *Polonia* Elgar turned aside one day to look at his Binyon music again. He " loved it himself, so there is hope." Lady Elgar went to the Colvins, at Kensington, to report. On April 25 Binyon and his wife, together with Streatfeild, were at Severn House and they heard the music in its then state. On May 2 an old Malvern acquaintance, Miss Burley, came ; the next day, in the uniform of a lieutenant of the Yorkshire Regiment, John Coates ; a few days afterwards de Greef. They all heard the Binyon music. They all insisted on its completion. So, on May 19, Lady Elgar—as usual—began to prepare the scoring paper for its orchestration. It was not, however, until July 29 that Elgar seriously began to work again at this setting and he was still disturbed at upsetting Rootham. The whole business was fraying his nerves so that at the end of October he could be reported as " not liking music at all & saying it was all dead etc." Robert Hichens, however, was the next important visitor. He felt *For the Fallen* to be overwhelming and " prayed E. to finish it." The next news of the " Binyon music " in Lady Elgar's diary is in February 1916. On March 11 a paragraph in *The Times* announced Elgar's *For the Fallen*. Rootham, whose work had by now been published, was very hurt, and in no way placated when Elgar told him that he understood that Rootham's only concern was that his setting should be published. This having been done Elgar—under the greatest pressure from Binyon, who only wanted Elgar's setting—considered himself free to proceed.

[1] Presumably " To Women " and " The Fourth of August " were already in mind.

In April Elgar broke down under the strain of work and worry. He was on his way to the Graftons for a few days respite but, feeling giddy, was taken from the train at Oxford by a Captain Dillon and put into a nursing home. He remained there for three days, Sir Maurice Abbot Anderson telephoning instructions to the local doctors from London, and then returned home. At this time Lady Elgar was also unwell.

Though still far from well Elgar travelled up to Leeds in time for the first performance of *For the Fallen* on May 4. The first London performance was at Queen's Hall on May 7. With it went *Gerontius*.

Thus a notable week, in which these works were performed every night, was inaugurated. This Festival, arranged in collaboration with Clara Butt's scheme of Red Cross Concerts,[1] was patronised by members of the Royal family. On one night Princess Henry and Queen Alexandra came, the latter taking pleasure in talking to Elgar of King Edward; on another the King and Queen. King George was said to have been much affected by *For the Fallen*, but *Gerontius* was not much to his taste. It was too long for him and as he had to leave promptly he incurred Lady Elgar's secret displeasure by showing restlessness. How different, sighed Lady Elgar, was it in the days of King Edward. At the end of the week Schuster thanked Elgar for *For the Fallen* " not only in my own name, but in that of the dear dead, to whom you have paid the noblest tribute it is possible to conceive. Their memory does not depend upon your work, but your work will ' remain '—with them—for ever." He added, as postscript, a quotation from a private in the London Scottish : " I know I am still more or less a stranger to Elgar's works—but through you I am learning to revere every note he writes. He is another Wagner, only kinder."

It was a year before the rest of the " Binyon music " was ready, the orchestration of the whole *Spirit of England* being completed on May 11, 1917. In addition to *For the Fallen*, which ended the work the cycle comprised *The Fourth of August* and *To Women* and the dedication was " to the memory of our glorious men, with a special thought for the Worcesters." The first performance of *The Fourth of August* was at Leeds on October 29. Embleton again reverted to the completion of the other trilogy

---

[1] Elgar attended a preliminary meeting on Mar. 21, at which the Dean of Westminster, Father Bernard Vaughan and Hon. Charles Russell spoke.

and said that " he must go on and they want the 3rd part Apostles."
They were in fact specific. March 1918 had been, courageously,
determined on.[1] *The Spirit of England*, in its entirety, was sung by
the Royal Choral Society at the Albert Hall on November 23. On
the same occasion Stanford's *Songs of the Sea* were sung. Lady
Elgar thought them " common " but when they were over " the
great music began—E. looked like the High Priest of Art . . ."

The adaptability of Elgar's genius has already been remarked
upon. There were other works of the war period to bear testimony
to this adaptability. Among actors and actresses Elgar had many
friends. One of these was Lena Ashwell, who in November 1915
was about to turn producer in the place of Basil Dean who was
called up for service in France. On November 10 she came to see
Elgar with a play for which she hoped he would write incidental
music. The play was *The Starlight Express*, an adaptation by
Violet Pearn of Algernon Blackwood's *Prisoner in Fairyland*. It
was a fanciful piece for children and might have been expected to
appeal strongly to the *Wand of Youth* side of Elgar. Lady Elgar
approved of the project—and of Lena Ashwell the actress. When
she was mooting *The Starlight Express* she was also playing, at
the Kingsway Theatre, the title role in *Iris intervenes*, " the only
play," commented Lady Elgar, " in wh. a woman has the sense to
say ' Nothing wd. make me believe it (tale about her husband) even
if it were absolutely proved I wd. not believe it.' A. clapped & was
joined by someone." On November 15 Lena Ashwell headed a
deputation—herself, Algernon Blackwood, and Sir Claude Phillips,
the Art Critic of the *Daily Telegraph*—to receive Elgar's answer.
As it happened he liked Blackwood immediately, Blackwood
telling him about rearing a horse to run in the Derby on dried
milk. Elgar went to Novellos and promised to adapt the *Wand
of Youth*. Actually his score, on which he worked steadily at the
end of the month and the beginning of December, was a new score,
although with quotations from the earlier work. Nor was the
score given to Novellos, but to Elkins.

The opening night was December 29. The theatre was the
Kingsway. Elgar refused to conduct—leaving this duty to Anthony
Bernard, nor was he even present. He disapproved—strongly—of
Harry Griffiths's scenery which Troyte Griffith acknowledged to be
unsuitable, even if beautiful. " Your friend," wrote Elgar on

[1] See Diary, Jan. 23, 1917.

December 28, " has entirely misused any chance this play had of success he's an ignorant silly crank with no knowledge of the stage at all & has overloaded the place with a lot of unsuitable rubbish & has apparently never read the play. He ought to be put in a Home ! " Elgar's mood was no doubt influenced by a domestic incident. Two days before the play opened Lady Elgar, involved in a taxi-cab accident, was brought home with slight concussion and was, accordingly, in bed for a little while. It was not, however, only the scenery that militated against success : the dramatised version of Blackwood's tale was but a travesty of the charming—if lengthy—original. The play came off, as anticipated, after an unprofitable month. Yet the day after the last performance Elgar regretted, very much, that it was the last.

It had all been very much worthwhile, however, for Elgar took much pleasure in the extracts subsequently recorded and he became much attached to Algernon Blackwood. It was on the following October 8 that Blackwood met Elgar " come up from Finchley Road with a toad in his pocket hkf.[?]. E. had bought it of some boys for 2d. He did not think it was happy with them. He put it in the garden & calls it Algernon. . . ." When Jack Littleton heard of this he commented " Toad & Verklärung," which might be construed as a sort of gloss on *The Starlight Express*.

At the beginning of February 1917 Mr. Elkin interested Elgar in a ballet proposal. The ballet, based by Mrs. Christopher Lowther on Conder's *Fan*, was to be put on at the Chelsea Palace Theatre towards the end of March, as part of a revue—*Chelsea on Tiptoe*—and in aid of charity. Elgar was delighted and set to work with a will. Lady Elgar considered his music " disarming & lovely." She was, however, horrified at inefficient rehearsal arrangements at Wyndham's theatre—Elgar being kept waiting for an hour before the first rehearsal, at the incompetence of the orchestra—even though this improved to be " more bearable," at the vulgarity of the remainder of the programme. Perhaps it was Monckton Hoffe's parodies of Chelsea worthies—Rossetti, Swinburne, Morris and Meredith, or Nigel Playfair's " Whistler " to which she took exception. For the rest the programme contained Ellen Terry as the Spirit of Chelsea, and Madge Titheradge reading a poem of Binyon. *The Fan* was danced by Ina Lowther, Gerald du Maurier, Ernest Thesiger and others. The scenery and dresses were by George Sheringham. And Elgar conducted.

While thus occupied Elgar was, for the first time, also testing the truth of Stanford's observation that he could express Master Rudyard Kipling in music. He was writing a song cycle—*Fringes of the Fleet*, which comprised four of Kipling's poems—" The Lowestoft Boat," " Fate's Discourtesy," " Submarines," and " The Sweepers." This was, indeed, a productive period for *The Spirit of England* was being scored at the same time. Elgar saw dramatic possibilities in his sea-songs and, after discussion with the management, it was decided that they should be staged as an act at the Coliseum. The singer was to be Charles Mott, if his calling-up did not prevent his engagement. In the end, but only after various alarms, Mott was available, through some wire-pulling in high places by Lady Maud Warrender.

On June 7 Elgar put himself in the appropriate frame of mind by going down to Harwich to see the Fleet, and at his first performance at the Coliseum on June 11 he submitted his act to the highest authority: as many admirals were present as Lord Charles Beresford—to whom the cycle was dedicated—and Lady Warrender could collect. All went well. In fact that is an understatement. Elgar had struck the right moment for buoyant defiance—the war situation was as serious as it could be and anxieties on the home front were innumerable and depressing beyond words—and his spirit instantly influenced his audience. Elgar was delighted and as once, a year or two earlier, he had shown his regard for the London Symphony Orchestra by taking them all to lunch at Gatti's, so now he honoured the theatre band and Arthur Croxton, a joint manager and secretary of the Coliseum, in the same place and in the same way. At the beginning of the second fortnight Elgar added one male voice chorus to the songs—a setting of Gilbert Parker's *Inside the Bar*. Thus stimulated *Fringes of the Fleet* went from strength to strength.

At first a three weeks' run had been intended, but the performance ran well on into July. Then followed a week in Manchester and a week in Leicester in August. Elgar was in excellent form although he was a little tired at the end of the Leicester week; but it came to Lady Elgar's ears that Kipling intended putting a stop to this exhibition of his poetry. In September *Fringes of the Fleet* went to Chiswick. Elgar, by now, was worried on account of Kipling's attitude and also because he could, having made approaches, get no satisfactory answer from him. However, two further weeks followed—one, when the Elgars were submitted to discomfort in their hotel and much harassing from marauding German aircraft, in Chatham ; the other at the Coliseum. After engagements in Leeds, Huddersfield, and the Albert Hall, the Coliseum management insisted on yet another week of *Fringes of the Fleet*. This ended on December 1.

By now Elgar's doctor was concerned about his condition and, unable to diagnose a specific condition, called in Dr. Hale White, Senior Physician at Guy's Hospital, to examine him. The specialist could find nothing organically wrong : but Elgar continued in poor health until the end of the year.

III

Elgar's commitments entailed both the giving and the receiving of hospitality and family habits in this respect changed only a little when once the shock of the outbreak of war had been absorbed. There is hardly a name in the previous part of this chapter which does not occur also on the list of guests who attended Lady Elgar's luncheon, tea, or dinner parties at Severn House, or elsewhere as host to the Elgars. There were, however, new contacts and old associations resumed. And an increasing number of visitors came in uniform. Among these was a future Master of the Queen's Music—Arthur Bliss, whom Lady Elgar regarded appreciatively as a composer (November 12, 1916, " A. to hear Mr. Bliss's Quartet. Liked it very much "), and respectfully as a soldier on account of the prisoners he captured and the wounds he sustained. There were also, on one occasion, Sarah's nephews—Sarah being an old and valued family servant—two boys who pleased because of their broad Gloucestershire accents and their favourable estimate of Sir Edward's courtesy in comparison with that of their officers. Musicians who came into the Elgar circle during the early years of the war also included Edward German, introduced by Landon Ronald ; Wassily Safonoff, the Russian conductor, who hoped that Sir Edward would be able to undertake a series of engagements in Russia ; Emil Cooper, conductor of the Russian ballet, who had introduced a number of his works to Moscow ; and Irene Scharrer, a friend of the Speyers ; Percy Scholes, then editor of *The Music Student*, was added to the list of those who came to interview Elgar in preparation for a special article on his life and works. One day Barclay Squire was doubly welcome. He, belonging to the British Museum group of friends, was *persona grata* for his scholarship, but on June 25, 1916, he contrasted favourably with the lawyer Sir Frederick Pollock, whom Lady Elgar had lately seen and who had the unhappy effect of saying " goodbye as if one were a toad." In this same year Yeats reappeared. He came to tea, but said nothing. Artists were frequent, especially Percy Anderson, Hugh Walpole's intimate friend and the distinguished designer of sets for the later Gilbert and Sullivan operas ; and Sir Philip Burne-Jones, son of Sir Edward and one of those who essayed a portrait of Elgar. At the Stuart-Wortleys' house in Cheyne Walk the Elgars encountered Frank Dicksee.

Art was one of Elgar's relaxations. He busied himself in designing friezes and in executing heraldic designs, in framing the Piranesi prints which Lady Elgar gave to him, and was in the Art Galleries as much as formerly. His visits to the theatre were also maintained, but too often Charles Hawtrey, Beerbohm Tree and Ernest Thesiger were squandering their talent on ephemeral shows or untimely plays of Shaw. There was one particularly upsetting piece by Shaw—*Augustus does his bit*, at the Royal Court Theatre in Sloane Square, and for the Stage Society, on January 21, 1917. The Elgars went for Lalla Vandervelde's sake, as she played " the lady." But to portray the British soldier, as Shaw did, as an idiot was hardly tactful at that time. On the same bill was Synge's *Tinker's Wedding*, with W. G. & Beatrice Fay, Arthur Cullin and Maire O'Neill, players whom at the time Lady Elgar much approved. Between Synge and Shaw Lalla Vandervelde recited poems by Cammaerts and Claudel. An odd assortment.

It was with his books that Elgar was happiest and in search of old editions he haunted the sale rooms. He talked endlessly to Colvin, and particularly about the Greek Anthology to which he once again turned for inspiration.[1] Lady Elgar turned authoress again and Streatfeild, having been shown a sonnet, took it to the Editor of the *Bookman*, when it was duly published on August 5, 1915. Streatfeild was always charming and able to express his gratitude for Lady Elgar's hospitality in the graceful manner. " This," he said to her after tea on one occasion, " is the most

[1] Diary, July 1917, " E. thinking of beautiful Scena from Greek Anthology— beautiful idea."

difficult house ever to leave . . . like the Garden of Armida, when you are in, you cannot get out."

Lady Elgar was always glad to return to London. She began to find provincial worthies monotonous and a little incredulous. Sir Edward was in Bradford to conduct in May 1916. He and Lady Elgar stayed with the hospitable and prosperous family of Behrens. They were, Lady Elgar noted, " obsessed by Bradford. Even said *have* you good Drs. in London ! This was Miss Behrens." The next day : " So nice to be in London again after Bradford's very local atmosphere." More and more, however, Sir Edward looked towards country life.

Worcestershire called. When in London Elgar read up the history of his county and was delighted when Alice Stuart-Wortley brought to him some relics, picked up in a sale room, and said to have been from King John's tomb in Worcester Cathedral. Elgar went down to Worcestershire four or five times a year, usually to stay with the Graftons, but often enough to see Frank and his wife, Lucy, the Leicesters, and Ivor Atkins. Uncle Henry Elgar died on February 24, 1917, and when Elgar went to conduct *For the Fallen* in the Cathedral a month later he had his affairs to clear up. February was a melancholy month in that year in the death of friends. The Duke of Norfolk died on the 11th and George Sinclair on the 12th. " E. keeps G's last letter in front of him on writing table & thinks much about him." Later in the year, when Elgar was away in Manchester, Lady Elgar went to Hereford to see her old house and her old friends. She also persuaded Willie Baker to motor her over to Hazeldine. " The great oak gone & the beloved ash perished. . . . The house charming & so much what we shd. like to have done & never could . . ." She planned where Edward's study would have been.

The Elgars were grateful to the de Navarros for looking after them on innumerable occasions. Mary de Navarro, two years younger than Elgar, was a fascinating hostess. Half English and half German she was educated in Kentucky. At the age of sixteen she went on the stage and enjoyed a brilliant career until she retired at the age of twenty-eight, to marry Antonio de Navarro, a Papal Chamberlain. She interested herself in singing, in music in general, in gardening, in reading, and—for she wrote *A few Memories* (1896) and collaborated with Hichens in making a dramatic version of *The Garden of Allah*—in writing. In 1915 she came from her long

retirement and appeared on the stage in various charity performances. The de Navarros' house and estate in Worcestershire was
a great social centre. It was there that Elgar met Maude Valerie
White—an unwitting collaborator as far back as 1885.[1] When he
was at Court Farm in the autumn of 1916 he found a congenial
companion for fishing and country walks and scholarly conversation
in Francis Mostyn, the Roman Catholic Vicar Apostolic of Wales
and titular Bishop of Menevia. From Court Farm, during that
visit, the Elgars went over to Spetchley, where Sir Edward had
received a brief part of his early education, to meet the Berkeleys, of
Spetchley Park.

Most of all Elgar enjoyed the Lakes. He went up there for a
little time in each of the first three summers of the war, enjoying
the remote beauty and literary traditions of that region and, above
all, temporary relief from the climate of war. " I am," he wrote to
Schuster in October 1916, " sick of towns." He hoped, in that
letter, that they might be away from London for a long time. In
May 1917 Lady Elgar and Carice—the merits of Sussex having been
extolled by the Colvins—discovered a cottage—Brinkwells—near
Fittleworth. This appeared the ideal country retreat, yet not too
far from London. They took it for June and also for some part
of August.

On June 7 Elgar wrote to Schuster ". . . we went to Sussex &
it's *divine* : simple thatched cottage & a (soiled) studio with wonderful view : large garden *unweeded*, a task for 40 men."

It was at Brinkwells that the last notable works of Elgar were
to be conceived.

---

[1] See Index of Works, p. 402.

CHAPTER XI

"...AND ALL *REMOTE* PEACE"

So the whole of my intimate past life is wiped out....
Letter from Elgar to Frank Schuster, July 12, 1920

*Could the motto " Fortiter et fide" go in: it suited dear A.
so well.*
Letter in re gravestone from Elgar to
A. Troyte Griffith, June 17, 1920

THE DREARY winter months of 1918 were made the more anxious by Elgar's state of health. He was, throughout January and February, disinclined to take interest in anything. He did, it is true, temporarily pull out of despondency when Lalla Vandervelde took him to lunch with the Bernard Shaws and when Lady Elgar persuaded him to see Pinero's *The Freaks* and two Old Vic productions —of *King Lear* and *The School for Scandal*. But otherwise he had no appetite, continual throat trouble, and was oppressed with a sense of great weariness. Sir Maurice Abbot Anderson, kind and considerate as ever, called in other opinions yet again. Elgar was X-rayed and treated for one complaint until on March 6 Mr. Tilley, of University College Hospital, discovered a diseased tonsil (the root of most of Elgar's ill-health throughout his life) and advised its removal. So on March 14 Elgar entered the Dorset Square Nursing Home where he was operated on the next day.

For days afterwards he was, despite the surgical success of the operation, in extreme pain. But gradually the pain subsided and visitors—Alice Stuart-Wortley with grapes, and Maud Warrender with roses—came to relieve the monotony. On March 22 Elgar, much depressed, went home. It was clear that he needed a change from the rigours of London life and so, early in April, he was

189

taken to the Hut by road—Sir Maurice, with permission exceptionally granted by the petrol control authorities, driving him. It was fairly quiet at the Hut but there were guests. Among them was only one who really caught Elgar's sympathy—Robert Nicholls, who read some of his poems to Elgar.

From the Hut Elgar went almost immediately to Brinkwells, where the greater part of the year was spent. The change quickly worked wonders. The quiet beauty of Sussex gave one kind of the refreshment; the war news, which was radiated each day from the post offices at Fittleworth and Pulborough, another. Ludendorff's great offensives had finally failed and the German tide was on the ebb; the American Expeditionary Force was landing in large numbers; Lloyd George survived, triumphantly, a political crisis; the great assault on Zeebrugge took place. Lady Elgar noted all these great events. Sir Edward stirred himself to fulfil a small commission from *The Teacher's World* to write a song—*Big Steamers*. This meant collaboration—at a distance—with Kipling, but this at this particular time was no obstacle: " anything for the cause," said Elgar.

There were, however, other matters on which he exercised greater enthusiasm. He cleared his workshop and set about various projects in carpentry, ranging from a stool for Lady Colvin to a table for the summer-house, which he also restored. Friends came with as much regularity as the distance from London allowed and, as the Elgars became accepted as resident in Sussex, a new group of acquaintances was assembled. Mr. Aylwin, the neighbouring farmer who put his transport—pony and trap, or horse and wagon— at their disposal when needed, and Mrs. Aylwin were delighted with Elgar's great interest in and knowledge of rural problems. Mark Holden, Elgar's odd job man—more fictional in rustic character than even fiction allows—became another particular friend. There were the Newburys at Fittleworth Rectory—Mr. Newbury's sisters then, by a coincidence, being in possession of Lady Elgar's old home at Hazeldine—to furnish welcome news for Lady Elgar of her old countryside. E. V. Lucas and his family and Sir Julian Corbett, Director of the Historical Section of the Committee of Imperial Defence, combined intellectual brilliance with easy manners and were as delighted to encounter Elgar as he was them. More formidable, but sometimes pressing in her invitations, was Lady Leconfield of Petworth House.

On the whole, however, in this year and the next, Elgar went to Sussex to avoid people rather than to meet them. The country-side was his great joy—and inspiration. He loved the setting and the ancient buildings of the downland villages—Petworth, Pul-borough, Storrington, Findon and Amberley; the larger monu-ments of Arundel and Chichester; the remains of antiquity that were to be seen near Stane Street. Most of all he loved the water—of streams and lakes in which he could fish—and the woods. To the trees in Flexham Park is attached a particular significance which must now be seen in the calendar of composition.

The wife of a creative artist may be, at one time, both the best and the worst of critics. In the technical sense Alice Elgar was no critic. On the other hand, because she had so completely lost herself within her husband's genius and career, she was able often to speak and sometimes to clarify his thoughts. This even extended to his own processes of composition. In her obituary in *The Times*, written by Fox Strangways in careful consultation with Elgar, it is recorded: " She was one of his best critics. He played over the Quartet to her, and she said little; but next morning he found pencilled over the close of the slow movement ' Is this quite ?—please ! ' and so we owe the fine close to her gentle correction."

The works of Elgar's last great creative phase are apparently more " abstract " than anything he had formerly published. Yet it may well be not that they are music for music's sake so much as the first results of a newly discovered philosophical centre. There are, in Lady Elgar's notes and also in the later imaginative literary essays of Elgar himself, stirrings of neo-pantheistic thought. In many ways of life and thought there was a patent withdrawal on Elgar's part from his former self.

It is clear that Lady Elgar assumed her husband's music of 1918–19 to be of some special significance, for her main diary entries become more precise and more definitive. As it happens she commenced 1918 with a singularly moving episode in which Landon Ronald was concerned. On January 6 he conducted the first symphony at the Albert Hall. Lady Elgar listened with pride, and taking something prophetic out of the work saw it in its present aptness—the " particular " being caught up into the " universal "— " The great tune so majestic & beautiful. Then the wild under-spirits & vain things conquered by it. Then the pagan tune absolutely a picture of the Huns & the great struggle ending in absolute triumphant victory for the great rights of humanity. So wonderful & uplifting." On the following evening Ronald called at Severn House. Taking Lady Elgar aside he said ' very shyly & sweetly ' ' do you know what I always want to do after the slow movement ? This,' crossing himself very reverently."

While he was in the nursing home Elgar began to consider his chamber music and even made tentative sketches. This was at least the third time in life that he had begun work in this medium. Three days after returning home the quartet began to go into definite shape. He had conceived, wrote Lady Elgar, " a remote lovely 1st subject." The next day he wrote hard for most of the day. But nothing more was done until August. On August 18 a piano arrived at Brinkwells in Mr. Aylwin's wagon. On August 24—a lovely sunny day and with the scent coming up to the room from Mr. Aylwin's new-cut clover-field " E. writing wonderful new music, different from anything else of his. A. calls it wood magic. So elusive & delicate." Work continued and Elgar was happy in it. On August 27 Landon Ronald came down. " He heard the new music after lunch and loved the mysterious orch. piece [1] & wants it dreadfully, & much liked the Sonata." The next visitor was W. H. Reed (who spent much time at Brinkwells during this summer). He and Elgar spent a large part of the rest of that week in playing the Sonata—so far as it went. One afternoon Sarah, the domestic, sat below the studio window " entranced." On September 6 Elgar wrote the dedication of the Sonata—to a very old friend, Mrs. Marie Joshua. Four days later Mrs. Joshua died. So on September 14 the Sonata was ended with an elegiac allusion. " E. writing end of last movement of Sonata, ended it with a wonderful soft lament something like ending of slow movement of 2nd symphony. This was after hearing with great shock & sorrow of sudden death of one of our dear & very kindest of friends Marie Joshua. . . ." The next day : " E. writing 3rd movement of Sonata growing most beautiful. Wrote part of Quintet wonderful weird beginning same atmosphere as ' Owls '— evidently reminiscence of sinister trees & impression of Flexham Park."

Just now Elgar was very much the woodman, having bought the under wood below the garden house and being occupied in

[1] 'Cello concerto (?).

Verehrter Freund!

Ich danke Ihnen herzlich für Ihren lieben Brief
und den erneuten Ausdruck Ihrer mir stets so
wertvollen Sympathie. Leider ist mein Sohn
krank und ich kann in den nächsten Tagen
nur schwer das Hotel verlassen. Seien Sie so
freundlich, mir mitzuteilen, wann und wo ich
Sie sehen kann. Mit besten Empfehlungen auch
an Ihre Gemahlin Ihr

unverändert verehrungsvoll ergebener

Richard Strauss.

A letter from Richard Strauss

Bernard Shaw and Edward Elgar; at Hereford, 1930

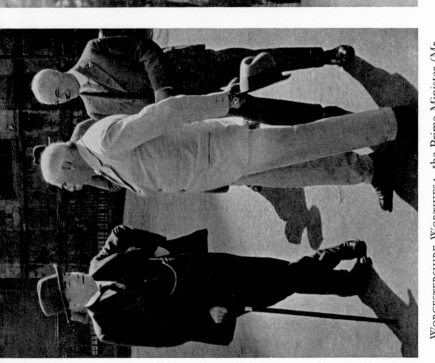

WORCESTERSHIRE WORTHIES; the Prime Minister (Mr. Stanley Baldwin), the Master of the King's Musick and Sir Ivor Atkins

clearing and chopping the brushwood and the chestnuts.[1] From woodcraft he turned eagerly to his music. " E. wrote more of the wonderful Quintet—Flexham Park—sad ' dispossessed ' trees & their dance & unstilled regret for their evil fate—or rather curse— wh. brought it on—Lytton's strange story seemed to sound through it too." The strange story relating to the withered trees in Flexham Park was a local legend. Once there was at that place a fraternity of Spanish monks. They, while engaged in ungodly ritual, were struck dead and transformed into dead trees. On September 24 Elgar was still with the Quintet—" the sinister trees & their strange dance in it—then a wail for their sin—wonderful." On September 27, however, " E. writing wonderful new music real wood sounds & other lament wh. shd. be in a war symphony." On into October Elgar alternated between quintet and quartet. On October 8 and 9 he was " possessed " with his music : " 2nd movement of 4tet varied by excursions to wood."

At this point work was interrupted by the need to return to London first for a private performance—at Severn House—of the Sonata by Reed and Elgar. This was on October 15. There were present Landon Ronald, who at once asked permission to give it at Wigmore Hall, the Fortescues, Schuster, Muriel Foster, the Colvins, Mrs. Thesiger and Button of Novello's, who had come early to talk over details of publication. A second engagement was a revival of *Fringes of the Fleet* at the Palace Theatre. And after that a concert on October 28 at Queen's Hall in aid of the Red Cross.

This was a sensational affair in which George Robey " conducted " (with great effect) the " Pizzicato " from Delibes's *Sylvia* and in which the orchestra, containing Elgar as cymbalist, Irene Scharrer, Myra Hess and Muriel Foster as nightingales, Albani, Ada Crossley and Carrie Tubb as cuckoos, Sir Frederick Bridge and Sir Frederick Cowen as rattles, Moiseiwitsch as triangle player, and Mark Hambourg with castanets, played Richard Blagrove's *Toy Symphony*.[2] Elgar, growing tired of cymballing, made his way to the first fiddles and seizing Max Mossel's instrument gave an impromptu cadenza.

A day or two later Elgar was at the Hut and so was Irene

[1] See *Elgar as I knew him*, W. H. Reed, p. 56 *et seq.*, and Lady Elgar's Diary, Sept. 16 *et seq.*

[2] A notice of this performance is in *Musical Times*, Dec. 1918.

E.   N

Scharrer. Elgar showed her sketches of his piano concerto, asked her to play them, and promised that when it was completed she should have the first performance. On Armistice Day Elgar went down to Brinkwells again—having hoisted the Union Jack at Severn House—and resumed work on the quartet and quintet. Once again he was interrupted because of the necessity to return to London. There was a performance of *Falstaff* at Queen's Hall on December 4. But there were other matters of a distressing nature.

A day or two before the Elgars were due to return to Severn House it had been burgled—the full extent of the burglary was only gradually discovered. Not only this but someone had been attempting to forge cheques in Lady Elgar's name, and she herself was still suffering from the after effects of a slight operation for the removal of a wart from her forehead. Over all lay the thought that very soon Severn House must be sold. Departure from Sussex meant the reinstatement of old problems—with some new ones added. Elgar, swift to change his mood, wrote gloomily to Schuster on December 3 that he must go to London—" & it means another interruption & the future is *dark* as A. poor dear is not well & of course, is bored to death here while I am in the seventh heaven of delight : so we may only return here to clear up—we shall see. But it seems that if I have to live again at Hampstead composition is ' off '—not the house or the place but *London*—telephone etc. all day and night drives me mad ! "

II

At the beginning of 1919 Lady Elgar listed what had been stolen—teapots, toast racks, dessert knives, socks, shirts, suits, trousers, shoes—and even braces. It is small wonder that she, still valiantly trying to act as the great hostess but feeling old and weary, should have lost heart : " A. seemed always to be having to do impossibilities." So she told Schuster, to which he replied : " But you always achieve them." In April it was decided that Severn House, the maintenance of which now appeared too burdensome, should be sold. This made Lady Elgar very sad—it represented the destruction of one of her ideals. But in this matter events moved slowly and, although prospective purchasers came later in the year to tramp speculatively through the property, others supervened. There were difficulties with servants—the continual difficulties but now intensified by the aftermath of war and the apparent decline of general morality. The butler-valet engaged—through some noble scheme launched by one of Lady Elgar's philanthropic friends—proved a failure. His successor was a rogue. He was incompetent and truculent and when, in June, Sir Edward remonstrated with him he put up his fists and offered to fight his employer. "An end of A's experiment. An entire and utter failure & lamentable expense. Entirely A's doing."

In July Sir Edward was at the Police Court to identify some of his stolen property. In September he was at the Old Bailey where the two burglars, formerly policemen, were tried and each sentenced to five years penal servitude. During the year food and fuel were scarce and industrial discontent evident. The strike of railway workers in September was the last straw for Lady Elgar : they were, she noted, "worse than the worst enemies—and they have *no* excuse." So many things added up to make life depressing. Sir Edward went to the Athenæum to lunch one day but found that temporarily members were using the United Services Club. When he arrived he found a general upheaval, for earlier in the morning Sir James Domville had committed suicide on the premises. Then there was the loss of old friends—Streatfeild in February, Lord Charles Beresford in September. And at the end of the year Lady Elgar, who to her friends was beginning to appear alarmingly frail, fell ill. To crown all the neighbours in Hampstead were having a new garage built and the noise of workmen and lorries was distracting beyond words.

Dismal events and gloomy forebodings were only part of the scene, but they cast heavy shadows and the other parts of life were overcast. Nevertheless outwardly the Elgars to the world were as before : he a great and opulent composer and public figure ; she a charming and well-versed hostess. Sir Edward, an ardent clubman, was elected to the Savile (through the good offices of Edward Speyer [1]), where he met many congenial spirits, including Robin Legge and Plunket Greene. In March he was elected to the Literary Club—this gave especial pleasure since he sometimes

[1] . . . "As to the Savile, there is not the slightest difficulty or awkwardness about my proposing you, & I will do so the next time I am there, which will almost certainly be tomorrow—or next day." Letter from E. Speyer to Elgar, Nov. 12, 1918.

regarded himself, with some justice, as a man of letters who had been sidetracked. Visits to the theatre continued to form a large part of recreation and among notable productions were those of *The Provoked Wife*—a Stage Society Production to which Elgar was taken by Ernest Thesiger, *Cyrano Bergerac* and *The Great Day* at Drury Lane. The Russian Ballet was at the Alhambra during the year. Elgar disliked *L'oiseau de feu* and *Petrouchka* of Stravinsky as much as he adored the Rossini of *La Boutique Fantasque*. Rossini was something of a hero at this time for Elgar had acquired some engravings of that composer, at which he grew accustomed to look with respectful admiration. There were a few musicians whose company Elgar enjoyed—Landon Ronald, Edward German, Frederick Cowen, Walter Damrosch, Harold Brooke of Novello's, and Adrian Boult, of whose gifts Elgar held the highest opinion, and a number of faithful executants. In general, however, his enthusiasm was rather more for artists like Lindsay Macarthur, William Rothenstein, who was commissioned to execute a portrait of Elgar for the new quarterly *Music and Letters*, or Roger Fry ; writers like E. V. Lucas, who was a competent billiard-player and therefore doubly welcome, Algernon Blackwood—" Starlight," Bernard Shaw, with whom a close friendship was beginning to develop, and among writers on music Hadow, Francis Toye and Ernest Newman ; or the miscellaneous men and women of affairs who crowded the salons at The Hut or at Ridgehurst.

Public commitments abounded throughout the year. In March Elgar was in Liverpool—where the Adelphi Hotel and the new cathedral of Giles Gilbert Scott excited his admiration—to conduct *Gerontius*. He was delighted to find in Arthur Catterall, who led the orchestra, one of his firmest admirers. In April Elgar was associated with a concert promoted by George Robey in aid of the Printers' Pension Corporation (for the support of Children of Printers who had fallen in the war). This, and other charitable calls, must have recalled the philanthropic causes for which he had played his violin in youth. Another cause to which he gave his name was the Hampstead General Hospital. The originator of the Appeal published in *The Times* on July 2 was John Galsworthy, who had, besides Elgar, as co-signatories Hon. John Fortescue and Gerald du Maurier. In the autumn an Elgar Concert—high with ceremony and attended by civic dignitaries and county worthies —took place at Dudley, the largest town in Worcestershire and where it was felt proper honour should be paid to a son of the county. Elgar went home with an illuminated address, industriously composed by the Town Clerk, and gratified that the War Memorial project centred on a concert hall.

In November he conducted in Amsterdam—where they asked that he should come back for two or three concerts in the next year —and Brussels. This last visit was arranged by Vandervelde, who wished respect to be paid by his fellow countrymen to one who had served their cause so well. Thus Elgar was made the guest of honour at a reception at the Ministry of Justice, entertained at the Hôtel de Ville by Burgomaster Max and taken round the battlefields. He reported that he had enjoyed himself, that he was impressed with the gaiety of the Belgians, with their taste for and enthusiasm in eating, with their apparent wealth. But there was another side : " The Belgians are putting up the most awfully shoddy ugly & degraded buildings (Louvain etc.) in place of the old, destroyed houses—the suburbs of, say, Wigan are noble compared to these atrocities. The B's swagger & do nothing but eat & drink—have forgotten the war & seem to detest the thought of English ! " So he wrote to Troyte Griffith.[1]

At the end of the year an article on Elgar, accompanied by Rothenstein's drawing, was published in the first issue of *Music and Letters*. This caused the greatest pleasure. Lady Elgar forgave Shaw all the plays she had disliked and wrote his essay down as " splendid." This was the second time this year she had had occasion to be grateful to Shaw. In March he had heard the Quintet and Lady Elgar wrote his opinion at once to Troyte Griffith. " Bernard Shaw told me there had been nothing like the opening of the Quintet since Coriolan & wrote a delightful letter to Edward about it." It was on January 6, 1920, that Elgar paid his first visit to Ayot St. Lawrence where, with Lalla Vandervelde, he had a delightful lunch with the Shaws.

Throughout January and February 1919 Elgar worked at his chamber music. Reed brought a quartet to try sections of the quartet and quintet and there were also rehearsals at the Snows— Jessie Snow at that time beginning her career as a chamber musician. Intimate friends—the Ronalds, Schuster, the Colvins, Lady Stuart of Wortley, the Fortescues, Lady Horridge—noted the progress of the works with delight and Lady Elgar thanked God " for such

[1] Dec. 8, 1919.

wonderful gifts given to E." On March 21 the Sonata was played
by Reed and Landon Ronald at the Aeolian Hall. As so often
Elgar was in a nervously exhausted state when the day came. He
returned from rehearsal depressed, " not liking his music. At last
was persuaded to go to concert. . . ." When on April 22 Schuster
had a performance of the completed quartet and quintet (by Albert
Sammons, W. H. Reed, Raymond Jeremy, Felix Salmond, with
William Murdoch at the piano) " E. could not stay in the room,
went into hall." The first public performance, by the same artists,
was at the Wigmore Hall on May 21. The playing was superb.
Elgar received a wonderful ovation.

Throughout the summer it was the 'cello concerto that mono-
polised Elgar's imagination. Felix Salmond came down to Brinkwells on numerous occasions. Elgar was so obsessed with this
work that he once again reverted to the habits of his youth, getting
up sometimes at 4 and sometimes at 5 o'clock in the morning to
work. On August 2 " F. Salmond left after lunch & seemed so
happy here *thrilled* with the thought of playing the concerto for
the 1st time & wildly excited about it, did not sleep all night
thinking about it." On August 8 Lady Elgar took the manuscript
—the last time she was to perform this office—to the Post Office
at Fittleworth. On October 26 the concerto was rehearsed at
Mortimer Hall. Coates, who was conducting the rest of the
programme, kept Elgar waiting for an hour after he was scheduled
to take over for the concerto. Coates was rather more concerned
about Scriabin's *Poème de l'Extase* and Borodin's B Minor Symphony. But for Salmond's sake Elgar was almost inclined to throw
his hand in. The performance on the next day was not as good as
it might have been. " The concert," wrote Alfred Kalisch,[1] " was
marked by two circumstances unfortunately characteristic of our
great country and this great metropolis. The announcement of an
important new work by our foremost living composer with the
composer conducting, did not suffice to fill the hall to overflowing,
and the principal new work was obviously under-rehearsed."

From November 16, 1919, to the end of the year Lady Elgar
was not well enough to leave the house. She was not, however,
considered to be seriously ill and Sir Maurice Abbot Anderson
could express himself as quite satisfied with her condition. She
did not herself feel more than " rather a poor thing "; but, intrepid

[1] *Musical Times*, Dec. 1919.

as ever, she determined to pursue her accustomed tasks. She persuaded Sir Edward to go to Felix Salmond's chamber music concert on November 30 at which the Fauré quartet played won his generous approval. She prepared him for a visit to Bishop Auckland and Middlesbrough, in which towns he was to conduct for Nicholas Kilburn. She looked after Beatrice Harrison, who came to rehearse the 'cello concerto in preparation for a recording, and assisted in editing the orchestral parts for this purpose. She discussed the desirability of purchasing Brinkwells as a permanent home when, as in the near future it would, the time came to leave Severn House.

At the beginning of 1920 it seemed that another year of struggle lay ahead. The year made an inauspicious start. Dry rot was discovered over the stables in some of the bedrooms—" a very disquieting worry & dreadful expense." But faith was undimmed. Elgar had been invited to contribute a foreword to a book on notation to be published by Novellos. He spent a couple of days on the task. " Will it not," asked Lady Elgar of herself, " be more read than the book ? " And then she felt so much better that she was able to go outside the house for the first time since November.

In the middle of January Elgar was writing music again. He was also going to the Zoo—a favourite occupation—and to the cinema. His interest in this which was already keen was strengthened in March by the fact of his being filmed himself. This was one tribute. There were others. On February 3 Elgar received his diploma admitting him to membership of the R. Accademia in Florence. The same evening came news of his election to the Literary Society. Two days later H. C. Colles came to say that Elgar was to be elected to the Council of the Royal College of Music. On March 18 he succeeded to Sgambati's place in the French Académie des Beaux Arts, his notice being signed by Widor. This, two days after a brilliant performance of the second symphony at Queen's Hall under Boult, was a crowning joy. " How beautiful to have this & the Symphony success—so thankful." These were the last words written by Lady Elgar in her diary.

III

Towards the end of January Lady Elgar's enthusiasms and activities were running if not with full at least with admirable vigour for a septuagenarian. She entertained Binyon, Steuart-Powell, Barclay Squire and other old friends. She went the round of club, dentist, and shops, and was glad to be able to travel by omnibus again. As Elgar was recording at Hayes on February 24 she went also and was pleased to see royal personages on a tour of inspection. On February 29 she had an afternoon party and Jelly d'Aranyi and Mrs. Hobday came to play the Violin Sonata and, as well, one by Brahms. Then came a visit to the theatre—*Candida*, " most interesting and touching, not very well done." Ten days later Lady Elgar felt unwell again and spent half a day in bed. But the next day she felt better, so much better that she determined to go to a dinner party given by the Fosters of Brockhampton. It was a pleasant party, the Petres of Ingatestone Hall, the Clanels, Lady St. Leonard's, Lionel Tertis and Sir Gilbert Parker being other guests. The next day Alice Stuart of Wortley and John Ireland came to lunch. Sir Maurice saw Lady Elgar and " relieved her mind of some anxiety."

On March 23 Elgar was at Leeds for a performance of *The Apostles*. Lady Elgar did not feel equal to the long journey, but insisted on attending a performance at Wigmore Hall of the three chamber works. This was her last concert. Elgar noted at the side of the entry made in his own diary (the first he had kept since 1889) ". . . thoughts of the 30 (weary fighting) years of her help and devotion."

On March 25 Lady Elgar felt compelled to stay in bed. Muriel Foster came to tea and had it in the sick room. Outside of the family and the medical she was the last person to see her. After March 25 Lady Elgar's condition deteriorated swiftly. On Easter Tuesday, April 6, the specialist came but only to say that nothing more could be done. On Wednesday Father Philip Valentine, the priest from Holly Place, Hampstead, came to administer the last sacrament. At ten minutes past six that evening Lady Elgar died. Immediately he heard the news Landon Ronald put aside his work and came to stay at Severn House for two days to look after his friend. This act of kindness was never forgotten.

The funeral took place at St. Wulstan's Roman Catholic Church, Little Malvern—a little way along the road from the old house of Craeglea—on Saturday, April 10, in the presence only of close friends of the family—with one exception. Stanford, who had not been on speaking terms with Elgar for 16 years, made an unexpected appearance. Whether this was an act of impulsive charity [1] or an histrionic means of closing a feud will never be known. Elgar himself was unaware of Stanford's presence until days afterwards. In deep distress he was in no mood to consider the motives of one by whom he felt he had for so long been wronged. Accordingly he expressed indifference to Stanford's gesture, distrust of his sincerity and resentment at past behaviour in a bitter note to Schuster.[2] He could, however, conclude : " For the good things he has done in the past I still hold respect."

Before and after the funeral service music from the slow movement of the Quartet was played. The arrangement that Sammons, Reed, Jeremy and Felix Salmond should travel down from London for this purpose had been made by Schuster. For this Elgar was profoundly grateful. He was also grateful to Troyte Griffith who took charge of affairs at Little Malvern.

Elgar's letters at this time indicate the desolation of his spirit.

To Frank Schuster :

> *Kirkland* [3]
> *Little Malvern, Monday* [*April* 12]

My DEAREST FRANK,

We have had a real rest. This is the quietest place ever known & we are the only people here—we can see the little grave in the distance & nothing cd. be sweeter & lovelier only birds singing & all *remote* peace brought closely to us. I cannot thank you for the quartet—it was exactly right & just what she wd. have loved—but once more you must please let me settle the acct when you know what it is : the boys played like angels.

As to our future we know nothing : Carice will stay here with friends & I shall lead a normal sort of life—at my sister's & round about until business calls me home.

[1] As Plunket Greene suggests.
[2] April 18, 1920.
[4] The old presbytery of St. Wulstan's Church.

I hope the day was not too tiring for you & once more heartfelt thanks. The place she chose long years ago is too sweet—the blossoms are white all round it & the illimitable plain, with all the hills & churches in the distance which were hers from childhood, looks just the same—inscrutable & unchanging. If it had to be—it could not be better.

The words do not quite suit but all the time the line from In Memoriam comes to me—" I think my friend is richly shrined "—& thank you for making the last plaintive little scene something far away from the commonplace.

Ever your friend

EDWARD

The Elms,[1] *Stoke Prior,*
Bromsgrove. Friday [17 *April* 1920]

MY DEAREST FRANK;

Thank you for your letter. I am doing my best here—the weather of course prevents my having any walks but Juno seems to know that something is wrong & never leaves me—such wonderful things are dogs. Here my dear A. never came so I can bear the sight of the roads & fields.

I am glad you saw the place she chose to rest in it is divine. I send you a poor p.c. with the old presbytery where C. & I stayed.

You speak of H. Sturgis—the news of his death comes as a great shock to me—he was always so pleasant & kind although he never really knew me. I shall be glad to hear anything of him & will—as you say—remind you of it.

After 37 years my poor old sister may have to turn out —everything being sold—& although the 70 acres or so of land has been let with an[r]. farm for more than 200 years the new rich refuse to sell the house & paddock separately—after 200 years ! All the consideration she was treated with as the widow of a respected (& beloved) manager is thrown to the winds—so I am in a sad house : the same fate is due on May 1 for my poor old *eldest* sister—stone deaf etc. her little house has been bought " over their heads " & she is turned out—nowhere to go ! So you see I am unhappy. You write to me of my music etc. like the good fellow you are—but I am plunged in

[1] The Graftons' house.

the midst of ancient hate & prejudice—poor dear A's settlements
& her *awful aunts* who cd. allow nothing to descend to any
offspring of *mine*—I had forgotten all the petty bitterness but
I feel just now rather evil that a noble (& almost brilliant) woman
like my Carice should be penalised by a wretched lot of old
incompetents simply because I was—well—I.

Don't talk to me of achievement. I drank spider juice for
my mother's sake, went thro' penurious times to buy my dear
wife a car for her old age—I failed of course & now I am going
to fail in settling the third woman for whom I ever entertained
real love—so you see I must revert to my old plan as soon as
convenient. But Juno's nose presses against me & says a walk
is near.

Love,

E. E.

To Troyte Griffith :

The Elms Stoke Prior
Bromsgrove. *Ap.* 19 1920

DEAR TROYTE :

I do not know how I shd. have got through the awfully
lonely time without your friendship & care. As the days go by
—(I am, with Carice, at my sister's)—the " blank " seems greater
and unbearable.

I wish you would see if the *next space* to the little lonely grave
is to be had & if so secure it for me : I shd. like to know this
at once & shd. be glad if you wd. have a simple (enclosing)
edging of stone put round the graves or the grave & unoccupied
space—if the latter is secured.

Carice & I send our love to you.

Yours ever

EDWARD ELGAR

Brinkwells etc. July 2 : 1920

MY DEAR FRANK

Many thanks for your note. We *are* sorry you have had the
trouble of going to Lincoln's Inn & we are very grateful. In
calculating the net result you forget alas ! the things which

dear A. had for life.[1]   Medley says the Indian raily. would realise about £400—but as it appears to pay 7½ p.c. at that price I will not sell it.   C. & I have now a comfortable two hundred a year ! and anything I can make—but that cannot be much now ; my race is run.   We are enquiring for a purchaser for the house—a former enquirer.   It is devastating that our landlord here has changed his mind & will not give the place up to us as he suggested nine months ago—which is piggish for us.   It wd. have been a shelter anyhow. . . .

Ten days later Elgar closed the chapter of his creative work. Or so he thought.

Brinkwells July 20 1920

MY DEAR F.

This is only to tell you of what seems to me to be a curious thing.   In my active composing life there are three places endeared to me because I worked much in them, viz : my sister's cottage, Birchwood (our old cottage) & the portion of the Wye where I fished—or pretended to—& wrote.   These are *all advertised* to be sold !   My sister's case is of course a disaster —that was advertised on Saturday—later in the day Birchwood —& in Country Life (also on Saturday) the fishing.   So the whole of my intimate past life is wiped out : isn't it a curious coincidence ?

Yours ever

E. E.

It was more than a year before Elgar understood the finality of Alice's death.   On October 22, 1921, he wrote to Troyte Griffith with whom he had been in constant communication about the design for a gravestone :

" I have at last realised that my dear wife & beloved companion has left me : until about two months ago I always felt—sub-consciously—that she *must* return as of old—now I know & submit . . ."

With that realisation emerged a new Elgar, but without the creative genius of the old.

[1] Schuster, together with C. S. Terry, was a trustee of Lady Elgar's estate.

CHAPTER XII

MASTER OF THE KING'S
MUSICK

*A certain unmistakeably royal pride and temper were
getatable on occasion; . . .*
> Bernard Shaw, in Music and Letters, Vol. I, no. I

IT WAS fortunate that at the time of his bereavement there were
engagements to keep Elgar from perpetual gloom. By himself he
was in despair, the emptiness of Severn House a nightmare. He
had postponed returning there for as long as he could. From
Worcestershire he went down to Kent, where he tried to look up
some " old Elgar things." Then he had to travel up to Newcastle-
on-Tyne, where he conducted the Leeds Choral Union in *The
Apostles*. This was in the Cathedral, on May 8—" our wedding
day 1889 " he noted. At the end of May he went again to Glamorgan
in order to conduct the London Symphony Orchestra at Cardiff
and Swansea in a series of performances, promoted by Cyril
Jenkins and Lord Howard de Walden—who had suddenly created
for himself a Welsh ancestry—in order to bring " new music " to
the people of Wales. Besides Elgar there were represented Bantock,
Julius Harrison, Cyril Jenkins, Vaughan Thomas, Delius, Holbrooke and Vaughan Williams. Elgar was a guest of Lord Aberdare
at Duffryn Castle.

For the rest of 1920 Elgar went away from London as much as
he could. He stayed in Malvern for a little, more and more coming
to depend on the calm, unemotional sympathy of Troyte Griffith
and able to discuss anything with him but—mercifully—music.
He went to Brinkwells, to the Hut, to Spetchley—where he was
delighted to find an old friend of Garmisch days, Father Barton,
installed as chaplain—and to Stoke Works. He retired into his
scientific hobbies, with microscopes and botanical specimens

littering the billiard-room, into carpentry, and books. He immersed himself in the theatre, especially enjoying the Hammersmith revival of *The Beggar's Opera* and the Stage Society's presentation of *The Knight of the Burning Pestle*, and the cinema. As often as possible he avoided musical engagements. So he missed the visit of the New York Symphony orchestra to London in June, even though Walter Damrosch, an old and devoted friend, was performing the first symphony. He was, perhaps, a little moved when Damrosch wrote to him on June 20 :

> DEAR ELGAR,
>
> Your glorious symphony went off magnificently, yesterday, and the audience was so wildly tumultuous in its acclaim that finally I had to lift your score from my desk and point to it to show to whom the real tribute was due. . . . My wife and I send you much love and . . . gratitude for what your genius has given to the world.
>
> Your old friend
WALTER DAMROSCH

There were invitations to go to Brussels and to Prague—due to the enthusiastic manipulation of diplomatic contacts by Lalla Vandervelde—but these were refused.

In the autumn the Three Choirs Festival, revived with much difficulty by Ivor Atkins, was again to take place at Worcester. It was a solemn Festival. Not only was it the first in which due honour could be paid to so many connected with it who had been killed during the war but there were Parry, Lloyd, and Sinclair, who had died, to be commemorated. Moreover there were none present who were unaware of Elgar's private grief. The programmes included Sullivan's *In Memoriam* overture, Parry's " There is an old belief," Beethoven's three *Equali* for four trombones— placed distantly in the Lady Chapel, Bach's *St. Matthew Passion*, Verdi's *Requiem*, Elgar's *For the Fallen*, *Gerontius* and *Music Makers*. It was gratifying to Elgar, who lived quietly in lodgings formerly occupied by his uncle Henry during Festival time and avoided all social activities, that the Bishop of Worcester—Dr. E. H. Pearce— was an understanding prelate and a keen musician. The bishop was, in fact, a member of the chorus and both he and the dean —Dr. Moore Ede—appreciated the connection of the great composer with their cathedral. On Christmas Eve Elgar went again to Worcester for the presentation of the robes of a Doctor of Music to Ivor Atkins, who was knighted in the New Year's Honours of 1921. In respect of both honours Elgar used his influence on behalf of his old friend.

After the Festival there were conducting engagements, contracted before the death of Lady Elgar, in Amsterdam, Brussels and Birmingham, and also some recording sessions at the H.M.V. studios at Hayes. He enjoyed going to Hayes, partly because the mechanical side of the business fascinated him and partly because of his friendship with Fred Gaisberg.

One other honour came during the year. The King of the Belgians made Elgar a member of the Ordre de la Couronne and on June 12 the faithful, industrious Carice went to the Embassy to collect the insignia. From there she went to the Czech Embassy for passports for the visit to Prague that never came off. The Belgian decoration gave great pleasure to Cammaerts and also to members of the Goossens family.

Even though Elgar freed himself as much as possible from music he was always at the disposal of those among the younger school who sought his advice. Albert Coates—despite the disapproval he had incurred from Lady Elgar in her last days—was most anxious to conduct as many works of Elgar as possible—in England and abroad—and, equally anxious to interpret them authoritatively, consulted the composer on many occasions. It was at the end of 1921 that Sir Edward characteristically wrote to Albert and Madelon Coates offering to them all assistance in a particular and tragic personal crisis. John Ireland came to see Elgar during 1920 about his own career, and Adrian Boult, rapidly developing into a notable conductor, was put up by him for the Athenæum. In November there was a banquet to Landon Ronald at the Connaught Rooms and Elgar made the effort both to attend and to make a speech. The new organist of the Chapel Royal—Stanley Roper—was busy in the reorganisation of his choir and sought advice both on this matter and also in reference to the institution of Sunday " abend —musik " in the Chapel Royal for Queen Alexandra. And there was Suggia asking for a testimonial in support of her candidature for membership of the Ladies' Lyceum. Among other guests at Severn House were the Silotis, Felix Salmond, Leon Goossens and Heifetz.

Composition—apart from a trifle revised for Heifetz—was disregarded. Elgar, in addition to his inability to settle to the ardours of solitary work without the guiding presence of his wife, was beginning to feel that in the post-war world of new ideas and techniques his own music was out of place. There were, however, those who hoped. Embleton made one of his periodic visits to London from Yorkshire and once again—on June 21—urged the completion of the trilogy : in this he was assisted by Reed who tried to encourage reconsideration of the sketches to this end that had been accumulating, reluctantly and slowly, during the years. Adrian Boult, on the other hand, hoped for a new orchestral work which he would be delighted to play.

Literature, however, was of greater interest than music and Elgar—indulging that part of his genius which he had frequently thought of as belonging to a literary scholar—listened to the aspirations of Robert Nicholls.

Lawford Hall, Manningtree,
Essex. Aug. 24th 1920

DEAR SIR EDWARD,

I was glad to hear that the Strauss Alpine Symphony was of interest to you & I would have written before had not my life been crammed to the brim with work & contemplation of work just lately. I am composing a religious play—religious in the sense that the main interest is not social or erotic but moral & full of psychological interest in which whole moral systems embroil themselves : such moral systems having been adopted as they normally are by the parties concerned for no intellectual reason but solely according to the suggestion of education and individual temperament. There are some pretty bitter doings in the play & I hope that, although my first stage effort, it may do something to help revive our unfortunate stage. Arnold Bennett approved of the first two acts—all that are on paper at present. By the way you must meet Arnold Bennett if you do not know him. He's musical & fond particularly of César Franck—which somehow I don't think one would expect in him. You must also meet Henry Head, a fellow of the Royal Society & one of the greatest psychologists in the world—there are other people who might interest you whom I happen to know through my literary jobs & with whom you are perhaps

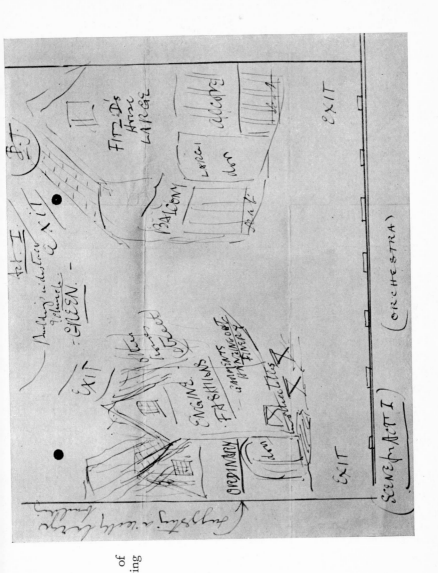

Set for Act 1 of
the opera; a drawing
by Elgar

The Malvern Hills; from a painting by A. Troyte Griffith

not at present acquainted—but I have selected these two as
worthy of you. I must try & fix up something so that you
three can meet. It would be jolly for us to contrive a circle in
which only the generous minded have a place so that all the
interminable & offensive literary & scientific squabbles should
be left outside & the great minds of the time (N.B. self as
onlooker?) meet not over solemnly for quiet & matured
jollifications together.

I have lately come on the programmes given by the Schola
Cantorum of New York under Kurt Schindler which I attended
last year [1] & remember how much I enjoyed two ballads of
Spanish Galicia by *Juan Montes* for Tenor Solo and Male Chorus.
They were in Gallegan dialect—how I wish somebody would
do them here—it appears Juan Montes, who died at the end of
the last century, is well known all over Spain but nary a tune
of his do we get in this country.[2] *Lluis Millet*, director of the
Orféo Catalá, sent these to Schindler. I've lately heard " All
creation soon must perish " from the Michelangelolieder of
Wolf & I never heard a more desolate majesty in song. Two
of the Spanische lieder also struck me very much. " Dereinst,
dereinst, gedanke mein," of the love songs & best-liked perhaps
of the lot " Wunden trägst du, mein Geliebter " from the extraordinary religious songs which are perhaps the most tortured
expressions of intolerable emotion I've ever heard. Yet when
I come to a final analysis I'm not sure I don't really like (of
religious music) Gregorian best of all—heard it in its purity &
perfection at the Abbey de Solennes where I have been staying
—there were especially two Kyries (the Deus sempiterne and
the Orbis factor) which transported me. What happens at
the Improprea [*sic*] on Good Friday I hesitate to think. It must
be overwhelming.

Yours sincerely,

Robert Nicholls

P.S. Sorry this is a drear dull letter but I have been overworking
lately.

One can see why Bennett found Nicholls " full of himself."

---

[1] Nicholls served on the British Mission (Ministry of Information) to U.S.A.,
1918–19.
[2] Passage marked by Elgar.

E.   O

However, the meeting with Bennett and Head was contrived at a dinner party—at the inevitable Schuster's—at the end of October. It was a success.

12B *George Street, Hanover Square W.*1
10.11.20

DEAR SIR EDWARD,

Many thanks. But when I suggested seeing you again I did so in the hope that you would come here. My wife being away in Scotland reciting French poetry before learned bodies. I propose to myself to have a little masculine dinner here during her absence. I wonder whether Tuesday 23rd would suit you? If so, I will ask Henry Head, as I particularly want you two. Later, when the household is reestablished, we will arrange to bring a wife into the equation.

With kind regards to Miss Elgar,

Yours sincerely,

ARNOLD BENNETT

In addition to Elgar and Head—who was a poet as well as an outstanding pioneer in nervous disorders—there were present at Bennett's party Barrie and Siegfried Sassoon.

Such entertainment offered great pleasure but for ever Elgar was pulled back to thoughts of home. When Arnold Bennett left the Potteries he left for good. Elgar, on the other hand, looked on great cities as places to be endured. Worcestershire and the friends of old time were never out of mind. After the 1920 festival he realised that he had missed speaking to some who would have appreciated his remembrance of them from time past. Old Sutton Corkran, who had from the first been assistant secretary of the Worcester Amateur Instrumental Society—which had given Elgar his first opportunities as composer and conductor—was there. Elgar saw him, but not to speak with. Accordingly he wrote from Brussels and received a grateful reply

Worcester,
Oct. 29, 1920

MY DEAR ELGAR,

Your letter from Brussels was very welcome. It is pleasant to think that your old friends are not forgotten & that changing conditions have not changed your affection for the past. .... I should dearly liked to have seen you at the Festivals & have had a chat about old times but I understand what your feelings must have been & how much sadness it would have evoked. ....

Looking at prints at a bookseller's one day Elgar came across one of Stourport in Worcestershire. He bought it and sent it to Julius Harrison who was born in Stourport. It now became one of his chief interests to collect memorials of his own county, until the house was overflowing with them. Like Lord Baldwin and Francis Brett Young he subscribed to a belief that Julius Harrison conveyed in his letter of thanks : " There is no county like it." In pursuing his local studies Elgar was, unconsciously, forming a new pattern of life—or, rather, reforming the pattern that had been broken by his vocation and his exile. In 1922 he came across a print relating to a parliamentary election in the City of Worcester in 1776, which he promptly presented to the Mayor and Corporation. Two years later he acquired a picture of Malvern by William Turner of Oxford ; this he deposited in the Public Library of Malvern in commemoration of the passing of the Malvern Hills Act of 1924, by which some part of this country became a national possession and amenity.

In the course of time Elgar went home to Worcestershire but not as soon as he would have liked. On the death of Lady Elgar he felt that his career as composer was finished. Within the year, however, the dying embers momentarily rekindled. In the months before he wrote of his final submission to the fact of her death he did turn again, fitfully, to *The Apostles*. So on May 9 he wrote to Troyte, from Severn House.

Strictly private

MY DEAR TROYTE,

The above looks rather forbidding & very unlike me—and you, but please observe the—well, injunction.

Carice is engaged to be married (*that's* no *secret*) & in due course I shall be alone—(I will not stand in the young people's way in the least—in fact I encourage them to get married as soon as possible [1]) but I seem to have a certain vitality & must work—with a pen if not with the baton. *Now!*

[1] Carice *m*. Samuel Blake, Jan. 16, 1922.

I want to know if you can find me a permanent (more or less) lodging at the Wells ? ? ! ! Is there a *remote* small house—cottage in the plain—to be bought or is there any *homely* little house where I could be the *only* lodger. It is possible that I may be finishing the III part of *The Apostles* & I want to be quiet & uninterrupted *generally*—of course I want to be near you altho' you may not desire my proximity when the divine *afflatus* is on —but we have got on well for about twenty six years & might continue to do so with due " deference " to one another —anyhow, dear old friend, I shd. like to be within reach of you.

What I feel now is that I am not young ! and I want to complete the great work ;—that I want to be near my dearest one's grave ;—& that I want you not too far off. Naturally I can't be definite and worries may come to put off composition again—but at the moment I feel that Little Malvern—near the church—I mean something not more than a mile or a mile and a half away is what I want. . . . Now dear Troyte, just think this over give yourself no *active* trouble—you might make a few enquiries of agents etc. *not mentioning me.* I am called now.

Best regards

Yrs. ever

EDWARD ELGAR

II

But events did not work out in this way. The urge to compose would never remain for long, and Elgar confided to Goossens that all that inspired him to think musically were the works of Bach. In 1921 there was a transcription of Bach's organ fugue in C minor, to which was added the fantasia in the following year. Eugene Goossens conducted the first performance of the fugue in October and hoped, as did many others, that it might herald a fresh period of masterpieces. Charles Macpherson, organist of St. Paul's Cathedral, a grandson of J. H. d'Egville of Worcester, and one who had as a young man been grateful for Elgar's efforts on his behalf,[1]

---

[1] Elgar had once shown Richter a score of Macpherson's *Psalm cxxxvii* with a strong recommendation.

wished for a piece for the Festival of the Sons of the Clergy. Lutyens, designing the Queen's Dolls' House, wanted a little piece. Dr. B. S. Siddall, conductor of the Choral Society of St. Helen's in Lancashire, and an old pupil of Lee Williams of Gloucester, asked for more part songs. But all proposals were met with prompt refusal. A couple of part songs, some very small incidental music for a play of Laurence Binyon, a few bars for the War Memorial Committee at Loughborough, and some indifferent, lack-lustre pieces for the Empire Exhibition at Wembley in 1924 were all that could be accomplished in those years.

On October 15, 1921, Elgar left Severn House and went to live in a flat at 37 St. James's Place. Although he still pined for the country he knew that he had a special place in the musical life of London which he could not abdicate. His prestige had been marked fittingly when, earlier in the year, Edmund Gosse had requested that a photograph should be deposited in the National Portrait Gallery. In 1921 Elgar declined an invitation to a reception in honour of Sibelius, but the following year he was delighted to be able, after so many years, to welcome Strauss again to London.

12 June 1922

Dear Dr. Richard Strauss,

I send you a word of warm welcome & an assurance that your return to our country gives the greatest pleasure to myself & to very many of my musical countrymen.

I hope we may meet soon. With cordial greetings.

Believe me to be
Your sincere friend
Edward Elgar

To which came this reply.

My very dear Friend,

I thank you heartily for your dear letter with its renewed expression of your sympathy and kindly feeling—always so precious to me.

Unhappily my son is ill, and I cannot leave the hotel, within the next few days, except with difficulty.

Will you be good enough to tell me when and where I may see you?

Convey my sincere compliments to your wife also.

I remain,

Your ever devoted admirer

RICHARD STRAUSS

Shortly afterwards Elgar, assisted by Bernard Shaw, entertained Strauss to lunch at the United Services Club.

Elgar was equally pleased to see the development of some (not all!) of the younger school. Arnold Bax and Arthur Bliss were specially indebted to him and demonstrated their gratitude.

Bax to Elgar:

155 *Fellows Rd N.W.*3
March 3, 1921

DEAR SIR EDWARD,

I hope you will not mind if I give myself the pleasure of dedicating to you a string quartet [1] of mine that is now in the press. I think I may say that I have always been one of the warmest admirers of your work, and beyond this I have never forgotten a wonderful day of summer twenty years ago when George Alder brought me to see you at " Birchwood." I was only seventeen then and much has happened since, but I should be very pleased if you will accept this simple work in memory of an unforgettable day and all the pleasure your own music has given me.

Yours very sincerely,

ARNOLD BAX

Bliss to Elgar:

21, *Holland Park, London*
Dec. 26 [1920]

DEAR SIR EDWARD,

I thought I should like to write and wish you the best of health and happiness for 1921, and also to thank you so much for giving me the chance of writing a work [2] for the Gloucester Festival. It is a great opportunity, and I look on it as one more proof of your generosity to us younger musicians.

[1] String Quartet No. 1 in G.
[2] *Colour Symphony.*

I do not think you realise what a fine and rare encouragement your presence is, when, as you did at luncheon the other day you gave the lead to younger composers. It is such a unique thing, this broadminded generosity, that I hope you will be long spared to make the music of Englishmen pre-eminent.

Yours ever

ARTHUR BLISS

The luncheon party, to which the letter refers, was held on December 16, at the Royal Societies Club. Besides Bliss there were present W. H. Reed, Adrian Boult, Anthony Bernard, Eugene Goossens—another newcomer as composer to the Three Choirs Festival—and John Ireland, who had sent his latest scores to Elgar for criticism. As he looked at the work of the composers among this group, and as he noticed the other names which began to appear prominently in the programmes of the twenties, the more Elgar felt out of touch with those modern tendencies which appeared to him either irrelevant or vulgar. Troyte Griffith once asked him what he thought of the folk-music influence; to which, magnificently, he replied " I am folk music."

Elgar was a craftsman. When he recognised the maintenance of old standards of craftsmanship—as he understood it—he was both gracious and generous. Thus, the playing of Thibaud and Heifetz, the honours bestowed on Landon Ronald and Dan Godfrey gratified him. In respect of the latter he was personally involved.

Dame Ethel Smyth to Elgar.

Coign, Woking.
March 14, 1922

DEAR SIR EDWARD ELGAR,

Though I think I only once had the pleasure of meeting you I feel sure you will forgive me for writing to ask if you will give your powerful aid to an attempt which I think will be successful—to get Dan Godfrey the " honor " he covets—& which he thinks will save his Orchestra from extinction (" compliment to municipal music " etc.)

I wrote, on the advice of a new acquaintance, Lord Riddell (who is a great friend of Mr. Lloyd George's) to L. G's secretary

Miss Stevenson—who used to be a great suffragist etc. and had told him she'd like to know me—I explained about Dan Godfrey —what a disaster it would be if that band were to collapse—what a fine record he has.   And then I went to see her about it & while I was there in came the P.M.—He had been very sympathetic about it, Miss S. said, & the advice I got as to procedure is this—to ask every one of weight in the musical world *to write direct to the P.M.* & say that D. G. really deserves an honour (I may add the question of the orchestra will be decided *in July* so the June Honours List is the one to aim at.)

Then, would anyone who writes thus to the P.M. kindly send a p.c. to me saying " *the letter has gone* ", for this reason. The next step (I am told) is to approach someone near the King—& that I can easily do through my oldest friend's son, Fritz Ponsonby.   One must be able to say " To my certain knowledge every one of weight has written to the P.M. recommending this candidate—*including* (here follow the names). *Then*, I am told, the thing is certain—And why I wd. ask for a p.c. is because many people really *do* mean to do a thing—but forget.   And such an omission would, if the person had been named as a supporter, tell against the candidate perhaps— People who promised & have written to say *the letter has gone* are :

Sir C. Stanford

Sir H. Wood

Prof. Bantock

Lord Shaftesbury

People who have promised one, & *will* write (but haven't done it yet) are :

Lord Howard de Walden

Sir Hugh Allen

Adrian Boult

and people I shall ask, & who will, I know write are

Holst and Delius

It would be an impertinence to speak of the weight your name wd. have—so I will only hope you will forgive this long letter from

Yrs. very truly

ETHEL SMYTH

Elgar's telegram promising support was dispatched immediately. Dame Ethel Smyth to Elgar :

Coign Woking
May 17, 1922

DEAR SIR EDWARD,
Whether the effort we have all been making to secure Dan
Godfrey official recognition will be successful I don't know—
perhaps the P.M. doesn't know himself yet ! But, thinking of
your kind wire I wanted to tell you this.

Yesterday I saw the Secretary at Downing St. who sees to
these things : he told me *as far as one could tell* it was a certainty.
The day before Lord Stamfordham had come in about it & had
been told of D. G's " formidable backing " etc. He then said
" well I think I'll just write to Sir E. Elgar. . . ." " There's a
letter from him " said Mr. Davies. . . .!! . . .

He told me I might tell D. G. that things are " very hopeful "
& both Lord Stamfordham & my old friend Sir F. Ponsonby
will watch the case when the list goes up to the King.

So I hope for the best. But Lord French told me the other
day *he* had found it next door to impossible to get an honour
for a soldier—that " the political fellows want them all . . . &
get them " . . . with many thanks

Yours very truly

ETHEL SMYTH

Elgar to Dame Ethel Smyth :

Brook's May 22 1922

DEAR DAME ETHEL SMYTH
Thank you : I know the magic of your own name would be
sufficiently thaumaturgic to influence an ordinary P.M. ; but,
like Falstaff, I fear the Welsh fairy : he may turn D. G. (who
sings no hymns) to a piece of cheese : but we must hope.

Believe me to be

Yours very faithfully,

EDWARD ELGAR

While this diplomatic machinery was working in the background

Dan Godfrey, true to form, was challenging the Easter holiday crowds at Bournemouth with a Festival of English music. Mackenzie, Elgar, Vaughan Williams, Ethel Smyth, Bantock, Holst and Eugene Goossens came to conduct their own compositions, among which were two very new works (the second having had its first performance at Bournemouth a few weeks before)—Vaughan Williams's *Pastoral Symphony* and Bax's *Tintagel*. Each of the visiting conductors received a formal letter of thanks from the Town Clerk —Elgar drew an inviting gallows on his copy, below the functionary's signature : the orchestra was saved from extinction : Godfrey was made a knight.

Elgar's influence was powerful, when he chose to exercise it, but a cold wind of indifference was beginning to blow on his greater works. It was commented, in 1922, that *The Apostles* was falling out of favour. On the afternoon of June 8 the Leeds Choral Union (*en route* to Canterbury, where another performance was given on the next day) sang the oratorio to a half-empty Queen's Hall. Bernard Shaw was furious and sent his apologies to posterity for " living in a country where the capacity and tastes of schoolboys and sporting costermongers are the measure of metropolitan culture." The *Musical Times* judiciously pointed out that on Thursday afternoons in June there was cricket either at Lord's or the Oval and that accordingly there could not additionally be expected a disengaged body of oratorio-lovers to attend Queen's Hall. In 1923 there were no excuses for increasing apathy. Correspondence in the *Daily Telegraph* and the *Musical Times* revealed that the symphonies were dropping out of the repertoire and that while a few enthusiasts were alarmed the general concert-going public were indifferent.

So, too, in a sense, was the composer. After Carice's marriage he spent much time in his clubs—to which was now added Brook's. This especially he enjoyed : it was, he wrote to Griffith,[1] " a haven of rest & quiet, with untold memories of Fox, Selwyn, etc. The house is interesting dates from 1764 & is about the best club in London." Two years later he was anxious that Griffith should join the Savile. At that time he was a member of the committee of the club and assured Griffith that there would be no impediment in the way of his election. " I have always wanted to make you a present—if you are elected (there wd. be no doubt *about* that) let me

[1] Jan. 30, 1922.

see you through the entrance fee & subs. ! [1] Among those whom he supported for membership of the Athenæum was Hugh Walpole, on whose behalf he was approached by Sir Frederick Macmillan.

Moving from one club to another Elgar inevitably made varied contacts. He became acquainted with Bruce Richmond, editor of *The Times Literary Supplement* (to which he wrote letters on a variety of subjects [2]), Owen Seaman, editor of *Punch*, John Drinkwater, Granville Barker, Squire Bancroft, Seymour Hicks, Lord Dunsany, H. Stevens, the auctioneer of 38 King Street, and Herbert Hughes. When he entertained Elgar often brought in Shaw to animate the conversation at one end of the table, while he himself managed the other. It was on June 17, 1921, that he entertained the whole company from the Hampstead Everyman Theatre to lunch at the Café Royal. He was then not so accustomed to Shaw as a guest as he was to become, and it was necessary for Mrs. Shaw to give instructions on diet. " I was almost forgetting about the food ! But, by great good fortune I have read your kind note again. I should advise you to order for G. B. S. some maccaroni cheese, or maccaroni a l'Italienne. All these restaurant cooks know it. Or a dish of eggs (curried, or in white sauce, or with tomatoes or " au gratin ' ! !) He does *not* eat fish ; ; & he does not eat a great many dishes. He eats vegetables, sweets & dessert just as we do—but not *green* vegetables for his special dish."

Some of the older friends—the Speyers and Schuster—were seen a little less than formerly. Too many memories of Alice attached to Old Queen Street, to the Hut, to Ridgehurst. But Schuster still accompanied Elgar to the theatre and Speyer, though going blind, wrote from time to time. Because of failing eyesight and the bad weather then prevailing Speyer, most regretfully, could not attend the luncheon to Strauss in February 1922. But he was busy as ever on musical projects, and was now compiling a biography of his father. " But it means something to get through such an avalanche of letters with my old weak eyes : over 100 from Spohr, 60 from Meyerbeer, and lots from Mendelssohn, Moscheles, Hauptmann, Liszt, and tutti quanti, not to forget some 60 from Aloys Schmitt. . . . When shall we see you again ? . . ." [3]

[1] Griffith declined the offer : he disliked London.
[2] " I saw your letter in the Literary Supplement of the *Times* & your bursting out as a Greek scholar. I never had any suspicion of this, & must declare that you are the most many sided musician that ever lived." Edward Speyer to Elgar, Aug. 10, 1923.
[3] Feb. 14, 1922.

The next year Speyer sent birthday greetings and looked forward to new effort on Elgar's part. " I, myself," he wrote, " was 84 last month so you, still, are only a mere boy from whom the world is entitled to expect many more glorious doings."

III

In April 1923 Elgar took a short lease of Napleton Grange, Kempsey, just beyond the boundaries of Worcester, and on the Tewkesbury Road. At the same time he maintained his two-room flat in St. James for the occasions when he must come to town. By a series of renewals of the lease, Napleton Grange was to be Elgar's home until 1927. Here the " country gentleman " picture began to take shape for the benefit of news editors. Elgar, now with hair and moustache to silver turned, but erect and with commanding presence, cultivated roses, walked the countryside with his dogs, and talked on crop prospects with slow-burring labourers : the great composer in retirement. There were occasions on which he forsook his friendly tweeds for more formal attire. But when he now conducted it was, as Constant Lambert said, as if one of the classical composers had appeared to conduct a work of another age. At the Proms. in the autumn the first symphony and the 'cello concerto were warmly received—partly out of chivalry because of their comparative neglect—but as relative antiquities. At the Three Choirs Festival he was by now an institution : at Worcester, indeed, he was the festival. And so it continued until—and, indeed, beyond—his death.

In November Elgar's perpetual restlessness asserted itself. He must have a change—and as far from civilisation and from music as possible.

He booked for one of the cruises of the Booth Steamship Company. He was a good sailor and—as he wrote later to Henry Wood in recommending the company, the boat, and the cruise —preferred a small boat of 7000 tons—the *Hildebrand*—to a large liner. His reputation as a good sailor was well tested, for out from Liverpool and well into the Atlantic was the worst sea that could be remembered in a decade. It was so bad that the Liverpool pilot, normally put off at Holyhead, had to be carried on to Madeira.

From Madeira the *Hildebrand* sailed to Para at the mouth of the Amazon, and then up river for a thousand miles to Manaos. Elgar loved it. He had congenial English companions—he kept away from foreigners and particularly the Portuguese !—and became very friendly with the ship's commander Mr. Mandrell. His high spirits found outlet in social functions on board and ashore and he congratulated himself that although in the jungle there were 20,000 varieties of insects—some which stung, some which bit, and some which did both—he escaped any injury. He returned to England at the end of December with the full intention of making the same trip again.

In 1924 a number of friends and acquaintances, who had occupied varying places of significance in Elgar's life, died : at the beginning of the year the eighty-year-old Nicholas Kilburn, much loved, and Mrs. Fitton—in her ninetieth year ; in March Frederick Bridge, who as organist of Westminster Abbey and conductor of the Royal Choral Society had had a long association with Elgar ; in March, too, Walter Parratt, remembered for his early encouragement, and Stanford ; last, in November, Fauré—his reputation then in the doldrums. Parratt had been Master of the King's Musick. In May, shortly after returning from a visit to Paris, where Embleton had taken the Leeds Choral Union and dissipated more of his fortune in so doing, Elgar was informed of his succession to Parratt in the Royal Household. His letter of appointment made it clear that rumours that Walford Davies, Parratt's successor as organist at Windsor, would succeed were without foundation. The emolument was £100 a year.

Although the Private Band had been discontinued Elgar was not disposed to treat his appointment as a sinecure. His historical interest led him to take a great interest in the King's Music Library (housed at the British Museum) and in the royal collection of musical instruments, which he had put in order. Otherwise he advised on appointments—as when in 1927 a successor was needed to Barclay Squire as Curator of the King's Music library—and honours—he was very annoyed when his recommendation in favour of Percy Pitt was ignored ; he kept the king informed— through Sir Frederick Ponsonby—of changes in the constitution of the Royal Philharmonic Society ; he arranged royal visits to concerts and made preparations for formal presentations on such occasions ; and, when the occasion demanded, he wrote ceremonial music. There was not much of this and what there was different from what he had formerly composed in the *genre*. The *Carol for the King's Recovery* (1929) and the *Nursery Suite* (1931), dedicated to the Princesses Elizabeth and Margaret, are of an intimate character and in this reflect the change in the relationship of the Crown to the people. Elgar was sensitive to the public mood of those times and when Leslie Boosey wanted words for the trio tune of the fourth *Pomp and Circumstance* March Elgar indicated that words more general than those which Benson wrote for the first were wanted—people being more shy in expressing loyalty, but not less loyal.

Elgar as Master of the King's Musick was also a godsend to the press. How finely his regal instincts and antecedents fitted him for the honour : poor Parratt had been but an organist who played chess. Sir Edward wore his decorations well and graced an occasion with courtliness. Indeed he was able to display how well he could live up to his own ideal, built on early education and respect for the public manners of the aristocracy. The older Elgars, like their class, honoured their patrons in understanding them to be patterns of propriety.

It is significant that his response to Schuster's news of Fauré's death was twofold. He wrote, on November 15, from Napleton Grange :

" My dear Frank

Thank you for your letter from Paris. It was very sad over Fauré's death—he was such a real *gentleman*—the highest type of Frenchman & I admire him greatly. His chamber music never had a chance here in the old Joachim days I fear ; I may be wrong but I feel that it was ' held up ' to our loss. . . ."

A week or two later he wrote again saying that he had passed Schuster's letter—suggesting the Fauré *Requiem* for the Gloucester meeting of the Three Choirs—to Brewer, noting that " my influence at the 3 choirs is nil." Brewer's answer was that while he would like the Fauré work as a novelty there was a strong feeling among the committee that the only *Requiem* acceptable as a " draw " would be Verdi's, and so it was.

The year ended with an interchange of good wishes between Schuster and Elgar, the former saying that he wanted only one thing in life—the conclusion of the trilogy. To which :

Dec. 30, 1924

DEAR FRANK,

I had a very quiet time only Troyte here & a dog or two. I fear you will have nothing more from " my pen "—but if that's all to look forward to you will not miss much : music is dying fast in this country.

Thank you—but I do not intend to stray far & the S. Coast [this in reply to an invitation to Brighton where Schuster was now living] will not see me again. Yes, the weather has been wonderful & I find I have driven 1500 miles about this dear old county in six weeks. I thought the notice of Puccini [d. Nov. 29] dreadfully inadequate.

Yrs. ever

EDWARD ELGAR

" Music is dying fast in this country ": for the next year or two this refrain runs persistently through Elgar's thoughts. He did write a fugue at Kempsey, which Ivor Atkins played in Worcester Cathedral when, on February 14, 1925, the new organ was opened and a year later he did once again settle down for a little to his oratorio. This oratorio, planned so long ago and with sketches spread over twenty years, was finally forsaken in the summer of 1927. On June 14 of that year poor Embleton—who, it transpired after his death in 1930, had beggared himself in the support of music—was told there was little hope of its ever being accomplished. Elgar felt himself to be far down the vale of years, and the climax of his career long past. As for his works he felt that each performance he heard might be, for him, the last. There was more in life than work—even if his work happened to be music.

37 St. James's Place
Thursday [April 27, 1926]

MY DEAR FRANK :

Your *very welcome* note finds me on the point of departing to the country where my dogs are pining for me so I am told. I am glad you were at the concert [1] probably the *last*—as I do

---

[1] " Sir Edward Elgar conducted the London Symphony Orchestra in a programme of his own works at Queen's Hall on April 26. It comprised the Overture ' In the

not take *much* interest in *much* music now. It is too unthinkably
sad about the Wortleys [1]—what can be said beyond that ?

It is curious that I do not *tire* now—3 hours solid rehearsal
Sunday ;—the like on Monday & the concert ; early on Tuesday
HMV (large orchestra) Wedy. afternoon also. Dinner on
Tuesday & theatre last night & I am 69 ! !

I want to see you some time but I will advertise my coming to
town. If you are going to be at Bray *solidly* I would love to drive
over to luncheon one day & return same day to Wrcr.

My love to you

Yrs. ever

E. E.

South,' the 'Sea Songs' (Miss Muriel Brunskill), the 'Enigma' variations, and the
first Symphony.

"Such an evening as that will in years to come be matter for the anecdotage talk
of the fortunate hearers. It is indeed a privilege thus to have great music interpreted
by its author when it so happens that he is incomparably its best interpreter. Sir
Edward has a drastic way of hacking at his music. All sorts of things which other
conductors carefully foster, he seems to leave to take their chance. He cuts a way
through in a fashion both nervous and decisive. At the end we realise that detail and
rhetorical niceties have been put in their right place, and that the essential tale has been
vividly told. Credit is due to the Orchestra for its response to Sir Edward's uneasy
wilful beat." "C." in *Musical Times*, June 1926.

[1] Lord Stuart of Wortley died on April 24.

CHAPTER XIII

THREE SCORE AND TEN

I think I could turn and live with animals, they are so
placid and self-contain'd.

Whitman, " Song of Myself," *quoted in Elgar's*
Christmas Card, 1929

It was for his wife's sake—so it was stated in her obituary—that Elgar departed from his earliest resolve to remain " Mr. Elgar " by accepting titles. After her death honours of one sort or another continued to accumulate. There were some he accepted with pleasure. On November 19, 1925, he received the gold medal from the Royal Philharmonic Society—and he enjoyed an informal supper party afterwards at Pagani's. During the following year this Society nearly, but not quite, persuaded from him the elusive pianoforte concerto. There were innumerable bodies which sought Elgar's patronage, and normally he returned a kindly but negative answer, saying that such duties were " outside my allotted sphere." When, however, the Choral Society at Kidderminster requested that he should become its President he accepted the invitation out of the great respect he had always had for his old fellow student Wadely, who conducted that society for many years. The third honour he especially appreciated was the bestowal, in 1928, of the W. W. Cobbett Medal for Chamber Music. For the rest he accepted without particular emotion the K.C.V.O. in 1928, membership of the American Academy of Arts in 1929, another honorary Doctorate—from London University—in 1931, a baronetcy in the same year, the first Collard Life Fellowship of the Worshipful Company of Musicians in 1931,[1] and a G.C.V.O. in 1933. Symbols of this order at this time seemed irrelevant, though

---

[1] Elgar became an Honorary Freeman of the Company in 1911. After his death his successor in the Collard Fellowship was Vaughan Williams.

if his daughter and his friends and relatives in Worcestershire were gratified so much the better.

There were some musical occasions, however, when acknowledgment of his genius moved him considerably. There was a B.B.C. performance of *Gerontius* on Good Friday, 1927, prepared with consummate care by Percy Pitt and showing Steuart Wilson as the latest in the great tradition of Gerontius singers, and later in the year a seventieth birthday celebration concert. This in some part made up for past neglect by the B.B.C. of Elgar's music.[1] Other proposals for marking his birthday he rejected. But that Brodsky should come out of retirement to play the violin concerto at a Hallé concert was deeply appreciated as a spontaneous token of affection. On August 17, 1932, Elgar made his last appearance at a Promenade Concert, to conduct the second symphony. In this way Henry Wood celebrated Elgar's seventy-fifth birthday.[2] The B.B.C., largely through Boult, also rose grandly to his seventy-fifth birthday ; not only was there a three day festival of his music, but the Corporation—Reith being urged by Bernard Shaw—also commissioned a third symphony, for which a payment of £1000 was made.

A chance remark by Elgar, taken up by the *Daily Mail*, suggested that a symphony was more or less complete ; but this was not the case, there only being various sketches.

The concert which made the deepest impression in these last years was that in Paris, on May 31, 1933, when Yehudi Menuhin, who had worked at the concerto for the past two years, and had already played it with Elgar at the Albert Hall, and in Belfast, was the soloist. For the boy Menuhin, Elgar had the most tender affection—which was reciprocated by all the members of the Menuhin family. The arrangements as conveyed to Elgar by Fred Gaisberg seemed to indicate that Paris—of all European cities the most antipathetic to English music—was about to make some amends for former indifference. It was arranged that the Diplomatic Corps should attend and with the highest backing a great occasion was ensured. Yehudi's father wrote with excitement and delight to Gaisberg : " I am happy to tell you that ex-premier Herriot (who expects to be the Premier again by May 31, and who at any rate is the power behind the " throne " now) has arranged

---

[1] See *Musical Times*, July 1923.
[2] See Gaisberg Music on Record, p. 245 *et seq.*

already for the President, Premier, etc., to attend the May 31 concert. Thus the beginning of the Gala affair is reassured, as it will be THE social event of the spring season, and the full house being Yehudi's always in Paris, we have every reason to believe that our dear Sir Edward Elgar will draw a lot of joy and contentment of this visit with us. Do please convey to him in your own way this message, as you will know how to break it nicely without at the same time making it appear that we pray about it.

For after all, things should come that way on the score of sheer merit of the dear lovely, fine soul that Sir Edward is."

This journey to Paris was made more memorable by reason of travelling by aeroplane—an experience which Elgar enjoyed. Then there was the visit to Delius, whom Elgar had only seen but not spoken to at the Birmingham Festival of 1912 ; Gaisberg had pointed out that Elgar could hardly visit France without paying a call on Delius. Generally not very enthusiastic about meeting other composers—lately he had escaped invitations in London to meet Ravel and Schönberg—Elgar gave way in the case of Delius. Partly out of sympathy for the lonely, paralysed state in which Delius then was, and partly out of an affection, lately revived by letters from his old host and companion Dr. Buck, for those parts of Yorkshire which he knew and which Delius, too, as a boy had known. Elgar took as a gift records of works by Sibelius and Wolf. The meeting was a great success.[1] Eric Fenby, Delius's companion and amanuensis, wrote on June 5 to say that he had had a long account from Mrs. Delius " of your kind visit to Grez . . ., and pleased to hear that you were surprised to find Delius as well as he is and in good spirits—both Mrs. D. and I have done our best to make life jollier for him during these trying years.

" They were both charmed with you." So did these two ships pass in the night, and speak to each other in passing.

At the end of October 1927 Elgar, no longer able to rent Napleton Grange, took another temporary home at Battenhall Manor, which was also on the outskirts of Worcester. A few months later there was another move—to Tiddington House, Stratford-on-Avon, the home of Lady Muntz. For some time Elgar had had an inclination towards Stratford. He had early memories, of sixty years before, of being taken there, and from that time dated his great love and knowledge of Shakespeare.

---

[1] See *Delius as I knew him*, Eric Fenby, (London, 1936), pp. 123–5.

Now, at seventy, he was hoping, perhaps, to fulfil another ambition
—to write incidental music for the productions at Stratford. At
the beginning of 1927 he wrote this to Mr. W. Bridge-Adams,
then director of the Memorial Theatre. While in Stratford Elgar
saw as many productions as he could, and entertained the players, but
wrote nothing. When eventually the new theatre arose, in 1932,
in the place of that which was destroyed by fire six years previously
he was so incensed at the monstrous architecture, as he considered
it, that he wrote a furious letter to the *Daily Telegraph*—he tore it
up before sending it—and vowed never to be associated with it in
any musical capacity. There was, however, one outcome of his
close association with the stage at this time : the incidental music
for Gerald Lawrence's *Beau Brummel*, which Elgar himself conducted
at the Theatre Royal in Birmingham at the end of 1928. The charm
and delicacy of this music was not entirely destroyed by a poor
theatre band and Elgar won high commendation not so much for
the quality of the music as for the spirit in which he had engaged
on it. " In accepting a task of secondary importance Sir Edward
showed once more that those who are best fitted to command also
know best how to obey." [1]

For the Worcester Festival of 1929 Elgar took a house on
Rainbow Hill—Marl Bank. Shortly afterwards he bought it and
moved in on December 3. That was his last home.

Living there the old times crowded back. " It is pleasant," he
ended his Foreword to Hubert Leicester's *Forgotten Worcester*,
" to date these lines from our eminence distantly overlooking the
way to school ; our walk was always to the brightly-lit west.
Before starting, our finances were rigidly inspected,—naturally not
by me, being, as I am, in nothing rigid, but, quite naturally, by
my companion, who tackled the situation with prophetic skill and
with the gravity now bestowed on the affairs of great corporations
whose accounts are harrowed by him to this day. The report being
favourable, twopence were ' allowed ' for the ferry. Descending
the steps, past the door behind which the figure of the mythical
salmon is incised, we embarked ; at our backs ' the unthrift sun
shot vital gold,' filling Payne's Meadows with glory and illuminating
for two small boys a world to conquer and to love. In our old age,
with our undimmed affection, the sun still seems to show us a
golden ' beyond.' "

[1] F. B. in *Musical Times*, Dec. 1928.

In these last years many events and persons came up from the past. Sir Robert Armstrong-Jones, a specialist in mental diseases, asked him his opinions on the therapeutic value of music in mental cases, arising from his former experiences at Powick ; but Elgar could not remember anything likely to be scientifically valuable. Herbert Sullivan revived memories of Sir Arthur's kindness and, no doubt, Elgar recalled that Sullivan, as Parry, nearly became a movement in the *Enigma*. A girls' school at Malvern—Lawnside— brought back recollections of early ambitions by inviting him to a ballet which they had made out of the *Wand of Youth* music. " I shall," he wrote back, " be delighted to look over the old music which gave so many young people such pleasure long ago, to myself I think more than most of the listeners." Some more un- fulfilled ambitions came to light. Sir Richard Terry had always hoped for a liturgical work (presumably a Mass) from Elgar, but Elgar had excused himself, shortly after the war, saying, honestly, that he could not undertake such a work unless in complete spiritual accord with the philosophy of the text. Among Elgar's earlier ambitions, as shown by his sketch books, had been just such a work. In 1928 Cardinal Bourne, Archbishop of Westminster, returned to another project, by which he hoped to elevate the standards of Catholic church music.

Elgar to Cardinal Bourne :

Sept. 18, 1928

MY LORD ARCHBISHOP,
    I am honoured by the request contained in your letter of the 16th. The question of a broad corporate setting of the *Te Deum* has frequently occupied my mind since 1870 but the irregularity of the text stands in the way. I will think of it again as you suggest.

Believe me to be
Your Grace's obedient servant
EDWARD ELGAR

A year earlier he had written to another Archbishop—Randall Davidson of Canterbury, who was celebrating the twenty-fifth anniversary of his succession as Primate. Elgar recalled the intention behind his oratorios and threw some light on his present convictions.

Feb. 22, 1927

MY LORD ARCHBISHOP,

Although your Grace has been so kind to me on every occasion on which I have had the honour to meet you I should not have had the temerity to address a letter to you on any ordinary occasion; but the anniversary occurring this year is unique: and so important that I venture to send respectful congratulations & deeply felt good wishes.

Bred in another form of religious observance I stand aside, unbiased, from the trivialities with which controversies are mostly informed; whatever differences exist there remains the clear, wide & refreshing Christianity, desired by all men, but obscured by the little darkness of their own imperfect vision. To the better understanding of such broad Christian feeling I am thankful to have been permitted, in a small way it is true, to exercise my art; in this spirit and in a spirit of humble fellow-ship I offer this tribute of deep respect—to an ideal great church-man, a staunch friend, and an embodiment of all that is good & true in Christianity past mere forms & observances.

> With every respect
> Believe me to be
> Very sincerely & affectionately
> Your Grace's obedient servant,
> EDWARD ELGAR

This was a letter which cost much effort and called for many alterations in the draft before the proper phrasing came.

In 1932 letters from and to Dr. Buck revived other and gayer days.

Marl Bank Worcester
19th August 1932

MY DEAR BUCK:

I have thought much of you & the dear old days lately. Your British Medical Socy. have been here, as you will know, un-veiling a window in the Cathedral to Sir C. Hastings: it is just fifty (! !) years since you were here & played in the orch:

—what a lovely time we had, the first of many adventures. In this August weather I always live over again the holidays I had with you & the taste of *grilled Ribble trout* comes with ineffaceable relish : nothing so good in eating or company has occurred to me since 1882.

Best regards
Yours very sincerely
EDWARD ELGAR

23 *August* 1932

MY DEAR BUCK :

It is splendid to hear you are still enjoying life in spite of livers and ducts or something : you may remember that I never could remember anything about the human form & to this day if you offered me £1,000,000,000 I cd. not tell you where my liver, or any damn thing lies.

It is marvellous that you remember the gorgeous doings after that Soiree ;—it was not *Louis* d'Egville but his cousin *Wm.*—it was a grand wind-up to a woolly concert.

Changes & many have been among us : poor old Frank departed this life three years ago.

I fear there is small chance of my travelling north again but I still hope for it.

Warm regards,
Yours ever,
EDWARD ELGAR

The long illness of his brother Frank had greatly disturbed Elgar and he had devoted much time to looking after him and his affairs and to taking him for drives in the country. For Frank Edward had an especial sympathy. He had succeeded to the family business and controlled it until 1918. He had conducted the local Civil and Military Band and had played the oboe in local musical events. He had also even aspired to composition. Troyte Griffith records this : " On the day that Elgar left Craeglea for Plas Gwyn he gave me a quantity of his own music and with it two pieces by ' Gustave Franke ' published by Boosey.[1] He certainly told me

---

[1] In Elgar's sketch books there is one fragment, headed " Franke." Of the two pieces the title page of one is among the Grafton papers : *Offertoire pour le violin*, Gustav Francke (op 11), dédié à Serge Derval, Anvers.

that he had written them himself to encourage his brother Frank to follow them up with others. He said that Frank Elgar was a good musician but had not enough energy or something of that kind. . . ." When Edward considered the minor career of Frank it was a case of " There but by the grace of God go I."

II

With the increasing loneliness brought by the deaths of members of the family and old friends—Lucy Pipe in 1925, Frank Schuster at the end of 1927, Frank Elgar and Brewer of Gloucester in 1928, Embleton in 1930, Wolstenholme in 1931, Percy Pitt in 1932—Elgar turned to his animals for companionship and to the countryside for solace. He withdrew himself almost entirely from London life, even cancelling his long membership of the London library. As a child Elgar had grown up to love horses and dogs. During his formative years as a composer and before his marriage the irrepressible Scap had cured many bouts of melancholy. Now at the end of life there were Marco, the spaniel, Meg, the Scottie, and Mina (the " subject " of his last published work), the Cairn. It will be seen that they reveal, anagrammatically—" Marc OM Enigma ! " Elgar was drawn into a rare and mystical communion with his dogs : they, he thought, perhaps alone could understand him. They, perhaps, knew that the guiding trait of his character was affection. In 1929 Elgar quoted a passage from Whitman's *Song of Myself* on his Christmas Card : he stopped short before the significant lines

> *So they show their relations to me & I accept them*
> *They bring me tokens of myself, they evince them plainly*
> > *in their possession. . . .*

In his 1932 Christmas card Elgar wrote a brief fable concerning the last creation of the Almighty which brought honour and happiness to mortals and immortals alike. God made a puppy.[1]

As with dogs so with horses. Elgar loved horses (see p. 174) for themselves. He also enjoyed horse races. For some years he was a member of the Worcester Race Course and he made oppor-

---

[1] This story which was subsequently published in the *Tail Waggers' Journal* will be among Elgar's writings published in a companion volume to this study.

tunities to attend at classic meetings elsewhere. " I expect," wrote
the ageing Cowen on June 1, 1932, " you are at the Derby & hope
you have backed the winner." Sir Edward rarely backed the
winner : in fact it was well known among bookmakers that any
horse fancied by him was almost certain to finish unplaced. So,
perhaps, it was that Elgar was the most highly thought of composer
among the bookmaking fraternity. Sometimes odd consequences
followed. One day a bookmaker asked a favour on behalf of his
clerk. Would Sir Edward give his autograph. The great man con-
sented. To his surprise—and gratification—the said clerk bought
along a full score of The Apostles to be signed. From his interest
in horses grew a late friendship with Mr. E. Somerville Tattersall
(of " Tattersalls ") whose correspondence blends his two main
interests in life in nice proportion. Tattersall was a great friend
of the Menuhins. Hence—

Tattersall to Elgar, January 13, 1934:

" Sir Courtauld Thomson says he (Menuhin) is as far in front
of the next violinist as Gordon Richards is in front of the next
jockey." Tattersall was much impressed by a performance by
Rosenthal of Chopin's E Minor Concerto. Therefore (February 2,
1934): "I see that Rosenthal was born at Lemburg—another sporting
name—so he ought to be a classic performer. Brunswick is quite
well handicapped in the Queen's Prize on April 2 at 8—6 with the
top weighters Loosestrip & Seminola 9—7." One of Tattersall's
horses, in delicate compliment, was named " Concerto "—and at
Worcester one memorial to the composer was the institution of a
race as the Elgar Plate.

This interest in horse racing was one side of his out-of-doors
life. It was part of the exuberance with which he used to astonish
and shock the sedate. On the other hand his reflective spirit sought
the quiet places in country life. He visited, wistfully, all the scenes
associated with his earlier achievements—Birchwood, Queenhill
Church and the Wye Valley. Any reference to a favourite landmark
touched his memories. So in 1931 when the County Surveyor for
Herefordshire, preparing a paper on " The Art of the Bridge
Builder "—for the Royal Society of Arts—wrote to him about his
reputed connection with Mordiford Bridge, Elgar replied, saying,
". . . Most of my ' sketches ' that is to say the original thoughts
reduced to writing, have been made in the open air. I fished the
Wye round about Mordiford and completed many pencil memor-

anda of compositions on the old bridge of which I hold many affectionate memories." [1]

Any suggestion that any part of his county was being despoiled was sufficient to arouse him to speech and action. In 1929 Bernard Shaw wrote an angry letter to *The Times* about the destruction of the northern contour of the Malvern Hills by quarrying. Elgar was among the first to jump to his aid in a supporting manifesto signed by many distinguished persons with interests in Worcestershire. When the old bridge across the Severn, at Worcester, was being widened he could not bear to see the old iron balustrades going carelessly away to scrap. So he bought two lengths of balustrade and embedded them in concrete in the garden at Marl Bank. One of the compositions of his last period—the *Severn Suite* —was composed out of this affection. For some years Herbert Whiteley had been pressing in his request for a work for brass bands to be used as a test piece at the Crystal Palace competition. In 1930—as a companion to his essay in Hubert Leicester's book —the *Severn Suite* came, with its local allusions in the titles of the first four movements as given in the version for orchestra : " Worcester Castle," " Tournament," " Cathedral," " Commandery."

In some ways Elgar resembled Hardy. In none more than in his feeling for nature. Mysticism enwrapped him at the end of his days as also in his eager years. But now the direction was changed. He felt the *lux perpetua* in the light of the sun, the *spiritus sanctus* in the winds that blew across the inscrutable, western plain, the *pater omnipotens* behind the change of the seasons. Elgar was long fascinated by the Saxon derivation of his surname and had formerly asked for Saxon emblems to be placed on the gravestone of his parents. Coming towards his own end he would seem secretly to have been moved by something akin to the beautiful, poetic, teleological speculations of the Saxons. Thus he felt that he would like to be buried among the flowery meadows and by the running waters where, downstream from Powick Bridge, Teme joined Severn. But that was not to be.

---

[1] Jan. 15, 1931. There is a note in the sketches of *Music Makers* (at 42 in the published score), " Mem : four trout (decent) three (small) put back. Mr. D. hooked a salmon & lost it. Mordiford."

III

If former pleasures were recollected in late life so too were previous distresses. In 1931 Professor E. J. Dent, Stanford's successor at Cambridge, contributed a brief notice on Elgar to Adler's *Handbuch der Musikgeschichte*.[1] It is, of course, reasonable that a critic should back his own judgment. Therefore if Dent found Elgar's chamber music " dry and academic " (though the latter adjective is, at least, surprising), his music in general " too emotional and not quite free from vulgarity " he was entitled to say so ; even though by suggesting that the latter defects were disapproved by " English ears " he assumed all the English to judge music from his own individual standpoint. He was not entitled to say that Elgar " was more or less a self-taught man, who possessed little of the literary culture of Parry and Stanford," for, by surveying all the available evidence, it is clear that in " literary culture " Elgar left Parry and Stanford far behind. That unhappy episode was the outcome first of the Stanford cult which was practised and preached in Cambridge at that time, and of the fashion of withholding approval from all living English composers who failed in showing a knowledge of the 16th century, and, second, a desire to embellish folk-song. There was an obligation on the part of Cambridge music students then to avoid all mention of Elgar. The name appeared to suggest something slightly indecent and the most kind hearted, but parochially minded, urged against the inquiring young, who persisted in looking at the score of the *Dream of Gerontius*, the fact of Elgar's interest in horses !

Dent's main charge was competently met by a furious body of distinguished musicians, critics, and men of letters, who published a protest. In addition to signing the joint manifesto Bernard Shaw wrote an individual essay in which he said that " Professor Dent should not have belittled his country by belittling the only great composer who is not dwarfed by the German giants."

Elgar showed no gesture while the battle raged. Two years later, however, he took exception to an injudicious remark of Herbert Thompson in a letter to the *Sunday Times*.[2] The occasion was the publication of Basil Maine's book on Elgar. Thompson

---

[1] This episode is dealt with in detail in Maine, *op. cit.*, p. 277 *et seq.*
[2] July 2, 1933.

felt that the case of Canon Hudson (a Cambridge amateur who was said to have been surprised that Stanford should have wished to present Elgar's name for an honorary degree) should have been mentioned by Maine as testimony to Stanford's high opinion of Elgar. Thompson commenced his letter—" I am loth to stir up muddy waters, but when my friend Mr. Ernest Newman calls attention to the disagreements between Elgar and Stanford. . . ."

Elgar thereupon drafted a reply, which, however, he withheld from publication :

SIR :

My attention has been drawn to a letter from a Mr. Herbert Thompson under the heading " Elgar and Stanford " which introduces the word " disagreements," a word to which in this connection I definitely object. There could be no " disagreements." Stanford (Mr., Dr. and Knight) at various times thought it well to avoid speaking to me for periods varying very considerably in length. It was a matter for comment that such periods of silence invariably began when some work of mine was produced.

I never refused to " shake hands " after these silences although the reason for them was never disclosed ; three men whom Stanford asked to " approach " me with a view to a renewal on his part of ordinary civilities were A. E. Rodewald, Hubert Parry and, last of all, Granville Bantock. On every occasion I hoped that the reason for " cutting " me might be told : Stanford only said " we (!) have been under a cloud."

I shook hands without comment but I am still without knowlege of Stanford's somewhat eccentric silences.

Mr. Thompson's reference to the Cambridge telegram shows that he knows nothing of the matter : at that moment Stanford was very friendly to me, but he did not wish to meet Sir Frederick Cowen who was receiving the Mus. D. at the same time.

Poor Cowen ! In these late days indigent, ill, and forgotten he was of no account in these contentions. But at the turn of the century he was so prominent as to be considered as a candidate for the conductorship of the Leeds Festival. Hence Stanford's desire to avoid him at Cambridge.

IV

Hedenteum Lodge, Bungay Suffolk
Dec. 23 [1931]

DEAR SIR EDWARD,

I am venturing to send you my edition of *Die Kunst der Fuge* as a Christmas card, in the hope that the features in it which will be new to you will not be a bore.

Bantock holds out to me a hope that we might meet in or around the New Year before I go north again. There are so many things I want (such as a pianoforte concerto) to wangle from you that I am ready to cast away all modesty and scruples and to use all manner of kunsterfuges—I mean subterfuges to get them. It is best to be shameless in this connexion; it would be an impertinence to pretend that I have nothing to gain from meeting you. For instance, a pianoforte concerto. Rumour asserts that you can't abide the pianoforte. However impertinent such rumours are they point to your having much the same view of my instrument as I have—viz. a dislike of chopsticks, and a hankering after the suggestive rather than the material range of the instrument. Etcetera, etcetera. But I must not intrude further.

Please forgive this note-paper [of the O.U.P.], but I had no bound copy of my " kunsterfuge " and had to go to the Aeolian Hall for one.

Yours very sincerely
DONALD FRANCIS TOVEY

It was gratifying for the old man to find that there were those who still esteemed his talent. Indeed after his seventieth birthday another generation was coming to maturity with a new approach to the music of Elgar, and with opinions untouched by the rivalries and controversies of the past. Donald Tovey, of course, was an old friend of earlier days at Ridgehurst, but he spoke with authority; and in writing of Elgar's works he had regarded them in their relation to the great European classics and not solely in relation to other English music of the twentieth century " renaissance." Of the younger conductors Sargent and Barbirolli were distinguishing themselves in Elgar performances, and Constant Lambert was

seeing the realisation of the ballet implicit in the *Nursery Suite*.[1]
It was a matter of surprise to Elgar that Siegfried Sassoon and T. E.
Lawrence (Shaw), leaders of thought among the young men of fame
in post war years, should be wholehearted in their respect and
affection ; that they should ask for new music from his pen. At
the same time Bernard Shaw was insistent that perhaps the best
was yet to be. The *Severn Suite*, which was dedicated to Shaw,
caught much of the old virility as the *Nursery Suite* was imbued with
all the former charm and whimsicality. In 1931 and 1932 Elgar
wrote a handful of songs and, as if in consideration of the prospective concerto, one or two piano pieces. By 1933 he was almost
back to his full working habits. He undertook his B.B.C. commission with zest. At the same time he began another work that
his older friends had hoped for for more than thirty years. For it
was as far back as 1901 that Speyer—in 1933 still alive and approaching ninety-four—had asked " How about the opera ? Could
the divine William not provide you with a libretto? It is true that
' Much ado about nothing ' has been done already, but you may, I
assume, find ' much to do about some other things ' ! "

Increasing intimacy with Barry Jackson and the steady pressure
of Bernard Shaw at last brought him to commence an opera. He
went back to the seventeenth century—but not to Shakespeare—and
from the reading of his youth he took Ben Jonson's *The Devil is an
Ass*, extracting from it, with Barry Jackson's help, a libretto. The
title of the opera was to be *The Spanish Lady*.

[1] Sadler's Wells, Mar. 1932.

CHAPTER XIV

UNFINISHED SYMPHONY

After many a dusty mile,
Wanderer, linger here awhile.

From the Greek Anthology

ELGAR ATTENDED his last Festival at Worcester in 1932. Of his own works there were included *Gerontius*, the first symphony, *The Music Makers*, *For the Fallen*, the *Quintet* and—a first performance —the orchestral version of the *Severn Suite*. Additionally the Festival opened with his arrangement of the National Anthem and the orchestral version, by Esser, of Bach's *Toccata in F*, played as a voluntary at the conclusion of the Sunday afternoon service, was one which Elgar had revised many years before to conform with Bach's own score. There were other links with the past. Among the first violins was one who was not a member of the London Symphony Orchestra : J. W. Austin. He, seated at the back desk, was the last connection with the former days when most of the orchestra was recruited locally. He was also one to whom Elgar willingly acknowledged gratitude, for his help in proof reading and copying. On Thursday morning Beethoven's *Equali* for four trombones were inserted between *The Music Makers* and Szymanowski's *Stabat Mater*. This addition to the programme was to honour Hugh Blair, who first had encouraged Elgar to great works and had remained his friend across the years.

During the Festival Elgar was inseparable from Bernard Shaw, who showed his appreciation of Elgar's attending the Malvern Festival by his presence at that of the Three Choirs. Elgar had opened a Shaw exhibition at Malvern in 1929 and it was then that Shaw publicly acknowledged that Elgar was a greater man than himself. Elgar looked fit and vigorous. As he walked down the centre aisle of the nave with Shaw he made a magnificent presence.

He conducted with more deliberation than formerly, relying on facial expression rather than on manual subtleties ; but he inspired performances of affectionate beauty.

Those who were most nearly concerned with his welfare—Carice, Miss Clifford his secretary, his Grafton nieces, Dick Mountford his manservant, Reed, Gaisberg—saw to it that his exertions were limited as much as possible. But, his mental powers being as lively as ever and his enthusiasm for music greater than for some time past, they looked forward, confidently, to more creative activity. Two months after the Three Choirs Festival Elgar learned of the intention of the B.B.C. regarding a third symphony. He immediately wrote to the promoter of this intention.

> *Langham Hotel, Portland Place,*
> *London, W.1.* 11*th Nov.* 1933
>
> My dear Shaw,
>   Landon Ronald has unfolded today the wonderful plan which you invented—I am overwhelmed by the loftiness of the idea & can only say *thank you* at this moment—My love to Charlotte & of course to you.
>
> Yrs. ever
>
> Edward E.

The great affection and profound regard which Elgar had for Shaw was the inspiration of his last months. The extent to which his philosophy of life (and of death) was affected by this friendship and respect may not be estimated, for there were some matters on which his eloquence found expression in silence. It should, however, be noted that he had seen every play of Shaw, that his intimacy had ripened over the last fifteen years, and that among the last works which Shaw gave him was *The Adventures of the Black Girl in Search of God.* The only way in which he could symbolise his gratitude to Shaw was in a major work. Therefore he must write his symphony. The opera was part of the same token.

At the beginning of 1933 Elgar, having obtained fresh supplies of manuscript paper from Italy and a new upright piano from Chappells, worked at his sketches with determination. He tired more quickly than formerly, however, and would break off after shorter periods to talk to the dogs, to walk in the garden, to listen to the gramophone, to read. But his spirits were high. He still

chuckled at his " japes." When an American compiler of a pre-
tentious symposium of all knowledge asked him to say what music
was he asked Troyte Griffith what he would say. What he did say
was faithfully transcribed to America. Elgar protested that what
he himself thought on this subject was of small importance : " I
will quote the words of the philosopher Arthur Troyte Griffith."
So while Professor Koons had Einstein on one branch of philosophy
he had Troyte on another.

Willie Reed was sent for in the spring to play through parts
both of symphony and opera. The former progressed rather more
favourably than the latter, for Elgar's knowledge of the theatre
made him a somewhat too dialectical partner for Barry Jackson.
Nevertheless a large amount of music in sketch form—much of it
taken from the work of earlier years—was produced for both
projects. The Shaws, too, came to study progress. In May, as
already described, there was the excitement of the journey to Paris.
Basil Maine's book duly appeared and also one which had been
on the stocks for some time by J. F. Porte. Numerous recording
sessions were held during the year and Gaisberg too looked for a
new masterpiece. " I had," he wrote on August 21, " a delightful
weekend at Marl Bank, and one that will live in my memory for
a long while, especially the Sunday afternoon after tea, when you
gave us a rare treat ; I feel greatly flattered at being able to hear
bits of the new work. It was like a door opening and letting rays
of sunshine into a dark chamber. There were sufficient jewels of
melody to stud a king's crown, but the greatest satisfaction was
to know that you are up to your highest form in the work you are
engaged on."

A week later came the Hereford Festival. Elgar stayed at the
Priory and was in genial form. He entertained generously and
the daily tea parties on the lawn were the last intimate recollections
of him of many of his old friends.

Early in October Elgar was taken ill. He had for a little while
complained of sciatic pains and had appeared more exhausted than
might have been expected after conducting at Hereford. In 1925
he had been a patient in the South Bank Nursing Home on account
of a minor operation. Now he was taken there again. Examination
revealed that he had a malignant growth. An operation was performed, but the most that could be hoped for might be a reprieve
for a few months, even a year. Reed coming down from London at

E.   Q

Elgar's urgent request was informed of this grave condition by
Dr. Moore Ede, son of the Dean and Elgar's doctor. Reed and
Carice engineered a conspiracy of silence so that her father might
be allowed to live his remaining days in some peace of mind.
Intermittently he suffered great pain. At the end of November he
collapsed and, unconscious, was given the last rites of the Roman
Catholic Church. But, unexpectedly, he rallied.

He knew now that he would never complete his symphony and
enjoined it on Carice and Reed that no one else should ever make
the attempt. A few years previously he had expressed himself
with some force when an American firm tried to interest him in a
competition for the completion of Schubert's " Unfinished Symphony." He had no wish that his own incomplete work should be
subjected to such " vulgar publicity." He was, however, unwilling
even as yet to accept the finality of incompletion. Deep down his
love for Shaw stirred him. On December 5 Shaw sent him a copy
of *On the Rocks*. The following day Elgar dictated his acknowledgment—and managed to sign it with his own hand.

> *Nursing Home, Worcester*
> *Dec. 6. 1933*
>
> My dear Shaw:
> Nothing could possibly give me greater pleasure than the
> receipt of your play *and* preface—(kolossel !)—& your wonderful
> letter. I fear it will be a long time before I can say I have
> read the whole of the printed matter, but I look at it with pride
> all day and dip into it occasionally. I am still in the depths of
> pain.
> It was good of you to speak to Sir John Reith about the
> symphony. The very pleasant arrangement made by you in
> the goodness of your heart for my peace of mind & betterment
> last year was turning out to be my greatest worry & disap-
> pointment. At present I can only wait and see & hope for the
> best, but I am low in mind.
> My love to Charlotte & kindest regards to you,
> > Always your affectionately
> > (*Signed*) Edward Elgar

Three days before Christmas he heard from the other Shaw—
T. E., 33871 A/C, of the R.A.F.

Cloud Hills, Moreton,
Dorset. 22.12.33

DEAR SIR EDWARD

This is from my cottage and we have just been playing your 2nd Symphony. Three of us, a sailor, a Tank Corps soldier and myself. So there are all the Services present ; and we agreed that you must be written to and told (if you are well enough to be bothered) that this Symphony gets further under our skins than anything else in the record library at Clouds Hill. We have the Violin Concerto, too ; so that says quite a lot. Generally we play the Symphony last of all, towards the middle of the night, because nothing comes off very well after it. One seems to stop there.

You would laugh at my cottage, which has one room upstairs (gramophone and records) and one room downstairs (books) ; but there is also a bath, and we sleep anywhere we feel inclined. So it suits me. A one-man house, I think.

The three of us assemble there nearly every weekend I can get to the Cottage, and we wanted to say " thank you " for the Symphony ever so long ago ; but we were lazy first ; and then you were desperately ill, and even now we are afraid you are too ill, probably, to be thinking of anything except yourself; but we are hoping that you are really getting stronger and will soon be able to deal with people again.

There is a selfish side to our concern : we want your Symphony III ; if it is wiser and wider and deeper than II we shall sadly dethrone our present friend, and play it last of the evening. Until it comes, we shall always stand in doubt if the best has really yet happened.

Imagine yourself girt about by a mob of young pelicans, asking for III ; and please be generous to us, again !

Yours sincerely

T. E. SHAW

It was just over a year previously that he had been taken to see Elgar by Bernard Shaw. The affection and tenderness which Hugh Walpole had noted so many years before came out in full measure in old age. For youth he held reverence. This is often the way with those whose careers, having passed through difficulty and disillusion, end in a success which somehow seems pointless—

si jeunesse savait et si vieillesse pouvait! The career of Yehudi Menuhin to Elgar promised a miracle. His love for Menuhin was profoundly touched by a New Year's greeting which was sent on a postcard from the liner *Italia* bound for New York.

29 December 1933

The quintet Mo Ma Ye He Ya Menuhin sends loving greetings and hearty wishes to their beloved friend Sir Edward! May you live in health to 120, and may our children's children learn to know the dear English gentleman of the warm heart and brilliant mind whom we all love so tenderly!

MOSHE MENUHIN

Dear friend, I hope that we will be able to see you very soon. Please get well and let us all be happy.

LOVE FROM YEHUDI

After Christmas Elgar was taken home to Marl Bank. Distressing bouts of pain and the consequential effects of heavy drugging left him for the most part hardly aware of what was going on around him. Gaisberg thoughtfully contrived to bring him all the happiness that lay in his power to give. He engaged Harriet Cohen and the Stratton Quartet to record the chamber works, and the proofs he had immediately sent down to Worcester for Elgar to hear. Troyte Griffith came in one day. On hearing the slow movement of the Quartet he said " Surely that is as fine as a movement by Beethoven." Elgar replied, " Yes it is and there is something in it that has never been done before." Griffith asked what it was. The old man returned to the teasing mood in which formerly he had treated his friend : " Nothing you would understand, merely an arrangement of notes."

Gaisberg made further plans. With the consent of the doctors and the help of Post Office engineers, he arranged that some parts of *Caractacus* to be recorded should be directed by Elgar himself from his bedroom. Although on the appointed day it looked as though he would be unable to endure the strain he revived considerably towards the afternoon. The engineers had done their work perfectly and, so far as Elgar was concerned, the London Symphony Orchestra was in his room.[1] There was an audience :

[1] See Fred W. Gaisberg, op. cit. p. 249 *et seq.*

Carice, Ivor Atkins, Troyte, Madeline Grafton, Miss Clifford, two
servants and Dr. Moore Ede. For more than an hour the rehearsal
proceeded and when it was about to end Elgar asked for the
" Woodland Interlude." This he had repeated. So he went out
of, and through, his music into the remembrance of his beloved
countryside.

There remained a few grey weeks of increasing distress. Sometimes he thought with terrible perverseness as pain drove him to
reproach even those he loved the most. When the spasms were
eased and he lay, half unaware, he was in tranquillity. Lady Elgar
would have heard premonitions of this final conflict within the
first symphony. It was at 7.45 on the morning of February 23,
1934, that Sir Edward Elgar died. It was the day of the month on
which, in 1685, Handel had been born.

Messages of sympathy came from all over the world. There
was a telegram from the King, and others from Paderewski,
Kreisler, and Richard Strauss with their heartfelt condolences.
Delius, to survive Elgar by a few months only, grieved the loss of
one whom he recalled with gratitude as "a great friend." Hamilton
Harty spoke of " a very great musician and a very great man ";
Sir Edward German of " a modest genius "; Sir Richard Terry of
" a noble life nobly lived." Vaughan Williams described his works
as " imperishable monuments." Constant Lambert said " he was
the first English composer since the 18th century who was the
technical equal of his foreign contemporaries. He put England
on the map again, musically." Lord Berners said that he was " the
first English composer since Purcell to make for himself an international reputation." It was, rightly, left for Sir Landon Ronald
to summarise the expressions of his colleagues and his own personal
sense of loss in a broadcast tribute on the night of Elgar's death.

Men of this acknowledged stature are rare. At their death the
place in which they are to be buried becomes, perhaps inevitably,
the subject of discussion and even dissension. So the final honours
become not necessarily those which the dead would have had
in their memory, but those which the most possessive section of the
community considers appropriate. This was well illustrated in
the macabre division of Hardy between Westminster Abbey and
Stinsford Churchyard. He himself had wished for entombment
among his ancestors in Wessex. As Hardy belonged to Dorsetshire
so Elgar to Worcestershire. In his case Westminster Abbey—

though some of his friends considered that he merited to lie near Purcell—was not possible. He had been born and bred as a Roman Catholic. He was the only English composer since the days of William Byrd to have given expression to Catholic philosophy and sentiment in a musical work of universally acknowledged greatness. In his later years Elgar had not been, as they say in a narrow sense, a " practising " Catholic, although he continued to support his old church of St. George's by donations to its charities. His withdrawal from formal modes of worship, however, was no escape from spiritual discipline. He sought truth in solitude. What distressed him most in the world was the lack of the greatest of the theological virtues—charity. Elgar had said that his burial place should be at the confluence of Teme and Severn and his interment without ceremony. It was, however, considered more fitting, after deep consideration, that he, a Catholic, should, in view of the grace vouchsafed to so many through his art, be buried according to his family tradition. Thus he was laid in consecrated ground and in the place he had appointed Troyte Griffith to obtain for him fourteen years previously, in the churchyard of St. Wulstan's, Little Malvern.

The funeral service, brief and simple, took place on the morning of Monday, February 26. Snow scudded over the hills at the time, but soon there was brilliant sunshine. A handful of the closest friends, including the oldest of all—Hubert Leicester, was all that attended. They wore no mourning. There were no flowers.

A Low Requiem Mass took place at St. George's, Worcester, at the same time. On March 2 the Cathedral Church of Worcester was filled by a vast congregation representing every part of national and local life. The Festival Choir and the London Symphony Orchestra were present and the life of one of Worcester's greatest citizens was magnificently commemorated in a service in which the main part consisted of his own music. On the previous day the Royal Philharmonic Society had given an *in memoriam* concert —the Prelude to *Gerontius*, the violin concerto with Sammons as soloist, and the second symphony. This was conducted by Boult.

In May 1935 the cottage of Broadheath, in which Elgar had been born, was purchased by the Worcester Corporation and, endowed by subscriptions, was entrusted to the care of a committee of trustees as a national memorial—" as dear to lovers of music—as the national monuments at Stratford, Chalfont and Grasmere are to lovers of poetry." Four months later, on September 3, the opening day of the Worcester Festival, a memorial window was unveiled in the Cathedral. This, according to designs by A. K. Nicholson, was based on the *Dream of Gerontius*. The unveiling ceremony was by the Lord Lieutenant of the County and in the presence of the Bishop, the Dean, and the conductors of the Three Choirs, as well as many others. After the dedication of the window the orchestra played the ninth of the " *Enigma* " *Variations*.

" The music ended, the Bishop and Clergy, with the Lord Lieutenant and those with them, returned to their places and the oratorio, *The Dream of Gerontius*, began. . . . "

CHAPTER XV

THE MAN HIMSELF

If I were not Alexander, I would be Diogenes.
Plutarch, Life of Alexander XIV, 3

A MAN is sometimes best to be judged not by what he is but by what he might have been. Often he becomes what he is in spite of himself: through influence or lack of influence; through opportunity or lack of opportunity. Elgar became a musician because his father wished it. Elgar Bros. was a settled, if not a particularly prosperous, concern and, after the custom of the period, the sons were expected to maintain it. Thus Edward and Frank were conditioned to their future state. A little lower down in the High Street the Leicesters similarly came to careers in a printing business. But for other circumstances Edward would have devoted a lifetime to the sale and maintenance of pianos and music, in which case he would, almost certainly, have achieved greater prosperity than he did. As late as 1891, indeed, Elgar was still helping behind the counter. Many years afterwards a member of the Yorkshire contingent which formerly helped the chorus—Mr. Arthur Walsh—recalled leaving a rehearsal of *Lux Christi* to buy a programme of the Festival. He was directed to Elgar Bros. "When I went in who should be behind the counter but Mr. Edward Elgar."

It was characteristic of one side of his nature that even then he should have been willing to help his father. But there was an impediment to shopkeeping. Partly inspired by his parents' unfulfilled ambitions for themselves—as composer and poetess respectively—and partly by a very shrewd estimate of his own worth Elgar saw within himself realisable aims. In the nineteenth century, taking a cue from Nietzsche on the one hand or Samuel Smiles on the other, one estimated the strength of one's will to succeed and acted accordingly. Elgar rated his very high. One part of this will to succeed is in persistence. But persistence is not enough. It is necessary to outflank opposition by making use of the weapons employed by the opposition. Elgar, whatever his native gifts, faced two main obstacles : social and intellectual snobbery. Of these the second was the more severe. A lifetime of struggle leaves its marks. At the end it was said, sometimes out of envy but not always without some truth, that Elgar's circumstances appeared ostentatious, that his disrespect for Art and for the " intellectual " was ungenerous and without warrant. Here we see the marks of the provincial who has captured the market from the vested interests. Who but a provincial could have written in his years of fame— " From among the crudities which one of the many—why are there so many ?—unbrilliant university men has used in reference to myself . . ." ? [1] But the fallacy that systems are infallible is unacceptable to those who live without the system.

Elgar's education was, for the most part, under his own supervision. He was a strict taskmaster. If (on the occasion of the conferment of the Freedom of the City of Worcester on Hubert Leicester) he appeared to consider that further public expenditure on public education was unnecessary it was not because he wished to deny advantages to others, but rather to demonstrate that opportunities are always to hand for the diligent and curious.

It was part of Elgar's early concern that he should move with ease among people of knowledge. The tradition of a cathedral city was towards book learning : the man of culture was remarked by his acquaintance with the classics, his knowledge of history. An independent love of books for their own sake has been noted among earlier Elgars and Greenings. Edward's accomplishment in letters was as astonishing as his tastes were wide. He left no page unturned in his effort to become a " scholar."

It may well be claimed that Elgar's library, built up from boyhood by inheritance, by the early investment of pocket-money and casual earnings, was a library for every taste : the deduction is clear. We may, then, show some of the limits of his reading habits and reflect on the injustice of the charge that he lacked literary culture.

On the classical side he possessed several editions of the *Greek Anthology*, including that in 6 volumes by W. R. Paton, the *Anthologia Polyglotta*, Homer's *Odyssey* in H. B. Cotterill's translation, and

[1] Foreword to *Forgotten Worcester*, H. A. Leicester.

Paley's *Greek Wit*. The chronicles—of Froissart, Holinshed and Baker—were to him, as Chapman's *Homer* to Keats, first causes of imaginative exploration. The cheap editions of the 1870s and 1880s were a godsend to the earnest student, and Elgar eagerly purchased the classics of English literature in the friendly formats of the " Chandos Classics," or the " Canterbury Poets," or the Tauchnitz edition.

One day, in 1880, in Birmingham for a rehearsal of Stockley's orchestra, he acquired Philip Bourke Marston's *Song-tide* : *poems and lyrics of love's joy and sorrow*, for he had the true bibliophile's incapacity to leave the second-hand dealer's shelves without purchase. Bray's edition of Evelyn's *Diary* was a great solace in the lonely days of early marriage and the pencilled glosses of Alice Elgar still remain. In boyhood Elgar read Adelaide Proctor, as a young man he admired the Tennyson *Birthday Book*, the slender poems of the Honourable Roden Noel, and the curiosities of *The Reliques of Father Prout*. In middle life he settled to a critical appreciation of Donne. In prose reading he graduated by way of Emerson, and Longfellow, and Mallock's *New Republic*, to Gray and Walpole, and the eighteenth century in general. Herein lay one of his deepest interests and in this field he exercised his most critical faculties.[1]

From Elgar's acquaintances in literature came some attractive first editions. Principal among these, of course, were several from Bernard Shaw : others from Binyon, E. V. Lucas—his *Hambledon Men* inscribed " from Edward II to Elgar I," Henry James, Emile Cammaerts, Sidney Colvin, Arthur Pinero—" with profound admiration and regard," and many friends with autobiographies of varying quality.

Croake James's *Curiosities of Law and Lawyers* stood among his *belles lettres* as symbolic of an interest, which he never lost, in a rejected career.

In fiction Elgar moved from Scott and Lord Lytton and those former set pieces—*Artemus Ward*, *Charles Anchester* and *Lorna Doone*—to Jane Austen, Anatole France and Samuel Butler, to O. Henry and Phillips Oppenheim, to Edgar Wallace and P. G. Wodehouse. He also possessed most of Hardy.

Elgar was a careful, studious reader, going through his reward-

[1] See *Gray, Walpole, West and Ashton—The Quadruple Alliance* : letter to the *Times Literary Supplement*, Sept. 4, 1919.

ing texts with a pencil in hand. His copy of Graham Tomson's edition of Selections from the *Greek Anthology* lies before me. This was one of his favourite books. Many versions of individual poems he collated with other translations and noted his preferences : thus Bateson's treatment of Anacreon's " Cupid, in a bed of roses " and Edwin Arnold's of " Love once among the roses " he thought inferior to that of Herrick, and Andrew Lang's " They told me, Heraclitus " to Cory's. Where there were alternative versions of particular poems in Bohn, or Loeb, or Richard Garnett, he catalogued them. He observed and underlined infelicities of vocabulary, dismissing Alma Strettell's and Robert Bland's attempts respectively as " wordy & poor " and " Wretched stuff." Likewise he marked for remembrance—he was apt at quotation—frequent words and phrases. He had that capacity, defined by Sir Richard Livingstone as necessary to the full appreciation of the classics, for seeing the relation between the poem and the incident or person to which it might be relevant. By his reading he often interpreted his own experience and gave play to his humour. On a sad stay-at-home piece by Agathias on the dull life of " poor women-children nurtured daintily " he inscribed " Suffragettes ! " As for Nicharcus's.

The screech-owl sings; death follows at her cry
Demophilus strikes up; the screech owl dies

he pointed an arrow at Demophilus and wrote on its tail " Henschel " [George]. Over and above these glosses he marked verses for setting and in some cases worked out the rhythmic scheme for music. The setting was a by-product of his reading rather than the reverse.

He had an eye for out-of-the-way pieces in old periodical literature (which drew him to the Club libraries and sale rooms in London), and would send E. H. Fellowes into the library at Windsor Castle for obscure authorities in and on the eighteenth century. This was the period of his choice, as is apparent in the vocabulary and rhythm of his own prose. There are also relics of eighteenth-century calligraphic habits in his hand writing. His acute knowledge of, and his researches into, Shakespeare are in his essay on *Falstaff*, but there may also be considered his " Scott & Shakespeare " (*Times Literary Supplement*, July 21, 1921). In 1930 John Murray tried hard to extract an autobiography from Elgar. That he failed is our loss.

Elgar's love of travel and of antiquity is reflected in his collection of guide books, and also in pencil sketches and diary notes of his travels abroad. He drew architectural features for his own record and for the enlightenment of his friends, and hinted at the depth of his archæological feeling when on his " true portraicture " [*sic*] of the Norman font in Burghill Church, Herefordshire, he put a note to Griffith—" What a pity I was not brought up to architecting." In the ancient buildings of his own countryside—and in those of Austria—Elgar appreciated sturdy craftsmanship. He was himself accustomed, from youth, to use his hands. He was ready at all times to turn to with saw, and plane, and chisel ; and he left various monuments of industry ranging from a pen-stand to a restored summer-house. This craft he learned from his father, who had once been apprenticed to a cabinet-maker, from Uncle Henry who built the coach house at Broadheath, and from Ned Spiers.

There was, he considered, merit in doing things properly. So when he took up rabbit-keeping and fish culture on Carice's account he added books on those subjects to his library. Curiosity led him to chemistry and biology and if memories of his experimental work are mostly of noisome smells and untoward explosions there was no lack of theoretical background : Griffin's *Scientific Text-Book*, Tilden's *Chemistry*, Ramsey's *Modern Chemistry*, Attfield's *Chemistry*, Crowther's *The Microscope*, Beck's *The Microscope* and Lankester's *Half hours with the Microscope* were all to hand. Compton Mackenzie alludes, movingly, to Elgar's romantic love of microscopic study in the first essay in his *Echoes*.

All the time that Elgar devoted to his " Ark " at Hereford and to his workshop at Severn House—where night after night he examined and documented botanical specimens—was an extension of his determination to answer riddles. His flair for solving puzzles of one sort and another was considerable. In 1898 he was engrossed by problems set in *Pearson's Weekly*, in 1927 by those in the *Observer*. In the one instance he was one week complimented on his success and presented with a pencil-case, in the other he congratulated " Torquemada " on his ingenuity and asked for his cross-words to be published collectively.

A willing victim of the problem-setter Elgar enjoyed turning the tables. Thus he would salute his friends with anagrams whenever he could. Or he would run his delight in mystification into practical joking. A favourite word of his was " jape." One jape, with a wry turn, took this form—masochistic in its reflection of what his detractors sometimes said.

> *Propriety Villa*
> *147 Precise Gardens, Parallel Road.*
> *Dec.* 6 : 1901

DEAR SIR :

I understand that you are a friend of Dr. Elgar's and I believe you with others have subscribed to a fund to provide him with robes suitable to his degree. My object in writing is to warn you not to make too much fuss of this young man & I wish you would warn Doctor Richter against playing his music. It is very bad for him and especially for other British composers. You will I trust forgive me, a stranger, for writing to you but I feel on the subject of Elgar's music very deeply. I was at Leeds festival with some friends when some piece of his was played by the band : my lady friends said it was very dry and I said so too. You will now see that you and your friend Dr. Richter are quite wrong in taking any notice of this young man whose music is dry. I hear he is very rude and conceited and that the receipt of the doctor's robes has made him worse —if this is possible—I enclose a temperance card and if you could get Dr. Elgar to sign it and to give up writing music I should be grateful and should feel I have not lived in vain.

With apologies for troubling you

> I remain dear Sir
> Yours truly
> (MRS.) LETITIA BARNETT

To Henry Ettling, Esq.

The author, of course, was Elgar, but he thought fit to reply to his *alter ego* by sending to Ettling a new " moral " coda for *Cockaigne* (facing p. 161). The " japes " in the music were various— ranging from the largest of all, the *Enigma*—to detailed references— by means of anagrammatic arrangement of note names—to persons he disliked in the demons' chorus in *Gerontius*. Outside of music the leg-pulling propensities were more obvious—and sometimes more embarrassing. In some ways Elgar never grew up. But that incapacity was not then so uncommon as, perhaps, it is in these days.

"Recollections of Edward Elgar remind me of the U.B.Q. (You Be Quiet) Club. This club was founded by my father and Archibald Ramsden, a well-known Yorkshireman of Park Row, Leeds, and Bond Street, London. Archibald Ramsden was a piano dealer by trade and a patron of the arts in his spare time. I believe he once owned Reynolds' 'Little Boy Blue.' He married the daughter of Sir Rowland Hill, inventor of the penny postage.

"Membership of the U.B.Q. Club was open to any of Ramsden's friends on payment of 5/- subscription, which carried with it the right of a free whisky and Polly whenever the member liked. Among the original members, besides Ramsden and my father were Hans Richter the great conductor, Nathaniel Vert, the famous concert agent and Elgar. They had a Ritual which took place at every gathering. Archibald Ramsden, the President, would take up a hugh shillelagh lying on the table and bring it down with a thump and surveying the gathering would shout ' *You* be Quiet.'

"During the existence of this Club several great artists were discovered. Besides this conviviality, the members met for the purpose of furthering the cause of music. If I remember rightly it was at an audition before N. Vert, my father, Ramsden and Richter that a young lady electrified everyone with her glorious voice. She was Clara Butt ! [1] "

Elgar categorised his mysteries. There were little mysteries : these were funny. There were large mysteries : these were challenging and sometimes painful. There was the ultimate Mystery. Here we return to his library shelves. There were numerous editions, including some modern translations, of the Bible and the apocryphal writings : a *Latin Manuale*, a *Vesperale Romanum*, a *Graduale Romanum*, and a German prayer book. There were volumes by R. H. Charles and H. B. Swete on the *Apocrypha* and the apocryphal *Acts* ; commentaries on the *Psalms* by Jennings and Lowe, on the *Minor Prophets* by R. G. Molton, on the *New Testament* by T. E. Page, J. Armitage Robinson, E. Robinson, P. W. Schmiedel and R. B. Rackham ; works on the *History of the Early Church*, the *Eucharist*, and the *Didache* by W. B. Frankland, Archbishop Whateley, W. A. Blake, H. Cox, E. Renan, Dean Farrar and H. Kelly ; translations of the *Hymns of the Early Church* by J. Brownlie ; more

---

[1] From the MS. of *Forty Years a Music Publisher*, Florian Williams.

general works on theology such as H. Latham's *The Risen Master* and pastoral essays by anonymous priests and published by Burns, Oates and Washbourne. There was also James New's *Traditional Aspects of Hell*, which Elgar—to Lady Elgar's discomfiture—would keep prominently displayed. Such was the reading which continued from the instruction of Francis Reeve and Father Waterworth to the composition of *The Kingdom*. Even in 1922 or 1923, the successor to *The Kingdom* not quite out of mind, he was studying Dr. R. H. Charles's commentary on the *Revelation*.

Like his *Greek Anthology* these volumes were annotated—and it is at the back of his *New Testament*, acquired in 1882, that the oratorios are detailed: I *The Apostles*, II *The Kingdom*, III *The Judgement*, *The Saints*, *The Vision*, *The Throne*, *The Holy City*, *The Fulfilment*. Of these titles proposed (*circa* 1909) for the third part of the trilogy that which Elgar marked as the best was *The Saints*.

Brought up as a Catholic in a devout household, and in a community where ancient traditions were strong, Elgar developed an attitude that may be defined as medieval. From this came a perfervid mysticism. On the other hand he was ardent in enthusiasm for the scientific developments that revolutionised the period in which he came to maturity. Most of us possess a medieval-renaissance, romantic-classic duality, but of the two warring elements one generally prevails : the other remains, but in submission. The source of much of Elgar's unhappiness as a man, as also of his genius, was this perpetual conflict, which was never resolved. In religion he moved away from " orthodoxy " not, I think, because he had too little faith but because he had too much. The pointlessness of sterile controversy, the officiousness and slick competence of so many of the professionally religious in all denominations, the supine acceptance of huge suffering as compatible with the ideals of Christianity, distressed him into anger or silence. It has been stated that Elgar " lost his faith." This is not so. " When in your last hour (think of this) all faculty in the broken spirit shall fade away and die into inanity—imagination, thought, effort, enjoyment —then at last will the night flower of Belief alone continue blooming, and refresh with its perfumes in the last darkness." Elgar carried with him this apothegm of Jean Paul Richter, copied from a copy of *Levana* which he found one day at Schuster's. He believed in God—but finally not in any theologian's concept—and he believed in the essential goodness of human nature in its many forms.

Elgar was an individualist and admired individualist qualities in others. His friendships, established, were durable and none was dissolved by any word or action of his. His gratitude and deepest affection was for those who first helped him—to Hubert Leicester, Hugh Blair, Troyte Griffith, Frank Schuster, Edward Speyer; for those who could treat him with natural equality—King Edward, Aylwin, the Sussex farmer, Lindsay Macarthur, Lord Charles Beresford; for those whose respect for his music was genuine and untouched by obsequience—Nicholas Kilburn, Ivor Atkins, Willie Reed, John Austin, Landon Ronald, Adrian Boult. He was devoted to his family and among great artists conspicuous for his domesticity. His loyalty to Lady Elgar was monumental. Her understanding of him in fundamental things was equally monumental. Lady Elgar had social values which might now be criticised as false; she was often outrageously wrong in her judgments; she was less of a writer than she thought herself to be. But the obverse was her adamantine devotion. She considered every material need of her husband and, with tactful charm and without jealousy, encouraged his friendship with those young and ardent women—to whom an artist is as a candle to the moth—whose presence entertained him and whose good offices frequently relieved the drudgery of composition. Some of these young women have fallen into autobiography and shown, perhaps, rather more of themselves than of their hero.

This naturally bookish man, for necessity's sake, made himself into a public figure. In public life he was, inevitably, variable. He would at one time enjoy the great social occasion, and enliven it with wit and eloquence; but at another would withdraw himself, not always with grace. At one moment he could be unconscionably gay and frivolous; at another shy, or subdued to the point of moroseness. He would ignore praise or censure, but again in the face of either display extreme delight or gloomy concern. He was exquisitely, painfully sensitive. He would laugh uproariously or weep unashamedly. In some ways he might be said by the less sensitive to have shown a lack of self-control, while others might remark that his public handicap was lack of sophistication. The comments of his acquaintances show those facets of character which they noted. Arnold Bennett, who at one time sought Elgar as an intellectual giant, at another set him down as " a disgruntled old man . . . full of affectations, always saying something silly." [1] Yet in the same period of his life Eugene Goossens could call him " an amazing, lovable man." Bennett noted the lassitude, Goossens the energy. It was at a Gloucester Festival that he, with Reed, Bliss and Elgar walked along the banks of the Severn. Elgar, he said, " not only outwalked us all, but completely outmatched us in matters of local history & topography." [2] It was, perhaps, Hugh Walpole who caught him most characteristically. Elgar frequently appeared to mirror the company he was with. In many ways Walpole and he were alike. So Walpole found him " as simple & full of fun as a boy . . . He was always to me kind & generous & even tender. Never anyone with less side." There are memories of his quiet generosity and of his lack of side. An old, retired nurse in Worcester, who had been of some service to the Elgar family, was surprised one day with the arrival of a new gramophone—a gift from Sir Edward. On one occasion in his last years Sir Edward arrived at the door of Messrs. Spark's music shop simultaneously with a tramp. Sir Edward opened the door, saying, " After you, sir ! " It is notable that no painter among all those who attempted his portrayal could do justice to Elgar. He was, said Griffith, himself a painter of charm and precision, too " various " for any painter to summarise his character.

There are few professions so arduous as that of music. Elgar has been criticised for his frequent avoidance of musicians and for his odd tastes in music. He was a law to himself—because he was practically the only British musician who determined to make a career in composition and in nothing else, when by it he knew he must earn his living. He planned his work and, on the whole, adhered to his plan rigorously. He sketched his music at various times—more often than not in the open air—but from 9 to 1 daily he made it a rule to write down his fugitive thoughts in permanent form.

" When he began writing he sat at his upright piano, trying themes and making notes on music paper and later he sat at a table getting up from time to time to try a few bars on the piano. But he often said that he realised his music as the finished orchestral effect not as the sounds on the piano.

[1] See *Arnold Bennett*, Reginald Pound, p. 344 (pub. London, 1952).
[2] See *Overture and Beginners*, E. Goossens, p. 193 (pub. London, 1952).

Orchestration was a carefully organised business. Lady Elgar prepared the paper for the full score and he worked methodically doing ten or twelve pages a day. When the parts came from the printers, he played through every note of every part on the piano with Mr. Austin playing the violin or viola, ruthlessly stopping in the middle of a bar, never wasting a second. They played the violin concerto on a Sunday at Hereford from 10 o'clock in the morning to 11 o'clock at night only stopping for meals. Elgar objurgating Novellos when he found a mistake." [1] But when he had finished work he was off-duty and more inclined to follow his other interests than to deal in the small talk of the profession.

He had an eccentric opinion that composers should be adequately remunerated for their work and he had a distaste for those, who while paying lip service, were only too ready to exploit the native artist. He felt it when incompetent performers reaped more from a single performance than the composer who had made their opportunity. In adopting this attitude he made enemies and ran into trouble with publishers and agents. But there were old memories which died hard : of the humiliation endured as a peripatetic fiddler, as the inexperienced provincial, or the visiting music teacher in the ladies' seminaries of Malvern ; if, he said, he had not had to teach he would have written *Caractacus* ten years earlier. Inevitably he compared his career with these of others who, with far greater opportunities, had achieved temporary success by membership of a clique rather than by virtue of their own merits. Standing aside from " schools " and " movements " Elgar was not obliged to consider at any time which were the proper names to applaud. So he approved Handel—" the greatest figure in religious music, for he had a sense of Beauty and Humanity which belonged so much to himself," [2] Bach—the slow movement of the concerto for two violins being "the most divine thing ever written," [3] Haydn, Mozart, Mendelssohn, Beethoven, Brahms ; Berlioz, Liszt, Tchaikovsky, Wagner ; Schumann, because he found affinity in Schumann's thought and expression ; but also Puccini, Delibes, Sullivan, German, Eric Coates. Debussy he did not much like finding his music " lacked guts." Of " modern men " and of pre-eighteenth-century music he was generally intolerant. He would, however,

---

[1] MS. notes of A. Troyte Griffith.
[2] See *Just as it happened*, Newman Flower, p. 264 (London, 1950).
[3] Letter to Troyte Griffith, Mar. 28, 1925, *in re* recording by Kreisler and Zimbalist.

find unexpected delight in jazz records, which he occasionally recommended to Shaw, and in the records of Jack Hulbert and Cicely Courtneidge. His eccentricities of taste were part of Elgar's humility. He himself had once written minstrel songs and was not the one to denigrate the neat musicianship and the social value of " light " musicians : it was pretentiousness in composition that he hated.

As a conductor Elgar was safe rather than brilliant, and an innate nervousness sometimes induced insecurity among players who were not familiar with him. He was impatient of professional incompetence and would not allow indifferent standards among amateurs. When the Worcestershire Philharmonic Society were insufficiently rehearsed—through the bad attendance of tenors and basses at afternoon practices—he refused to conduct the winter concert of 1902 unless the committee would postpone the perform-ance. As this was not practicable he withdrew, Granville Bantock taking his place. There was another, similar, episode during the rehearsals for the Three Choirs Festival in July 1921 at Hereford.

" The Worcester contingent had received their copies in good time, and by the time the combined rehearsal was due to take place, Worcester knew the work quite well. It was learnt afterwards that Gloucester and Hereford had only received their copies a few days previously, and it was fairly obvious that these two contingents would be ' all at sea ' with what was an entirely new and very difficult work to read at sight. This fact was only discovered afterwards—when it was too late to remedy.

" The *Music Makers* was down for rehearsal by the Three Choirs (or contingents), and Sir Edward stepped up on to the conductor's rostrum, facing with eager (if that is not too strong a word) looks at his chorus, who were about to let him hear what they could do with this work, to which they were hitherto strangers.

" A start was made, but many stops had to be made to correct mistakes and false starts. We of Worcester knew our work, but it was soon evident that the other two choirs were entirely lost, and they entirely overwhelmed all the good work we were doing. Alto-gether it looked pretty hopeless ; Elgar was at first disappointed, and then incredulous, and at last he was furious, until he suddenly threw down his baton and remarked in a quiet and cutting tone :
You don't appear to know anything about the work. That will be all.'

" He immediately got down from the rostrum, and walked out of the room, at the Shire Hall, and we never saw him again on that occasion. I believe Sir Ivor Atkins privately explained the cause of the disaster to him, and the work had a splendid performance at the Festival in the following September.

" In rehearsals Sir Edward was never ' fussy,' and he did not worry over trifles so long as the general effect was satisfactory, and it was more due to Elgar's personality, and the choir's great admiration and love for the ' master,' that his works always had first-class performances at concerts and festivals ever afterwards." [1]

Elgar frequently and unostentatiously went out of his way to assist amateur musicians. He founded the Malvern Concert Club in 1903 and—impatient of committees—laid down a constitution which was that later adopted by the national Federation of Music Clubs. In 1906, after his experience at the Morecambe Festival, he was anxious that the village singers of South Worcestershire should hear the really superb singing of the Hanley Cauldon Choir. Because they could not afford more he charged 1s. a head and helped to defray some of the expenses by entertaining the choir to lunch. In this is shown his characteristic practical sense and his generosity.

Human nature consists of paradoxes threaded on inconsistencies. Elgar's personality was more subtle than most and defies easy definition. He was infuriating, lovable, proud, modest, gregarious, solitary, gay, morose ; a dreamer, a man of affairs ; it depended when and where he was encountered. He was as Griffith wrote " a very complex character ": to which should be added Griffith's summary of the fundamental Elgar as he knew him—" a good hater but a better friend." The music of Elgar is, in large part, the reflection of his character. He himself knew this and refused John Murray's invitation to write his autobiography. He would have written a good one, but he felt it superfluous. When asked the meaning of his 'cello concerto he replied : " A man's attitude to life."

[1] From MS. by Hugh F. Bradburn.

PART TWO

PART TWO

CHAPTER XVI

IN SEARCH OF A STYLE

Le génie n'est qu'une grande aptitude à la patience.

du Buffon

I MUST confess that in childhood it was often encouraging to feel that great composers were not entirely remote, nor entirely inaccessible. A stray minuet, air, gavotte or sonata—by the age of twelve we had ourselves and our Sunday visitors introduced to the small talk at least of Beethoven, Handel, Bach, Mozart, Haydn.

It is not necessary, of course, to write domestic miniatures in order to become a great composer. But it helps. It helps to avoid sententiousness ; it helps the perspicacious artist to see the other point of view ; it helps, in the long run, to accomplish gracefully. In Elgar's domestic music there is an abundance of charm and affection—very much the reflection of the man (and boy).

Elgar the composer made his début, according to the records, at the age of ten. Then he sketched some of the pieces which grew up, over a period of thirty-seven years, into *The Wand of Youth* Suites : *opera* 1A and 1B. The earliest sketches still extant, however, date from ten years after the production of the children's play and betray the further skill which, by 1879, he had acquired. The first manuscripts then to be considered as representative of the boy Elgar are those of *The Language of Flowers* and *Chantant*, the first a song, the second a pianoforte piece. It may strongly be suspected that the somewhat lengthy apostrophe to the forget-me-not, which is the substance of the poem of the first, was also the original work of Edward W. Elgar (the author is veiled on the title page beneath " Percival ").

As music *The Language of Flowers* has its defects. Downstairs in the shop in High Street were available all the best ballads—of

Bishop, or Loder, or Hatton (to quote the best and not the worst). Edward had little difficulty in reaching their general standard, and in the comfortable atmosphere of D major. But there are hints of more than mere imitative competence. Quite without relevance to the general tenor of the scheme the pianoforte stretches up, sequentially, and with a slight hesitancy of rhythm leaves an unmistakeable imprint (Ex. 1).[1]

Chantant is equally trivial and equally impressive. Here is a piece in A minor—air, air with variation, middle section, air, coda —of methodical pattern, and ranging from *pp* to *fff*—also largely drawn from the downstairs stock. But the middle section stands still in long chords which ask for the *sostenuto* of strings and, as a tenor fragment wanders loose, for the guiding voice of a solo viola ; there is some warming exchange of courtesies between rival dominant sevenths above a pedal ; before the final cascade of semiquavers there is, sudden and surprising, a silent bar. The boy had an ear for the effective disposition of sounds. At the same time he recognised sterner ideals, for a fugal exposition in G minor— for organ—is representative of deeper studies.

This, we may presume, was as far as his father and Uncle Henry could help Edward along the career of composition. He arrived, however, at the age of fourteen with at least a keen sense of moral propriety in music : his grammar was impeccable. From then his progress depended on himself.

To become a composer, granted some basic aptitude and a lively imagination, it is obligatory only to follow one principle : to compose and to go on composing. It is in the going-on that difficulties arise. Elgar went stolidly on for thirty years. At the end of thirty years his apprenticeship was over and he enjoyed some general recognition. The characteristic of his long initiation was his readiness to accept all obligations and commissions. So his style in all its branches begins to emerge from his Worcestershire background.

The disadvantage of having an overworked father he turned to profit by a not altogether altruistic keenness to undertake such of the back work as his father would delegate. For some occasion in 1874 at All Saints' Church a string orchestra was employed. Edward, by now ardent as fiddler, wrote an introduction to the anthem and

[1] This and subsequent references in chapters 16–23 are to the musical examples which appear consecutively from page 383 to page 397.

scored it—with one eye on Haydn, and a consequent duplication of the 'cello line by the violas. But Anglican Church anthems were poor things. The choir at St. George's might not be more than mediocre but at least they sang—as a matter of routine—selections from Vincent Novello's prolific catalogue of Catholic music and, ceremonially, the masses of Haydn, Mozart and Hummel. Assiduously Elgar, first as assistant and then as principal organist of St. George's, set himself the dual task of increasing his own knowledge and expanding the horizons of the faithful and not too critical.

Mozart himself was not quite clear as to what the middle movement *Allegro* of the Violin Sonata in F (K.547) was meant to be. Manifestly it was no violin piece so he arranged it for pianoforte. Elgar had other ideas. Within the framework of the movement he set a choral insertion—a complete *Gloria in excelsis Deo*. From this exercise he turned to Beethoven. Similar but more extensive joinery fitted together sections of the fifth, seventh, and ninth symphonies into a *Credo*. (The arranger was put down as " Bernhard Pappenheim.") The *Allegretto* of the seventh symphony furnished material for the opening—the viola and 'cello countersubject branching out at "et ex patre . . ."; the major middle section, translated by Elgar to F major, taking up at " genitum non factum." The *adagio molto* of the ninth, now in A flat, was introduced at the words " et incarnatus." At " et in spiritum " the opening music returned, going, however, by way of D major to A major, in which unaccustomed splendour the second " subject" of the first movement of the fifth symphony (Fate being debarred from knocking at the door) took over the " vitam venturi."

Two points emerge. Elgar shows in these pieces an emotional appreciation of Mozart and Beethoven, and also his attitude towards the function of the choral unit in choral-instrumental work. The choir does not exist to state the words, which are in any case so familiar as to need no direct statement, but musically to express their significance. This is even clearer in an original *Credo* of 1877 where the chromatics of Beethoven's *Mass in C* have left their mark. We begin to understand the glory, but the necessary limitations of *Gerontius*, *The Apostles* and *The Kingdom*.

By 1878 Elgar took his courage in both hands and began a *Salve Regina* without the assistance of Mozart or Beethoven, but with some reference to the plaintive Mendelssohn of " Lord, bow thine ear " in *Elijah*. A curious key contrast occurs in this *Salve Regina*, for the middle section counters the main key of D major with A minor, in which two solo sopranos are set above and in contrast to tenors and basses in unison. In passing one is bound to observe a poignant descending seventh within the shape of the melody. This is probably the work which was performed at St. George's on June 6, 1880. In that year Polly Grafton copied Edward's *O Saluturis hostia*, a fluent piece which moves confidently to pious conclusions in evocative harmonies, handed into the English ecclesiastical system by Vincent Novello from Steibelt, Reinagle, Himmel, Spohr. Elgar followed the approved scheme, but by moving his voices—the sopranos being taken up to most unchristian heights—took the self-satisfaction out of the conventional chords of sevenths and ninths. Another *O Saluturis* of 1882, anticipates " Nimrod " and the final chorus of *The Kingdom* in breadth, simplicity, and tonality. On his *Ave Verum*—" in memoriam W. H. obit Jan. 27, 1887 "—Elgar noted one of the other main influences of English Victorian music : " Very Like ' Love Divine ' in *Daughter of Jairus*, Stainer." Within his organ loft Elgar broke new ground gently, but in private he sketched more striking possibilities. There is, for instance, in his sketches of 1882 a neat sequence—for the opening of a *Gloria*—which, pivoting on the mediant of each successive key passes from D major to F sharp major to B flat major and thence to the original key in the space of a dozen bars. But wisdom prevented such extravagance from exciting the liturgy and only the fragment remains. There were, however, less ambitious essays. Two hymn tunes written in 1878 enjoyed a more or less extended life, one—a " children's hymn " going *via* the *Westminster Hymnal* ultimately into the first movement of the *Nursery Suite* of 1931.

As in church so in his secular sphere Elgar showed apostolic zeal in making the classics available to his compatriots. There exist arrangements of almost everything from obscurities by Leybach to the last movement of Beethoven's violin sonata (Op. 23), for the wind quintet which met at the Leicesters on Sunday afternoons ; the tenth *concerto grosso* of Corelli and Handel's *Ariodante* overture stand prominently among arrangements for the Instrumental Society ; reductions for pianoforte of favourite passages of Wagner (*Tannhaüser* Act II, entry of the minstrels) and Schumann (the *Scherzo* of Op. 52) for private instruction. Ballads were reconstructed with fine and florid obbligati for Grainger the grocer to play; and when Mann Dyson, the lay clerk, decided on a solo from Weber, or Fred Pedley on one from the Christy Minstrel anthology, Edward was to hand to accommodate the accompaniment to the available instrumental resources. Once or twice he caught at folk-song, but his enthusiasm in that field was limited. In 1881 he began a *Fantasia on Irish Airs*, in which a pianoforte introduction of affecting eloquence, and with some regard to the *Ave Verum* style, breaks off at the entry of the solo violin with a modified form of Tom Moore's " The Valley lay smiling before me." This in turn is succeeded by two bars of variation. Some, no doubt, would discover Elgar's affection for the principle of monarchy in this subject, for was it not the song of " O'Rourke, Prince of Breffni " ? It was some nine years later that English folk-music—*pur sang*—made its brief appearance. Dr. Buck, ardent on the antiquities of Yorkshire, commanded an arrangement of " Clapham Town End " and received it by return of post. But that was as far as Elgar went in that direction.

The classical composer in one particular may be defined as one who works to order. Mozart thus obliged the freemasons on one hand, the Haffners on the other; for Elgar the City and County Pauper Lunatic Asylum and the committee of the Amateur Instrumental Society are substituted. The main part of his obligatory composition up to the time of his marriage lay in polkas, quadrilles, marches, minstrel songs and curtain-raising overtures. In the whole mass of this music one admires the monotonous efficiency, the facile setting down of commonplaces, the almost contemptuous ease with which material was poured into the rigid forms. Such discipline was useful in imposing appreciation of formal design and also aptness to purpose. It was not an inspiring occupation but once or twice personality showed through. The beginning of the *Christy Minstrel Overture* remains to display something of the impertinence of *Cockaigne*, and most of the *March: pas redouble*, played by the Amateur Instrumental Society in 1882, in which is the essential spirit of *Pomp and Circumstance*.

This march was scored for a reasonably full orchestra, but the Volunteers who engaged the band for their minstrel show were economical. Elgar's resources, therefore, comprised strings—but without double bass—flute, cornet, tambourine and bones. In the second bar of the overture the bones are marked *tremolo*, one effect which escaped even the imagination of Berlioz. Elsewhere Elgar dealt with almost every conceivable variety of ensemble. Within limits, for orchestras of Wagnerian stature were beyond possibility, he had more opportunities for experiment in instrumental sonorities than most composers. But, since his music was utilitarian, his effects must succeed. Thus there arose another stringent discipline. From this experience Elgar developed the capacity to think his music in terms of the instruments by which it was to be played. Scores began to take shape in which the desire to exploit tone colour took precedence and in which there was no suggestion of previous working-out at the keyboard. In larger pieces areas of score are blocked out. An overture with no more than a tenuous line of melody and an occasional chord to keep the tonality secure, but with leading ideas pencilled in at proposed entries will show the intended activity of the main groups of strings, brass and woodwind. It is, however, in the fugitive thoughts that the individual quality of Elgar clearly emerges in exquisite and whimsical fragments. So an air for oboe—with his brother Frank in mind (Ex. 2) ; a *Scene* in which the woodwind come and go above a tonic pedal sustained by muted lower strings (Ex. 3) ; a *Serenade* for cor anglais, where the characteristic mysterious tone of the instrument is increased by attendant bare fifths in the strings. Noted down in the same casual way are passages for " the play ": in 1879 the opening of the *March* (*Wand of Youth* Suite II) and of *Moths and Butterflies* (Suite II), and of the *Wild Bear* (Suite II) ; in 1881 the *Minuet* (*Wand of Youth* Suite I) in its entirety, but in short score.

Apart from these essays Elgar's personal interest in the violin was carrying him to little extravaganzas with which he himself might dazzle the neighbours. Among his earliest violin pieces stands the *Romance* dedicated to Oswin Grainger which, although not published until 1885, was composed in 1879. The violin part was completely done before a pianoforte accompaniment amplified the score : such was Elgar's estimate of the relative value of the partners in this ensemble. As a fiddle teacher he further felt obliged to write numerous studies, polonaises, and so on, which, on the whole, are an index to him as performer rather than as composer.

A young man in Elgar's circumstances was, sooner or later, bound to entertain wistful thoughts about the large works which would, God willing, take their place with the masterpieces of the past. Accordingly, he privately examined all conceivable avenues

of expression. As with folk-song so with the "modal idiom."
He at least noted the names of the ecclesiastical modes—with
their supposed derivation from more ancient Greek modes. These
were, characteristically and painstakingly, noted in Greek. Fugue
was a form which often curiously and fantastically fired his inspiration, and he worked, on and off, at fugal expositions which he
made less academic by writing as for strings. The ultimate way to
magisterial success, he decided, was through sonata form. In this
case he must, then, try his hand at symphony, string quartet, or
possibly other forms of chamber music. Taking the pattern of the
first movement of Mozart's G Minor Symphony (No. 40) and constructing a work of the same proportion, in the same key, and with
similar rhythmic figuration seemed a good way of starting. So,
in the winter of 1878, Elgar commenced this project. It did not
go very far, breaking off in full score at the entry of the "second
subject." The interest of this attempt lies not in what is like Mozart
but in what is not—in the incidental figures (Ex. 4 a, b), the one
with an air of expectation the other with a sense of swagger, and in
the scoring which runs to four horns—keeping them in fuller
occupation than ever Mozart would—and requires some early and
significant *divisi* passages.

Elgar made at the same time various attempts at string quartet.
As to form he was content with the conventions. This is, after
all, the safest way to develop in logic and fluency. In melodic
outline and in details of scoring, however, he allowed some freedom
to his personal inclinations. The result, up to a point, is arresting.
In incomplete first movements of two separate works, one in
D minor, the other in B flat major, vigour presides at the outset
(Ex. 5 a, b). In both cases the result is patently orchestral and, as
often in the case of Mendelssohn, the first violin line is overem-
phatic. Elsewhere among these sketches of the 1878–79 period
lies a theme, designated for string quartet, which may well have
been intended to balance 5a in a last movement (Ex. 5c).

Attainment in classical forms, though generously received in
more or less academic circles, was not enough. Romantic moods
weighed heavily on the young composer of 1878. Elgar knew his
Schumann—whose cross rhythms and deliberate counterpoint
inform the second subject of Elgar's D minor string quartet—and
his Berlioz: he had acquaintance with the pictorial moods of
Beethoven and had read a little of the style of Wagner. With an

ear for words, an eye for pictures, a deep sense of the mystery of antiquity, he needed little encouragement to attempt the more alluring aspects of what was then modern. So from the simple chanson-type " air de ballet " and the orderly minuet he proceeded to ballet. There are a number of ideas for this purpose noted side by side with the *Wand of Youth* music, which itself is impregnate with the spirit and movement of ballet. That they never reached fulfilment is not, perhaps, surprising ; but they represent one ideal which found other outlet. It was, for instance, recorded by Troyte Griffith that Elgar himself saw in the "*Enigma*" *Variations*—the substance of a ballet which, had the music been by a Russian he grumbled, would have been used for that purpose.

Elgar was a constant traveller in " realms of gold." With Tom Moore as his guide he inspected *Lalla Rookh* and commenced two separate pieces (intended as movements of a suite ?) on that gorgeous subject ; but again the project was stillborn. The locality of the poem was left until another occasion, for which *The Crown of India* was composed. From India Elgar turned to Hungary where there were Liszt and Brahms and, for that matter—since precision in geography was immaterial—Dvořák, as models ; so an *Ungarische* for violin and pianoforte was sketched, coloured by syncopation and an occasional augmented triad. Among these experiments stand others, more technical but more revealing. Chordal progressions worked out to extract the fullest flavour from their incidence. Some of these were hardy annuals; some—as a trite set of dominant sevenths, labelled " Les Cloches," merely tawdry ; but occasionally more striking ventures into chromaticism occur, as (Ex. 6). This hint of Wagner's " heavenly wanderer " (as yet not arrived in England) seems to have been intended for the Serenade for cor anglais and orchestra. It is a glimpse of the more mature Elgar, the same sequence appearing midway through the third scene of *The Black Knight*.

It is clear that Elgar was both opportunist and idealist—the two facets meeting in his passing sketches. In the six " shed books " are the outlines of the complete composer. The earliest pieces go back to 1871. In later life Elgar looked over these pieces again from time to time, so that old inspirations were repolished for *Rosemary* and for the *Starlight Express*. In 1930 recollection brought back a children's hymn for the *Nursery Suite* and, at that time, among his earliest essays he set the outlines of " The Merry Doll." Later still the " shed books " were drawn on for the opera *The Spanish Lady*.

The " shed books " show a composer of dances, marches, " morceaux de salon," and choral music ; they show aspiration towards the higher forms of chamber music and symphony (there are, besides the Mozart imitation, a couple of likely themes labelled respectively " 1st subject " and " 2nd subject ") ; programme music is there too. What is lacking is assurance in the use of vocabulary. Yet the basis of the familiar vocabulary of the Elgar of later years is recognisable.

In melodic outline there is already a feeling of spaciousness : no mincing behaviour with the point of a pencil but large, bold sweeps of a sizeable brush (see 5a, b, c). A melody which is worthy of repetition is repeated. Both 5a and 5b having been presented are immediately swept up into a second statement in octaves. Some of the characteristic intervals are shown (see Ex. 3, 4b and 5b ; the latter with a four note gesture which turns up again in *Froissart*). The sequential organisation is apparent (see Ex. 2). Some of these habits were caused by environment. The studious use of sequence is straight from the text-book : the ranging leaps of melody from playing the fiddle. In the emphasis given to melodies by an added top octave can be heard the provincial *chef d'orchestre* intent on audibility above the babble of provincial conversation. Tonally one would note, without further comment, that approximately two out of three ideas are set down in the minor.

The two poles of Elgarian rhythm may be described as pride and prejudice. Elgar had a flair for the obvious (see 5b). Equally he had a distaste for what was obvious, so, by holding melody notes across the accent he brought into his style a curiously nervous manner, which often is allied with whimsical notions of tonality. One rhythmic feature to be expected is the triplet. Here we may quote from 1879 (Ex. 7a, b). This, in the second form, is the phrase with which *The Black Knight* commences. Elgar discovered his plagiarism long afterwards : " how strange," he commented ; which shows how much a composer may unconsciously repeat. It is worth comparing Ex. 7a and 7b with the final version in the score of the Cantata.

Between Ex. 7b and Ex. 6 lies the harmonic territory still largely to be explored. In the former is the flamboyant—in small extravagances of period practice and in the frequent pressure of appogiaturas ; in the latter the mystical. It is not, however, the existence of chords in themselves that is musically interesting, but their situation. Elgar in a famous *obiter dictum* once suggested that music could be picked up in the air. The idea is sound, for music, so far as the creative musician is concerned, cannot be thought of in a paper existence. Much of Elgar's genius lay in his appreciation of sound effects on the ear. So, with a double intention, we may quote the introduction to an unfinished Easter Anthem, dated April 7, 1879 (Ex. 8). Clearly there is no considerable originality here—unless in the deferred phrase ending : but the siting and the spacing of the chords yields a suitably sombre atmosphere for the opening words—" Brother, He died for thee . . .". In relation to music in general this excerpt is of no great consequence, but for a community which approved Goss, Stainer, Barnby and Ouseley, it is almost outstanding. It is not far from this to the first 3/4 section in the *Light of Life* " Meditation," nor, in the matter of atmosphere, to the beginning of the " Prelude " to *Gerontius*. Ex. 8, in fact, shows up in its atmospheric finality as a *leit motiv* ; but it is homeless. Elgar's own reference [1] to the subject of *leit motiv* is here apposite : " I became acquainted with the representative-theme long before I had ever heard a note of Wagner, or seen one of his scores. My first acquaintance with the *leit-motive* was derived (in my boyhood) from Mendelssohn's *Elijah* and the system elaborated from that, as my early unpublished things show."

[1] *Musical Times*, Oct. 1900.

CHAPTER XVII

MUSIC FOR ORCHESTRA

Elgar was the last serious composer to be in touch with the great public.

Constant Lambert in Music Ho!

ELGAR'S ORCHESTRAL music falls into two main groups : one containing the non-symphonic, the other the symphonic. Within the latter group should be included what may be defined as the nearly symphonic. The range in this chapter is from *Salut d'amour* and the three *Characteristic Pieces* which comprise *Opus* 10 to the " *Enigma* " *Variations* and the *Introduction and Allegro* for strings. The larger works—those in symphonic manner—are reserved for later consideration ; not because they are of necessity more important, but because the intention behind them suggested that they ought to be. Such a work as *Cockaigne* may, if the skill and imagination are present, be written without *arrière-pensée*, but such as the 'cello concerto only from deep reflection and great spiritual energy.

The music with which we are immediately concerned may in turn be divided into six classes. There is, in continuation of many of the earlier unpublished sketches, a considerable amount of " domestic " music, in which Elgar's ingenuousness is frequently and charmingly uncovered. There are, for example, 'cello obbligati to popular ballads written for Dr. Buck, a tiny piece " for Dot's nuns " (1906) and a movement " for the Barbers " [1] for violin, mandoline and guitar (June 15, 1907). There are some evident " pot-boilers"—not, perhaps, so many as might be expected from the notoriety of the few. In them he shows his lack of what is sometimes now irreverently named as " ghastly good taste." There is descriptive music and a solid, impressive block of ceremonial music. One or two pieces qualify solely as " music for orchestra.'"

[1] See Index of Works, p. 406.

Finally there are a small number of transcriptions. This categorisation, naturally, is not ultimately binding, for many works may qualify for inclusion in more than one class. But it is a convenience to be able to distinguish the several main causes of Elgar's instrumental style.

His intimate music has an especial charm not only for its own sake but for its relation to his monumental works which often display their highest quality in intimate moments. In the " *Enigma* " *Variations* he stands mid-way between the delicacies of the *Wand of Youth* and the more comprehensive character of the symphonies and concertos. The *Variations* and the children's play music, however, are only two out of a number of works which are, so to speak, conversation rather than rhetoric.

In his smallest pieces Elgar reveals his affection for the instruments of the orchestra—an affection which extended also to the players of the instruments. It is notable that he was always at pains to allow independence to each timbre in his ensemble so that no player would ever feel ignored. Elgar's writing for strings and for brass has generally been extolled, largely, I suspect, because in those departments his style is most clearly that of a virtuoso. His woodwind writing is not less meritorious. It is, however, less ostentatious. So we may see it in quiet animation in his conversation pieces. There is better music, no doubt, than is contained in his Opus 10, but there is not so much that between 1883 and 1899 could have been so enchanting for amateur orchestras—such as he had in mind—to attempt. All three pieces were dedicated to Lady Mary Lygon. They were scored for a full-sized band, with double woodwind, four horns and the customary complement of trumpets and trombones ; but for the benefit of Worcester and Malvern, when without supernumaries, it was noted that the pieces might " be effectively performed by an Orchestra consisting of 1 flute, 1 oboe, 1 clarinet, 1 bassoon, 2 horns, 1 trumpet (cornet), drums and strings." However—" any other instrument in the Score may be added with corresponding gain in effect."

Of the three pieces the *Mazurka* is the least rewarding, for a persistent rhythmic figure stands in the way of melodic digression —and it is in his digressions that Elgar is often at his most characteristic ; but in the middle, in D major in contrast to the main key of D minor, the oboe, sometimes joined by flute and sometimes answered at a lower octave by clarinets and bassoons, picks up two points of rhythm and turns them to its own advantage (Ex. 9).

The *Sérénade* (formerly *Intermezzo*) *Mauresque* is an evocative adventure in G minor—major—minor, with a flattened sixth and a sharpened seventh standing prominent in the melodic contour of the minor section. The major section, based on a fragment which has its modal implications and is related to the *Grania and Diarmid* music, sets the woodwind chorus in apposition to the strings.

The *Gavotte* 1700-1900 follows the same formal pattern. It is in neat ternary form with a tidy coda and again the key contrast is between tonic minor and major : here again the key is that of G. The eighteenth century is represented by a tune in the minor, with slender thematic connections with the " Gavotte," also in G minor, in the 3rd *English Suite* of Bach. This is developed in easy counterpoint which has the effectiveness of Handel rather than the studiousness of Bach. Elgar, as always depending on ear rather than eye, was masterly in producing the effect of counterpoint without too much regard for academic scruples. In this work, for instance, the " filling-up " parts should be studied, for none, however insignificant intellectually, are without purpose to the ear or interest to the player. The cymbals strike twice ; the triangle and bass drum have a single note apiece. Here is an authentic mark of Elgar. From the *Gavotte* to the late Handel and Bach arrangements is a far cry but the same tendency to recreate brilliance from the past is present. I commend the *Gavotte* to the amateur band.

A composer who imitates another composer does so at his peril : he may easily produce either a travesty or a parody. Elgar's imitations, however, have the quality of commentary. This is certainly true of the *Minuet* in the first *Wand of Youth* suite. Here are gravity and tenderness—qualities which Elgar shared with Handel. This minuet—an authentic survival from his boyhood sketches—may be compared with that in G minor in the first of the second collection of Handel's suites for harpsichord. Strangely the comparison, with Handel's wide leaps and cumulative sequences, shows Handel for once as more Elgarian than Elgar.

The *Wand of Youth* music was published when the composer's career was approaching its zenith. It is, however, representative of his youth. It is—as Barrie's *Peter Pan*, which was produced two years before the first performance of the *Wand of Youth*—true to child thought, and unsentimental. The difference between this music and that of the three *Characteristic Pieces* lies less in manner than in matter. In those the main discussion was often commonplace. Here, however, there is nothing that is not engaging and original. The pieces are grouped thus—I " Overture," " Serenade," " Minuet (to which " the two old people enter "), " Sun Dance," " Fairy Pipers (who charm the old people to sleep)," " Slumber Scene," " Fairies and Giants ": II " March," " The Little Bells," " Moths and Butterflies," " Fountain Dance," " The Tame Bear," and " The Wild Bear."

This is " programme music," but it is not tied to a connected narrative, nor to what—in the first degree—may be considered as real. Therefore all that may be expected is a series of impressions —impressions such as may easily arise from a quick survey of the titles.

The greatest beauty comes from the most insubstantial subjects ; and it is in a capacity for understanding and portraying the properties of imagined images, which are none the less real for being imaginary, that Elgar excels. For imaginative truth there may especially be noted the clarinet melody of the "Serenade" (given, in recapitulation, to the fiddles), reflective but also a little *giocoso* ; the movement of the muted strings in the " Slumber Scene ", and the sense of tranquil darkness induced by the two bassoons and the single horn which thicken the harmony ; the distant, because muted, play of arpeggios in the " Fountain Dance."

The relation between the remaining music and the titles needs no underlining. It is clear in each that the gist of the matter is contained in the first bar or two. Take the opening of " Moths and Butterflies " or " Little Bells." The first shows apt movement, and, leaving a striking bass note behind, is aerial. It is, perhaps, tinged with regret ; for moths and butterflies are but ephemeral creatures. The second achieves its pretended tintinnabulations in piccolo, flute and clarinet. It is not merely a matter of choice of instruments, however, for the whole atmosphere is destroyed if the undulating six note group which commences is replaced by a regular four note group of semiquavers. So, throughout, melody, harmony and instrumentation are inseparable.

The idea of a work of art (it is called by various names by philosophers) exists in general in the artist's mind before it assumes particular shape. A non-musical idea (which may be concerned with love, or hate, or life or death) must by a musical mind be transmuted into a musical idea. A musical idea, however, exists only when it is patterned according to musical conditions. So while it is true that in any one of the *Wand of Youth* pieces the first bar or two is evocative it is also true that full significance is only apparent when the pattern includes a contrasting phrase, for pattern is based on variety as well as repetition. Elgar was content with the musical forms that he inherited. Sometimes, as in the present pieces, this was advantageous, but sometimes not. The *Wand of Youth* pieces, therefore, fall naturally into ternary form, or binary form, and they exhibit familiar modes of development. In this orderliness Elgar respected the model of Mendelssohn, whom he also resembled in other ways : spiritually in his understanding of the " elfin and spirit life," technically in his talent for *scherzo*, in his bright-coloured orchestration, in his whimsical treatment of minor tonality.

The *Nursery Suite* is an addendum to the *Wand of Youth* suites. Some of the music, as has been shown, comes from the early period. Three pieces are of equal quality—" The Serious Doll," " The Sad Doll," and the " Waggon Passes." The other pieces are good, except the tedious index of melodies interspersed with violin cadenzas which is the " Envoy," but somehow lack the inevitability of the earlier suites. In the *Nursery Suite* it is, as in a poem by Charles Lamb,

> ...... *most sweet to muse*
> *Upon the days gone by; to act in thought*
> *Past seasons o'er, and be again a child.*

Elgar shared with Lamb a rare ability to retire into what was. Indeed he equally shared Lamb's capacity for living not only what had been, but also what might have been. One illustration of this is in *Dream Children*, two of the most exquisite pieces ever written. " We are nothing ; less than nothing, and dreams. We are only what might have been, and must wait upon the tedious shores of Lethe millions of ages before we have existence and a name." Another turn and we are within the atmosphere of *The Starlight Express*, the interludes in *Falstaff*, the visionary music of *King Olaf* or *The Music Makers*, the Fantasy of *The Apostles*, or within *Gerontius*: Elgar's dreams were frequent.

There are thirteen pieces in the *Wand of Youth* suites. There are—after the theme—thirteen pieces in the *Enigma Variations*—plus one. The extra piece in the latter work stands apart. It is that which makes the complete sequence into a concert work and it " represents " the composer ; the others, as hardly needs saying, " representing " a number of his friends. The *Wand of Youth* pieces are variations, not on a theme but on an idea : the idea, or perhaps the ideal, of childhood. The idea behind the Enigma set was friendship. The work remains unique because this idea is felt to pervade the whole of the music, which in tenderness, wit, boisterous humour, gravity, valediction suggests some part of the relationship known to have existed between the composer and those signified at the head of the separate variations. The last variation was at first shorter [1] and, in scale, more in proportion to its fellows. Richter and others asked that it should be rewritten so " that it would make a better concert piece than the first which was played at St. James's Hall. The first was more intimate, he [Elgar] told me [2] that it meant something of this kind ' Well we have had a very pleasant evening. I am glad to hear what you all think about it. Good night.' "

Elgar considered the *Variations* with lasting pride. " Well," he said, rather grudgingly towards the end of his life, " they may live." He insisted, however, that " they ought to be considered as absolute music and that any personal allusions only concerned his subjects and himself." [3] At Marl Bank one day he and Griffith were discussing the work and " how (it) could be produced as a ballet (which Elgar said would have been done long ago if they had been written by a Russian); he said he visualised the scene as a banqueting hall. He or I suggested that the Enigma might be a veiled dancer. But when I said that she would unveil at the end and the orchestra would play the theme, he shook his head." [4]

It is commonly supposed that the " enigma " concerns a theme to which the actual theme on which the variations are based was a counter-subject. Elgar himself suggested that this was the case, even going so far as to say that " it was so well known that it was strange no-one had discovered it." Since on one occasion he set " God Save the Queen " as counterpoint to the 5/4 melody in Tchaikovsky's *Symphonie Pathétique*, and on another incorporated

[1] See pfte. arr. pub. 1899 (Novello), which has the original ending.
[2] Troyte Griffith MS.
[3] *ibid.*   [1] *ibid.*
[4] *ibid.*

Mendelssohn's *Wedding March* within his own *Cockaigne* it is not to be taken as impossible that the theme of the *Variations* began in this fashion, but the earliest existing sketch (facing p. 145) puts difficulties in the way. The middle section was originally planned as an 8-bar phrase and its reduction to 4 bars leaves any supposititious counter-theme adrift.[1] I am unconvinced that the enigma, or the whole of the enigma, lies in this matter of " theme " at all. Elgar's occasional Schumanesque and cryptical disposition of notes—shown by the immurement of some of those he disliked within the demons' chorus of *Gerontius*—suggests other avenues for the musical detective. But the best " jape " of all is the absence of any enigma—except the one Enigma of existence : the *Variations* were within the period of the composition of *Gerontius*.

In the works written before the *Variations* there are suggestions as to the musical pattern that might be followed, and these may be used as evidence against special artifice in the invention of the theme. There is predominantly the matter of key. The characteristic of the *Variations* is a Schubertian contrast between minor and major, which is at once stated in the theme. There were numerous occasions previously on which G minor was relieved by an episode or movements in G major. This sequence is, for instance, in the " March " and the " Tame Bear " of the *Wand of Youth*, the song *Like to the damask rose*, the *Organ Sonata*, the *Mazurka* and the *Gavotte* of the *Characteristic Pieces*, *Lux Christi* and *King Olaf*. *The Black Knight* reverses the process—G major—G minor—G major. The second movement of the *Organ Sonata* further exploits the subsidiary keys of the *Variations* and in the same sequence : C minor, C major, and E flat major.

The first noteworthy melodic shape in the Enigma theme is in the interval of the minor third. This is exploited forcefully in " The Wild Bear," and gracefully in the halting cadence of *Virelai* —where a dominant thirteenth extends wistfully—as at the end of Variation VIII. The other striking intervals of seventh and sixth are scattered throughout *King Olaf*, *Caractacus* and *Lux Christi*. Here, for example, is an unmistakably Elgarian gesture from the

[1] Such attempts as are made in Richard Powell's *Elgar's Enigma* (*Music and Letters*, Vol. xv, no. 3) reveal a degree of mathematical prestidigitation uncharacteristic of Elgar as composer. There should be remembered the captivating wit of Father Ronald Knox, who once proved, by an admirable show of logic, that Queen Victoria wrote *In Memoriam*.

last-named (Ex. 10).[1] In the E flat section of Scene IV of *The Black Knight* and again in the major opening of " The Conversion " in *King Olaf* are foreshadowings of the deep but simple dignity of " Nimrod." But the closest connections are with the *Gavotte* (Op. 10, No. 3), of which the melody is the melody of the "Enigma" before crystallisation (Ex. 11). The salient points are marked, but the general contour is suggestive. Further details are germane to the matter in which the Enigma theme extended in some directions (Ex. 12a, b and c). And at the end there is a fine full brassy *Largamente* which, *mutatis mutandis*, fits into the final triumph of Variation XIV.

In a sense then the *Variations* existed before they were written down. This is the case with all major works of all major composers. The occasion arises to call out accumulated experience. The only experience that Elgar lacked was in writing variations, for previous attempts had not extended further than the incomplete *Fantasia on Irish Airs*, the even more incomplete variations on the *Nursery Suite* hymn tune, and a set of variations for wind quintet on the " Evesham Andante."

We return to the matter of personality—and personalities. The *Variations* were " dedicated to my Friends pictured within." We cannot escape this matter of " picturing." Elgar was even specific in the notes which he prepared for issue with pianola rolls. [2]

In " C. A. E." (Caroline Alice Elgar) he stresses the " romantic & delicate inspiration " that she was. " H. D. S-P." (Hew David Steuart-Powell) was a pianist. The music, suggesting a Toccata, " humourously travesties his characteristic diatonic run over the keys before beginning to play." " R. B. T." echoes Townshend's dramatic impersonation of an old man. " W. M. B." recalls William Meath Baker *forcibly* [or does Elgar mean forcefully ?] reading out the arrangements for his guests and leaving the music room " with an inadvertent bang of the door." R. P. A. was a man of feeling but given to whimsical and witty remarks. "Ysobel" (Isobel Fitton) played the viola and the prominent viola part was contrived as an exercise in crossing the strings. (Years afterwards when conducting a performance of the Variations in Worcester, Elgar was astounded that Miss Fitton, despite " Ysobel," still

---

[1] No. 3.
[2] Republished, with additional material, by Novello & Co. Ltd. as *My friends pictured within.*

made the errors that he had sought to overcome.) "Troyte" in the "uncouth rhythm of the drums and lower strings was really suggested by some maladroit essays to play the pianoforte." "W. N." was "really suggested by an eighteenth-century house." "Nimrod" (Jaeger : "the dear friend, the valued adviser & the stern critic ") "is the record of a long summer evening talk, when my friend discoursed eloquently on the slow movements of Beethoven. . . . It will be noticed that the opening bars are made to suggest the slow movement of the Eighth Sonata (Pathétique)." "Dorabella "—"the pseudonym adopted from Mozart's *Cosi fan tutti* suggests a dance-like lightness." The first few bars of "G. R. S." are detailed precisely. Sinclair's bulldog Dan falls into the Wye (bar 1), paddles up stream (bars 2 and 3) and gives voice to a rejoicing bark on landing (2nd half of bar 5). "G. R. S. said ' Set that to music.' I did." [1] "B. G. N." (Basil Nevinson) played the 'cello. *** (Lady Mary Lygon) was on a sea voyage, so the throb of liner engines is admitted and, above it, a quotation from Mendelssohn's overture *Calm Sea and Prosperous Voyage*. As some doubts have, from time to time been expressed regarding the "portraiture " of Lady Lygon it may be said that Elgar's first sketches define this movement—" L " (for Lygon). In the sketches for the finale he suggests, but does not act on the suggestion, the re-introduction of " L. M. L." (Lady Mary Lygon). The same sketches show that one variation, not used, was headed " Kilburn," which, perhaps, is why *The Music Makers*, so intimately connected with the *Variations*, was dedicated to him.

"E. D. U." (cf. " Edoo," in the diaries, for Edward) shows what the composer, " writing at a time when friends were dubious & generally discouraging," intended to do.

To square that with the proposal that the work should be regarded as " absolute " music is, manifestly, difficult. Yet one point is immediately clear. In the majority of cases (R. P. A. is the clearest exception) there is no portraiture but a recollection of an incident or, in the case of the musical, a habit. To think of likenesses to specific people in terms of music is misleading. For instance Troyte, the scholar and artist, was quiet and seemingly aloof : his variation is, accordingly, the antithesis to his personality. As for Dorabella she was not " like " the music of her variation

---

[1] Further illuminating episodes in the career of Dan are shown in the Appendix on p. 398.

(there is yet to be born the woman who corresponds to that ideal of grace and beauty) ; but her attitude to Elgar, and his to her, in conversation and correspondence held for each both lightness and delicacy. The truth is that the capacity to write such music was already present and as the items flowed so did they appear to conjoin with everyday experience. A line of poetry stands for years and then it is seen, as Newbolt puts it somewhere, to be touched to truth by life. The last word on this matter shall be Elgar's.

On October 24, 1898, he wrote to Jaeger, " Since I've been back I have sketched a set of Variations on an original theme : the Variations have amused me because I've labelled 'em with the nicknames of my particular friends—*you* are Nimrod. That is to say I've written the Variations each one to represent the mood of the ' party.' I've liked to imagine the ' party ' writing the var. him (or her) self and have written what I think *they* would have written—if they were asses enough to compose. It's a quaint idea & the result is amusing to those behind the scenes and won't affect the hearer who ' nose nuffin ' What think you ? "

In Variation I the melody, enhanced by wide-spaced figuration in the strings, inspires a " fountain dance " in slow motion. Variation II, the theme in the bass, shows Elgar as contrapuntist. But the counterpoint has a ghostly quality, which is increased by the allusive chromatics, and is far from any solemnities of the study : it was not for nothing that Elgar did most of his sketches out of doors. Variation III has light and darkness, a delicate oboe fancy catching sunlight, as does the clarinet tune of the *Wand of Youth* serenade, and more morose qualities coming in the middle section through the lower woodwind. The bassoons link the middle to the final section when the flute edges the oboe tune. Next comes a study in energy, the theme being rhythmically transposed into a 3/4 *Allegro di molto*.

Variation V commences a new chapter. Hitherto the tonic key has been maintained. But here C minor, characteristically deferred by the long omission of the leading note, supervenes. The melody is given to 'cellos and basses, helped by bassoons. Above is a long, rich counter-tune in 12/8 time. At figure 17, after the contrasting glitter of chattering woodwind, the bass and the treble of this counterpoint change places, the original theme now showing in woodwind and horns *above* the 12/8 melody. The rapid passage again appears before the dominating idea resolves, above a drum roll, into C major. In this key Variation VI—the viola solo, though contrasted with occasional arpeggios from the clarinet—is held. Variation VII follows in the same key. Then the melody is reduced to a rhythmic pattern except when the scale passage (based on bars 7–10 of the original theme) rushes impetuously forward. The Beethovenian energy of the basses and drums was previously hinted at in the last movement of the *Organ Sonata*. Attention in this variation should be directed to the *brillante* runs of the strings : Tchaikovsky never achieved more incisively than this.

The pretty antiphony of strings and woodwind of Variation VIII may be seen in simpler form in the middle of the *Sérénade Mauresque*, where, however, there was no comparable comeliness of rhythm. The sequence of sixths in which first the clarinets, next the flutes, and then the violins rise and fall is a conspicuous feature of Elgar's style. The ornamentation (cf. Example 12c) which is noticeable is also a feature of his style, but it is not always employed so tactfully as here. Without a break, the music swivelling round on G to the new key of E flat major, Variation IX follows.

This is one of the simplest and most moving utterances in the whole of music. It is achieved first by the transplanting of the original theme into E flat major (with intervals that previously were minor now appearing as major and dignified by the slow tempo), then by the inversion, in the middle, of the formerly rising scale, and finally by the superb orchestration : strings, commencing *ppp* ; strings with woodwind and horns ; a momentary exposition of the middle register tone of strings and horns with a descant of oboe and clarinet ; full orchestra rising to a climax of enormous weight ; finally a *diminuendo* to *pp* and a last chord held by divided strings with clarinets and bassoons merged in the lower harmony.

After this Variation X, elfin-like, shows fluttering fiddles, muted, and woodwind, over a *pizzicato* bass. The key is G major. G minor is vigorously asserted in the gruffness of Variation XI, more plangently in the romantic lower string melody of Variation XII. It was Variation XIII which especially called for Richter's commendation at the first rehearsal. This, in G major but with lovely shifts to A flat and E flat, is another masterpiece of simplicity. The original theme has all but disappeared except in veiled hints to its melodic features ; but a new melody, given to the clarinet, attracts attention (Ex. 13). One bar shaped this way in the early *Chantant* had set the germ in Elgar's mind. At a later date he was to extend it further in the *Introduction and Allegro*. In Variation XIV the old *pas redouble* manner, which had gone also into *Caractacus* and the *Imperial March*, asserts itself. But in this movement Elgar does not fail to be truthful to himself in emphasising the melancholy of some of his moods, as between figures 72 and 74.

Elgar was right in supposing that the *Variations* might endure. Why this should be is no easier to say than in the case of any work which survives its own day. Part of the reason, however, must lie in the essential intimacy (which word is underlined by Elgar's use) of the music. So various are the moods of the movements yet so personal that each listener will understand, now and then, facets of himself—but shown in the ideal and, therefore, the absolute.

In an illuminating sentence in his *Music in our Time* Adolfo Salazar comments : " Poematic symphonism leads to ballet if it is built in regular periods, to pantomime or the drama if it develops freely." (By " poematic symphonism " is intended music of symphonic scale which is illustrative.) We have seen that Elgar in fact saw the " regular periods " of the *Variations* as possible for ballet. We know that he hankered, all his life, after the opera he never completed. Even without the opera the strong dramatic force is revealed in oratorio and overture. We may truly say of one overture—*Cockaigne*—that it is within the field of pantomime— at least as understood by Salazar. We may conclude that in Elgar is a characteristic romantic composer. So, I think, to the English he may still appear : certainly fifty years ago he was the arch-romantic to the conservative native. Yet Salazar can temper his appreciation of Elgar with the reservation that he is " cold, courtly, and wholly well bred." If this criticism is at all valid we must find in Elgar qualities which were out of their time, qualities which to the full-blooded romantic are not congenial. Such as has been previously suggested lie in Elgar's reticences. It sometimes appears that he has withdrawn from the subject of his expression to think about its deeper nature. He will often give the impression of standing still, but sometimes there is a splendid spontaneity uncomfortably checked.

This is the case in some of the descriptive music which at first gives such splendid promise.

Elgar's three concert overtures—*Froissart*, *Cockaigne*, and *In the South*—are outstanding in English music in brilliance and in picturesqueness. One—*Cockaigne*—is outstanding in all music of this type. *In the South* only just falls short of the highest standard. Behind them stood various essays in bold illustration, ranging from the *Ungarische* and *Lalla Rookh* sketches, and the *Paris* pieces for Powick, to *Sevillana*, *Spanish Serenade* and the *Serenade Mauresque*.

When he began *Froissart* Elgar for the first time settled on a subject which fitted him, for Froissart the chronicler was within his own experience. Quoting from Keats's lines for Georgiana Augusta Wylie he set above his manuscript

> *when chivalry*
> *Lifted up her lance on high*

and immediately brandished his strings aloft (Ex. 14). After this gallant entry the succeeding parade of melodies is disappointing. The first brilliance is exhausted after thirteen bars and then an *andante* section follows wherein nostalgia is revealed in a broad theme (relieved by a horn call borrowed from *Scheherazade*) which itself dissolves into chromatic *longueurs*. By way of a *stringendo* and some vaulting rhythms in the strings the music is returned to *Allegro moderato* and to a stock-in-trade military pattern (Ex. 15). The first *andante* theme is next interposed, fully scored. And so to a modulation to the dominant where the clarinet states the second subject. This holds some of the pattern of the early B flat quartet (see p. 384, Ex. 5b). The development section of the overture in detail is interesting for its ingenuity as well as its felicitous scoring, but the ear already bewildered by so many various themes is only perplexed. If the middle course of the narrative is tedious it is dispelled by a coda which recaptures the *élan* of the opening.

To achieve a good start and an inevitable finish is, as any composer knows, more than half-way to distinction. It is one of the delights of Elgar that his genius is so often at its height at these crucial points. So far as *In the South* is concerned he gets off the mark immediately with a boundary. (This, however, was really scored at Hereford—see Appendix, p. 400, where the opening of the overture is shown as " Dan triumphant.") After a brief flourish, 'cellos and violas, horns and some woodwind with trumpets at the end cut through a series of diatonic triads illumined by violins in bowed tremolo. At that point the matter is briefly summarised by a vivid burst from the full orchestra. Then a counter-tune, shaped a little after the drooping pattern of Saint-Saëns's *Le Cygne*, appears above. Out of this the music develops easily, splashed with rapid runs from harps and strings, until (at figure 6) *nobilmente* directs attention to a spacious passage in which a descending scale over a fairly static bass presses forward to this rhythm (Ex. 16). Now the composer (who always considered that if a thing was worth saying once it was worth saying twice) returns to his initial outburst of joy. This subsides into an exquisite glimpse of his pastoral style (Ex. 17), which is outlined by woodwind and characteristically set in sixths. A repeated C in drum and basses (Elgar's drum parts are often in intensity nearly allied to those of Beethoven) begins to prepare for a new key—F major. For a moment the bass continues in three-time while a new, emotional melody is established, in the strings, in 2/4, *poco meno mosso*. This episode—the emotional quality written into extensive directions—dissolves into quietness in the four-note descent of Ex. 17 shared between violins, flute and horn. Against it, distant, stands the opening *motiv* of the overture given to clarinet.

This, in the classical sense, is the exposition. Now comes the development, in which the key sequence is wide of the obvious— F major, F minor, A flat minor and major, E major, C major, A major. Two features stand out. First a passage—" the glory that was Rome "—indicated as *grandioso* and vibrantly scored for lower woodwind, brass, harps and strings. The second violins play *sul G*, and are supported by 'cellos in unison (Ex. 18). Another melody arrives when the tonality moves to C major. This, one of Elgar's imitation folk-tunes (by some it was at one time even considered as an authentic folk-tune), was separated later from the parent work and issued as a *Canto popolare*. The sheer loveliness of the scoring—with strings divided into many parts, discreet shading from woodwind, the little *angelus* chime of the glockenspiel, the haunting clarinet echo of the first triplet figure—disguises the slenderness of the music at this point. From here (the scoring remains soft and seductive) the direction is homeward. Through A major the quasi-folk-song goes to E flat, wherein the final section of the overture reviews all the previous material.

If one cares to regard it that way *In the South* is a conducted tour of Italy. For Baedeker, the conscientious traveller should carry Tennyson's *The Daisy*, Byron's *Childe Harold*, and, according to an undated letter to Troyte Griffith, the fourth book of the Aeneid ; works from which Elgar quoted—or intended to quote—in explanation of his episodes. It will be found, however, that the guide-books are a hindrance rather than a help for, while they draw attention to the weakness of the work in including (as in *Froissart*) too many episodes, they neither explain nor enhance the evident qualities of joy, pride, and wonderment. In passing, however, a stylistic similarity to Byron may be noticed in the keen-edged verve of Elgar's exhilaration.

In effect *In the South*, completed when Elgar should have been at work on a symphony, has symphonic properties : notably the " motto theme " device is employed to effect unity and there is extensive development of all the melodic material. But the work occupies almost a thousand bars, at the end of which the listener may be forgiven if he feels that his excursion, while pleasant in so many aspects, has been too exhausting. Even so Elgar did not use all the ideas he had garnered. An ear for the common speech of music caught an Italian errand boy unawares. So in his sketches reposes this example of the ebullience of fifty years ago (Ex. 19).

Cockaigne, only just more than a third of the length of *In the South*, concentrates but does not unduly compress its material. Thus the picture, while full of entertaining detail, is firmly held within its frame. *Froissart*, which occupied almost the same number of bars (340 as opposed to 351), is less effective because the melodies are less memorable and, generally, less spontaneous. In *Cockaigne* more than in any other work of Elgar is the snook-cocking aspect of his character. At a period when respectability settled on "serious" music like a blight it demonstrated, without loss of artistic dignity, his capacity for instruction through amusement. When settled in Severn House at the height of his career Elgar would sometimes rush off to a little shop in Fleet Street where he could buy delicacies formerly enjoyed in Worcester but unknown to Hampstead. He came home with black puddings.

Much of *Cockaigne* expresses this impudence : so we notice the effect in the *scherzando* opening of the stutter of repeated semiquavers, the " urchin theme " (at figure 7 of the score) with its implicit tribute to Wagner's apprentices, the brass band *motiv*, with cornets in full cry (after figure 17), and a battery of percussion in attendance. The disappearance of this theme, in modified form (between figures 21 and 23), while an excellent example of " development," in the academic sense, is an even better example of Elgar's quick understanding of the nearness of laughter to tears. Clarinets urge their distant tune in G flat against a persistent bass F. The basses move to G in the hope of meeting the clarinets in the matter of tonality ; but the clarinets, obstinate and self-contained, promptly settle in A flat.   At the same time the violins, *pp*, set above this little conflict a fragment based on the *tranquillo* music (before figure 5) of an early tender episode, and lead into a reflective contrapuntal passage, not unlike the " Cathedral " music of the *Severn Suite* and noted in the sketches as " church " music.   The delicacy and affection of this part of *Cockaigne* is one of its most memorable features.   From a note on the manuscript it would appear that Lady Elgar had a hand in the tune, for it reads " Braut's part." For the rest we have pure Elgarian romance in the " lovers' " theme (see figure 5) and a *nobilmente* allusion to civic pomp (figure 3). Apart from the comedy of keys as expressed in the disappearing band Elgar is less unexpected in tonal contrasts than in the majority of his extended works.   C major is firmly in view and digressions are almost exclusively made to the flat side of the key—to E flat, B flat, G minor and D flat.   The climate is a little colder than in Nuremberg.   A sequel to *Cockaigne* was intended—a nocturne in C minor.   Some few sketches, probably from the end of 1902 and the early part of 1903, show the contrast—" Cockaigne No. 2 : city of d[read]ful night."

Cockaigne shows *Pomp and Circumstance* in undress.   It was not always thus.   Elgar's five great marches,[1] the centre of his devotion to traditional ceremony, were inspired by the spectacular.   As near as makes no odds they are the musical counterpart to the Changing of the Guard and the Trooping of the Colour.   It has, ignobly, been said that Elgar's music of this order is " imperialistic " or " militaristic."   This is nonsense.   Like many of his countrymen, Elgar was thrilled by the colour and precision of English military pageantry, and to express his appreciation in terms of music was no more unnatural or improper than that he should similarly honour his friends, or commemorate his delight in places.

In one way or another Elgar had been writing marches from his earliest years.   In the old *pas redouble* of 1879 is the prototype : a lively opening, a broad middle theme and a *da capo*.   The elements in that work and in other similar sketches of the same period will be discovered in more authoritative setting in the *Imperial March*

---

[1] Among the sketches are rejected openings for at least half a dozen other *Pomp & Circumstance* marches.   Another march, complete but in short score, exists in MS. in the possession of the Elgar Trustees.

of 1897 and in the last, highly coloured scene of *Caractacus*. The *Imperial March*, like *Froissart* in B flat, is curiously ambiguous. It glows with colour, but the colours of sunset rather than of high noon. The opening *pomposo* commences almost sombrely with clarinet and horns and the vigour of the succeeding *animato* (note the carillon effect of horns and trombones) is short lived. The trio tune in E flat suffers from nervous debility and is unable to escape from the ineffectual repetition of (Ex. 20). One of Elgar's mannerisms in scoring does not assist. The clarinet—so often called on like the bright boy of the class, who generally pleases his teacher by giving the right answer—merely adds a degree of unctuousness to a flaccid melody. The same reliance on this tone colour is also apparent in *Pomp and Circumstance Marches* Nos. 1 and 4—the most popular of the series. In these works, however, it is the low chalumeau register of the clarinet which is exploited, not, as in the *Imperial March* the weak middle of the instrument.

The *Pomp and Circumstance* marches should be seen as a whole if the answer to the customary strictures on Elgar's period pompousness is to be found. No. 1 is undeniably brilliant and in the famous central tune (which is not improved by the necessary substitution of crotchets for minims in its form as " Land of Hope and Glory ") inspiringly comprehensive. This is a fact which, however unpalatable to the specialist critic, remains a fact. " A tune like that," said Elgar, " comes once in a lifetime."

At the head of his Marches Elgar set as motto a verse from Lord de Tabley's *The March of Glory*: an oddly fiery piece from a poet who was scholar and recluse. The first march has proved itself as

> *A measure that sets heaven in all their veins*
> *And iron in their hands.*

An observation by Elgar on politics and music (see p. 301) should, however, be heeded by the Conservative Party who have appropriated " Land of Hope and Glory " for their own. But the second moves away to a mood which sets " glory " at a distance. The key is A minor and the main theme of the first part is set in E minor. The trio, in which swords might appear to have been beaten into ploughshares, is in A major : a beautiful sequence of woodwind thirds above a bass which, moving in triplets, carries on from the rhythmic figure of the E minor melody. The third march is also

E. T

in a minor key—C minor, with a ghostly introduction, *ppp*, from which all brightness is excluded until, at a contrasting *fff*, the violins and upper woodwind introduce an exhilarating *motiv* based on an Elgarian commonplace (Ex. 21). The trio, in the solemn movement of the staccato bass and in A flat major, reads as a rejected thought for the motto-theme of the first symphony. Memories of this are in the equivalent portion of No. 5, which was composed many years later. The fifth March, matching the earlier pieces in rhythm, shows an austerity in its counterpoint which is to be seen also in the carol " I sing the birth " of the same period. Hereabouts it might appear that the voice of Stravinsky had been heard (Ex. 22). The fourth March has the exultancy, but with some of the fierceness subdued, of the first.

All in all there is more in these works than meets the ear. Aimed at " the people "—precisely the same " people " who were simultaneously being informed by others that their birthright was in folk-song—they did, in part at least, reach their objective. In the end, however, the proper Elgar is in the second march rather than the first.

Sir Walter Scott commented on one occasion in his *Journal*: " The Big Bow-Wow strain I can do myself like any now going ; but the exquisite touch, which renders ordinary commonplace things and characters interesting, from the truth of the description and the sentiment, is denied to me." We accept Elgar's ability in the Big Bow-Wow strain. In contrast to Scott—though we should not accept Scott's self-denigration as final—he could, however, make commonplace things interesting. We are readily aware of Elgar's commonplaces : *Liebesgrüss* (*Salut d'amour*), *Rosemary*, *Chanson de matin*, *Chanson de nuit*, *Sérénade lyrique*—and all that. These, pallid for the most part and (with one or two notable exceptions) forgotten, were admittedly pot-boilers. If they are worthy of passing attention it is on account of their scoring, which is often delicious, as in *Sérénade lyrique*, and sometimes, as in *Chanson de nuit*, of such inspired quality as to obliterate the tenuous quality of the music. But occasionally a musical idea may appear as not very different from the musical idea of more important essays.

In the two outstanding works for strings, the *Serenade* and the *Introduction and Allegro*, the basic material is commonplace enough. The *Serenade* was composed as an offering to Alice on the third anniversary of her wedding and the original score notes " Braut helped a great deal to make these little tunes." What is not common-place is the attitude to the material. The *Serenade*, in E minor, is an early work, as Elgar's published works go. It still retains the accent of some of the first violin pieces and, indeed—in the slow movement—of some of the wind quintets ; but it has authority in the complete mastery of the medium. The first page of the first movement, the whole of the slow movement, and the coda of the last movement in particular are fine examples of technical achieve-ment. The music appears to belong to the medium for which it was composed and for no other. We are some considerable way from the sinister trees at Flexham, but the rhythm which is announced by the violas, and which pervades the first movement and the end of the last, foreshadows the apprehensiveness that colours some part of the chamber music. In key and in melodic outline the first movement is within the territory of the *Romance* (Op. 1). The expression, however, is more terse and, therefore, more arresting. The usual transition to the tonic major introduces a passage of less distinction, though the manner in which it moves back to the opening is a neat piece of craftsmanship. The *Larghetto*, in C major, is passionate yet refined : an elegiac piece with wonderful instru-mental variety—look, for example, at the last, brooding 14 bars—and with solemnity in its cadences. In 1879 Elgar dealt thus with a slow movement melody (later used for *Cantique*) in C major (Ex. 23). The Elgarian impulse is within the fourth bar. But compare Ex. 24 where the same figure no longer stands alone but as an inevitable link in an unfolding scheme. Within this is passion. For refinement we observe the meticulous balance of the movement and the cool originality of some of the harmonic progressions, which, almost imperceptibly, slip away from the routine of the text-book. Those who know the little GEDGE *Allegretto* will observe that the notes with these names are prominent in the outside movements. While those who know the *Introduction and Allegro* and, for that matter, the last section of *Gerontius* will heed the tranquil manner of Ex. 25, with which the second melody of the slow movement commences. In the last movement another familiar shape is unostentatiously present in the declining $d^1 s l m$ pattern.

It is with this, but in G minor and dynamically stated, that the *Introduction and Allegro* begins : one of Elgar's most masterful openings. This work has some claim to be considered as the most perfect that he wrote. Certainly it is the most classical. Here attention should be directed to the poise of the music, to the inevitability of the formal scheme. Yet the form is Elgar's own : it is not a design to which he compelled himself to conform for the sake of conformity. The plan is tripartite and broadly symphonic. The first section and the last contain the same material, but in the middle, where otherwise (see the overtures and symphonies) he would develop his arguments more or less according to tradition, he interposes an unexpected and independent section. It is this section, paradoxically, which ensures the unity of the whole. In general Elgar was too disposed to vary, to qualify, to restate themes which had already undergone, even in exposition, a fair amount of analytical commentary. "I am," he wrote to Jaeger in January 1905, "doing that string thing . . . no *working-out* part but a devil of a fugue instead, G major and the 2nd divvel in G minor." The fugal episode, described as *fantastico* in the sketches, at the same time prevents repetitiveness and " brings out much tone for the strings." Here we may consider the disposition of the strings. There is a string quartet (*concertino*), and a full body of strings (*concerto grosso*) which is sometimes divided into eight or nine parts. The model for this is, of course, the eighteenth-century *concerto grosso*.

The work commences as has been stated with a large gesture which sweeps down over three octaves. This is succeeded by an upward, but more interrogatory, movement in the solo quartet. The two ideas intermingle and a figure in the bass becomes noticeable for its urgency (Ex. 26). This figure asserts itself as a countersubject during the fugue, where, however, it appears spontaneously to grow from the fugue subject itself. At the thirteenth bar a long sustained B flat first appears in the solo viola. Beneath it the lower strings of the main group leave the tonic key and reach down to that of E flat major. Then the viola continues its statement of a melody of equal simplicity and lyrical beauty. When Elgar re-created an eighteenth-century form, as has already been seen in the Gavotte of Op. 10, he did not feel obliged to crib. In this lyrical passage (which grows to dominate the whole work) of the *Introduction and Allegro* there is, however, a hint at least that Elgar might have had Handel's G Minor *Concerto grosso* (Op. 6, No. 6) somewhere in mind ; for Handel, in that work, subsides into similar eloquence in E flat major in his *Musette*. But there is another cross-reference. When in Cardiganshire in 1901 [1] Elgar heard some distant singing. He developed an independent, quasi folk-song, tune out of what he heard (cf. *canto popolare* of *In the South*) and set it in his sketch book at the end of 1901 ; but there it was intended for full orchestra. This derived melody was infected some time later by another *al fresco* singing party, to which Elgar was audience, in the Wye Valley. The next stage was the lyrical melody of the *Introduction and Allegro*. At (7) the passage previously and a little tentatively given by the solo quartet at (1) emerges, now *allegro*, in G major. Here again is the characteristic Elgar antithesis. At (10), and still in G major, yet another passage commences—of repeated, excited semiquavers. Discussed first by quartet and then by the violins of the orchestra they increase in intensity until everybody is involved. Then *nobilmente*, and heralded by sweeping scales, the opening of the work reappears in major guise. There follows a comprehensive survey, in the major, of all the melodic material.

After the fugue the first section is freely recapitulated, but with the themes, on the whole, in reverse order. The feature of the recapitulation is the impressively radiant extension of the quasi-folk-tune : *ff molto sostenuto* ; *largamente* (violins *sul G*) ; *stringendo* ; *con fuoco* ; orchestra *pp*, with quartet riding out *f* and *espressivo* ; then, in brief decoration, *fff*. At (32) the orchestra commences its final sweep. After the prevalent major third of the previous melody the arpeggio figure first heard at (1) follows naturally. Imperiously it asserts control, and the music goes up in triumph. At the end a brief dominant seventh ; a rest ; a bar occupied by G in three octaves ; a comma ; a final *pizzicato* chord. Each note in this work merits consideration. That, perhaps, is the true summary of musical excellence, for there are not so many works of which it can be said that they possess neither one note too few nor one too many.

---

[1] On the front page of his first sketch book (dated Nov. 19, 1901) Elgar wrote " Ynys Llochtryn." This refers to Ynys Lochtyn, an islet off Llanganog in an isolated and beautiful part of Cardiganshire.

CHAPTER XVIII

MUSIC FOR VOICES

*The passions, whether violent or otherwise must never be
expressed to disgust—and music, even in the most terrific
situations, never give pain to the ear, but ever delight it and
remain Music.*

(*Quotation from a letter of Mozart to his father* (1781),
kept by Elgar on his desk.)

CHORAL MUSIC is what the English write about when they wish to
answer the charge of being unmusical. In these circumstances,
however, it is advisable to be general rather than particular—to
fall back on the Middle Ages and the time of the Tudors, to refer
to Purcell and to Handel, then—*longo intervallo*—to Stanford, Elgar,
Parry and Vaughan Williams. To be particular leads to embar-
rassment. Were the exponents of Hatton and Hullah, Stevens
and Stewart, Callcott and Carulli, Pearsall and Pinsutti as exemplary
in the matter of taste as we might like to believe ? The answer is ;
no. Choral music, especially in the nineteenth century, was an
ancillary occupation. Glee Clubs existed for the cultivation of a
proper discrimination in beer and whisky ; Ladies' Choirs for the
interchange of gossip ; mixed groups for the support of charities.
Music came in on sufferance—" it must never give pain to the ear
but ever delight it. . . ." The catalogues of the most successful
publishers of the period are full of pieces that were as innocuous as
they were profitable.

Elgar was not immune from the influence of such music nor did
he dispute its social and local value. He was a faithful supporter
of the Worcester Glee Club, going there not so much for musical
instruction as for convivial company. As a composer he was not
slow to see the opportunities that such societies afforded ; anything
from three to five guineas for thirty or forty bars was riches. So

the pragmatist turned out songs and part songs which were precisely designed for inclusion in the lists of John Beare, Joseph Williams (the trade connection between these firms and that of Elgar Bros. was an asset to the young composer) and of Messrs. Novello.

At this point we begin to dismiss works; such as *How calmly the evening*, *O Happy Eyes*, *Love*, *A Christmas Greeting* (with its incorporation of Handel's "Pastoral Symphony"), some of the Greek Anthology settings, and *The Shower*. These are period pieces, neither better nor worse than the average. But we must not proceed too fast. Elgar had too much musical personality to stay in any department merely with the mediocre. Besides, his intimate acquaintance with provincial music quickly taught him that the choral unit afforded many possibilities of fascinating experiment in tone painting. It was not long before he became aware of the great technical proficiency of the choirs which primarily existed for competition. Thus a close inspection of his now most unfashionable works will reveal something of his style that is at once characteristic and important. His best choral works (excluding for the time being those, of a larger scale, which require orchestral accompaniment) show a remarkable diversity and his initiative lifted the part song on to an altogether higher plane.

Elgar brought to the art of the English part song an influence from the field of orchestral music. Thus we notice many effects. In *Weary Wind of the West* the basses divide into 'cello and double bass type of foundation for the last two pages. In *After many a dusty mile* the 2nd bass line also takes on the character of a 'cello tune. *Feasting I Watch* catches aptly the manner of a brass ensemble, while the conclusion of *It's Oh! to see a Wild Wind* is as for muted strings. In *Angelus*, a companion piece to those in Brahms's *Marienlieder*, and the only completed piece in an intended suite,[1] an orchestral analogy does not work, when sopranos and basses are in octaves (the same device is more tellingly applied to the setting of Byron's *Deep in my soul*); the result is not as if violins and 'cellos were playing the passage. In *The Fountain* sopranos and contraltos are sometimes *divisi a 3*. These passages of cold chords above a pedal bass and a slightly moving tenor melody are beautiful and evocative—if somewhat too extravagant, according to present standards in these matters—for Vaughan's pellucid verse.

[1] " Choral Suite—I *Intro.*, II *In a Vineyard*, III *Angelus*, IV *Dance*, V *Vintage*, VI *Envoi* "; titles in sketch book 1909 (?)

In *Owls*, a ghost of a piece, singers are presented with extremely difficult problems of nuance and intonation. In this Elgar's imaginative dread of darkness and obscurity, pain and death is set out in broken fragments of melody and in peculiarly Debussy-like sequences of sevenths. The piece is in C minor, but avoids the key almost entirely, ending on a major third of D and F sharp. In *O Wild West Wind*, written at the same time, there is also a trace of Debussy in the transition to sadness on page 5. This work, notable for its general congestion, otherwise shows an orchestral *nobilmente* and an onomatopoeic use of a secondary seventh, with many marks of expression, to illustrate the " wind." The work in which inspiration and virtuosity are properly used is *Death on the Hills*. This is a horrific picture of Death—in person—abroad in Russia (the words are translated from Maikov), and choosing his prey against the pleadings of the old on behalf of the young. There are premonitions in this music, which was composed in 1914. Elgar herein shows his capacity for understanding any march *motiv* : the work is labelled *quasi alla marcia*. But this is a funeral march. The high voices are isolated poignantly on two occasions : the harmony ranges from the startling impact of Ex. 27 to the modal austerity of Ex. 28 : at the end a woeful monotony of chanting voices accompanies the voice of death, speaking in meas-ured crotchets in the bass. This, of its kind, is a great work. It is more than thirty years since Langford drew attention to the high qualities of Elgar's greater part songs, but now and then they are " in difficulty so far overshooting their mark that they are in bulk still insufficiently known."

Experiments in tonality showed more than once in the part songs. The most striking example being the bitonal *There is sweet music*, which throughout, is simultaneously set in A flat major and G major. There is also some carefree experiment with time signa-tures—4/4, 5/4 and 10/4. In neither tonal nor rhythmic respects can the experiments be counted as successful.

Some of Elgar's part songs plainly show their descent from those which were in vogue in his youth. In them may be seen the last of the Victorians. In others, particularly those for male voices, is the influence of the German *liedertafel* ; Cornelius and Bruch show through the ambitious ranges of the *Wild West Wind* and the too inflated *Go Song of Mine* ; elsewhere the alternate gloom and hearti-ness of Schumann. Late in life, however, Elgar made one attempt

—almost his only attempt—to come to terms with the new asceticism that he generally deplored in his younger compatriots. The carol *I sing the birth* is out of character—modal and largely spread in single lines ; the direction that the unharmonised phrases "should be sung in a very free manner, without any rigid adherence to tempo" carries towards Holst and Vaughan Williams and the *Oxford Book of Carols*. Thirty years before Elgar had momentarily, and privately, flirted with another promising fashion. For his *Christmas Card* of 1897 he set—*a capella*—a traditional poem. Thus he renounces the allurements of his own age in favour of the plain triads of the *stilo* Palestrina (Ex. 29).

Paradoxically, had he been a member of the Church of England Elgar might have learned more of the ancient glories of the Catholic Church than he did by belonging to that Church. As it was he based his church music on the frequent pleasantries that were in the repertoire of St. George's. His few published motets move with easy grace and sometimes involve the devotional spirit of the Italian masters of the eighteenth century : there may be instanced the ending of the *O Salutaris*, where the trebles move up over an octave and a half, against a descending bass, before dropping to the final *ppp* chord. This sounds like sanctuary music but, going beyond the norm in colouring, it looks towards the seraphic chorus of *Gerontius*. Among the small works of Elgar there is one which shows him, as it were, leaving *Gerontius* behind. In 1909 he set Newman's elegiac *They are at rest* in memory of Queen Victoria. This is among his neutral tones. Colour has been deliberately withheld. The result is impressive.

Unaccompanied choral music, however, was not Elgar's most effective métier. He was generally happier when instruments were available. So on the one hand are the miniatures like *Fly, Singing Bird* (where the practice of adding violin obbligatos to his friends' singing asserts itself), *Spanish Serenade* (an excursion in search of local colour similar to the *Sérénade Mauresque*), or the *Songs from the Bavarian Highlands* ; on the other, pieces for church performance—*Te Deum and Benedictus*, and the two *Psalms* which read like episodes from an incomplete oratorio. In small scale pieces Elgar too often tried to put a quart into a pint pot. In his "Bavarians" he was content with general impressions and refrained from referring to every detail. So they survive and may not unworthily be set beside similar works by Brahms.

Among the forgotten works of nineteenth-century Germany are the choral ballads of Mendelssohn, Marschner, Schumann, David, Wolf, Humperdinck and others who sought to domesticate the mysteries of the romantic movement. Elgar, in *The Black Knight*, took up where the Germans left off. The legend of *The Black Knight* was told by Uhland. Elgar unfortunately used Longfellow's translation and this militates against any present-day performance. So far as Elgar was concerned the libretto was little more than a fitting commentary to an ardent example of programme music. He described the work as a symphony for chorus and orchestra, set it in four movements, and carried the narrative through the orchestral texture by means of a few *leit motiven*. The most striking of these is the grisly figure employed by bass clarinet and horn to signify the mysterious stranger (Death) who arrives (at the Feast of Pentecost) to turn the happy festivities at Hofburg into tragedy. Elgar could blow the trumpets on the battlements, mysteriously march his Black Knight into the second movement, rock the castle walls with chromatic tumult to perfection. But, as Spitta said of Schumann's *Paradise and the Peri*, there is too much music about.

The one movement which is free from this stricture is the third, where the spirit of the *Bavarian Songs* is foreshadowed. Here, with sequences of sixths in the orchestral score, with deft choral dance movement, is at first grace and charm. Then, introduced by the sequence of chords shown as Ex. 6 on p. 384, the mood changes unmistakably but not too much. The key now is G minor; a heavier dance is maintained by the orchestra; the chorus ejaculates without elaboration, only reaching lyrical utterance when the guests see the roses fall faded from the princess's hair. The last page of music fades and falls like the roses and the mystery is shown by a characteristic use of the chord known in the text-books as that of the Neapolitan sixth.

In *King Olaf* the librettist is still Longfellow (with some help from H. A. Acworth). The libretto follows its long course with relative modesty and obtrusive diction is somewhat less noticeable than in *The Black Knight*. The story too is of a higher dignity, even though the hero's character is enveloped in a mass of improbabilities. Elgar, with more space in which to move, begins to approach the outskirts of his greatest work. The chorus " I am the God Thor," strenuous and fierce, is a brilliant piece of savagery that must have struck ears accustomed to the tame paganisms of Barnett, Smart, and Cowen, with much force. In the central episode of the attempt on Olaf's life by Gudrun his bride (treachery stirred by the death of her father Ironbeard in the Conversion Scene) the restlessness of Elgar's personality is communicated to the music. So the beauty of the quiet moonlight, the " tide of dreams," the rising determination of Gudrun, her passage by Olaf's bedside, his awakening and expostulation with Gudrun, and his escape, are set in a constantly changing pattern of rhythms and chords which are dramatically apt and musically logical. It does, unfortunately, happen that the text hereabouts is at its most banal. Why, said King Olaf to Gudrun, are you there ? She answered

> *'Tis the bodkin that I wear*
> *When at night I bind my hair :*
> *It woke me falling on the floor;*
> *'Tis nothing more.*

That, perhaps, is not the stuff out of which drama is made.

Elgar's genius, however, did not generally shine in dramatic exposition. *Caractacus* was once staged in Liverpool,[1] but the sole effect was to show how devoid of compulsive dramatic movement it was. It is essentially—and the same applies to almost every choral cantata based on a historical text—a series of tableaux, decorative but episodic. In themselves, however, the episodes may possess great quality. So it is in the case of " Thyri," the ballad in which is described the marriage of Olaf to the beautiful Thyri (sometime the unhappy betrothed of King Burislaf of Wendland). In this movement the freshness of the themes, the buoyancy of the rhythms and the sweetness of the texture are lovely : as a welcome to a bride nothing could be more acceptable (Ex. 30). The ballad has a refrain—

> *Hoist up your sails of silk*
> *And flee away from each other.*

This refrain provides another *motiv* (Ex. 31). The interplay of the

[1] " I also recall that when my brother John was busy, in the 1920's with the Liverpool Repertory Opera Elgar helped greatly in the adaptation of *Caractacus* as an opera. He was in Rome when the work was produced yet I recall the receipt of a most encouraging telegram." Letter from J. Raymond Tobin to the author.

two themes is spontaneous and engaging, and not least moving is the preservation of the rhythmic pattern of the tenor part of Ex. 30 against the alteration of the melody for a melancholy reference to Thyri's betrothal to Burislaf.

In truth, however, we can never, at any time, be particularly concerned as to the destiny of these Norse heroes and heroines. Longfellow is unlikely to stir enthusiasm, while Elgar with enthusiasm for everything else forgets that character should be central. He still delights in the reflection of light from armour, in the clash of swords, in the movement of ships, in " the image of gold in the sun," in the sharp air of winter, in the fragrance of incense from swinging censers. So the *mise en scène* within the music is exact and expressive. It is small wonder that for long *King Olaf* was the delight of choral societies ; for the freshness of the choral technique, the practicability of the lay-out, the contrast of high voices and low voices, the sensuously spaced chords (see the " sleep " chord of No. 7) are unforgettable.

If there are present reminiscences of Handel and Mendelssohn —and a memory or two of the Nordic dialect of Gade—there is also Wagner. *King Olaf* is shot through with *leit motiven*. Since there are some seventy of these it cannot be said that their employment leads to any unity. The more these themes crowd in, one on the other, as at King Olaf's death, the more irrelevant they seem. The new academicism of the late romantics becomes as frustrating as the old conventions which it was designed to displace.

Caractacus like *King Olaf* falls short of its heroic theme and is to be remembered only for the occasional moments : for the entry music, somewhat after the march in Berlioz's *L'Enfance du Christ*, the setting of the mystical circle of the Druids, their dance and invocation, the Arch-Druid's remembrance of " the hearts of ancient heroes " in Scene II, and the Severn music of the introduction to Scene III. Curiously, however, *Caractacus* enjoys at the present time some esteem in Soviet Russia but not entirely on account of its musical content.[1] The material is there for a symphonic poem, in which it could more happily and briefly been collected. In comparison with *King Olaf* the choral writing is less interesting and the motto-themes of even less intrinsic importance.

[1] " In a Moscow radio programme in English last night devoted to the works of Sir Edward Elgar, a Russian authority, Mr. Igor Belzer, said the anniversary of the British composer's death was being widely celebrated in Soviet musical circles.

" Among Elgar's most popular works in Russia, he said, was the *Caractacus* cantata

The conclusion of *Caractacus* is an expressive piece of immodesty in praise of Britain. Unless we except an odd reflection, in the bass, of the major section of the *Enigma* theme and a triumphant exposition of the opening of " Nimrod " (see p. 60 of the vocal score) there is nothing to be noted but enthusiasm. Since the words are our guide we stand now in mortification at their sentiments.

Since self-praise became unfashionable *The Banner of St. George*, of which the sentiments are those of the conclusion of *Caractacus*, has also been out of favour. This is as well for among Elgar's works it must take the lowest place. It is merely dull. It is an odd fact that when Elgar deliberately sought to express the conventions of patriotism—as in the *Coronation Ode*, the *Crown of India* and the Wembley music of 1926—he ran out of inspiration. For one performance these pageant pieces serve well enough, but that is their limit.

Profitable patriotism of the sort that elevated the members of the Conservative Clubs of the nineties are no great incentive to art. Elgar expressed himself in his sketches of the *Crown of India* : " There is *far too much* of the political business." So it is not surprising sometimes in this genre he was as perfunctory as Purcell in parts of *King Arthur*, or Handel in *Judas Maccabaeus*, or Brahms or Stanford in occasional pieces now forgotten. But if it is desired to see how tasteful Elgar really was among the captains and colonels reference should be made to *The Absent-minded Beggar*, a joint production of Kipling, Sullivan and the *Daily Mail* in aid of the dependants of those fighting in the South African war. The glory of arms was of no great interest to Elgar—unless, as in the historic pieces, it was as viewed through the eyes of Scott or Harrison Ainsworth, or unless he was able to meditate on the many aspects of " glory."

With *The Spirit of England* we become aware of Elgar's deepest feelings. Here, outside of the oratorios, he is in his splendid elegiac mood (in the expression of which he had few equals), at the height of unassuming dignity, and most poignant. It is, wrote one critic, the music of " patriotism without vainglory and sorrow, without self-pity." [1] Of the three pieces, which are for tenor or

---

which ' gave musical expression to the courageous struggle of the British tribes headed by Caractacus against the Roman invader.' " *Glasgow Evening Citizen*, Feb. 24, 1954.
[1] *Elgar and the Public*, C. W. Orr, *Musical Times*, Jan. 1931.

soprano solo, chorus and orchestra, the most moving, though not the most familiar, is the second—" To Women." This is a work of understanding of the living rather than of commemoration of the dead. It is full of sympathy, of hope, but not of false optimism. It is akin to Brahms's *Song of Destiny* in key and disposition, but the mood is more grave than Brahms allows in the first part of that work. In " To Women " Elgar, for once, does not direct *nobilmente*, but there is no music of his which is quite so incomparably noble. The lines of nobility are in the commanding sweep of the solo voice, the chordal underlay, the allusive orchestration (which carries over one theme from "The Fourth of August"), and the higher emotion of the chorus which sets off the tragic impersonality of the solo line. " For the Fallen," for obvious reasons, has been more frequently performed than its companion pieces. In the aspiring parts of this work the same melodic curve serves as in "To Women " and it is, as the whole sequence, characteristically, a march ; in this the 3/4 middle section serves as a trio. At one point especially Elgar shows marvellous restraint and imagination. " They went with songs to the battle." In Rootham's setting a *quodlibet* of popular songs accompanies this passage. Elgar, on the other hand, starting his voices on a monotone (he was less bound to four part harmony than any other English composer of his time) sets behind a remote hint of a march, empty, slightly fantastic, and showing the comfortless edge of a diminished fifth. So the present reality of war is set in terms which give no glory, no splendour ; only a sense of inexorable destruction contrasted with human determination. This is shown by the chorus, which borrows the ugly diminished fifth and inverts it as an augmented fourth. In the recollection of the dead, however, there is great dignity— commonplace chordal sequences losing any hint of the commonplace by their juxtaposition and their spacing—and in the conviction of their immortality an ineffable radiance.

In some details *The Spirit of England* recalls *Gerontius*. There is another work—to some Elgar's finest choral work excepting *Gerontius*—which is also reminiscent : *The Music Makers*. O'Shaughnessy's Ode is not distinguished poetry, but the vision which inspires it, if unacceptable to the rationalist, is one which has frequently been the guiding star of poets and philosophers. Shelley, in a memorable passage in the *Defence of Poetry*, says, more succinctly, what O'Shaughnessy writes. Elgar catches the meaning behind the verse and directs it into music. "Poets," he asserts with Shelley, "are the unacknowledged legislators of the world." Whether this is true or not is irrelevant. Elgar believed it to be.

The Music Makers[1]—which was composed over a number of years —was dedicated to Nicholas Kilburn. This goes some way towards explaining its form. Kilburn was one of Elgar's oldest and dearest friends and had intimate associations with all his great works. Some of these are directly recalled in quotations from the *Variations*, *Gerontius*, and the violin concerto. So Elgar, back to the intimate, cryptic manner, recommends his own first choices to his friend, and attaches, by verbal label, additional significance to particular phrases. Elgar thought it a good work—" good (enough for me) " he wrote. On Christmas Eve, 1912, Kilburn, having grown to know the work in rehearsal, wrote to Lady Elgar. . . .

" I have desired to tell him and you that my Choral folk love the Music Makers. All three Choirs alike who have now tasted it.

The strong virility and charm of the music appeals to them, and the interest is manifestly sincere and alive. 'Tis delightful to find difficulties which do not dismay, but give zest; stimulating even the stodgiest !

Whole tone scale, the obliquely intertwined tune, and the quotations, all a quaintness and a delight. With what genuine fitness of feeling dear " Gerontius " themes here take their place."

After his performance Kilburn wrote again—" Especially did I strive to impress on all concerned the importance of a subdued mystical treatment of certain parts of the words. Sing and play, I said, as though you were in *dreamland* then all will be well. I mean at ' our dreaming and singing ' and ' Oh, men, it must ever be ' and at the *Choral* commencement and ending of the work."

It is clear that Kilburn understood the poetry of the music—and was less concerned with the poetry of the poetry. In *The Music Makers* Elgar expands his technique of song writing. He is relatively indifferent to niceties of accentuation, preferring to use the voice as a musical instrument and to translate the poet's vision directly into terms of music. It has lately been the fashion to decry *The Music Makers* because of the text; but musical criticism is not literary

[1] It seems that work started on *The Music Makers circa* 1903, although, owing to Elgar's habit of filling up blank pages at odd times, the contiguity of some sketches with those of *The Apostles* and *The Kingdom* is not conclusive. By Feb. 21, 1908, however, Littleton of Novello's wrote to Elgar that he had obtained permission for the use of the words. Much of *The Music Makers* was sketched by Mordiford Bridge.

criticism, and so long as we accept Schubert despite Müller then we must accept Elgar despite O'Shaughnessy. In the case of a narrative work (e.g. the earlier cantatas) the matter is different because the function of the words is different. Here the musician creates his own narrative—out of music. The main course of the musical narrative is so marked by self-quotations.

It is not long before the orchestral introduction shows the shadow of the " Enigma " theme. The voices enter, as is frequent with Elgar, unaccompanied :

> *We are the music makers*
> *And we are the dreamers of dreams.*

The gravity of F minor displays the " seriousness " which Samuel Langford discovered as Elgar's conspicuous quality. As the last word dies away the opening theme of *Gerontius* is quoted. In the background of the solemn opening there are further references to the " Enigma " theme as the isolation of the artist is expressed. The genius of the work lies precisely in this insistence on solitariness ; but solitariness is not mere loneliness. Behind the solitary worker lie the thoughts and aspirations of generations :

> *The soldier, the king, and the peasant*
> *Are working together in one*
> *Till our dream shall become their present*
> *And their work in the world be done.*

During this passage Elgar reduces the picturesqueness that has intervened—with a phrase of the *Marseillaise* " fashioning an Empire's glory ", and the busy-ness of his voices ; a falling third comes familiarly ; a chord of G major changes to G minor (49) ; the contralto solo enters and leads to a great moment of reflection (Ex. 32). Later as " we dwell in our dreaming and singing, a little apart " the " Enigma " theme is again shown, to be followed by a brief hint of the violin concerto. At the end of the work—as " the dreamer slumbers and a singer sings no more" and hope is in the future—there is quoted the " *novissima hora* " *motiv* from *Gerontius*, which, by coincidence, is also present (in simpler form) in the *Minuet* which Elgar had written, years before, for Paul Kilburn.

Quotations do not occupy as much space as significance in *The Music Makers*, but their presence is made to appear as inevitable by the unified design of the whole work. There is a symphonic quality present which shows the accomplishment of what had been attempted in *The Black Knight*. The opening themes, first of the orchestra and then of the voices, run throughout, binding more technically what is already imaginatively united by the allusions. There is an incredible variety in detail, but the details are sorted into four main groups of ideas which contrast as distinct but connected movements. The first section incorporates four stanzas, the second section one stanza, the third and fourth two each. (There are other possible divisions, but this appears to be the most convincing.)

The variety of the choral writing sets off the deep spiritual quality of the solo part which, designed for Muriel Foster, is heroically intense—an *helden*-alto role as it were.

Elgar's frequent distaste for solo singers was well known. Outside of his oratorios and other choral-orchestral works they as a class have little for which to be grateful to him. Songs with pianoforte accompaniments did not interest him. When he did write songs it was with muted enthusiasm, and he was content to stay on the level of Cowen and Sullivan, Henschel and Bantock. One of Elgar's earliest published works was " The Wind at Dawn," entered for a competition organised by the *Magazine of Music*. It was a prize-winning entry, bringing the composer a welcome cheque for £5. So far as the publishing house was concerned it was the very thing to achieve popular acclaim : Elgar knew all the devices to screw out emotion and applause. So it continued. The dramatics of " Like to the damask rose," the strummed lute of " Queen Mary's Song," the *grandioso*, *tutta forza*, *largamente*, *accelerando* and *ritardando* of " The Poet's Life," the alternating languors and excitements within Op. 48 and Op. 60 are all part of the general style of the period. So far as songs were concerned it was a bad period.

It is always noticeable in Elgar's songs that he appears to emphasise how much better he could have succeeded had he had an orchestra available. So in *Sea Pictures* the difference is evident. Here, seizing the imagery, he has drawn and painted engagingly. Putting aside obvious differences of style there may be caught some of the fancifulness of Delius in insubstantial moments of orchestral ingenuity : we notice the light fleck of the flute and the splashing

E.   U harp in " Sea Slumber-Song," or the little wave-figures that characterise " In Haven " and " Where Corals lie." The poetry of this song cycle is generally indifferent. Thus we are brought to the point at which Elgar is unfavourably compared with more "literary" composers. For him, however, a poem which was artistically successful in its own right was not necessarily material for musical setting. In fact, as hinted in the Shelley superscription to the second symphony, a great poem could only be expressed in music which, following the aspirations of the verse, developed its own life. The words of minor poetry, on the other hand, may more easily be assimilated directly to music ; for, while they may annotate mood and atmosphere, they will, by reason of poetic indifference, make no impediment to the music. This is the case in *Sea Pictures* where neither the words nor the vocal part—which, however, is allowed moments of effectiveness—are of independent importance. This goes some way towards explaining the total effect of *Gerontius* on those to whom the argument of the work is unacceptable.

CHAPTER XIX

AD MAJOREM DEI GLORIAM

This is the best of me: for the rest, I ate and drank and slept, and loved and hated like another: but this I saw and knew; this if anything of mine is worth your memory.

Written by Elgar at the end of the MS. of
The Dream of Gerontius

I am not at all sure if I shall ever complete my task, but it is the work to which I devote my best thoughts.

Elgar to Rev. W. E. Torr, c. Oct. 28, 1905

IN 1850 Millais exhibited " Christ in the House of His Parents " at the Summer Exhibition of the Royal Academy. It is well-known that the hypocrites descended on this work in force, finding in it " a pictorial blasphemy," and re-titling it " The Carpenter's Shop." Among the severest critics was Charles Dickens who issued a violent denunciation in *Household Words*. The main charge against the painting—which would now appear only extraordinary for its lack of revolutionary character—was that Christ and his family were represented as living characters. Pre-Raphaelite religious painting mostly fell short of the ideals entertained by the Brotherhood, but there remains on the part of Rossetti, Millais and Holman Hunt a poetic and living quality that may occasionally appear as even exquisite ; in two pictures of Rossetti especially—the " Girlhood of Mary Virgin " and " The Annunciation "—there is the authentic mark of genius.

It is not far from the tremulous beauty and delicate execution of Rossetti to some scenes in Elgar's oratorios. In the " Mary Magdalene " music of *The Apostles*, in the scene " At the Beautiful Gate " in *The Kingdom* there are to be experienced similar tenderness of feeling, grace of portraiture, and idealisation of beauty. In such moments of quiet inspiration it is evident that personal emotion moved Elgar, and not the graven imagery of conventional piety.

Elgar was the second great English composer—Handel being the other—to have genuine appreciation of the visual arts. He had a great affection for the pre-Raphaelites, which, no doubt, was stimulated by acquaintance with Alice Stuart-Wortley, who was a daughter of Millais. An affinity between him and them was recognised by Canon Gorton. Writing to Elgar, after the first performance of *The Apostles*, Gorton proposed that he should look at the work of " a kindred spirit " in Ford Madox Brown's " Christ in the Temple," in the Birmingham Art Gallery. The analogy of spirit may be arguable : not so, however, that of technique.

The hallmark of all the pre-Raphaelites was precision in method and accuracy in narrative. This was a source both of strength and weakness. So it was in the oratorio style of Elgar. Millais, in search of detail, worked on his canvas in a carpenter's shop, Holman Hunt twice visited Palestine in order to achieve verisimilitude in local colour. Elgar's reading in the history of the Early Church transcended that expected of ordination candidates, while his researches in liturgical music—both of the Catholic and Hebrew faiths—went a great deal further than was required for the "Shofar" theme and " Constitues eos " in *The Apostles*, or " O Sacrum Con-vivium " as quoted in *The Kingdom*. It is noteworthy that these two oratorios, which in manner and intention most nearly accord with pre-Raphaelite practice and intention, are less great than the one which is free of detailed references. In *Gerontius*, however, a broad humanism—to the expression of which Millais aspired—is apparent.

" There is," wrote Jaeger,[1] of the " Sanctus fortis " section of *Gerontius*, " nothing in this movement suggestive of ' sacred ' music as the term is generally understood. Neither Gregorian nor Anglican ritual music is laid under contribution ; nor are the styles of the recognised masters of sacred music hinted at. There is, moreover, nothing to show that the composer considers Geron-tius either a priest or a saint. On the contrary, he seems to look upon him as an ordinary man and a sinner, who, after leading a worldly man's life, is now ' near to death ' and repentant. The

[1] *The Dream of Gerontius*, Analytical Notes, p. 13.

music is individual, a personal reflex of the composer's feelings, and filled with a full-blooded romantic fervour, rising to moments of exaltation and ecstasy, as that of an old man feeling momentarily young again in the remembrance of his youth's steadfast faith and ardent hope."

Gerontius still stands as a unique expression of one man—the most subjective extended study in the history of English choral music.

Thus we have the two poles of Elgar's oratorio style : the meticulously calculated descriptiveness of *The Apostles* and *The Kingdom*, and the intense and often painful characterisation of *Gerontius*. Other composers, whose example Elgar admired, come to mind—Berlioz of *L'Enfance du Christ*, Bach of the *Passions*, Schumann of *Faust*, and Verdi of the *Manzoni Requiem*. None of them were general influences in that style of English oratorio which, mercifully, Elgar destroyed ; for the aim of the nineteenth-century composer of " sacred music " for English choral societies was respectability. Elgar came on the scene, with the wrong antecedents, very much as one of the " inspired cads " whom the Rev. F. D. Maurice looked for to revive English Christianity, and *Gerontius* appeared almost as blasphemous as " The Carpenter's Shop." But before *Gerontius* there was *Lux Christi*.

Lux Christi is no great work but Elgar, while keeping to the safe path of choral propriety for a Festival Choir, displays sufficient evidences of imaginative originality to emphasise the commonplace character of other " new " works of the period. The episode on which the oratorio is based is that of the healing of the blind man in *St. John's Gospel*, ix. The title phrase is not only the inspiration of this one work, but also of the later *Apostles* and *Kingdom*. The verse from which the title is taken is marked by Elgar in the *New Testament* in which he planned the last two oratorios of the trilogy. In a prominent *motiv*, first seen on p. 27 of the vocal score, and later appearing in the last aria of Jesus—" I am the Good Shepherd," there is the germ of the triplet-marked theme, representative of the " New Faith," which dominates *The Kingdom* and, as the sketches show, was to have carried on to the third part of the trilogy. *Lux Christi*, with its careful selection of the sayings of Jesus (the " Good Shepherd " section is taken from its immediate biblical context) may well be seen as a first contribution to the great saga of Christianity which had been intended from Elgar's earliest years. As often happens the intention of the oratorio was obscured by a well-meaning librettist whose irascibility in the face of constructive criticism was a grave disadvantage both to composer and publisher. (The words of the Mother of the Blind Man, which caused some offence, are characteristic of the opaque theology that was thought to be proper for musical setting.)

As in his secular cantatas Elgar is faithful to the principle of *leit motiv*. So, if inclined, the sedulous student of *Lux Christi* may point to the exposition of demonstrative themes in the introductory orchestral *Meditation* : at letter *B* the " blind man " motiv, given by the horns ; at letter *C* his " longing for light " in a brief passage in G major—expectation held out in rhythmic hesitancy—which, however, develops passionately towards E flat major ; at letter *E* a cognate tune—but with conventional rhythm, which appears later as accompaniment to " I am the Light of the world "; finally at letter *G*, where G major is re-established, a phrase (with Elgarian syncopation) which is used to point to Jesus as the giver of light. This last appears again in the *Apostles* (p. 4 of the vocal score) with the same purpose.

This method of composition, which Elgar faithfully followed in all his large choral works, is fraught with difficulties both for composer and listener. The one, being consistent, is frequently forced into musical situations which are created by forces outside the music and which are, accordingly, irrelevant : the other is often compelled to halt his imagination while the reference is checked against the index. In one work—*Gerontius*—Elgar vindicated the system because the whole is so evidently greater than the parts. In the other oratorios this is not so. There are, however, other reasons than this loyalty to Wagnerian design. In *Lux Christi* the most frequently quoted *motiv* is the last. After its appearance on every page—sometimes in deep disguise—one is tempted to consider whether it has, in fact, made any contribution to the musical or dramatic development at all.

Lux Christi, however, is more than a mere period piece. It is the first extensive piece in the post-Handelian tradition of English oratorio music to protest a composer's enthusiasm for his subject, while registering his claim, by due consideration of the choral desiderata, to belong to the tradition. " I thought," said Elgar, " a fugue would be expected of me. The British public would hardly tolerate oratorio without fugue. So I tried to give them one. . . . There's a bit of canon, too, and in short, I hope there's enough counterpoint to give the real British religious respectability." It is not, however, for the apt academic touch at " The wisdom of their wise men " nor for the less necessary imitative technique of Nos. 3 and 8 that the oratorio is (if at all) regarded.

There are moments of quiet originality which are more striking. There is the distant entry of the chorus of Levites which overlaps the end of the *Meditation*; the *Enigma*-related phrase which introduces Jesus (see Ex. 10, page 384); the choral climax in ten parts at " the eyes of the blind shall see "; the graceful, fluid instrumental undulations behind " As a spirit didst Thou pass " which carries through to the angelical chorus of *Gerontius*; the extension of the triplet figure as mentioned on p. 271. The orchestration throughout is vivid and the choral writing is not restricted by the limitations of four part harmony. Elgar, like Fauré, knew how to make effective use of unison writing.

Elgar wrote *Lux Christi* because he felt that he ought to write an oratorio. *Gerontius* he wrote because he must. Successfully to set Newman's poem it required, wrote Jaeger, " poet, a mystic, a dreamer of dreams."[1] All these Elgar was. But he was also patently practical. *Gerontius* overwhelms by its mysticism, but convinces by its authority. In short, Elgar, perceiving its essential fugitive quality, gives to the poem shape and significance, while matching theological convictions with musical assurance.

At the time of writing *Gerontius* Elgar fully accepted the teaching of the Catholic Church and he undertook its composition inspired by religious as well as musical ideals. This is equally true of the subsequent oratorios but in them the didactic impulse may be seen to dominate. *Gerontius* submerges the narrowly doctrinal within the dramatic and lyrical nature of the music and the development and conclusion of the music itself seem to carry the fears and hopes of humanity, in view of death, as profoundly as can any verbal dogmas. It was at the end of the score of his *Te Deum and Benedictus* that Elgar inscribed " inter spem et metum ": the motto would have better fitted *Gerontius* which is so finely poised between those two conditions.

Newman's poem is specific, theologically unimpeachable. After death comes Judgment. Beyond the Judgment are the communion of saints—to be entered only after purgatorial refinement—and the

[1] *The Dream of Gerontius*, Analytical Notes by A. J. Jaeger, p. 3.

convention of the damned. In precise and often frightening terms
Newman sets out the logic of a particular theology. Elgar by trans-
lating the poem into music removes the substantial argument of one
particular creed and indicates a series of spiritual crises which, in the
" Angel's Farewell," are resolved into a state of perpetual beauty.
Elgar was a Catholic and he was a Romantic, and the end of *Gerontius* reads very much like a Keatsian conclusion : truth becomes
beauty. But a great work of art bears many interpretations. So
one man may be content with the poetry of *Gerontius*, another
with its fidelity to the moods of the poem and, therefore, with its
nearness to Catholic feeling and tradition. In the particular case
of Elgar—as indeed in that of Berlioz, who in his *Memoirs* paid
tribute to the poetical and colourful atmosphere of the Catholicism
of his early experience—the capacity for poetical expression arose
largely from early environment. Thus, in the way in which
" Proficiscere, anima Christiana," " Praise to the Holiest," and the
" Angel's Farewell " show in melodic shape, rhythmic outline, and
essential simplicity their connection with the early pieces written
for St. George's Church, we recognise one cause of Elgar's distinction from other English writers of " sacred " music.

In *Lux Christi* Elgar had been more or less content to follow
the main conventions of English oratorio style. He wrote a series
of choruses, recitatives, arias and duets, each complete in itself.
In *Gerontius* he broke away from the conventions and, following the
principle of Wagnerian music drama, constructed a completely
unified whole, in which no single section was independent. The
gain was enormous. For without opportunity to isolate individual
movements the listener is compelled to follow the course of the
work as a whole. The Wagnerian influence is apparent in other
ways. There are, as always in Elgar, " leading themes "—seventy-
six of them. These, perhaps, are not of the greatest consequence
except insofar as they may possess especial musical virtue. More
significant is the manner in which the orchestral and vocal
textures are integrated. This was a stronger break with English
practice, for, in general, composers of oratorios had concentrated
on making the orchestra discreetly subordinate, and the voices
obedient to the academic strictures which governed " part writing."
Elgar sent proofs of *Gerontius* to his friend G. Street Chignell,
organist of St. John's Church, Worcester, and asked that grammatical
errors should be pointed out. When they were he often left the

music without alteration.[1] The point was that every part of his
ensemble should be equally effective.

It is customary to print in programmes the text of *Gerontius*.
The words so printed form a convincing narrative, but by comparing them with the whole of the original poem it will be noticed
that the finest parts are excluded. Elgar's judgment in literary
matters is nowhere more apparent than in the compilation of this
libretto, for philosophically and poetically superior as are the
omitted lines they are too self-sufficient to prompt musical setting.
Yet it may well be felt that Elgar's music takes cognizance of the
whole poem and not merely of the dramatic excerpt which is set.
To read the whole of Newman's *Dream of Gerontius* is an aid to
understanding the spirit of the music. We may examine one
instance.

There is, says the Angel of the God to whom Gerontius passes
for judgment,

> *. . . a pleading in His pensive eyes*
> *Will pierce thee to the quick, and trouble thee.*
> *And thou wilt hate and loathe thyself; for, though*
> *Now sinless, thou wilt feel that thou hast sinn'd*
> *As never thou didst feel; and wilt desire*
> *To slink away, and hide thee from His sight:*
> *And yet will have a longing urge to dwell*
> *Within the beauty of His countenance.*
> *And these two pains, so counter and so keen,—*
> *The longing for Him, when thou seest Him not;*
> *The shame of self at thought of seeing Him,—*
> *Will be thy veriest, sharpest purgatory.*

The duality of this passage lies beneath the last utterance of Gerontius—" Take me away "—in the orchestral texture, where the
conflict of earlier " leading themes " is emphatic.

The course of *The Dream of Gerontius* is indicated in the "Prelude"
by a succession of themes which occupy key places in the work.[2]
As the *Prelude* ends the " Judgment " theme overlaps a rising and
falling pattern in the violins which carries urgently and with anguish

---

[1] See pp. 46 and 48 of the vocal score of *Gerontius* where may be discovered conse-
cutive fifths and octaves, and a " doubled leading note."

[2] The principal themes of Elgar's major choral works are admirably laid out in
the *Analytical Notes*, to which the reader is referred (see Bibliography).

into the death scene. *Gerontius*, interpreted by Elgar as neither grievous sinner nor saint but as everyman, feels the " chill at heart " of imminent dissolution and, with great fear, hears " a visitant . . . knocking his dire summons at my door." " Assistants " pray for the dying Gerontius in an evocative passage which, commencing *a capella*, rises to passionate entreaty. Gerontius delivers his faith in the fierce exultation of " Sanctus fortis "—an episode which, in fervour and in garish colour, recalls Verdi. This is music which out of its context might well be considered as vulgar : but in relation to the character of the dying man experiencing one last savage emotional outburst it is sublime. Gerontius collapses into momentary quiescence : a wonderfully spacious sequence of common chords in the strings, divided into fifteen parts, spreads over " the sense of ruin " a feeling of eternity. Another spasm—of terror— follows and innumerable and uneasy images are presented in a welter of orchestral timbres. The " Assistants " pray again for the soul of Gerontius and in a litany the semichorus interpolates mystical " Amens " between the recitations—to organ accompaniment—of the main body of the chorus. Gerontius, wearied, approaches his end. Elgar leaves the words " and I fain would sleep, The pain has wearied me " in simple recitative. As Gerontius commends himself to God the " Sleep " and " Miserere " themes, the latter incomplete, convey his soul.

The last section of Part I is a march. The Priest and the chorus of Assistants send the immortal part of Gerontius forward with a great pæan of faith and praise. As the sound of many voices— of chorus, at its climax in 8 parts, and semichorus—goes into the far distance the music appears not so much to end as to embark on an endless career, which the human ear is unable to pursue. This is one of the greatest moments in Elgar. Here is the culmination of all the feeling in myth and religious dogma that creates the pageantry with which communities take leave of their dead.

Some foreign critics of the present age (in contrast to their compatriots of an earlier period) find Elgar " cold." It is fair to see some substance for this charge in the second part of *Gerontius*, which is dominated by the lyrical quality of the Angel's music. The realisation of the supernatural atmosphere in which the second part of the oratorio is set is of the most extreme beauty. The music at the outset is the definition of silence (Ex. 33). But not only of

silence : of lightness, of freedom, of deep rest. Into this silence
the Angel enters, quietly triumphant at the arrival of another soul,
but gravely tender at its bewilderment (Exs. 34 and 35). We are,
perhaps, brought back to the delineations of Rossetti : so Jaeger
wrote . . . " As we come under the witching spell of this inspired
and absolutely original song, our thoughts seem to wander, we
know not why, to some saintly picture by a pre-Raphaelite
painter." [1]

On its way to the throne of God the soul of Gerontius is
carried past the dispossessed demons, " chucked down by the sheer
might of a tyrant's frown," who mock at their supplanters as
" psalm-droners, and canting groaners . . . and pious cheat . . . and
crawling knave." Elgar's demon music catches the considerable
and unexpected anger of Newman's verse. Moreover the intellectual argument which Newman contains in the passage is reflected
in the intellectual calibre of the music at this point. The first impact
on the ear is of the shattering intensity of the orchestration, which
at the definition of a saint as :

> *One whose breath*
> *Doth the air taint*
> *Before his death;*

calls for strident triads outlined by 3 flutes and glockenspiel,
3 trumpets and 3 trombones, over a pedal note sustained by the
lower strings, drums and organ. The following satanic sneer—
" Ha ! ha ! " is accompanied by the jingle of bells. The choral
interjections, separated by rests, varied in rhythmic energy, thrown
from register to register, and culminating in acrid and bare fifths—
at (38)—are equally cataclysmic. But within this tumult the
exposition of a double fugue conveys a sense of intellectual power.
At the same time we are shown Elgar's mature conviction that fugal
form should be the composer's servant and not his master.

With regard to fugue he had an original and unexpected attitude.
An early fugal sketch of 1879 (later used in the *Spanish Lady*) was
set for strings *tremolando*. The fugue of the *Introduction and Allegro*
was at first marked *fantastico*. In *Falstaff* a fugato treatment
of Falstaff's " boastfulness and colossal mendacity " theme is
introduced at (44) to illustrate the discomfiture of the thieves

[1] *Op. cit.*, p. 25.

in Eastcheap, and the even more mendacious Meercraft of *The Spanish Lady* is similarly shown—*fugato*. Here, in *Gerontius*, at " Dispossessed, Aside thrust, chucked down " in a complete realisation of the dramatic potential of the most exacting of musical forms.

The demons are left behind and from the noise of their sullen accents Gerontius is taken towards the realm of the Angelicals ; their song floats to him first from the divided soprano and contralto voices of semi-chorus and full chorus above the murmuration of high strings, woodwind and harps. No tonal detail is overlooked. Soft chords are held by the organ, of which the registration—" gamba tone "—is laid down in the score. The hymn grows in power, and, twice, the full resources of voice and instrument are unloosed in ringing chords of C major. Any other English oratorio composer but Elgar would have set this hymn in a more respectful metre : Elgar goes from 3/4 to 4/4 and 9/4—using some ingenious cross rhythms at the " double agony in man "—and thereby achieves an engaging lightness of movement. It has been said that this great climactic section is ineffective. This may be the verdict of the eye. It is not the verdict of the ear. As this part of the work ends—on a third tremendous outburst in C major from the choir, now divided into eight parts—the Angel prepares Gerontius for the final stages of his journey. The Angel of the Agony, accompanied by the priestly quality of trombone chords implores Jesus on behalf of all souls in travail : from the earth come strains of the *Kyrie Eleison*—the words now " Be merciful, be gracious ; spare him, Lord "—as sung at the deathbed : Gerontius seeks his final immolation, his last utterance being prefaced by a majestic statement of the " Judgment " theme (which in *Gerontius* has something of the same authority as the " motto theme " of the first symphony). As Gerontius leaves the souls in purgatory chant part of the ninetieth psalm ; above this rises the solacing melody of the Angel's farewell which loses itself in a faint, but clear echo of the chorus of Angelicals.

Of the music of *Gerontius* it may be felt that it is of that order which Sir Thomas Browne thought to " arch over this world with another and diviner." It is music which commands attention and holds an audience spellbound because it possesses a rare perceptiveness. It is one integrated whole, with all the details of technique subdued to the visionary end. Thus dramatic virtuosity balances lyrical aspiration, and imaginative sensibility is checked by intellectual precision. "But this I saw and knew": Elgar rightly estimated its value.

Gerontius, from the time that Father Knight presented the poem to Elgar, was twelve years in coming to fruition. The succeeding oratorios were in gestation for an even longer period. The idea of composing a vast musical study of the origins of Christianity was established in boyhood, and reading to that end was spread over many years. One powerful influence, which Elgar acknowledged, was Handel's *Messiah*. This, too, was a comprehensive study of the early days of the Christian faith, and culminated, in the third part, in the "extension of the Kingdom." *Messiah* has a masterly libretto which is not too precisely detailed and it leaves adequate space for Handel's musical development. In constructing the texts for *The Apostles* and *The Kingdom* (and the third work which was never completed) Elgar made the error of compiling a too comprehensive verbal picture. So it is that the works become—as is not the case in *Gerontius*—congested with detail. Jaeger made a virtue out of this [1]; but against the common conclusions of æsthetic theory. If, however, *The Apostles* and *The Kingdom* are to be considered—relatively at all events—as failures they are noble failures, and if *Gerontius* had not been written they would still appear as supreme in the tradition to which they belong.

It is clear that the works were long in mind. The book on which Elgar made his first notes (though at what time is not possible to determine) was a *New Testament* (Authorised Version) which is dated April 1882. Some early thoughts for the projected *magnum opus* were used for *Lux Christi* and from that work (1896) one theme passed into *The Apostles*, where it was labelled as the "Light of Life" theme. The next extant sketches date from 1901. In November 1901 the "Morning Psalm" began to take shape. Precisely to date sketches is generally impossible because of Elgar's habit of returning to blank staves when pressed for space. But it is clear that as *The Apostles* progressed so too did *The Kingdom*. For instance the draft of the setting of the "Lord's Prayer"—as it is in *The Kingdom*—appears between those of "Land of Hope and Glory," which we know to belong to the early part of 1902, and the Op. 45 part songs, written in the same year. The arrangement

---

[1] cf. *The Apostles, Analytical Notes*, p. 9, in respect of the Angel's solo—". . . a picture quite pre-Raphaelite in its finish of detail."

of " O Sacrum convivium " is, in fact, dated at Rodewald's house at " 66 Huskisson Street, Liverpool, Dec. 1. 1902." Other parts of *The Kingdom* which appear to belong to the period 1902–3 are the " Prelude " (but marked " Overture "), the " Pentecost " scene and the scene in " Solomon's Temple." As for *The Apostles* a casual observation throws one theme back probably as far as twenty years : the " Judgment " theme—a sequence of augmented triads which accompanies, in the brass, these words of Christ " And whatsoever thou shalt bind on earth, shall be bound in heaven "—is noted in the Sketch Book (No. II) as " old," which Elgar frequently applied to surviving fragments of his thoughts of the years up to 1882.

There were, however, to have been three oratorios. The three were planned simultaneously. One note [1] shows the main lines of the scheme thus :

The Development

I.	Peter Weak & tried	John Love	Judas	B.V.M. Mary	Mary Mag. Sinful & repentant	Jesus
II.	Peter tried & strong	John	Simon Magus etc.	B.V.M. the mother Sapphira	Mary Mag. At peace & serving	The influence always present
III.	The spirit of robust faith St. Everlasting life	The spirit of trusting love	Antichrist Everlasting fire	Barren Women Everlasting fire	Good women Everlasting life	Worthy is the Lamb

Of the concluding part of the trilogy there are many literary but few musical remains. Among the former are glosses on a variety of theological works and sermons (the last work consulted by Elgar having been published as late as 1922),[2] and on the libretti of Philip Armes's *St. Barnabas* and Benedict's *St. Peter*; there are many selected scriptural passages, and the main outline of at least one part of the libretto for the oratorio. Among the latter it is shown that the " Shofar," " Wayside," " Joy," " Gospel " and " New Faith "

---

[1] B. M. Add MSS. 47905, f.7.
[2] See p. 255.

themes [1] were to be carried forward to the end of the trilogy. One or two new themes were noted. Of these the most significant is that specified as " The Judgment " (Ex. 36). In Add. MSS. 47905 this is indicated as the Introduction to the oratorio and continues as shown in the quotation. The idea of the Last Judgment was obsessive : there are other " Judgment " themes in *Gerontius* and *The Apostles* ; and in the last weeks of his life Elgar scribbled the phrase as shown above, handed it to Reed, and said, "This is the end, Billy." It was, however, not as Reed supposed, the end of a symphony ; but the end of a life.

Beyond this there are an " Antichrist " theme, some incomplete choruses based on Zechariah XII, 10, and on James I, 18 ; and a final " Alleluia" (Ex. 36a) to blend with the " Alleluias " of *The Apostles*.

It may be seen that Elgar chose to set to music virtually the whole of the *New Testament*—or at least so much of it as would with music give such total effect. Immediately the difficulties become apparent. The multitude of persons and incidents necessary to give a comprehensive view far exceed the potential capacity of six hours of performance. The brief *schema* quoted on p. 318 shows how Elgar proposed to concentrate his expression : on the one side on the life, teaching, death, resurrection and eternal influence of Christ, and on the other on the conflicting emotions of Judas Iscariot, of St. Peter, and the perpetual antagonistic forms of Antichrist. Elgar in his reading, in his long correspondence with Canon Gorton, in his earnest conferences with Dean Armitage Robinson prepared himself for his task with assiduity. The libretti of *The Apostles* and of *The Kingdom* are admirable—fluent, colourful (the colour often coming from the judicious quotation or paraphrase of apocryphal writings) and convincing. They are, however, too studious and too compact.

The Apostles is divided into seven scenes, the first three con-stituting Part I of the oratorio. Scene I is introduced by a Prologue in which an orchestral introduction leads to a solemn " chorus mysticus "—" The Spirit of the Lord is upon me." The " Spirit of the lord " theme which is first delivered by the orchestra is reminiscent, in wide scoring—the strings divided into fifteen parts— and in diatonic harmony of that in *Gerontius* which holds before the

[1] The two latter marked as for the final oratorio in a sketch dated " Oct. 13, 1913."

dying Gerontius the vision of eternity.[1] The chorus is couched in the grave language of the concluding chorus of Schumann's *Faust*. Behind it stand some of the themes which play a great part in the development of the work : of these the most pregnant are those known as " Christ, the Man of Sorrows," the " Gospel," and " Christ, the Son of God." The first, sharp and dissonant, is beautifully recollected in *The Kingdom*, when St. Peter repeats the words of Christ, " Where two or three are gathered together in My Name there am I," in the Upper Room. The second, urgent and expansive, is also given prominence in *The Kingdom* where it reappears (together with " The Apostles " theme) at the outset of the Prelude. The third of these Prologue themes is one which is outstanding by reason of its exquisite tenderness, by its extraordinarily complex simplicity (Ex. 37). This use of plain chords is one of the most striking elements of Elgar's harmonic style.

The Prologue sets the spiritual standard of the work : what ensues is to be seen as evidence of the Spirit of the Lord. Scene 1 begins with a Nocturne, Christ praying in the mountain preparatory to calling the disciples. At the time of sketching this section Elgar was also engaged on another work—*Cockaigne No. 2*, also conceived as a night piece. Above the shifting colours of the orchestral score an Angel, introduced by a thematic fragment borrowed from the Angel of *Gerontius*, proclaims the prophetic words of Isaiah, as quoted by St. Matthew (XII, 18)—" Behold My Servant . . ." As the dawn breaks the watchers on the Temple roof hail the rising sun. The Shofar—an ancient Jewish ritual instrument which Elgar somewhat academically revives in his score —sounds, and the Temple choristers sing their Morning Psalm within the Temple. Here Elgar employs an ancient Hebrew melody for Psalm XCII and, with other figures intended as Oriental, comes very near to the spirit of Bloch's *Sacred Service*. (In a letter to Miss Adela Schuster[2] Elgar, noting events in Germany in 1933, comments : " The Jews have always been my best and kindest friends." There is a parallel here also with Handel.) The Scene ends with a long chorus celebrating the calling of the disciples. In his first sketch Elgar marked this chorus—" The Lord hath chosen them "—*grandioso*. The chorus is relieved by comments from

---

[1] Jaeger names this (without Elgar's authority, I think) the " Sense of Ruin " theme. He is wrong in being too readily influenced by the words and by being, at this juncture, insensitive to the spiritual point at issue.

[2] Mar. 17, 1933.

St. John, St. Peter, Judas and the Angel and it may be noted that in his frequent use of such contrast Elgar repeats with voices the *concertino-concerto* effect of the *Introduction and Allegro*. " By the Wayside," the second scene, is a setting of the Beatitudes. This, apart from the beautiful opening—akin to that of Part II of *Gerontius* —is dull. The following movement—" By the Sea of Galilee "— on the other hand is fascinating, and gives a passionate portrayal of the supposed character of Mary Magdalene, her past exposed in the abandon of the " Fantasy." A project under consideration at the same time as *The Apostles* was the Rabelais ballet : some of it is here. Some juggling with St. Matthew's text makes Mary Magdalene a spectator of the storm at sea and the miracle of walking on the sea in which St. Peter shows his insufficient faith. A fine piece of imaginative writing leaves the storm music to represent not only the natural storm but also the tumult within Mary's heart. This dramatic and intense episode resolves into a long passage " In Cæsarea Philippi " which is an anticlimax, the music straining under the tyranny of too much mere theology and ending in utilitarian chorus writing. The centre of this section should be the asseveration " Thou art Peter . . .", the phrase of such deep Catholic significance, but the contrition of Mary Magdalene is the most memorable moment.

Part II of the oratorio commences with the " Betrayal." Herein Elgar brilliantly, and dramatically, illustrates his liberal conception of the character of Judas.[1] In this scene orchestral virtuosity reaches its zenith in the picturing of the " Silver Pieces " by piccolo, flutes, oboes, bassoons, harps, organ, cymbals, triangle and glockenspiel. The effect of the striking realism that shows vividly the soldiers, the rabble, the high priests, again detracts from the subsequent episode—" Golgotha," in which the last moments of the Crucifixion defy description in Elgarian terms. Or is it that Bach has said the last word on this in the music of the *St. Matthew Passion* and the *Mass in B Minor*?

In the Easter music of Scene VI there is a moving blend of evocative dawn music (borrowing from that of the opening of the

---

[1] " I was always particularly impressed with Archbishop Whateley's conception of Judas, who, as he wrote, " had no design to betray his Master to death, but to have been as confident of the will of Jesus to deliver Himself from His enemies by a miracle as He must have been certain of His power to do so, and accordingly to have designed to force Him to make such a display of His supernatural powers as would have induced all the Jews—and, indeed, the Romans too—to acknowledge Him King." Elgar, as reported in *Strand Magazine*, May 1904.

oratorio), quiet gaiety and mystical adoration. As in the angelic chorus of *Gerontius* the alleluias of *The Apostles* move fluidly in triple time. The last scene is of the "Ascension" which is concluded by an example of choral writing unique in its disposition for a semi-chorus of female voices, a chorus of female voices, four soloists—Mary, Mary Magdalene, St. John and St. Peter, and a chorus of male voices to represent the Apostles.

In *The Apostles* the prevailing mood is one of gravity. In *The Kingdom* there is lightness of touch and radiance of thought. Elgar, thrilled with the joy of the Early Church, allows poetry to master dogma and sets the whole story within an atmosphere of soft brilliance. *The Kingdom* is a continuation of Elgar's pastoral idiom, the idiom that characterises the finest pages of *King Olaf* and *Caractacus* and the early morning scenes of *The Apostles*.

The Kingdom has its first scene set in the Upper Room in Jerusalem to which the apostles and the holy women repaired after the Ascension and where Matthias was chosen in the place of Judas. The narrative of the first chapter of the *Acts of the Apostles* is amplified by quotations from *St. Matthew* V, 14, from *St. John* XIV, 6, XV, 1 and *St. Mark* XIV, 22. These quotations fill a gap in the narrative, by skilful recapitulation of the most lyrical sayings of Jesus, and, at the same time, stress the Eucharistic purpose of the oratorio as a whole. Scene II shows the lame man at the Beautiful Gate of the Temple (*Acts* III, 2). The time is the morning of the day of Pentecost. In Scene III the story of the visitation of the Holy Ghost on the day of Pentecost (*Acts* II) is set out in detail. The next Scene (*Acts* II, 41, III, 2, 6, 9, 10, 12, IV, 1) continues the story of the healing of the lame man into that of the arrest of St. Peter and St. John. The last scene describes the witness of the apostles (*Acts* IV, 7, *et seq.*) and concludes with a celebration of the Eucharist. Here Elgar engaged in much research on the *Didache* (the writings which incorporated the Eucharistic doctrine and tradition of the Early Church) and made numerous attempts to translate for himself the prayer running through the "Breaking of Bread" movement. In the end, after Gorton too had made suggestions, a translation by W. B. Frankland [1] was used. There follows the Lord's Prayer—sketched in February 1902.

The more tumultous character of *The Apostles* is seen to fall in place as part of the complete scheme which Elgar had in mind;

[1] *The Early Eucharist*, W. B. Frankland, M.A. (London, 1902).

but the length of the work, the complexity of its structure, and the dark character of much of its harmonies and rhythms leave an impression of restlessness and turgidity. *The Kingdom* is infinitely more convincing as music, and it is by musical standards these works must be judged. With less impediment in its text *The Kingdom* moves more exquisitely and more rapidly : as in *Gerontius* there is an awareness that indisputably reflects the individual vision of one mind. Other composers might have written *The Apostles* ; none but Elgar could have made *The Kingdom*. Why then is this oratorio to be set below *Gerontius* ? The reason lies in the episodic character of *The Kingdom*. *Gerontius* is an irrefragable unity. *The Kingdom*, in some respects like *King Olaf*, is a sequence of rare and beautiful lyrics, but without the one beating impulse that commands attention from beginning to end. The unity of *The Kingdom* is achieved by the text, but only then by reference to special literary and theological factors. As always motto themes are repeated and this at one time was thought to be an infallible method. Some of the themes, however, stand too prominently in their own independence to merit repetition. This is especially true of those of the " New Faith " (Ex. 38)—carrying unmistakable Elgar characteristics in the triplets, but too commonplace for its purpose, and of " Penitence "—where repetitiveness becomes wearisome. A further weakness of *The Kingdom* lies in the setting of the " Lord's Prayer " which falls between two stools at a moment of spiritual climax : it is neither ecstatic nor solemn ; the choral writing is undistinguished.

The first scene, on the other hand, reveals choral writing of a magnificence that is not surpassed in *Gerontius*. As the Prelude —which also is of the most rewarding quality, ardent in feeling, flexible in expression—finishes, the unaccompanied voices enter. The texture is bright and the statement diatonic. The first command —" Seek first the Kingdom of God "—falls into St. Peter's greeting, and the reflection of the sayings of Jesus is introduced by a tenderly beautiful meditation in the orchestra on the traditional, plainchant, melody " O sacrum convivium." This, by association, concentrates attention on the spiritual centre of the whole oratorio. One other plainchant melody has previously been indicated in " The Prelude. This is the hymn " Constitues eos," [1] out of which the Apostles " motto theme was contrived. This opening movement

---

[1] " the Gradual in which power is promised to the Apostles and their successors for all time ". Elgar in a prefatory note to *The Apostles*.

of *The Kingdom* has its lightness enhanced by the relative economy of the orchestration, in which two solo 'cellos—alternating at times with solo violas—are prominent, by the eager lucidity of the solo passages ascribed to St. John and to Mary Magdalene, and by the interlude of remote Alleluias.

In the " Scene at the Gate Beautiful " lie the quality of delicacy and the virtue of pity. This extraordinarily gracious music—a duet for the two Marys accompanied by strings, woodwind, horns and harp—is one of the notable monuments in the Romantic tradition and nowhere does Elgar show better his faculty for simple expression. Threaded into the texture of the movement are the themes of the " Temple Watchers " and the " Morning Glory " from *The Apostles*; but the orchestral idea which holds the gaze is that of the " Temple Singers " (Ex. 39).

The Pentecost movement, alive with light from beginning to end, is equally imaginative but of the virtuoso order so far as its scoring is concerned. It is tempting to dwell on the startling verisimilitude of the music which illustrates the " mighty wind " or "the tongues of fire," or indeed on any textual detail of this section; but it is the spacing and adaptability of the voices which is most significant. As in the last chorus of *The Apostles* there is great diversity. Solo voices are freely employed and—in contrast—the male voice chorus of the apostles, a four or six part mystic chorus of women's voices, and a full chorus which ranges from four to eight parts. The voices throughout are employed with full regard to their colour potential and as partners with the orchestra. The moment to which all else leads is the noble deposition of St. Peter—" Ye men of Judea . . ."—in which the authority of the priest in *Gerontius* is exalted as befits the chief of the apostles. " Men and brethren," say the people, " what shall we do ? We have denied the Holy and Righteous One . . ." The anguish of the negligent as expressed in Elgar's questing chromatics and uncertain rhythms furnishes a masterpiece of dramatic intelligence. " Repent," says Peter. " Pour upon us the Spirit of grace " call the people. And so it is that the movement ends in a glorious burst of repentant faith and thankfulness for the gifts of the Holy Spirit.

The fourth movement is dominated by Mary's soliloquy. This has an oriental richness (assisted by the quotation of two Hebrew melodies—the Hymn of Weeping ('Al Elleh) and the Hymn of

Parting (Ham abdil) but also comprehension of the particular nature of Mary : consider the queenly delivery of :

" The Gospel of the Kingdom shall be preached in the whole world,"

which leads to a great statement by orchestra of the theme associated with the " Beatitudes," first heard in *The Apostles*. Consider, on the other hand, the motherly sweetness of Ex. 40, and finally the soaring cadence in which Mary sends as a prayer her song to God. Here ends the great music of *The Kingdom*. There remains the relatively uninspired final movement, the result of Elgar's struggle to fulfil his contract with Birmingham. Writing against the clock is not always the best incentive.

CHAPTER XX

THE SYMPHONIC COMPOSER

To prove the greatness of a work of art is a task as
hopeless as it would be tedious; but, like the candidate who
failed in geometry, I think I can make the greatness of
[these] appear highly probable.

D. F. Tovey on Elgar's Falstaff
(*Essays in Musical Analysis*, iv. p. 3)

WHATEVER OPINIONS are held regarding the quality of Elgar's first symphony one fact is indisputable. It was the first English symphony to live. From the middle of the nineteenth century until 1908, the year in which this work was first produced at Manchester, the byways—as well as the highways—of English music were littered with the emaciated corpses of countless symphonies. It is not, perhaps, generally realised how industrious were native composers. That so many works were so proudly welcomed may stand as a warning to those critics whose charity to new music outstrips judgment. In 1867 Sullivan's " Irish " symphony, played at the Crystal Palace under Manns, gave rise to hopes of a new symphonic master. The first of Cowen's six symphonies came in 1869. In 1872 Sterndale Bennett's G minor symphony fetched " the warmest demonstrations of applause " at a Philharmonic Society concert. In 1885 Ebenezer Prout conducted his third symphony at the Birmingham Festival. From about this time until Elgar's emergence in the field Stanford and Parry—eventually with seven and five symphonies respectively to their credit—held a new monopoly. Two colourful composers, both Scotsmen, with an eye on newer developments in Europe, were Mackenzie and William Wallace. The latter was the first British composer to go over to the manner of the Lisztian tone poem. But from all this welter of ambitious composition not one single piece has survived.

Some brief explanation will serve, by antithesis, to show what Elgar had that his predecessors had not. Prout, Stanford and Parry knew what architectural features should be shown by a classical-style symphony. In an academic way—not unlike their contemporary and native architects, who were slavishly devoted to the copy-book—they built substantial monuments according to precept. Prout and Parry, however, had a moral distaste for glamorous orchestration and were pleased to make a virtue of dullness : they were oblivious of the necessity for orchestral music to be heard as well as seen. Stanford, in whose works are pages of imagination and charm (as in, for example, the " Irish " Symphony) was unfortunate in feeling obliged to accommodate his volatile talents to German discipline. He failed to understand that Stanford was Stanford and Brahms was Brahms. Sullivan, Cowen and Mackenzie each had an ear for orchestral colour, with a welcome appreciation of bright tones, but lacked sufficient thematic invention and harmonic variety for large operations. Most of these men had a little of genius but none the complete faculty.

Against the British school of the late nineteenth century stood formidable foreign competition. To succeed in the open market the British composer must appear as an equal in the company of Schumann, Liszt, Franck, Brahms, Bruckner, Dvořák, Tchaikovsky, Mahler and Sibelius—to mention only the greatest. He must, moreover, furnish an independent point of view—failure in this respect having already caused the extinction of so many native hopes. Yet he must be sufficiently aware of the emotional impulses of the time and of the guiding principles of musical appreciation to be able to establish contact with his prospective audience.

Elgar's qualifications may be briefly recollected. He had proved his mastery in expression, having few peers and no superior in the matter of orchestration. He understood both the architectural qualities of one tradition and the expressly dramatic qualities of another. He knew the temper of the community in which he lived, partly through his own powerful emotional reactions to popular thought, and partly through a shrewd estimate of his own and other people's failures and thwarted ambitions. He was staunchly traditionalist in some respects, but radical in others. Above all he reserved the right to inquire—there was something of Voltaire in his make-up—and to hold an independent opinion. A symphony is, or should be, a vehicle for expressing facets of personality and, through the single personality, of the corporate body of the society in which the personality is moulded. A symphony, or any epic work of art, is the synthesis of individual facets into an artistic unity, which itself may, under certain conditions, hold its own separate existence in its own sphere—of music.

I will not believe that music exists entirely abstractly : it is apparent that in the main stream of European music there is a definition and record of European culture and aspirations to culture. Elgar, himself, believed something of this and certainly in regard to his own music. On one occasion, it is true, he publicly extolled the " abstract " as an ideal. This utterance, given once and in academic society where he was notably ill at ease, was made because he felt it the correct statement in regard to time and place. It had an intellectual flavour and could pass as a generalisation without protest. It may also be said that Elgar had no relish for the detailed incidents which those who mistook realism for reality attached to every bar of certain of his works, notably the *Variations*. On a more private occasion he defined the 'cello concerto as " a man's attitude to life." With this in mind we may pass to the five major works which, together, display this " attitude to life " in full.

In three of the five works the composer suggests the outward influences on his attitude. The second symphony ostensibly commemorates loyalty to an idea—that of monarchy—and to a person, King Edward VII. Within the elegiac slow movement, however, the commemorative principle is not limited, for during its composition there was also present the desire to honour the memory of Rodewald. The violin concerto with its "soul of . . ." is an idealisation of a relationship. It is no accident that this should take the form of a concerto which, materially, is a study also of musical contrasts and affinities. The symphonic poem *Falstaff* is immediately symbolic of Elgar's (and his country's, he would have liked to think) reverence for one part of our antiquity, for which Shakespeare stands as a monument : we all possess some sort of proud response to this name whether acquainted with the dramatist Shakespeare or not. But *Falstaff* is also a scrutiny of a historic character in whom we may or may not see some part of ourselves. In no absolute sense of the word are these three works " abstract."

Lady Elgar sketched some sort of " programme " for the first symphony (see p. 191). Because she was imprecise she is helpful. She shows, for instance, that the " motto theme " was employed in this work not merely because such usage had distinguished the forward-looking music of the more adventurous among late nineteenth-century composers, but because the idealistic conception of the work as a whole required it. Similarly the obscure tonality of so much of the first movement was due primarily to an intention to indicate a state of unrest rather than to engineer new harmonic method.

The thesis of a symphony is epitomised in melody. The melodic material is that which is first to be apprehended and longest held in memory. In an extended work, however, the merit of one melody is relative to the merit of the others. So that which forms the basis of the last movement of Beethoven's ninth symphony is not especially significant except insofar as it stands in that particular work. There are innumerable instances of melodies which are similarly apotheosised by musical environment : those, for example, which dominate the first movement of Schubert's " great " C major symphony, the last movement of the " Jupiter " symphony of Mozart, or the third symphony of Brahms. The essence of a symphonic melody lies first in clarity and, second, in potential expansiveness. The symphonic line is not end-stopped. The symphonic idea—in whatever art it appears—is an exordium : thus, for instance, while their own especial grave magnificence is individually evident, we understand the first four lines of *Paradise Lost*.

Elgar's statements are, in this sense, of symphonic nature. The first symphony commences—*Andante, Nobilmente e semplice*—with a broad proposition which is, by the directness of its rhythmic pattern, arresting. The restraint, however, which allows it first only in two part counterpoint and entirely diatonic is the measure of its future development and growth. This is an enigmatic clause which relates to the future. In the second symphony the exhilaration of the first leaping phrase (closely related in rhythm and melody to the middle tune of the *Sérénade mauresque*) makes a quite different impact. Here it is as though the listener has arrived in the middle of a narration. The first bar—a single line of sound momentarily poised on the spring-board of the dominant—comes, as it were, out of past experience immensely athletic: in the violin concerto a similar urgency is at once achieved. In the 'cello concerto and in *Falstaff* the first moods are again interrogatory. That of the former is gravely suited to the character of the solo instrument, which, virtually unaccompanied, at once asserts its presence. Part of Elgar's genius lay in his complete appreciation of the quality of the sounds he noted down, so that at any time it is easy to be turned aside from the intellectual nature of a melody by the dress it assumes. The *Falstaff* theme—the first of that work—is darkly amusing, as it swaggers through eight bars in 'cellos, bassoons and bass clarinet, careless, and, in its chromatic inflections, more than a little cynical. So far as he could Elgar herein contained Sir John " in a green old age, mellow, frank, gay, easy, corpulent, loose, unprincipled, and luxurious : " of this definition at least half lies in the instrumentation. Going back to the first statements in the other symphonic works this will be found to be generally true. This is the first point of departure from the conventional English academic evaluation of symphony in which " subjects " are appraised according to their appearance on paper.

Although Elgar was prolific in melody he was not (in his symphonies) in the habit of stopping the impulse of his idea to draw attention to his obedience to formal limits. Thus the passage of his movements, the separate parts subtly interwoven, is inevitable—inevitable in a Wagnerian manner. The influence of Wagner should neither be over-estimated nor under-estimated. Apart from certain clear harmonic practices and an equally clear reliance on *motiv* this influence accounts for the plastic quality of Elgar's music. Elgar absorbed the spirit as well as something of the technique of Wagner, and in seeing symphony in the light of this enthusiasm he created a new type of symphony ; more original than that of Franck, more technically accomplished than those of Bruckner, and more objective than those of Mahler.

Elgar was accustomed to detraction. What infuriated him—and Jaeger—was the singular aptitude of hostile critics to set up Aunt Sallies at which to shy their irrelevancies. " No musical composition," wrote Charles Graves in the *Spectator* after his first hearing of the first symphony, " certainly no symphony, can be pronounced great which is not based on the bedrock of noble melody. . . . The chief or ' motto ' theme, which runs through the entire work . . . is sentimental rather than noble, and it owes its effect more to harmonisation and presentation, to orchestral trappings and dynamic contrasts, than to its intrinsic majesty or beauty." Graves—and others who subscribed to his opinion—was perhaps, unaware of Mozart's reaction to the " orchestral trappings and dynamic contrasts " of the Mannheim school. It was eleven years earlier that Jaeger had made this wise comment: " The critics don't lay half enough stress on the *feeling* in the music, the emotional qualities which alone make music *live*. Our Editor and other good folks keep on saying ' very clever, *very* clever ' etc., etc., and I say ' Hang your cleverness, *that* won't make any music great and " alive." ' "

The first symphony at least possesses " feeling " and a sense of " aliveness." If it is clever it is clever in unexpected ways. Elgar himself had something of contempt for academic ingenuity, relying, as did Handel, on the listener's capacity for catching the significance of a hint. Thus his counterpoint is frequently satisfying because of its incompleteness as, for example, in the mysterious and reflective imitations of the last movement of the symphony (130). Here as in the " fantastico " fuguing of the *Introduction and Allegro* and of the demons' chorus in *Gerontius* the form of expression is controlled, intuitively it would seem, by the dominating idea. The dominating idea is clearly indefinable (that is why " form " is a godsend to the casual *cicerone*, and " cleverness " to the learned), but it lies somewhere within the general region of " wonderment."

Theodore Watts-Dunton, the notable Victorian reviewer of Swinburne and Morris, of Meredith and Rossetti, in the *Athenæum*, was at the height of his reputation in Elgar's formative years as a composer. Elgar shared many of his views on Romantic poetry and supported his æsthetics. The " Renascence of Wonder " was no unfamiliar phrase and to view Elgar in the light of Watts-Dunton's definition of wonder is to appreciate his frequent intention. " There are," wrote Watts-Dunton, ". . . different kinds of wonder. Primitive poetry is full of wonder—the naïve and eager wonder of the healthy child. It is this kind of wonder which makes the *Iliad* and the *Odyssey* so full of delight. The wonder of primitive poetry passes as the primitive conditions of civilisation pass. And then for the most part it can only be succeeded by a very different kind of wonder—the wonder aroused by a recognition of the mystery of man's life and the mystery of nature's theatre on which the human drama is played—the wonder, in short, of Aeschylus and Sophocles." [1]

The passage from the development of the final movement of the first symphony to which reference has been made stands signi-

[1] *Poetry and the Renascence of Wonder*, Theodore Watts-Dunton (London, 1916), p. 240.

ficantly in the movement not because it is an effective piece of
musical " development "—in the restricted use of that term—but
because it lies between the two types of wonder, and bridges the
gap. These are the poles of the symphony. Thus the pattern of
the melodies is made to conform to an imaginative rather than an
academic design : on the one hand are those which are " naïve
and eager," on the other those which are Aeschylean. To the
first category belong the " motto theme "—its essence is also
in the third *Pomp and Circumstance March*, the trio tune of the
Funeral March from *Grania and Diarmid*, the trio tunes of the
second, *Scherzo* movement, and the opening melody of the *Adagio*.

This melody is a transformation of the theme which, in semiquavers, is stated at the beginning of the *Scherzo*. In his reference
here to the favourite device of the nineteenth-century Elgar shows
how the same object will appear differently according to the angle
of view.

The main part of the first movement is occupied by restless,
inquiring melodies, which strive in the spirit of Gerontius towards
the unknown. From this point the music moves through a wide
and unexpected range of keys and through a series of rhythmic
alterations and tempo directives which are not the less effective for
appearing inevitable.

In the last movement the progress back from darkness to light
is impressively conclusive. At the outset the emptiness of the music
seems absolute. At the sixth bar, however, the shape of a march
tune is drawn by bassoons, double-bassoon and divided 'cellos.
Six bars later the motto theme begins to show again, but tenuously
in some—not all—of the violins. This is a vision on the horizon.
Before its final achievement lies a stormy passage through a tempest
of agitation. The prevailing rhythmic figure of dotted crotchet
and quaver is one which had also appeared in similar context in the
first movement. At (130) agitation has subsided and the music is
poised in readiness for its *résumé*—or " recapitulation." The future
has been glimpsed some bars previously at (129) where the " motto
theme," delivered only by the back desks of violins and violas,
emerges in the key of A flat minor. The music hereafter keeps
within earshot of this key until in great glory the motto-theme
arrives at (146), to command the listener to the end.

One outstanding feature of this symphony in relation to the
greater part of English symphonic music is its orchestration, which

exists not so much in its own right as in expansion of the ideas of
the music.   Clearly it is brilliant and colourful but, as in the case of
Wagner, high skill is devoted to a higher end.   Certain passages in
which Elgar's genius for orchestral statement is at its most remarkable may be shown from (29) to (31) where high strings and woodwind alternate in a cold climate and where a solo violin rides high
—and, being in B minor, towards the violin concerto; from (54)
to the end of the movement where flute, clarinet and horns in wide
octaves show the " motto theme " against the same figuration;
from (91) to the end of the *Scherzo* with special reference to the
extinguishing effect brought about by a Haydnesque disappearance
of instruments from the score; from (98) where the arabesques of
clarinet and violin intertwine; from (102) where the intensity of
the strings is enhanced by an unexpected entry of the harp.   The
characteristic of these passages is the economy of the scoring; so
it is on account of the contrast with such delicate episodes that the
full panoply of Elgar's grand manner of scoring gives the effect of
opulence.

The corollary to the first symphony is the violin concerto rather
than the second symphony, for the concerto adheres more firmly
to the symphonic ideal.   Additionally, it continues some of the
thoughts exposed in the first symphony.   For instance, in the
strenuous rhythm of the first paragraph is an extension of the
vigour of the symphonic first subject, while the slow movement
makes tranquil company with the symphonic *Adagio*.   As a movement this must be ranked as one of the most beautiful slow passages
in all music.   It possesses greatness in its simplicity.   Simplicity
applauded as a virtue may, however, mislead; for the movement,
not being merely statuesque and therefore cold, moves on and is
thus moving.   Nowhere does Elgar show a more complete understanding of the potential equality of all keys under the suzerainty
of the tonic, for despite a wealth of modulation the overall tranquillity is never disturbed.   Nor can any other slow music exceed
this in ineluctability of organic growth, as shown in the achievement
of climax.

These great instrumental works of Elgar's middle years represent the fruition of their composer's earliest ambitions.   Perhaps
the completion of a great violin concerto meant most to him, for
he was at heart ever a fiddler.   Away back in 1891 he had first
essayed such a work.   Again in 1901 he had taken up the project

anew. Of this there remains (Ex. 41). Therein lies impetuosity. The stretch of the violin part, the groups of semiquavers at the bar ends, the striding bass, recollecting pedal exercise in the organ loft, all denote Elgar. But the idea after germination emerged more complex, more subtle, more personal (Ex. 42). This possesses a highly personal quality, accumulated experience, and wisdom.

As in the first symphony the concerto is prolific in melody, yet the individual melodic fragments appear to bear particularly close relationship to one another so that the unity of the work— accomplished in the symphony by the employment of a master theme—is evident in feeling as well as in form. So far as the formal design is concerned the last movement, conspicuous in concerto history by reason of the wonderful accompanied cadenza, ties up the plan by recollection of material from the previous movements. It is noteworthy, however, that this occurs inevitably, the recollected phrases seeming to belong equally to the third movement as to the concerto as a whole. It may further be noted that the flowing second subject of the first movement—with a side glance at the main tune of the *Introduction and Allegro* [1]—anticipates the intention of the opening of the slow movement.

As for this slow movement the impulse appears to have come from a sketch for another work. While in Italy in 1909 Elgar was contemplating a suite of part songs. Among his sketches lies Ex. 43. This landscape sketch is refined in the concerto, but the atmosphere is not very different (Ex. 44). Elgar's themes are invariably striking—so much he owed to Wagnerian practice—but what is more striking in his most important works is his extension and development of his themes. In some works, for instance *The Apostles* and *In the South*, the process of development is self-conscious and unity is established only by the compelling logic of sure-footed orchestration. In the violin concerto, and later in the 'cello concerto, the sequence of ideas is inescapable in all aspects of the music. In this sense the two concertos are truly classical. To consider whether they are " programme " music therefore may seem an irrelevance. Yet Elgar's genius was such that he could only reach the summit of musical expression under the influence of powerful catalytics.

Here we may return to the inscription at the head of the concerto. In this the significant word is " soul." At the time when Elgar

[1] Note also the persistence of the ⌐⌐⌐ figure as in the *Introduction and Allegro*.

was engaged on the sketches of the concerto he was also busy with
Falstaff and the second symphony—works which are also—and
more specifically—concerned with aspects of human character.
But there were other essays. Among these is Ex. 46. This is
inscribed "To Adela Schuster" and represents—according to a
pencilled note on the same page of MS.—a passage for *Music
Makers*. (There is, at least, a hint of " Nimrod " in this reflection
of late Beethoven.) Later on in his sketches Elgar added another
" soul " motiv (Ex. 45). This bears a general resemblance to the
end phrase of the first subject of the first movement of the concerto, particularly to the sequential developments of this phrase in
the course of the concerto. Thus we may see the broad influence
which excited itself about Elgar during this period of his life : the
" soul " of the concerto was not one specific soul, but a composite
spirit to which Jaeger, the Schusters—both Adela and Frank, and
Julia Worthington—and no doubt others—contributed.

On November 4, 1910, Kilburn added a postscript to a letter
to Elgar : " I want *please* to know what those words inscribed on
the first page of the Concerto mean. Do tell me." Elgar replied
by return of post : " Aqui esta encerrada el alma de. . . . Here, or
more emphatically *in here* is enshrined or simply enclosed—burial
is perhaps too definite—*the soul of.* . . .? The final ' de ' leaves it
indefinite as to sex or rather gender. Now guess." Elgar could
not supply the answer, for no one answer would fit. So may
Tovey well say in respect of the violin concerto :

" Of all external subjects for music the illustration of human
character is the most purely musical ; if indeed it can be an external
subject at all. Music either has character, or it is meaningless, and
the character either has human interest or none. . . . The soul of
the music is musical, and we need no further external programme." [1]

The sketch book which has formed the basis of these observations is labelled " Opera in three Acts—Edward Elgar—Careggi—
May, 1909." This, perhaps, was due to the visit of " Mr. Welch of
the U.S.A." (see p. 148). Nothing very much came out of this
(though it seems possible that some sketches may have been used
in the *Crown of India*) but that opera was very much in mind just
at that time is indicated by a memo accompanying a rough drawing
in the next sketch book, which was bought in Florence : " N.B.
The arch of this church must not be later than 1450 (*circa*). So

[1] *Essays in Musical Analysis*, iii. p. 152 *et seq.*

don't get too crockety. Avoid romanesque." In this idea of an opera clearly lay something of the glories of King Henry V. The idea, however, was not fulfilled in an opera but in *Falstaff* on the one hand and in the second symphony on the other.

The programme of the second symphony is kingship. The dedication to King Edward VII, however, must not be taken in a too narrow sense. Elgar had in mind more kings than one. For instance the second subject of the last movement of the symphony as stated in a sketch book (No. II) in the key of B flat is annotated —" Hans himself ! " Richter to his intimates was known as the " King." But this sketch is further revealing. It is placed among other sketches belonging to the years 1903–4. This in itself— because of Elgar's habit of returning to blank pages—is not con- clusive ; but the page shown in the illustration opposite p. 145 surely is conclusive. The top stave shows the projected *Cockaigne No.* 2—in C minor. On the next stave is a " gloomy " theme dated May 8, 1904, which foreshadows the slow movement of the second symphony. On the right hand side of the page is a " com- passion " motiv. The bottom three staves show in an early state the passage in the slow movement of the symphony which com- mences at (74). The note " Sym. II " has been written in at a later date than 1904.

From this it would seem that the second symphony was that undertaken, but abandoned, in 1904 ; that it was the one in mind for Leeds, and the promised offering for Richter. Indeed it may be that which can be traced back through the Jaeger correspondence to the " Gordon " project.[1] Moreover the apparent fact that this was a first essay in symphonic form may well account for its struc- tural simplicity relative to the more complex work in A flat.

In 1903–4 and again in 1909 Elgar was in Italy and the influence of the country was, as has been shown, very strong. It is, perhaps, no accident that *In the South* and the second symphony are in the same key. In the Sketch Book X (1909) is noted a diminished seventh chord—" in all keys and confused." Beneath it is a further note " I wish I could get the (1000000) frogs in the Vineyard into the score of Sym. II—a fine sound. Aristophanes etc." Where the frogs went, if anywhere, in Elgar's score is anybody's guess

---

[1] cf. letter of Nov. 11, 1898, from Elgar : " Now as to Gordon : the thing possesses me, but I can't write it down yet. I may make it the Worcester work, if that engage- ment holds, so don't, please, pass on the idea." On Nov. 9, 1901, Elgar recorded discussion of the possibility of a " festival " symphony with Rodewald.

but if attention is drawn to the wonderful, ardent, yet sinister scoring in the third movement between (119) and (122) the reference—with its implications—may be apt. This Rondo, one of Elgar's most powerful and original movements is, in any case, said to have had a specific Italian origin.

The Rondo merits close study, however, as a critical rather than as a descriptive piece. Formally compact—note the union of the sections, the interplay of themes and the quotation of the striking, ghost-like melody from the first movement—it throws out challenging cross-rhythms and unexpected harmonic sequences.

In the surrounding movements the moods are almost ingenuous, even though the opulence of orchestration seems to contradict this. The first and second movements are to be seen as well as heard : they are militant and solemn in pageantry. Yet the poetry is inescapable : the poetry of (Ex. 47) which is the second subject of the first movement ; of the movement of strings (Ex. 48), which extends an idea formerly tried in the incidental music of *Grania and Diarmid;* of the counterpoint in the funereal march (Ex. 49). In such moments is music's analogy to Tennyson—" first and foremost a lyric, incantatory poet. The music, the smooth, singing rhythms, the honeyed epithets, the consciously-wrought beauty are complex, dream-inducing, bracing." [1] But in Elgar there was something also akin to Browning : in this symphony in the third movement.

At least once or twice (in the appearances of the episodic theme in C minor, its development and dissolution) the Rondo of this symphony puts us in mind of *Falstaff* and especially of Elgar's quoted commentary on that work : " Sir John Falstaff," he concludes his Analytical Essay, " might well have said, as we may well say now, ' we play fools with the time, and the spirits of the Wise sit in the clouds and mock us.' "

Falstaff is an eloquent expression of Elgar's outlook. It is thought by many, indifferent to a distaste for symphonic poems frequently expressed in these days, that this is his greatest work. That we may doubt for, all in all, *Falstaff* appears perhaps too clearly as an opera without words, abbreviated to the length and adapted to the scheme of a symphony. The listener may follow the systematic guide to *Falstaff* provided by Elgar as for the *Musical Times* of September 1913. If he does he will appreciate the wit,

---

[1] *Notes on Tennyson,* R. G. G. Price, *Punch,* vol. ccxxvi. p. 589.

delicacy and gravity with which Elgar contrives his delineatory phrases, but he may well miss the real point. Elgar's conception of the character was based on an estimate by Maurice Morgann (1726–1802), in his Essay on the *Dramatic Character of Sir J. Falstaff* (1777):

"He is a character made up by *Shakespeare* wholly of incongruities—a man at once young and old, enterprizing and fat, a dupe and a wit, harmless and wicked, weak in principle and resolute by constitution, cowardly in appearances and brave in reality; a knave without malice, a lyar without deceit; and a knight, a gentleman and a soldier, without either dignity, decency, or honour."

The work is divided into four main sections, with two interludes. It runs, however, without break. The sections concern:

I. *Falstaff and Prince Henry.*
II. *Eastcheap—Gadshill—The Boar's Head, revelry and sleep.*
III. *Falstaff's March—The return through Gloucestershire—The new King—The hurried ride to London.*
IV. *King Henry V's progress—The repudiation of Falstaff, and his death.*

At the end of Section II is the "Dream Interlude—Jack Falstaff, now Sir John, a boy, and page to Thomas Mowbray, Duke of Norfolk," at the end of the following section the Interlude in Shallow's orchard in Gloucestershire. These exquisite, nostalgic miniatures—the one fluttering by in muted strings, the other pointing rural detail in pipe-and-tabor music and reflecting on the scene in a characteristically Elgarian string passage—are of the quality of the *Wand of Youth* music.

It is the string music from the Orchard scene which, after the animation of the king's march, the dismissal of Falstaff and the passing of the royal cavalcade, introduces the heart-breaking recapitulation. In these final bars the significant Falstaff themes are recalled in gaunt scoring. "The broken man weakens until, with a weird, final attempt at humour . . . we enter upon the death-scene. . . . True as ever to human life, Shakespeare makes him cry out even at this moment not only of God but of sack, and of women; so that the terrible nightmare version of the women's theme (from Section II) darkens (or lightens, who shall say?) the last dire moments. Softly, as intelligence fades, we hear the complete theme of the gracious Prince Hal (the "second subject" of Section I), and then the nerveless final struggle and collapse ; the brass holds *pianissimo* a full chord of C major, and Falstaff is dead.

In the distance we hear the veiled sound of a military drum ; the King's stern theme is curtly thrown across the picture, the shrill drum roll again asserts itself momentarily, and with one *pizzicato* chord the work ends ; the man of stern reality has triumphed." [1]

This conclusion is one of Elgar's great inspirations. It is, despite the intellectual energy at which he himself hints, music of feeling. It is no commemorative music. Nor is it heroic. In this lies its distinction, for others have remembered the deaths of great men in music. The death of Falstaff is a continuation of a study commenced in *Gerontius* ; but Falstaff is a secular man. This music, the part of the essay in which Elgar describes it, and the story of Elgar's final years might well be set side by side, at least for contemplation—and in an orchard.

What Elgar finally stated in 1913 he had wished to state for many years. Like the idea of the great oratorio that of Shakespeare was long with him. Sketches, indeed, were made for a *Falstaff* work as early as Septmber, 1902 ; but in them there are only stray resemblances to the final work in key, in occasional details of rhythm or contours of melody. It may, however, be deduced that the conception of the character was infinitely less complex than that which finally prevailed. The *Falstaff* of 1902, together with the *Rabelais* ballet and *Cockaigne* No. 2, projected in the following year or two, would not have been a great work. Indeed it would seem that even up to the last the appreciation of the essential nature of the work was developing until the whole was completed at the zenith of inspiration. In (or about) 1909–10 Ex. 50 stands as the "honest gentlewomen's" theme whereas the last revision left an infinitely more penetrating version (Ex. 51).

There is an almost unique inevitability about Elgar's music. Almost every work, good, bad, or indifferent, which he wrote, should have been expected. So far as he was concerned all his large projects were in mind in youth and, as is discovered from his sketches, were considered through the years. This will be found to be the case even with the chamber music, which, of the

[1] *Falstaff*, Analytical Essay, pp. 14–15.

same period of production as the 'cello concerto, caused some surprise on its appearance. The one unpredictable work, however, was the 'cello concerto. This was not an instrument in which Elgar had shown particular interest. No one pressed him to it as to the pianoforte concerto and the opera, which come in and out of the story for nearly thirty years. There are no hints in earlier designs of such a work.

The origin of the 'cello concerto lies within the tangled skein of Elgar's imagination. In a sense it was a work which he wanted, or indeed, needed to compose. After the war of 1914–18, having accomplished all that his earliest visions held, he would almost certainly have renounced composition altogether but for the still ardent aspirations of Lady Elgar. To fulfil her expectations was a first duty. But the mood in which he found himself was opposite to the moods in which the other symphonic works had been developed. Ascetic is as good a word as any other to epitomise his post-war spiritual climate. Being true to his feelings was part of Elgar's romantic heritage and truth of this order is the compelling influence of all his writing. So we recognise the accent of the concerto. The striking feature is the manner in which the basic Elgarian technique is adapted to a new purpose : the style is familiar and of a piece with the rest of his output, but the gravity of expression is no less powerful than that achieved by writers of a more deliberately contemporary order.

The 'cello concerto, confined to half an hour, is the most succinct of Elgar's large works. It is that in which as much is implied as directly stated. It wears a cloak of shyness—Tovey's word—and it is this which leads Tovey into stating [1] that it " well represents its composer's Schumannesque mood." Schumann, indeed, is the one composer to remember as a potent influence on Elgar—more potent than Wagner because Elgar's moods, whims, interests so much overlapped those of Schumann. It is the spirit of Schumann that may appear to speak through the allusive humour of the second scherzo-type movement and through the solemn, questioning, song-without-words that is the slow movement. Schumann's own 'cello concerto in A minor (Op. 129) may conversely be felt as one of the most Elgarian of his compositions. It is also a terse, undemonstrative work. There was, however, one other composer whose example Elgar must have had in mind—

[1] *Essays in Musical Analysis*, vol. iii. p. 200.

Dvořák, the hero of his youth. His 'cello concerto was surely an incentive. Comparison of the last movements of Dvořák and Elgar shows their contiguity of outlook.

Because it is so spare the formal structure of the concerto is of great interest, particularly as the relationship between rhapsody and logic is so happily balanced. The 'cello begins the first movement with a sombre recitative-like theme of four bars, which runs then into a prominent tune, reaching back to the first movement of the *Serenade for Strings*, in 9/8 time, and entrusted to the viola. This theme, intensified, continues until minor tonality is replaced by major. Once again the clear habits of older time come to mind and, according to those habits, a recapitulation ensues. This occupies hardly more than 100 bars. The *Scherzo*, in G major, follows almost immediately with the text, so to speak, delivered twice by the soloist before the movement gets under way. The main concern of this movement—despite a lyrical second subject which arrives in the untoward key of E flat major—is with a *perpetuum mobile* of semiquavers. Somewhere behind this is a similarly persistent pattern in the *Introduction and Allegro*. In this movement there is no turning aside, no digression. The slow movement is even more single-minded and extends one melody over 60 bars. The key is now that of B flat major, but ending on a chord of F major. The last movement takes up from this point as if following a conversational aside. The first eight bars move from B flat minor to the dominant of E minor where, again, the 'cello indicates the main impulses subsequently to be studied in a passage which is half recitation and half cadenza. A short chord of the dominant—one of the few moments in the concerto where the entire orchestra is playing, followed by a pause, prefaces the movement proper.

This final movement is sent on its way by a dactyllic subject which is poised between grave and gay by characteristic Elgarian restraint. As before, the soloist takes the lead and so it is when the second subject—" slightly suggestive of dignity at the mercy of a banana-skin," writes Tovey—arrives in contrast. The development of this exposition follows classical principles, but the tautness of the thought is emphasised by much thematic imitation in the parts which surround the energetic figuration of the 'cello. It is at the end of the recapitulation that Elgar turns aside, as though content to have shown so much of formal propriety for so long, and considers propositions that are both new and old. That Ex. 52

should arrive and passionately grow into Ex. 53 is unexpected in the sense that no other composer would have taken the same course. Within Elgar, however, the references are not obscure : we are returned to the neighbourhood of the " Death " and " Angel of the Agony " themes in *Gerontius* and the " Golgotha " music of *The Apostles*. From this the 'cello proceeds to announce the first four bars of the concerto and sixteen bars thereafter suffice to conclude the rondo movement and the complete work.

If Elgar had completed his third symphony it would have been performed within a year of the first performance of Vaughan Williams's fourth symphony. The comparison would have been instructive, for Vaughan Williams is not one who would readily turn his back on a definition of any work of his as " a man's attitude to life." When Vaughan Williams's fourth symphony appeared it was construed as a return " to the world of action—and a violent world he found it. . . . It belongs to an unlovable age, which it interprets and criticizes implacably." [1] No one was more aware of the unlovable qualities of the early thirties than Elgar. So the beginning of the third symphony—with a sidelong glance at a newer style than his own—runs tumultously (Ex. 54). This is the obverse of the opening of the second symphony and an eloquent commentary on the days that were gone.

Eight bars of this movement are scored. For the rest all that remains of the symphony is in various passages indicated in short score.[2] The exposition of the first movement is fairly complete but there is a gap until the reappearance of the second subject in the recapitulation section. Of the second movement—an *allegretto* " in place of Scherzo "—the opening passage, light with semiquavers, yet with gaiety modified by muted strings and by the key of A minor, exists, and two episodes of much less intrinsic interest. The main *Scherzo* tune was also intended as part of *The Spanish Lady* ; but where it should belong in the opera is not made clear. Eighteen bars of a spacious *Adagio* (with versions in two keys— of E flat major and D major) and some small subsidiary passages were written for the third movement. Of the Finale the outline of an exposition (in C major) can be pieced together.

There remain the " Judgment " theme (Ex. 36)—which was

[1] *Sixteen Symphonies*, Bernard Shore, p. 285.
[2] The whole of the material of the projected symphony is at present in the British Museum. There are, however, facsimiles in W. H. Reed's *Elgar as I knew him* and copious analysis.

the last music written down by Elgar. W. H. Reed thought it might have been intended for the final movement of the symphony, or alternatively for the *Adagio*. Whatever its intended situation the reference back to it across the years helps to explain the curiously moving episode which supervenes in the finale of the 'cello concerto. Among the sketches for *The Spanish Lady* lies the beginning of the " Judgment Theme "—two notes only. It is detailed " Sym. III Intro." I think this was an interim proposal and that when the symphony began to take final shape the idea of such an introduction was dropped. But the significance of the extra-musical idea in the symphony was clearly great.

The third symphony would have been listed (as Elgar noted in his own private catalogue) as Op. 88. The opera was to have been Op. 89 and the pianoforte concerto, so frequently discussed, Op. 90. Had Elgar been given six more working months both the symphony and the opera would, so far as may be judged, have been finished— or so nearly finished that their completion by another hand would not have been impossible.

The pianoforte concerto, on the other hand, in its fragmentary condition bears no signs of the eagerness characteristic of the other unfinished works. It is evident that this was an intention to please other people rather than an irresistible inspiration. It is significant that the most nearly finished movement is the slow movement—but the genius of the pianoforte being outside Elgar's sympathy the resulting nocturne type piece is not particularly rewarding either for player or listener.

The first movement is based on material discarded from the second symphony, or perhaps even retained as possible for the third symphony. The available material shows these outlines :

Theme 1 (Ex. 55). This, originally marked sym, is repeated *ppp*, with rather fuller chording in the pianoforte. Then the upper strings state it yet once again making for a cadence on C major. Theme 2 (Ex. 56) which is specified as " 2nd theme." There is also a version of this theme in E flat, and a number of subsidiary themes, of which the eventual place in the scheme is impossible to determine. The slow movement commences (Ex. 57), and changes after sixteen similar bars to Ex. 58. This movement is conventionally constructed in the classical " abridged sonata " form. The finale begins with a slow introduction in which the brass is conspicuous. Then a theme as for a rondo breaks out Brahmsianly (Ex.

59). The first motiv is now placed in C minor. After three bars
the sketch breaks off and of the future course of this movement
there is no suggestion. So we are left with a puzzle of tonalities
—C minor, D major, G minor and, in addition to the principal
themes, a dozen disparate ideas springing from the stray thoughts
of more than twenty years.

CHAPTER XXI

CHAMBER MUSIC

*What an outlook! A sonata for V. & P.!!! and a
Piano & String Quintet!!!?
    At last we chamber music people get also our due from
one whom we so much admire in his choral & orchestral
works.*

                    Dr. Adoef Brodsky to Elgar, Dec. 30, 1918

ELGAR'S CHAMBER MUSIC arrived in 1919 with apparent unexpected-
ness : this, it was suggested at the time, was out of character. It
is immediately clear that the sonata, quartet and quintet do represent
facets of the composer that had hitherto been hidden. The medium
—and no man ever studied his medium with greater care—was held
partly to account for this. But the overall tautness of effect and
economy, amounting almost to austerity, was—and is—startling.
A generous survey of Elgar's output, in which many experiments
are to be noted, puts this in perspective. But there is a practical
consideration of some importance.

It will have been seen that Elgar continually set down fugitive
ideas in his sketch books against the time when they might be
incorporated in some work or other. It would sometimes seem
that he found it difficult to resist certain passages which were,
accordingly, given houseroom. So in *The Apostles* and in *Falstaff*
(some, but not I, would quote also the first symphony), in the unfinished pianoforte concerto and the opera there is thematic congestion. This is not the case in the chamber music.

This, together with the 'cello concerto which shares the same
economic quality, was conceived in Sussex. The sketch books in
which so many phrases familiar in other works lie were not at
Brinkwells. Thus Elgar was not able to consult what he had in

reserve. It is, of course, clear that what had been committed to paper was also in mind—but in a general rather than in a particular way and there was not the temptation to work in ideas for their own special attractiveness. In fact had the sketch books been to hand it is almost certain that some previous attempts at chamber music would have made fresh appearance. In 1920 Elgar began a trio for violin, 'cello and pianoforte. He went back to an essay for the same combination which he had begun in 1878 and reworked it. After revising two-thirds of a movement, however, his interest dwindled and no more was done. What was accomplished was strangely, almost pathetically, immature.

Wordsworth's thesis concerning the recollection of emotion in tranquillity is apt to Elgar's Op. 82, 83 and 84. The emotional quality of the music is beyond question: the slow movements of the sonata and the quartet and the first movement of the quintet stand out as landmarks in modern chamber music. It may well be that these movements were directly stimulated by the legend of the dead trees in Flexham Park, but their origins lie further back than that. Elgar, as every other great composer, was half craftsman and half seer. It was a late response to his earliest ambitions as a craftsman that was fundamentally responsible for the chamber music. This was encouraged by the frequent presence in the household of W. H. Reed, whose charm and sympathy were transmuted into authority and beauty in chamber music performance.

The direction which Elgar's career took during the years in which he established himself was inevitable. Choral and orchestral music offered the possibility of at least a modest livelihood: chamber music did not. So Elgar was compelled to put on one side for many years the fulfilment of some of his earliest ambitions. It should not be forgotten that during his long obscurity his chief pleasure in music was in chamber music ensembles, with the Leicesters, the Whinfields, the Fittons, and the Bucks, as well as with the members of his own family. It was evenings with Mozart and Haydn, Beethoven and Brahms, Mendelssohn, Schumann and Dvořák that gave him technical accomplishment.

Even in the slightest domestic music his eye was discerning. Thus the large corpus of unpublished wind pieces composed for the Sunday quintets cannot be faulted on technical grounds. The *Promenades, Intermezzi* and *Harmony Music* are scrupulous in regard to instrumental aptitude on the one hand (as, in recent years, the enterprising Mr. Parr has demonstrated in performances in Sheffield) and in formal propriety on the other. At the age of twenty-one Elgar could wind up sonata form with the most earnest German academicians—Thuille, Rheinberger and company, who also went in for wind music—and make a single movement—*Harmony Music V*: *Allegro moderato*—last for twenty minutes. This movement he called " The Mission." Feeling, no doubt, that some of his movements required further exploration he bestowed sub-titles with Schumannesque eagerness. An *andante con variazioni* becomes an " Evesham Andante," an *adagio cantabile* " Mrs. Winslow's Soothing Syrup," an *allegro maestoso* " Hell and Tommy," a *Promenade-moderato*, with unconscious respect to Moussorgsky's Exhibition "Madame Taussaud's (*sic*)." None of this music—although one *Sarabande* fits magnificently into *The Spanish Lady*—is remarkable except for the devotion to technique which it symbolises. Each piece is beautifully and finely finished. One hopes that it was played as efficiently as it was written.

There is, however, one little work from this period which deserves resuscitation—the fugue in D minor for violin and oboe composed for Frank Elgar and Karl Bammert in 1883. This brief work is an early example of Elgar's quality as contrapuntist—a quality often overlooked—but also it shows the laconic manner which in later life might otherwise appear as uncharacteristic.

In 1878–79 Elgar was engaged in exploring the possibilities of chamber music for strings as well as for wind. To that period belongs a quartet, to which reference has already been made and from which episodes were drawn at the end of his life for the opera, and the trio which also came to light at a later time. In 1887 there is reference to another trio, this a conjoint affair as a letter [1] to Dr. Buck shows. In this too is the authentic voice of the craftsman:

" The Trio [apparently written by Dr. Buck, who was a composer in a modest way] came safely to hand & we have played the slow movement several times in private & the verdict is—gigantic! It is too monstrous however for three instruments. Fiddle, 'cello & piano all seem to distend themselves frog-wise 'till they burst in a vain endeavour to represent an orchestra. Since I received it I have added a ' Scherzo & Trio,' which is *jam*. The Scherzo is new & very difficult, but goes with a swing wh : would make you dance to Pen-y-Ghent & carry a cage of parrots as well (do you

[1] Jan. 7, 1887.

remember our exploit ?) [1] the Trio (mea culpa) I have transferred bodily from the little thing I wrote for you on my first visit to Giggleswyke (*sic*) ; and I humbly ask pardon but think it too good & sugary to be left to your tender mercies only. I hope to play this with you some day."

A year or so later there was another attempt at string quartet, of which traces exist in a small manuscript book. There are some parts of a first movement *allegretto* in 9/8 time and in D minor ; of an *adagio* in B flat major ; of an *Intermezzo* in F major ; and of a lively Haydnesque finale in D major. The *Intermezzo* was almost immediately transcribed for organ and may be found among the *Eleven Vesper Voluntaries* published by Orsborn and Tuckwood in 1891.

Elgar admitted into his final catalogue as Op. 8 a string quartet which together with Op. 9, a violin sonata, is noted as destroyed. In his own list this quartet is shown as also eligible for wind. It seems not impossible that the quartet in question is that from which the *intermezzo* leads a cloistered existence in other dress.

This is not the end of early quartet writing for in a sketch book of *c*. 1905 there are a few bars in E minor—with similar descending and overlapping arpeggios to those in the quartet of 1918–19— labelled " Old Quartet "; which type of reference generally throws back to *c*. 1878–80.

From about 1905 other material began to accumulate for the string quartet which Elgar wished to write. This time there was a stronger incentive, for he had become acquainted with the Brodsky quartet—an ensemble which he wholeheartedly admired and was responsible for inviting to Malvern. In the autumn of 1907 a good deal of time was spent in composing a quartet, as the diaries show. But, again, other affairs supervened and the work was left undone. And, again, there appear to be no extant sketches.

Finally we arrive at 1918 and to the fulfilment of the ambition of thirty years.

If the works of that time do not directly employ material from earlier days they do at least catch the spirit of yester-years. The relation, for instance, between the first movement of the quartet and that of the *Serenade for Strings*, or the *Romance* (Op. 1) is estab-

[1] " I have often heard my father laugh over this same incident. He & Sir Edward were carrying the parrot in a cage which was slung on a stick between them. As they crossed Settle Bridge the bottom dropped out & they walked on leaving the parrot sitting in the road behind them." Mrs. M. Greenwood to the author.

lished both in key and rhythm. One may look behind the strange pattern of the introduction of the quintet and discover stray forecasts of this mystery in the note-similar A minor phrase of the second of the violin studies of Op. 22 or in the second notable turn of melody in the *Idylle*. In the second subject of the first movement of the violin sonata can distantly be seen the second subject of the *Romance*. The animation of the piano part of the last movement of the quintet is the animation attempted in *La Capricieuse*. It is experience—experience of life—that has transmuted these early aspirations. But as formerly the work is that of one who loves chamber music for its own sake.

The violin sonata is a work at once powerful and fascinating. Power lies in the structure of the music and in the heroic properties of the violin part, fascination in the quality of the *Romance* and in the oblique harmonies which set so much of the music in interrogatory mood. There is, perhaps, some thinking-up of Brahms—of the violin sonata in D minor (Op. 108)—and of Mendelssohn, whose Op. 44, No. 2 has its affinities both with Elgar's sonata and quartet. It is inevitable that if similarities of phrase or rhythm are looked for that they will be found. Accordingly the fact that Elgar's first movement melody—there are, as normal, two " subjects " but the second at (5) clearly derives from the inversion of the first shown at (3)—is prominent in Mendelssohn need not be laboured : even though close attention to the three note descent which falls into the *Variations* from *Calm Sea and Prosperous Voyage* is a major concern in development. Nor need the vitality of the " trochaic " rhythm, generally supposed to be an Elgar characteristic, in the first movement of Brahms. But Elgar here is at one with the classics. He could, however, have learned from Brahms how to blend with violin the sonorities of the pianoforte. Throughout the sonata Elgar hands out to his pianist the stock-in-trade of the text-books. It serves, of course, for the continuity of the fiddle part is compelling ; but under close scrutiny the manner of the pianoforte, now apologetic, now oppressive, is repellent. On the other hand Brahms might very well have been glad to have written so miraculously for violin.

The sonata is in E minor. The first movement apparently commencing in A minor, or near A minor, in an allusive way again reminiscent of Mendelssohn, becomes an extensive plagal cadence. Thus by concentration on subdominant tonality the way is prepared

for the slow movement, which is justly respected even by those
who generally dislike Elgar. This is a personal utterance, owing
to no one and, for that matter, influencing no one. It stands alone.
In the poetry of the opening, which is temporarily keyless, the
descending feature of the first movement becomes infused with
nervous movement. The whole, despite the limpid second subject,
characterised by leaps of a fifth and a fourth and by the unusual
key of B flat major, has a spectral quality. It is a night piece such
as might put us in mind of Whistler, or of the unwritten *Cockaigne
No. 2* which Elgar had intended as a nocturne.

The *Romance* ends in A major. So the E major opening
of the finale falls happily. The placid, contrapuntal progress over
a pedal bass catches memories of Elgar the organist and there is
a Franckian serenity, enhanced at the third bar by the cool interpolation of a flattened seventh. Hereabouts Elgar's affection for
sequence gives great beauty to the score. It is not long, however,
before a more strenuous motiv supervenes. The two themes are
exquisitely balanced and the tranquil attitudes are enhanced by a
late reference to the middle movement. In the coda-cum-recapitu-
lation the two main themes are metamorphosed, the first now
appearing in the minor and the second in the major.

If the slow movement of the sonata may be construed as a
nocturne then that of the quartet—*piacevole*, in three time, and in
C major—might well represent an *aubade*. Here, in fact, if not in
name, is Elgar's real *chanson de matin* ; and, as if to lay emphasis,
at (27), where the first theme reappears, the first violin counter-
subject unmistakably, but fortuitously, quotes from Op. 15, No. 2.
The second violin has a field day in this movement—though the
equality of the participants is maintained scrupulously throughout
these ensemble works—for the opening tune is his and his alone.
Beneath, the viola and 'cello play respectful counterpoint. When,
eventually, the first violin enters an octave above the second the
dynamics are reduced from *p* to *pp*. The artless run of this movement
is the kind of music which everybody who has slight pretensions
to composition feels he should be able to write : yet it eludes the
common grasp. The detail—again pre-Raphaelite in execution—is
exquisite. The least of effects illustrates this : the muted return of
the theme beneath the high E of the first violin, or the handling of
the cadence, which again is plagal.

The outside movements of the quartet are of less immediate

interest. Or is it that they run too close to the spirit of the *Intro-duction and Allegro* for comfortable comparison ? The first move-ment, built on a restless modal group of E minor, D major, G major and B minor chords, on a downward-reaching arpeggio pattern in 12/8, on a declamatory rhythmic figure—at first divided between 'cello and upper strings—and on a broad, swinging phrase still in E minor, is a masterpiece of terse development. Despite the final flings of *appassionato, nobilmente* and *con fuoco,* however, there is some element of factitiousness : the penalty, perhaps, of too little variety in the exposition. I suppose this is that part of Elgar which critics sometimes discern as frigidity. The last movement is imaginatively greater. It ranges further in melodic invention. The urgent rhythmic beginning recalls a bar or two that Elgar once—about 1905—set down as for a *Fantasia* for strings, for Richter. Rhythmic excitement, carrying to a significant dipping third in the far distance of E flat minor, temporarily subsides when the second subject, in the atmosphere (rather than the key) of A major, brings some exquisite and wayward elements in which, however, the lyrical is tempered by some palpitating chording. At (45) the viola announces a new motiv in semiquavers : for Elgar a hard, remorseless tune, which, intermingling with the previous themes, assumes importance and leads to a vigorous ending. As in the slow movement there is one moment of highly imaginative scoring (Ex. 60). Basil Maine [1] observes : " All that has gone before in this and the earlier movements has been essentially the music of daylight and the open air : so much so that this sudden break in its genial warmth is strangely sinister, as if it were a capricious and wilful disturbance of the clear, delightful atmos-phere." Here he sees the influence of environment, of the sinister trees.

It is with a dark gesture that Elgar commences his quintet (Ex. 61). It will not go unnoticed that the signs of this disturbing vision show themselves within the slow movement of the quartet. But here the mystery is intense. So it remains through the course of a movement which in some ways may be ranked as Elgar's greatest single movement. Elgar was no great tragic artist—in the sense that Beethoven and Bach were : in the quintet he approaches tragic greatness as Shakespeare in *King Lear* was allowed to approach it by Johnson :

[1] *Elgar—His Life and Works,* ii. p. 267.

" There is perhaps no play which keeps the attention so strongly fixed ; which so much agitates our passions and interests our curiosity. The artful involutions of contrary characters, the sudden changes of fortune, and the quick succession of events, fill the mind with a perpetual tumult of indignation, pity and hope. There is no scene which does not contribute to the aggravation of the distress or conduct of the action, and scarce a line which does not conduce to the progress of the scene. So powerful is the current of the poet's imagination, that the mind, which once ventures in it, is hurried irresistibly along."

In the commencement of the quintet is time for reflection. The initial motiv disappears into the darkness of the lowest strings of viola and 'cello, muffled by octaves in the bass of the pianoforte, and admits at (1) a contrasting idea : a question on the upper strings which is partly answered by an eager response by the 'cello. Here we are seeing the work as a whole, for this second section— which is used throughout the movement—is essentially the introduction to the last movement. At (2) the time is changed to 6/8 and a fierce episode shows a prominent descent of chords in the pianoforte, somewhat derived from the opening bars of the pianoforte part ; against it is an urgent counter-theme in the strings, again largely in octaves. A dramatic pause prefaces a long development section in which freedom from conventional key sequences and textural procedures is balanced by an extraordinary devotion to the essential qualities of the principal themes. Two variants of the opening statement of the strings show Elgar's uncanny perception of the personality of a theme (Exs. 62 and 63). The same pianoforte figuration lies below both. W. H. Reed finds something " Spanish, Moorish, or possibly Oriental in character " in the first of these : the monks of the Sussex legend were Spanish, so it is that Elgar recaptures something of the exotic idiom of the picturesque pieces of early years. This idiom also affects the last movement at (49).

The first movement ends as it began. The *Adagio* opens in serene contrast with a viola melody of disarming loveliness in E major : not what would at once appear as a tune by Elgar, but, on reflection, a descendant of the *canto popolare* of *In the South* (Ex. 64). From this the whole movement stems, coming at (35) to a passionate climax in E minor.

The final movement is a brilliant dissertation on Ex. 65. This is the answer to the interrogative passage from the first movement with which the last movement begins. Other themes are grouped around, including the pianoforte octaves from the first bars of the quintet, but they are subsidiary to this powerful champion which rides to eventual glory *grandioso, animando* and *sonoramente*.

There are but few pianoforte quintets in common use. Elgar's is one of them. Compared with those of Schumann, Franck, Dvořák, it stands as at least co-equal. Less intense than Schumann's, less gracious than Dvořák's, less doctrinaire than Franck's, though with affinities with all three, it occupies an empirical position. It is romantic, even impressionist ; yet formally exact in the manipulation of detail and the siting of effect : it is at once outspoken and reticent ; the string parts are those of a virtuoso composer, the pianoforte part the reverse. Yet in this last point a particular excellence emerges. W. W. Cobbett points out how " the piano part is written in a style quite new to chamber music, not in the concerto style usually adopted by composers for piano and strings, but as one part in five ; a highly artistic, if not a pianistic conception." [1]

In all the chamber music Elgar's style is notable : in the quintet the ideas are worthy of the style.

[1] *Cobbett's Cyclopedic Survey of Chamber Music,* i. p. 377.

CHAPTER XXII

INCIDENTAL MUSIC

Whosoever is " wumbled " let him listen to Sir Edward Elgar.
                                        The Times, Dec. 30, 1915

IN GENERAL there is a no more unprofitable occupation for a British
composer than writing an opera. So Elgar never did. What
he did and what he wanted to do are, however, of different orders.
His ambitions led him towards ballet and—in a less direct manner—
towards opera, but his opportunities stopped short at a charity
piece on the one hand and various sets of incidental music on the
other. Beyond this there was the matter of reputation. Elgar's was
zealously guarded by his friends and any tendency on his part to
leave the high road reserved for great composers was resisted. The
ballet that he wanted to write is a case in point.

On November 19, 1903, Elgar added a postscript to a letter to
Troyte Griffith :

" I spoke to [Harry] Higgins Royal Opera & he is keen to
produce ' rabelais ' on the lines I suggested ! New costumes &
everything—' like a shot.' We'll have some fun one day."

In the light of the *Wand of Youth* pieces and of the *Variations*,
especially bearing in mind Elgar's own wishes in respect of them,
a ballet (assuming the availability of dancers) might have been
expected about 1903. But the subject ! As soon as intimates heard
mention of Rabelais cautionary voices urged that such a source of
inspiration would destroy any reputation. So there was no ballet.
There were preparatory sketches, however, and Elgar had his
private laugh in the end, when one of his Rabelaisian tunes was set
into the *Coronation March* of 1911. There it lies at the outset, now
maestoso, in triple time—in triple time because it did not set out on
its career as a march tune.

That there was no Rabelais ballet is, I suspect, our loss ; for
the subject is one which Elgar could, more effectively than almost
any other composer, have transmuted into theatre music.

Elgar possessed a consummate appreciation of the theatre.
When he was required to write incidental music he hardly ever put
a foot wrong.   Some of his pieces held only transient value, but
given the particular occasions to embellish or enliven they are
immediately effective.

His first music for the stage was for *Grania and Diarmid* and it
won George Moore's high regard.   " Elgar," he said, " must have
seen the primeval forest as he wrote, and the tribe moving among
the falling leaves—oak leaves, hazel leaves, for the world began
with oak and hazel."   In fact Elgar achieves all this with a juxtaposition of A major and A minor tonality divided among the horns,
and with a single phrase delivered by the clarinet.   The Funeral
March has outlived its first purpose and is now in the general
repertoire of funerary pieces.   It is a rich obsequy, fit for the heroic
Celtic theme which Yeats and Moore celebrated, and given the
proper dignity of antiquity by being cast in a modal atmosphere.
The Aeolian mode turns up—as it does sometimes in Mendelssohn
—as though it belonged to the age and had not been im-
ported by special licence.   There is, too, a magniloquent trio in
this march, wherein may be heard the distant tread of the first
symphony.   Here Elgar shows how two parts may sound like ten
(Ex. 66).   But the gem of the collection is the song " There are
seven that pull the thread," in which Elgar unusually refers to the
idiom of folk-music.   This delicate evocation—with the thread
pulled through by violins and violas, and sun-in-water reflected in
snatches of clarinet, with a whimsical and recurrent phrase in the
upper strings (related to a passage in the second symphony) and
an occasional harp chord to give the wash of elusive and Irish clouds
—is Elgar's most perfect song.   It bears comparison with Schubert.

In the early months of 1912 Elgar, having moved into Severn
House and being conscious not only of its nobility but also its
expense, was glad to undertake Mr. Oswald Stoll's commission to
compose the music for a grand, honorific masque to celebrate the
impending royal visit to India.   Henry Hamilton's libretto, a period
piece but not unaware of the masque principles that inspired various
poetasters at the Caroline court, filled Elgar with some alarm on
account of its political emphasis, but caught his fancy in its pic-

turesque possibilities. Having excised the more stilted lines of
the verse he reviewed his task. With a month in which to execute
it the temptation to fall back on old material was strong. So he
examined former sketches and—she being presumed as a competent
authority on oriental matters—consulted the Ranee of Sarawak.

The " Dance of the Nautch Girls " was a diverting essay
in the New English style (Ex. 67). There is no reason to
suppose that in 1912 it appeared un-Nautch-like. But its first
version (*circa* 1909) suggests that it was, in fact, contemplated as an
episode for *Falstaff*. (A somewhat cryptic note is inscribed—
" Sneak's horse.") *Falstaff*, as has been shown, was commenced
in 1902. The opening bars of " India greets her cities " are a relic
of those days, and foreshadowing of Sir John's " mendacity "
theme. An interpolation of 12/8 time during the apostrophe of
Benares also belongs to 1902, where it neighbours a grotesque
little motiv which found its place ultimately in the *Fan* ballet.

A hint of the march theme of the " Entrance of Calcutta " is
also among the 1902 sketches, but in 4/4 time and with a note by
Elgar for the benefit of musicologists—" fools would say this is
like ' Land of Hope.' " Something nearer to the final form of the
Entrance music is on another piece of paper (stuck to the sketches
of 1912) where it was at some time labelled " Suite." Reference to
the illustration facing page 145 will show that the music for the
" Entrance of Delhi " is an episode from *Cockaigne No. 2*. " All
this," wrote Elgar, as he looked at the music after ten years " is
quite good enough for something serious."

In the " Crown of India " march there are two prominent
themes. The first, a sweeping tune in E flat and beginning *nobilmente* after a fanfare of trumpets, comes from the period (1903–4)
in which the second symphony was beginning to form. The
connection between this tune and the symphony is apparent.
Elgar's memorandum read " Symphony ? " The middle tune of
the march comes from a sketch formerly noted as " March No. 4? " [1]

For the rest it would appear that some superfluous material
from *The Apostles* was incorporated into the *Crown of India*. The
" March of Mogul Emperors " is first discovered among oratorio
drafts and there is also a motiv at first designated " Jews " and after-

[1] In addition to the *Pomp and Circumstance* marches as at present constituted Elgar
made numerous other drafts over the years, and it was, indeed, expected by his publishers that there should be a set of six.

wards marked " Coliseum Masque," but in the end left unattached
to any work.

Clearly, despite the skilful spread of motiv, there is no genuine
consistency in the *Crown of India*, but vivid flashes of imaginative
treatment, combined with instances of tenderness and charm—as in
the *tempo di menuetto* (*antico*) for the " Entrance of John Company,
for which Elgar specified " pigtail stuff here," and in the " Interlude "—compensate for the " Ave Imperator " temper of much of
the work.

Elgar's adaptability, combined with his capacity for seizing
the significance of a dramatic idea from the point of view of the
audience, and his amazing craftsmanship, would have qualified
him as an ideal composer of film music. This is shown in two
works of the period of the First World War—the *Starlight Express*
and the *Fan* ballet.

The *Fan* has a fortuitous connection with the *Crown of India* in
using an old tune which was also considered for use in the masque.
This, however, is the only connection, for the ballet is light and
fanciful. Shepherds and shepherdesses, and young men and
maidens dressed in the period of Louis XV, frivol and languish by
turns with, or on account of, Echo and Pan. To this company
are added nymphs, satyrs, dryads, butterflies, and the winds. The
plot is involved as mortals and immortals fall in and out of love,
and thunderclaps spasmodically register Pan's jealousy (because of
the promiscuous habits of Echo) and wrath. Elgar setting his
field between the *Wand of Youth* and " Dorabella " catches these
pretty artificialities. His score, faithful to décor, has something of
Ravel ; though when he speaks of a *jardin féerique* it is with an
English accent. The courtly minuet is shown in Ex. 68.

The *Fan* is as pretty a score as one could wish for, with elegance
and wit in strings and woodwind, and delicate stabs of irony in
brass and percussion. The *Starlight Express* is equally enchanting,
but of graver significance : it is another contribution by Elgar to
the kindergarten. There have not been many composers with such
understanding of children's tastes. He was interested in what
children appreciate rather more than in what they ought to appreciate. Consequently he could be, by turns, playful and serious,
without losing either dignity or understanding. The grace of his
intimate correspondence with his daughter when a child and the
puckish sympathy which endeared his drawings to other particular

children is reflected in the score which he wrote for the *Starlight Express*. " Whosoever is ' wumbled,' " wrote *The Times*, " let him listen to Sir Edward Elgar." The same article defined the score : " Take the best bits of the ' Wand of Youth,' the orchestral pieces called ' Dream Children,' and the ' Dorabella ' variation, dip them into the ' star-cave ' so that they come out all fresh and glistening, and you have a fair notion of the spirit of Sir Edward Elgar's music to the ' Starlight Express.' "

As it happens the thesis of Blackwood's *Prisoner in Fairyland*—the book from which the libretto of the play was made—is, with mystical and quasi-philosophical embellishments, that of the Elgar children's play : grown-ups are " wumbled "; the secret of wisdom and happiness lies in the imagination of children. Blackwood pursues, *longo intervallo*, Yeats, Maeterlinck, and Barrie, to the stars, whence he scatters star-dust on an uncomprehending world. Blackwood's delicate prose can carry a willing reader, but the play version by Miss Pearn is a grievous impediment. It may be suspected that Elgar was persuaded to write his score by the attractive personality of Blackwood rather than by the libretto with which he was presented. As it is Elgar's music almost makes the work as a whole credible. It is an example of his capacity to restrain the too imaginative impulse ; with one foot on the ground he strengthens the whimsy with something that is substantial.

Eight parts of the *Starlight Express* have been recorded. It is clear from his songs that had the opportunity ever come he would have composed a masterly comic opera. There is something owed to Sullivan, to Messager, to Gounod, in the impulsive sweeps of melody, infectious rhythms, and dramatic authority to be found in " The blue-eyed fairy " and the finale to Act III (Exs. 69 and 70). The orchestration, with eager percussion and punctuating brass behind adventurous woodwind and facile strings, is of Elgar—unmistakably. One tiny point will illustrate the genius of orchestration. In the bar in which Ex. 70 finishes cymbals and a bass drum sound *pianissimo*, off the beat, to indicate far-away colours and mysteries.

The amiable character of the songs of the organ-grinder—who stands chorus-like outside the action, as a link between auditorium and stage—and the tenderness and brilliance of the soprano part hold the play firm. There are innumerable instances, however, of the composer's ability to transcend the stage set. The clarinet takes up the curtain on Act I with the pastoral theme (Ex. 71). Against the end cowbells sound faintly on the stage. Where Elgar could once write for mandoline and guitar (see page 406) here he is required to work a barrel organ into the score—with attendant clarinet and viola. In the gay, picturesque " Song of the wind " there is—for the record of the orchestral historian—a wind-machine. The most striking bit of scoring, however, is the most slender : night coming on (Ex. 72).

For the second time " Little bells " from the *Wand of Youth* appears among our quotations. In fact this *motiv* is the binding feature of the score. Elsewhere " Moths and butterflies " and the " Sun dance " are directly introduced, while the influence of *Dream Children* and of the " Bavarians " is also apparent. The *Starlight Express* was a Christmas play, and into the fabric of the Finale is worked the tune of the " First Nowell "—with seasonal bells and organ.

Fringes of the Fleet, technically a work for the theatre, is one of Elgar's " tremendous trifles." Comparison with Stanford's *Songs of the Sea* and *Songs of the Fleet* is inevitable. The difference between the respective sets lies in circumstance and approach. Stanford wrote for the choral society and from a general enthusiasm for maritime tradition, Elgar for the gallery of the music-hall and under the impact of daily tragedy at sea. It would be the height of bad taste to condemn Elgar's songs by reference to the wrong standards. Rough, powerful—bawdy if you like : but how immensely telling. And how true to Kipling's style and idiom. In the " Lowestoft Boat " Elgar's mock-shanty catches the pawky humour of the poet, in " Sweepers " his resolution, in " Submarines " his gravity. The last song, built on one recurring figure in the accompaniment, is immeasurably moving by any standards. It is a rare thing for a distinguished artist to be able to go on tour and appear in twice-nightly shows. That Elgar could do it is a measure of one part of his excellence.

After the war there were slight scores, of no great significance, for Binyon's *King Arthur* and Bertram Matthews's *Beau Brummel*. The minuet from the last was recorded and enjoyed a certain independent popularity, but the main importance of these works lay in the material provided for the subsequent project for the theatre.

CHAPTER XXIII

UNFINISHED OPERA

But I have now a project of mine own.

Ben Jonson, *Epilogue*
to The Devil is an Ass

ON SEPTEMBER 23, 1932, Elgar wrote, from Worcester, to Barry Jackson :[1]

MY DEAR BARRY J. :

I did not refer to the other B(en) J(onson) because I thought the idea did not appeal to you at all.

My feeling has always been that the Elizabethan (for short) dialogue is splendid for recit. I never thought of " Pug " remaining in at all. It seemed to me that a first act (scene exactly as you say) might be made. I am not sure if anything could be made of the " cloak " affair : but the " projectors " (Stock Exchange) might be very evident, all this, these, and the " title " scramble, are of all time : for lyrical moments I had marked out several things from the Masques, but I cannot find (at this moment) my " cut up " copy of Gifford's edn.[2]—I had adumbrated two acts exactly as you say : the first act wd "grow" easily I think & the chorus might be *plausibly* introduced for any effect of movement—not as you will feel—static.

A small chorus—not a huge crowd.

The period dresses appeal to me for opera &, padded out as you cd. do it, might make a " *warm & full* " thing—

I do not see any real fault with characters pairing off as you

---

[1] Sir Barry Jackson has given his account of his collaboration with Elgar : see *Music and Letters*, Vol. xxiv. No. 1.

[2] *The Works of Ben Jonson* with a Memoir by William Gifford, pub. 1838, 1858, and 1860. Elgar used the edition of 1858.

feel they will do. Meercraft (good bass) Dotterel (Beckmesser Baritone) appeal to me to " characterize " musically.

Dear Barry, do not give yourself too much trouble over it : just think of it occasionally.

My difficulty in trying to " plan " it years ago was the end —the actual wind-up—this you may be able to " see "—I don't know if clubs were " raided " at the time of B. J.—but that wd. make a tremendous scrambling finale—last ensemble.

Ever gratefully yours
EDWARD ELGAR

The long ambition to write an opera was crystallising. Recognising the need for a practised (and practising) hand to tidy his own thoughts, and those of Ben Jonson, Elgar, urged by Bernard Shaw, talked the matter over with Barry Jackson, who, at Birmingham, was conveniently near. Barry Jackson undertook to collaborate with enthusiasm and, as Elgar realised, with generosity. Having arrived at the point of enlisting support Elgar moved quickly. A second letter followed on September 26.

MY DEAR BARRY J :

In case you shd. pursue the other B. J. I am sending you Gifford—a copy I got for a shilling or two to " cut up ";—I do not treat books badly as a rule but this edn. is of no great character.

I had suggested, to myself long ago, that Wittipol might be a woman (contralto, as in Rosenkavalier) this might upset the disguise however : of course the contralto business gives a lovely air of *unreality* (in the best sense) to anything e.g. Handel's operas etc.

Best regards
Yrs. ever
EDWARD ELGAR

Work proceeded and Elgar was not displeased with his music. On January 23, 1933, he reported :

MY DEAR BARRY :

It quite cheered me to see you & Scott on Saturday & to know that you liked my new tunes—a little anyway. I feel

somewhat shy of writing at my age but on listening to it I fail
to notice any marked senility.

Do not think for a minute about " B. J." in the midst of your
vast undertakings—I have plenty to go on with [1]

Best regards to you both

Yrs ever

EDWARD

Had there not been a symphony to write Elgar would un-
doubtedly have completed the opera : without the call of the opera
there would have been a symphony. With six more months of
life both symphony and opera would have been completed. The
evidence of the sketches is that Elgar would himself have preferred
to leave the opera rather than the symphony as his swan song. The
symphony would have been one more symphony, whereas the opera
would have shown (as indeed the remains indicate) a personal
attitude in a form in which achievement was secretly desired for
half a lifetime at least.

The *Spanish Lady* project is one memorial of Elgar's literary
experience, which is revealed not only as wide but also as deep.
Outside the ranks of literary specialist scholars there can have been
few whose acquaintance with the works of Ben Jonson was so
extensive as Elgar's. In the narrow sense Ben Jonson is not the
obvious source for an opera libretto. Plot, counter-plot, philosophy, religion, scholarship, all expounded with torrential eloquence
and invested with scholarly glosses, add up to an alarming complexity. Elgar saw in *The Devil is an Ass* inspiration for *Cockaigne
No. 3* (which the opera in effect would have been) in the gallimaufry
of persons and incidents set amidst the squalor, intrigue, and
bawdry of Jacobean London. Some persons, some incidents, as
his observations show, belong to all time and the quippish Elgar
noted some points which came within his own personal experience.
Of share-pushing, for example, he had melancholy memories. On
another level the mock-Spanish episode threw him back to his own
earliest musical extravaganzas. Outside of the single play Ben
Jonson, of course, offered incomparable lyrics.

There was a certain propriety in the Master of the King's Musick
returning to an author whose masques, as set by Robert Johnson,
Alphonso Ferrabosco, Giovanni Coperario, John Adson—and

---

[1] Symphony III.

others of that lively company—were for so long the focal point of English royal music. In fact it was from such works of wit and fancy, beauty and slap-stick, that native opera promised to flow. Elgar, whose frequent chair may now be seen in the Crown in Worcester, could with ease have occupied one in the Mermaid.

Having himself selected episodes from *The Devil is an Ass* Elgar proceeded to ransack Jonson's other works for dialogue, description, and lyrics. The libretto eventually owed to researches among the following: *Bartholomew Fair*, *The Silent Woman*, *The Case is altered*, *Sejanus*, *The Staple of News*, *The Magnetic Lady*, *The Alchemist*, *The Sad Shepherd*, *The Gipsies metamorphosed*, *The Fortunate Isles*, *The Masque of Beauty*, *Pleasure reconciled to virtue*, *Neptune's triumph*, *Love freed from Folly*, *Hymenaei*, *The Forest*, *Underwoods*, as well as Beaumont and Fletcher.

Originally it had been intended to preserve Ben Jonson's dialogue, but Barry Jackson persuaded Elgar of the impracticability of this; so the whole scheme was skilfully streamlined in order, as Jackson said, " to give the composer as much chance to enlarge to his heart's content on whatever aspect of this or that scene appealed to his imagination."

The story, as adapted from Jonson[1] (reference to the text of *The Devil is an Ass* will show the extent to which the original has been modified), was as follows:

ACT I

A Street in London. Fitzdottrel's house; Engine's house, where Meercraft lodges.

The act opens with scenes of crowd life. Lady Tailbush, followed by her suitor, Manly, comes to visit Meercraft, to whom she serves as patron and dupe. The business between her and the charlatan is " beauty preparations." After this episode the main imbroglio develops. Fitzdottrel intends to marry his ward, Frances, beloved of Wittipol. The latter plays upon her guardian's vanity by presenting him with an extremely gaudy cloak purchased from the second-hand clothes-dealer Engine. In return for this gift he is to enjoy ten minutes' conversation with Frances. Fitzdottrel is to stand by, while Manly,

---

[1] Quoted, by kind permission, from Sir Barry Jackson's synopsis in *Music and Letters*, Vol. xxiv. No. 1.

Wittipol's friend, is to see fair play. After Wittipol's departure Engine introduces Fitzdottrel to Meercraft, who, among other rogueries is a bogus company-promoter. The foolish guardian falls an easy prey to him and in return for a hundred pounds, a ring and a promise of a possible elevation to the peerage enters into a scheme for the reclaiming of the fenlands by means of windmills. The finale entwines the last two episodes, showing the rogues and the guardian drinking to the success of their schemes while unseen to them Wittipol serenades Frances at her window.

ACT II, SCENE I

A front scene depicting Engine's backyard.

News has been spread about that a Spanish lady has arrived in town with details of new fashions and behaviour from foreign lands. Fitzdottrel determines that his ward shall become her pupil in order that she may be a credit to him when he has been created a duke. Meercraft promises to convey a ring on his behalf in order to obtain the stranger's good graces. This Spanish lady is something of a myth, but as she is due to appear at Lady Tailbush's—the rendez-vous of a ladies' club—something has to be manœuvred. Engine produces a Spanish dress for Wittipol from his shop and equips himself as duenna. The two, shepherded by Meercraft, who has also been dressed in some of Engine's second-hand finery, start off for the party at the club.

ACT II, SCENE II

The Reception at Lady Tailbush's

Diversified crowd movement culminating in the arrival of the Spanish lady and her duenna. " She " creates a great impression and Fitzdottrel has no qualms in leaving his ward in " her " hands for instruction. To the astonishment of Frances, Wittipol discards the Spanish dress, and it is not long before Manly appears with a priest. By the time the company has reassembled and danced a saraband the ceremony is complete. Fitzdottrel raises great confusion on failing to find his ward. He calls for the Spanish lady, but is presented with the discarded dress. The lovers, now united, return, and all join in the Epithalamium.

In Elgar's notes there are these precise observations on the

chief characters and their musical potential ; also their possible
relationship with characters from *La Tosca*, a work for which
Elgar had the highest regard :

(1) Fitzdottrel (45) [1]: A wealthy, rather short-sighted uses glasses,
middle-aged fool; vain and stupidly cunning. Basso cantabile.

(2) Meercraft (30) : A plausible rogue. Smartly dressed (flashy :
dagger). Shrewdly cunning.—Baritone (distinto) *Scarpia.*

(3) Trains: his servant—Tenor

(4) Everill : Meercraft's cousin, debauched—Baritone

(5) Wittipol (22) : A sprightly young man (sword)—Tenor *Cara-
dossi*

(6) Manly (26) : A more solid young man (sword)—2nd Tenor
Spuleta

(7) Engine (50) : A rogue of lower birth than Meercraft, and older.
Sardonic—Basso profundo—*Angelotti*

(8) Pug (35) : A manservant

(9) Frances (20) : A young lady of great estate and ward to Fitzdottrel who would wed her—soprano *Tosca*

(10) Lady Tailbush (30) : A lady of fashion desirous of freedom and
and fortune—mezzo-soprano (contralto).

(11) Lady Eitherside (45) : Very stout—high soprano. unexpected.

Further, Elgar showed the desired range of the several voices
and the normal " reciting-note." Pug, noted above, enjoys improved status in Elgar's libretto, for in Jonson he is an emissary
of Satan, detailed to stir up trouble in the world. Of the minor
characters not mentioned in the list are Ananias, a Puritan (borrowed, by name and outlook, from *The Alchemist*), and the Parson-
Prelate (as from *The Magnetic Lady*).

There were, when Elgar was finally compelled to relinquish
his work, numerous details unsettled ; and minor characters and
small episodes exist in alternative versions : but the main body of
the scheme was firm enough and for almost every important
situation there is an outline, at least, of the music.

There are approximately one hundred and eighty fragments of
the music of the opera extant ; the effective number being perhaps
half, by reason of the large amount of duplication caused by the

[1] Age in parentheses.

copying and revision of rough sketches. The existing music is interesting not only for its own sake but for its relation to the whole career and working method of the composer. It is, therefore, of especial importance to examine it in some detail.

The sketches proposed by Elgar for *The Spanish Lady* have been numbered, so far as is possible, according to their probable place in the opera. Some themes have been omitted from the main scheme because it is not possible to determine their ultimate situation. It is doubtful whether Elgar himself was at all certain in regard to most of these.[1]

ACT I

(1) A minor, 4/4, *allegro:* 11 bars, the last two cancelled, in short score (1) but with indications as to scoring. This is headed " Overture," but the sketch is an old one (between 1902 and 1910). The first 8 bars, however, were copied (1932–33) into—

(1a) The indication is now *allegretto* and the proposals for scoring more frequent. " Overture " is omitted, but this inscription—" Humourous (Street etc) TAVERN MUSIC "—shows that it was intended if not for the overture at any rate for Act I. The motiv, in any case, would have been worked into various apposite points in the final score.

(2) D major, 3/4, *moderato:* 7 bars, headed " OVERTURE." With this is a derivative passage (2a) which corresponds with 54.

(3) F major, 4/4, *dolce:* 7 bars, headed " Comedy Overture," repeated in C major in 3a. For the ancestry of this passage see 14e.

(3b) F major, 4/4, *allegro molto:* 7 bars, headed " Comedy Overture," showing a vigorous variation of the theme of 3.

(4) B flat major, 4/4 : 6 bars, headed " ACT I INTRODN." In the last two bars a fresh theme in A flat major, but going towards E flat major, is introduced.

(4a) B flat major, 4/4 : 4 bars ; an early version of the theme of 4 and headed " String orch.," and possibly belonging to the period of the *Introduction and Allegro* and the unfinished *Fantasia* (see Index of Works, p. 410.) for strings. This has been copied and revised (1932 ?) at the foot of the page with the second theme of 4 added, but in the key of B flat.

[1] Most of this material is in short score : when it is otherwise is detailed.

(4b) C major, 4/4, *allegro;* 7 bars; another version of the same headed " Strings & PF." On a separate sheet the material is briefly developed, in F major, to lead into the second theme of 4 in B flat major.

(4c) B flat major, 4/4, *allegro:* the same themes, differently treated, the second now marked *giocoso.*

(4d) a later copy of 4a and 4c, with no alterations.

(4e) C major, 6/8, *giocoso:* 12 bars, being an extension of the second theme of 4. There is a stave for a vocal part above with a final note only of a singer's phrase overlapping the beginning. Followed by 4 bars of first theme in D major, but with key signature cancelled and a memo " no sig." The whole is headed " Act I ? " with " Concerto[?] " —i.e. pfte concerto—mostly obliterated.

(5) F sharp minor, 2/4, *con fuoco:* 20 bars of fugal exposition, copied from a sketch of 1881–2, and now headed " Act I Sc. I."

(5a) F sharp minor, 2/4, *Quick:* 39 bars of " *Pas redouble* " march of 1882, now headed " Act I, Sc. I." Both pieces probably intended for a crowd scene.

(6) A trumpet call for Trains (C major) with a trumpet call for Everill (C major, but ending out of key with an unexpected F sharp) to blow on Trains's trumpet.

(7) E minor, 3/4, 9/8, *allegro molto:* 5 bars, the fourth cancelled and reworked in pencil. This excerpt is headed " Finale." The corner of the page has been torn away, taking with it an inscription. This, however, ended ... " t " (possibly ... " et "). The date would appear to be circa 1907 and the passage, which is fugal, may have been designed as the concluding movement of a string quartet. Recopied to—

(7a) and now marked 3/4, *allegro:* the fourth bar, copied from the earlier revision of 7, is cancelled in favour of a modification of the original 4th bar in 7. The music is now headed " MEERCRAFT " and the scoring is shown. As usual with Elgar a sinister character is identified by a fugal motiv.

(8) E minor, 2/4, *giocoso:* 4 bars. The fair copy at the top of the page is of a pencil sketch at the foot. Between the two lies one bar of an unidentified *scherzo.*

(8a) a copy of 8, but headed " MEERCRAFT, ACT I." At the foot of the page the *scherzo* motiv is copied. As this page is of the 1932–3 period it is clear that it was intended to incorporate the *scherzo* in the opera.

(9) A minor, 4/4, *armonioso:* 8 bars of accompaniment for a recita-

tive. Only three notes of the recitative are shown. Headed " Act I MEERCRAFT," and copied from Sketch book IX (1909).

(10) G major, 2/2 : 15 bars taken from an old sketch book (circa 1885 ?). Formerly in E flat major and probably to be used as a song. Following are 9 bars, *marziale* ; and at the foot of the page three chords *solenne*. The first theme copied for the opera to 10a, the second, with the *solenne* sequence, to 10b. More material for march on 10c and 10d. In the first act of the opera there was opportunity for such music for the entry of a group of sailors, at what point never seems finally to have been resolved.

(11–11e) F major, 3/8 : extensive material for a country dance which was intended to be played from time to time during Lady Tail-bush's first scene. The sketch marked 11c is extracted from Sketch book X, purchased in Florence in 1909. This sketch originally adjoined the notes made in 1909 regarding an opera (see p. 335). The country dance is more or less complete.

(12) A minor, 3/4, *lento* : 7 bars *plus* 11 bars, opening melody for bassoon. The whole headed " ANANIAS." This was copied from the Florentine Sketch book where it was shown as for " India's Song " in the *Crown of India*. It was there marked by Elgar—" trifling : good enough."

(13) B flat major, 4/4 : 18 bars, of early date. Inscription torn away, but remaining direction " Bagwig, Groombridge, Bannister (rowdy) ". The whole copied into—

(13a) C major, *allegro molto* : marked " Act I, crowd etc." At the bottom of the page is a fanfare motiv (a fantastic sequence of minor and unrelated triads) continued to 13b, where " Act I MEER " is stated.

(14) F major, 2/2, vivace : 35 bars of a bourrée-type piece, headed " Strs & Pfte " and later, " Act I Lady TAIL." This is a copy of a piece called a Gavotte in Shed book IV (1879). Sections of this piece are shown on sheets 87a–87d. 87a has also a quotation from the *King Arthur* music ; an eight bar phrase of a *tarantella* which was to be used in the opera ; and an attempt to solve an anagram.

(14e) consists of five pages pinned together. The first two deal with the material of 14. On the remaining pages are versions of 3a and 3b. The first of these is marked " Oboe [Ct] ? "

(15) A minor, 6/8, *tarantella*, leading through D minor ; 16 bars, followed by passage in B flat major, 3/4, *allegro* ; about 30 bars of a song—" Hang up those dull and envious fools "—for Lady Tailbush.

The words of this song, entitled by Ben Jonson " In defence of their
inconsistency," are from *Underwoods*. They are happily introduced as
Lady Tailbush encounters her suitor, Manly. In his typescript of the
libretto Elgar marked the song " Important, with D.C. 1st verse."

(16) C major, 6/8, *vivace* : 8 bars of duet, preliminary sketch of
16a, but with 2 bars—the second theme of 4—noted to be inset somewhere.

(16a) C major, 6/8, *vivace* : a duet (most of this is in draft) for Lady
Tailbush and Meercraft, on the subject of beauty preparations—" If
once we have it under seal," the words partly from *The Sad Shepherd*.
The figure with which the accompaniment commences is used again in
the introductory music to Act II.

(17) D major, 4/4 : 4 bars of recitative, transposed in

(17a) into C major, with words for Meercraft added. He boasts of
his prowess in making money, and that so far as Lady Tailbush is concerned (she being now off-stage) he " will coin her out of cobwebs."
At this point Everill enters, shabbily dressed, and soliciting Meercraft
for money. After some palaver Meercraft assists him with a coin, in
return for Everill's aid in his own devices. This is set out in the most
extended piece of recitative in the opera. The recitative, however, had
a previous history. It was conceived for the " Solomon's Porch "
Scene in the *Kingdom* and for St. Peter to deliver. Having been excluded from the oratorio it was ready-made for the opera. There are
other jottings for this movement in 18 and 19.

(20) E flat major, 3/4, *slow* : 4 bars ; followed by a chromatic passage
in the same time and key, but marked " quick." At the bottom of the page
is a phrase of three bars for oboe and strings [?]. This page represents
casual ideas eventually impressed for the opera, the second theme being
repeated in 20a and attributed either to Everill or Meercraft. Probably
it is an " Everill motiv." Inside the ms. marked 20 is a first sketch
(never completed) of the setting of Belloc's *Tarantella*—another Spanish
subject.

(21) G major, 2/4 : 14 bars of figuration also shown as for Meercraft
and Everill.

(22) B minor, 4/4 : labelled " Frances " and already referred to
on p. 335, where it is " The Soul."

(23–23f) On 23 the motiv to be played while Frances appears on
the balcony is the *scherzo* theme already noted in 8. At the bottom of
the page the introduction to the " Echo song " begins. This is a setting,

in D major, of " When Love at first did move From out of Chaos "
(*Masque of Beauty*).   It is Wittipol's song, with echo phrases supplied
by Manly and Engine.   The song is virtually complete.

(24–24d) D major, 3/8, *vivace* :   extensive but very rough sketches
of " Frances' great song "—" Her Man," the words from *Underwoods*.

(25) 10 pages devoted to Frances's song (see 24), with some parts
of the accompaniment developed, and with one page copied as for
violin solo for the use of W. H. Reed, who was often at Marl Bank to
play through parts of the opera and the symphony.   One page in this
set suggests an early date, the music being designated—" Str. & piano."
This is cancelled and " B. J." (the mark set on all sketches approved for
The Spanish Lady) superimposed.   On the last page is a fair copy of

(26) D minor, 3/8 :   9 bars, originally entitled " Callicles " (see
Index of Works, p. 421), but with " Frances " now written in its place.

(27) the same, but a later copy ;   headed " any key."

(28) D major, 6/8 :   3 bars, also " for Frances."

(29) B flat major, 2/4, *allegretto* :   *lento* erased :   about 12 bars to
cover stage business—i.e. " accpt. for trying on cloak " (Fitzdottrel).

(30–30d) G major-G minor, 3/4, *allegro* :   song for Engine, with
male voice chorus for the last part of the act.   A setting of John Hay's
Memento mori, called by Elgar " Engine's Toast Song."

(31) Another copy of 30, but containing this note by Elgar : " Mem :
some by-play during this song.   *Ananias* walks across & eventually
sits outside the open window.   Engine offers him a drink—which he
refuses ' Against the Spirit ' [Ananias' perpetual refrain]—but eventually
takes a glass or two or three & is cheered up considerably by this depressing song & joins in the refrain."

According to another note Fitzdottrel is also drunk & trying on a
coronet against his elevation to the Dukedom of Drown'd Lands, as
promised by Meercraft.

(32) D minor, 4/4 :   6 bars of " Curfew " chorus copied from

(33) on which are two tentative pencilled *incipits* for two *toccatas* for
organ, dating probably from *circa* 1885.

(34–35) various fragments of " Curfew " music, with a passage
of 2 bars to be sung at the same time by Frances and Wittipol.   It is
indicated that there should also be heard as from the " Ordinary "
the " Tavern music " as in 1a.

(36) music for bells.

(37–38) motivs designated for Act I, the first to be found in a sketch book of 1881.

ACT II, SCENE I

(39) C major, 4/4 (? in 12/8), *vivace* : about 19 bars, commencing as 16a ; formerly headed " Brass," now " Intro. Act II."

(40) D minor, 3/8 : 8 bars scored for strings of

(41–41g) a fairly complete set of sketches for the " Burlesco," Act II, Sc. I, in which Engine, Wittipol and Meercraft were to join, having determined the plan of campaign in regard to Wittipol's appearance as the " Spanish lady."

(42) C major, 3/2 : Sarabande copied from " Shed Book " III of 1878, where it was drafted as for the Wind Quintet (see Index of Works, p. 408).

ACT II, SCENE II

(43) G minor-G major-E flat major, 4/4, *adagio* : 17 bars of duet for Lady Tailbush and Manly—" Oh Manly ! "

(44–44f) G major, 3/4 : an almost complete setting of " Still to be neat, still to be dressed " (words from *The Silent Woman*), preceded by brief recitative. Sung by Manly. On the back of one sheet—" Old Sketch."

(45–45g) E flat major, 2/4 : Fitzdottrel's entry music and his song " Modest and fair " (words from *The Silent Woman*). Practically complete.

(46–46f) see 42 : the same music, but intended to play an important part during the entry of and presentations to the " Spanish lady."

(47) E flat major, 3/4 : fragment of full score of *Bolero*, 1st violin part complete.

(47a–47p) sketches of *Bolero* in short score, with some stage directions.

(48) A minor, 3/4, *allegro moderato* : 11 bars of *scherzo* movement, movement of Symphony III, 1st violin part only, here headed " B. J." and " W. H. Reed, 5th Feb. 1933 "; inside a corrected 1st violin part of *Bolero*, and, on back page, of " Burlesco " here entitled " España."

(49) E flat major, 2/2, *allegro* : 17 bars of accompaniment with blank stave for voice. Headed " This is she ? ", a song considered for introduction into the opera.

(49a) an earlier copy of the same music with " str. & pfte. trio no. 5 " crossed out. Barry Jackson points out a similarity between this song and the " Shepherd's Song " (Op. 16, no. 1, pub. 1895). In fact the present music may be assigned to *circa* 1880–85. A pencil note in the libretto after the recognition of Wittipol by Frances reads " [Wittipol] with his arm round FRANCES sings love song (1886)." Perhaps " Like to the damask rose " ?

(50) F major, 2/4, *allegro* : a two-part chorus and dance for girls— " How old may Tailbush be," based on an early setting (1895 ?) of William Watson's *April* for 2 sopranos, 2 violins, and pianoforte. (cf. *The Snow* and *Fly, Singing Bird.*) Cover note by Elgar—" Odd ! ")

(51) B minor, 4/4 3/4 : 14 bars for 'cello with accompaniment for pianoforte. An early piece re-used in 1928 and, therefore, headed " Brummel motif."

(51a) the same in 7/4 time, but marked " Act II Sc 2, Empty stage (FRANCES & WITTIPOL)."

(52–52a) G flat major, 4/4 : duet for Frances and Wittipol, during which Wittipol unmasks and divests himself of his other disguise. In the score are some indications for a distant chorus. Dated 20 Jan. 1933. Early sketches used in writing this movement.

(53–53a) G major, C major, *allegro* : 4 bars for Act II, Sc II with pencil note " B. B." (Beau Brummel ?)

(53b) the same with a second theme of 4 bars.

(53c) D minor, 2/2 : 16 bars from string quarter in D minor (" Shed Book " II, 1878) marked " on stage Act II."

(54) as 2a, but marked Act II, Sc. II. This music may have been intended for the wedding scene, for a note on the reverse begins " After the wedding hue & cry for Meercraft & Co. . . ."

The fragments numbered from 55–79 are of varying interest, but all were under consideration for the opera. 57 is marked " Fitz " and was probably for Act I. 55 is another excerpt from an old pianoforte trio. 56 is marked " SYMPHON " and also " B. J." 59, 61, and 66 are marked " K. P." (Keith Prowse, with whom Elgar was under contract to write a number of pieces in the last year or two of his life). 61 also appears among other sketches as for the pianoforte concerto and the opening of the finale of this work (see p. 393) is shown among the " B. J." pieces. 63, 67 and 67a are entitled " Walsingham "—though unrelated to the traditional ballad tune of that name—and marked with the characteristic *fantastico*. 79 gives themes variously intended for *The Apostles*, for *Falstaff*—but not used in these works—and for an " Old Quartet." There is also a memorandum of tunes to be consulted in the old " Shed Books."

The story of English opera has been for long one of almost continuous frustration. It is impossible not to believe that Elgar's opera would have exercised a profoundly healthy influence on the modern attitude. His genius was such that no music he composed could ever sound ineffective. The sketches of *The Spanish Lady* reveal a plenitude of musical ideas that, being intrinsically interesting, fulfil the libretto without obscuring it. There is, overall, a fine, but eloquent, simplicity that would have made certain episodes, at least, irresistible. The settings, for instance, of " Modest and fair," the " Echo " song and the love duet of Act II possess something of the inevitability of early settings of Jonson by Robert Jones or Thomas Ravenscroft. From the first the opening may be quoted (Ex. 73) from the last the end (Ex. 74). Within the first there is room for the inflection and gesture of the actor to symbolise the playful mockery of Lady Tailbush by Manly—and everybody else : within the second an infinite tenderness.

There is hardly sufficient material to show how the characters would have come to full dramatic vitality, except in the case of Meercraft. Elgar, as he wrote to Barry Jackson, loved the old swindler that Meercraft was ; so he portrays him in motivs which, flavoured with gin and bitters, are acrid but attractive. See Ex. 75 : there is a moral in the association of fuguing with Meercraft. A second Meercraft motiv develops fantastically in the brass (Ex. 76). The extensive duet between Everill and Meercraft is linked together by the recurrent, and formerly apostolic theme (Ex. 77). For grim humour there is also Engine's *Memento mori*, a song at once defiant and pathetic—pathetic in the *meno mosso* and *lento* which Elgar (there is a sombre and personal note here) attaches to " thoughts of dying. . . ." Lady Tailbush, the lady of fashion, is aptly introduced by music more gallant than she probably deserved, and Frances begins passionately and exquisitely to shine through the few bars in which she is contained.

Description in music is shown by Elgar to be a matter of relativity. It is a relief to discover that in many cases where an image is to be invoked the music existed before the image. So the " tavern " music only becomes tavern music when placed in a score relative to other and contrasted themes : the English country dance sounds impeccable, but it sprang from some Italian atmosphere ; a Puritan, thematically, is metamorphosed from a city in India. Elgar, by adroit craftsmanship, gives the illusion of reality. In short he is eminently a man of the theatre at heart.

The " tavern music "—a motiv to run at any rate through the first Act—is an excellent example. In itself it is amusing, though tinted with sadness, but not definitive : *à propos* of the stage set —with the Ordinary and the crapulent rabble of familiars half in, and half out, and half seas over—it is exceedingly apt (Ex. 78). Of the dances, which are an important feature of the score, two are outstanding : the *burlesco*, sardonic, restrained but vital ; and the *sarabande*, a noble piece even if not marked *nobilmente*, which, like another dance by Elgar, pays its service to Handel, losing nothing of its individual character in so doing. This piece, like other parts of *The Spanish Lady*, Elgar had carried with him for more than fifty years. In this way the *sarabande* ends (Ex. 79).

The Spanish Lady, as it is, is rather nearer " ballad opera " (in no deprecatory sense) than " music drama." The way in which Elgar would have connected and developed his material is not evident ; thus more cannot be said than that it would have been a work with impressive moments. There is, however, one marginal indication in the libretto of a motiv, fully to be heard at a later point, which is dramatically interpolated. When in Act II Frances is in conversation with the " Spanish lady " she thinks the voice familiar. Wittipol (alias the " Spanish lady ") shows her the ring (as detailed in the synopsis) and says :

> " But since you come to know me nearer lady
>   I'll beg the honour you will wear it for me
> (aside)   It must be so."

Against these words the orchestra is to play the opening of the love duet.

On February 18, 1933, the Elgar household noticed an announcement in the press to the effect that Richard Strauss was at work on a libretto, by Stefan Zweig, based on Ben Jonson's *Silent Woman*. It "filled us with dismay," wrote Miss Clifford, "but Sir E. declares it is simply his usual ill luck." Even so he persisted to the end, and the most moving pages of manuscript are those which show what must have been nearly the composer's last thoughts. The generally bold hand and music script had become crabbed and uneven. The idea is of a march (68–68b). But the idiom is neither of the old " pas redouble," nor yet of *Pomp and Circumstance* ; there was still enough spirit left to try new tricks (Ex. 80).

CHAPTER XXIV

EPILOGUE

A composer of a regal order.

Clue for a crossword puzzle

TWENTY YEARS after his death the reputation of a composer, more often than not, is at a low ebb. Of Handel at such a time no more was generally performed than two oratorios and a few choice excerpts ; of Bach virtually nothing. The low esteem in which Mozart, Haydn, and Beethoven were held by the *cognoscenti* was deplored in his youth by Mendelssohn ; while as for Mendelssohn himself it has taken a good half-century for the critical winds to veer again in the direction of favourable. In the end some composers ride contemptuously over the waves of fashion, weathering the rough waters of hostile criticism.

It is, now, just over twenty years since Elgar died. His reputation is immune from transient and wayward criticism, for some part of his music, adapting itself to succeeding climates of mood and opinion, is, for the English people at least, indispensable. *Gerontius*—old controversies so far forgotten that it is now sung in Welsh at a Royal National Eisteddfod—is immovable among the first half-dozen or so of great choral works ; the *Variations* are accepted as unique both in conception and in beauty ; the violin and 'cello concertos have their place among the classics ; *Cockaigne* is a programme builder's *sine qua non* ; the symphony in A flat and *Falstaff* are the proudest extended works in the English symphonic repertoire. These are the works for which Elgar is esteemed, and on account of which he must be considered by the musical historian for at least another generation.

But greatness lies in more than this. It is by his less ambitious pieces that Elgar has " gained the Empire of the ear." Two *Pomp and Circumstance* marches, and a handful of other tunes, have passed into the currency of common musical understanding. While others were arguing and cerebrating he, simply and correctly, deposed : " I am folk music." That is inescapable.

For some time a favourite vogue word, in the weekly causeries that comprise so much of contemporary criticism, has been austerity ; so much so that one of our younger symphonists is generally commended for being austere and nothing but austere. Now Elgar knew a great deal about austerity, but he kept relatively silent on its virtues. Music for him was a serious matter: so serious that it should embrace the whole, and not only part, of life. Thus the fastidious, out-of-joint with life, will complain of his vulgarity.

There is no doubt that a session at a Kitchen Concert, or a soberly bibulous evening at the Worcester Glee Club, or an hour's entertainment among the members of the U.B.Q. fraternity, would have offended against some personal ideas of desirable recreation ; just as a reception presided over by the gentle, inebriate Elia— furiously punning the while, or half an hour with Ben Jonson, or ten minutes of Rabelais would have led others to beg respite. But there, in those occasions, is one half of being. That half Elgar could express with infectious, modest, power.

That is one way towards Romanticism—to the teeming, human side of Romanticism ; and Elgar was a Romantic. He was, in some ways, the heir to Berlioz and Liszt ; he was in debt to Wagner ; he was the contemporary and friend of Richard Strauss. The technical affinities between Elgar and these composers are readily apparent. The language he used was akin to that of Bruckner and Mahler, and there is, too, the impress of Brahms. But, independent, Elgar made his style conform to his matter so that in no place can it be easily urged that the style is that of any other man.

Bernard Shaw appreciated the true quality of Elgar: we may refer to a post-card which he sent to the composer on January 25, 1930 :

> " Harty and his Manchester men pulled off a stupendous per-
> formance of the Elgar symphony last night: they seemed really
> to know it bit by bit instead of merely reading it : it was not a
> matter of the notes producing the effect (which they often don't
> [*sic*] if the players don't mean anything except to earn their
> salaries) but an *intended* and exhaustive real performance. H. H.

was a dripping rag at the end; but he had mastered and was
feeling every phrase: he was kinder to some of it than you
would have been yourself.

"As to that fortissimo in the rondo, which is like nothing
else on earth (Beethoven nowhere!) You should have heard it.
I never heard it before.

"I write this as, if there was a question of a new record of the
symphony, and you were not yourself disposed to conduct, it
might be useful to know that you could trust H. H. and the
Hallé band. Also it is pleasant to blow off steam after an exciting evening.

G. B. S."

In another way Shaw repeats Jaeger's thesis on "feeling"
(see p. 331) and points to the heart of the matter. For Elgar's
music is, of all English music, the music of feeling; but of a
variety of feeling. Further he knew more than most composers of his age and of his kind when to put an end to "feeling." In a letter to Robert Elkin he once said that he could
criticise no music but his own. It may frequently be felt that
his emotional appreciation of a situation is also subject to self-
criticism. In this he stands a little apart from some of the other
romantics—Liszt and Strauss for instance, and close to Schumann,
whom he so much admired and resembled. This leads to a certain
hesitancy, which may be seen in almost any slow movement, or,
in a lesser way, in a characteristic rhythmic retardation. It is frequently noted that Elgar had a *penchant* for the direction *nobilmente* :
it is less frequently observed that he had a contrasting affection for
fantastico. Between these two extremes is a point of view. That
point of view, positive and appreciable, is what we should mean
by Elgarian.

Up to a point music shows a man's appetite for life, his attitude
to life, his interpretation of life. Of all these one may disapprove ;
but there may still remain an indefinable quality to compel admiration. It is easy to put this down as musical quality *per se*. Thus we
regard Elgar's expert orchestration, his melodic invention, his
harmonic adventurousness, his fluency—which depends greatly on
the sympathy of the interpreter—as the stigmata of mastery. We
may equally and judiciously note the defects. Square rhythms
prevail for too long ; clichés in rhythm and harmony alike are not

infrequent ; " It is as difficult," it was once written in the *Pall Mall Gazette*, "for Elgar to leave a sequence as it is for a bicycle to leave the tram lines." The merits of the manner do, in fact, heavily outpoint the defects. But finally to adjudge a great composer in this way, as though a candidate for honours in some competitive examination, is as presumptuous as it is unrewarding ; for manner and matter meet together in a still more indefinable quality : that we call individuality. On this point we may read a summary by Samuel Langford :

"Elgar's music may, under certain conditions, be felt as cold ; but it also has in its coldness a great intensity. . . . To hear him begin, say with the overture to ' Gerontius ' is to experience a chill seriousness which no other experience in music can afford. . . . It is true of him as of Beethoven or Wagner that he comes out of each work a new man."

Elgar was the first composer of English birth since Purcell to appear on the stage of European music with unmistakable authority. With what authority has been related. It cannot, however, be overemphasised that fifty years ago the great men of Germany, Russia, Italy, and America greeted him as a peer ; and that the stature of his music was often revealed for the first time to his compatriots by foreign artists. Before him English music, harnessed to alien systems and weighted with stringent morality, stood immobile. For practical purposes it did not exist : England was a land without music.

Elgar picked the same native affection for colour and beauty out of English life and thought that had formerly infused the poetry of Keats and of Shelley. He brought into music the love of the commonalty that was in Dickens. His Catholic heritage was at once advantage and disadvantage. Immediately he was, by reason of his antecedents, debarred from opportunities open to others. On the other hand he was brought up to be unafraid of colour. The English musical renaissance is normally attributed to Parry and Stanford, from whose artistic integrity one would not wish to detract : more properly a new and vital impulse came much earlier, with Vincent Novello, who was himself the friend of our great Romantic poets and essayists.

The importance of Novello as editor and scholar has been insufficiently recognised. He it was who showed anew the virtues of grace and fluency through his issues of the masses of Haydn and

Mozart, and of the Italian masters of the seventeenth and eighteenth centuries. It was Novello who first popularised the choral master-pieces on which the common love of music in Victorian England was founded. It was, perhaps, because Novello and Elgar were of a different religious persuasion from most of their colleagues that they were able to adopt an emancipatory attitude. The organ loft of St. George's, Worcester, looked out on a different world from that of Worcester cathedral. Had he regularly occupied the latter the genius of Elgar might well have been stifled. True, he would have escaped the charge of vulgarity ; but posterity would hardly then have noticed the name of Elgar among the legions of the anonymous. The epitaph on the musicians whom Elgar displaced may be taken from Zola : " Behind those fine doors of lustrous mahogany there seemed to be veritable abysses of respectability."

"I suppose," wrote Dr. Vaughan Williams,[1] " one may say that when one has cribbed from a composer one has learnt from him. Certainly many of my generation and of the next below me have learnt much from Elgar in that way. I am astonished, if I may be allowed a personal explanation, to find on looking back on my own earlier works how much I cribbed from him, probably when I thought I was being most original." It is evident that during the past forty years the influence of Elgar has been con-siderable in particular instances : in the works, for example, of Bax, Ireland, Bliss, and Walton There has, however, been a more general influence, which has affected the whole conception of musical composition in England. Music, especially orchestral music, is now for the ear, whereas formerly it was for the eye. This, too, is engagingly illustrated by Vaughan Williams : " After the first performance of ' The Kingdom ' a distinguished musical amateur, one of those who have not got beyond worshipping orthodox technique for its own sake, complained to me that the double choruses in this work were not really in eight parts at all. I think he somehow felt that he had been cheated and was inclined to ask for his money back. If he had known a little more he would have remembered that Bach in the ' Matthew Passion ' owed him just as much hard cash as Elgar."[2]

[1] *Music and Letters*, Vol. xvi. No. 1.
[2] *ibid.*

II

To work one's way up from the bottom : that was the ambitious phrase that once sounded in the ears of the penurious young. That was what Elgar did. On his way through the music of church services and country concerts, of provincial societies and girls' schools, and of a Pauper Lunatic Asylum he learned how music affected the common ear. For music which fulfilled this purpose he had respect ; but he was aware also of the needs of the uncommon ear. He was himself a very ordinary person ; those who deprecate him because " he tried to be a country gentleman " forget that that is precisely what he was. In some ways, however, he was extraordinary and he had faith in the illimitable imaginative and intellectual capacity of his fellows.

The story of his career is simple, but not unaffecting ; it is a record of doggedness, of pride, of modesty, and of awareness. The achievement was that of Edward Elgar, but not quite of him alone. The course of his career was charted by William Henry and Anne Elgar, as they dreamed and governed their children with wisdom and humour. Besides them, and the devotion of wife and daughter, there was the influence of the community in which he was nurtured.

The visitor to Worcester is less conscious of a proprietary interest in Elgar than is the case in Stratford-on-Avon, or Salzburg, or Bayreuth, on account of Shakespeare, Mozart, and Wagner ; the citizens take him for granted. Ted Elgar, a clever young man, went away from Worcester and returned, full of honours, in old age. There were many who were not quite sure what it was all about. But there is general approval that the cottage at Broadheath is honoured, that the County Council mark the signposts from Crown East and Martley to " Elgar's Birthplace," that a portrait by Philip Burne-Jones and a bust by Donald Gilbert are in the Guildhall, that the name of Elgar stands mid-way between those of Nelson and Churchill in the list of Honorary Freemen of the City, and that the memory is reverenced each three years at the Festival. Elgar is one of Worcester's great men ; not the only one : his especial greatness concerns a larger community.

The High Street, between No. 10 and the cathedral, is little changed from the days of Elgar's youth. The country round Claines, at Birchwood, at Broadheath, and beside the rivers between Powick and Kempsey, is still serene ; and indifferent to the swollen suburbs still mercifully distant. From the west the evening light comes from behind the Malvern Hills ; it sweeps over Elgar's familiar territory, catching the wooded knolls, the orchards, the ancient cottages of black and white, until it falls into, and reddens, the Severn beneath the great tower of the cathedral. The imagination takes fire : once or twice genius is stirred and the vision is taken into poetry or music—

> *Ac on a May morning on Malverne Hulles*
> *Me bifel a ferly, of fairy me thoughte;*
> *I was very forwandred, and went me to reste*
> *Under a brod banke, by a bornes side;*
> *And as I lay and lened and loked in the waters,*
> *I slombred in a sleping, it sweved so merye.*
> *Thanne gan I to meten a merveillous sweven,*
> . . . . . .

MUSICAL EXAMPLES

Permission to quote from published works has been kindly granted as follows: by Novello and Co. Ltd., for examples 9-18, 26-28, 30-35, 37-40, 42, 44, 47-49, 51-53, and 60-66; by Boosey and Hawkes Ltd., for 20-22; by British and Continental Music Agencies Ltd., for 24 and 25; by Edwin Ashdown Ltd., for 67; and by Elkin and Co. Ltd., for 68-72. The remaining examples, from unpublished sources, are quoted by permission of the Trustees of the Elgar Will.

Ex. 5b
cont.

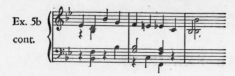

Ex. 5c

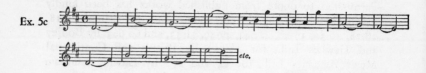

Ex. 6

Ex. 7

Ex. 8

Ex. 9

Ex. 10

Ex. 11

Ex. 12

Ex. 13

Ex. 14

Ex. 15

Ex. 16

Ex. 17

Ex. 18

Ex. 19

Ex. 20

Ex. 21

E.

Ex. 22

Ex. 23

Ex. 24

Ex. 25

Ex. 26

Ex. 27

Ex. 28
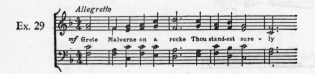

Ex. 29

Ex. 30

Ex. 31

Ex. 32

Ex. 33

Ex. 34

Ex. 39

Ex. 40

and the pa-tience,— and the pa-tience,— which are in Je-sus;—

Ex. 41

Ex. 42

Ex. 43

Ex. 44

*this bar is crossed out in the sketch

Ex. 54

Ex. 55

Ex. 56

Ex. 57

Ex. 58

Ex. 59

Ex. 60

Ex. 61

Ex. 62

1st & 2nd Vl.

Pfte.

Ex. 63

1st Vl.

2nd Vl.

Viola

Cello

Poco meno mosso

Ex. 64

Adagio

Ex. 65

Allegro
Str. in octaves

Ex. 66

sul G

Ex. 67

Ex. 68

→ then to D major

Ex. 69

There's a fair-y that hides in the beau-ti-ful eyes of the chil-dren who treat her well;

Ex. 70

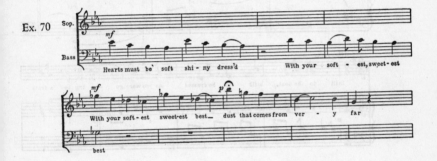

Sop.

Bass

Hearts must be' soft shi-ny dress'd   With your soft-est, sweet-est

With your soft-est sweet-est best— dust that comes from ver-y far

best

Ex. 71

Freely and carelessly   ten.

ten.

Ex. 72

(recit.)   accel.   rit.

The sun has gone, The tide of stars is set-ting all our way,   The

Viola & Cello only

Plei-a-des call soft-ly to O-ri-on   As night-ly they have

Viola & Cello only

2nd Vl.

cantabile

Ex. 72 cont.

called these mill - ion years

Ex. 73

(recit.) angrily

If you think you do please me in this, you are de - ceiv - ed

Allegretto

Still to be neat, still to be dressed As you were go - ing to a feast

Ex. 74

Orch.

Ex. 75

Allegro

2nd Fag.   2nd Clar.   Oboés enter

Ex. 76

Cor. etc   Tr.

Ex. 77

Ex. 78

Ex. 79

Ex. 80

APPENDIX

Inscriptions by Elgar in G. R. Sinclair's " Visitors' Book "

George Robertson Sinclair (1862–1917), of Irish extraction, was educated at the Royal Irish Academy of Music, St. Michael's College, Tenbury, and at Gloucester Cathedral, where he was assistant-organist under Dr. C. Harford Lloyd. Before becoming organist of Hereford Cathedral in 1889 he held posts at the church of St. Mary-le-Crypt, Gloucester, and Truro Cathedral. Through his energy and initiative the organs at Truro and Hereford were rebuilt. Sinclair was a practical musician of integrity who did much to raise the standards both of programme and performance in the Three Choirs Festival. He is now principally remembered on account of his bulldog Dan—his inseparable companion—and his friendship with Elgar. Dan is immortalised in the *Enigma Variations*, but otherwise commemorated in the inscriptions made by Elgar when he was Sinclair's guest at Hereford.

Of these inscriptions No. 3 is the theme which later was used as the " prayer " theme in *Gerontius*, No. 5 is the opening passage of the overture *In the South*, and No. 7 occurs in Elgar's " Sketch Book II " as an " Antioch " theme for the oratorio that was to follow *The Kingdom*. In fact Elgar later cancelled the title of this motiv. These inscriptions, which antedate the composition of the works in which they were ultimately to be found, show how Elgar accumulated ideas and found their appropriate context subsequently.

The last quotation in the " Visitors' Book " is of the " fellowship " theme of *The Apostles*—a graceful gesture.

June 5-7, 1897

FROM 'THE MOODS OF DAN, ILLUSTRATED'. No. I He sleeps

Dec. 18-20, 1897

From 'The Moods of Dan, Illustrated'. No. II He capers

April 19-20, 1898

From 'The Moods of Dan, Illustrated'. No. III He muses
(on the muzzling order)

Oct. 29-Nov. 1, 1898

From 'The Moods of Dan, Illustrated'. No. IV

July 8-10, 1899

FROM 'THE MOODS OF DAN, ILLUSTRATED'. No. V Dan
  triumphant (after a fight)

July 11-13, 1902

FROM 'THE MOODS OF DAN, ILLUSTRATED'. No. VI Dan
  wistful (outside the cathedral)

Aug. 27-31, 1903

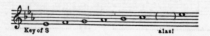

April 11-14, 1903

FROM 'THE MOODS OF DAN, ILLUSTRATED'. NO. VII NEW
SERIES. RETROSPECTIVE. THE SINFUL YOUTH OF DAN

June 29-July 2, 1904

INDEX OF WORKS

Comments made by the composer on his manuscripts are
indicated thus—[E]. Dates of composition are in (parentheses); where Elgar specified the day on which a work
was completed this is prefaced by "fin."; the longer
periods occupied by some larger works are calculated from
the Sketch Books and other sources.

I. ARRANGEMENTS

ANTHEM, arr. for strings and with an original introduction: (1874);
1st Perf. All Saints Church, Worcester, 1874; introduction only
extant.

VIOLIN SONATA (OP. 23) (last movement) Beethoven: for wind
quintet: (1878).

OVERTURE, ARIODANTE, Handel: for small orchestra: (1878).

"O 'TIS A GLORIOUS SIGHT," *Oberon*, Weber: (1878); arr. for Mr. F. J.
Pedley.

CONCERTO X, CORELLI: for wind quintet: (1878).

"ADESTE FIDELES," for orchestra: (1878).

ALLEGRO, FROM VIOLIN SONATA IN F (K. 547), Mozart: arr. as GLORIA:
(*c.* 1880). *1st. Perf.* St. George's Church, Worcester.

THEMES FROM SYMPHONIES V, VII AND IX, Beethoven: arr. as CREDO:
(*c.* 1880). *1st Perf.* St. George's Church, Worcester. "arr. Bernhard
Pappenheim." [E].

SCHERZO (OP. 52), Schumann: arr. for Pianoforte: (*c.* 1880).

"ENTRY OF MINSTRELS," *Tannhäuser*, Act II, Wagner: arr. for pianoforte: (1883). "Memento 1879–1883" [E].

MELODY, C. W. Buck: pianoforte accompaniment: (Sept. 15, 1885).

"ABSENT AND PRESENT," M. Valerie White: 'cello obbligato: (Sept. 9
1885); end note—"Lobster cutlets! Oh!!!!!" [E].

"OUT ON THE ROCKS," C. H. Dolby: 'cello obbligato: (Sept. 12,
1885).

"CLAPHAM TOWN END," Yorkshire folk song: for voice and pianoforte: (1890); "An old Yorkshire ballad taken down from the singing of old Tommy Kerr [?] as he got it from his grandfather. Harmonised in strict accordance with the spirit of the age." [E].

"GOOD FRIDAY MUSIC," *Parsifal*, Wagner: for small orchestra: (1894); *1st Perf.* Worcester High School, June 13, 1894.

"THE HOLLY AND THE IVY," for chorus and orchestra (1898); *1st Perf.* Worcestershire Philharmonic Society, Jan. 9, 1899.

2 CHORALES from *St. Matthew Passion*, Bach: for str., 4 cor., 3 tromb., tuba: (1911); *1st Perf.* Worcester Festival, Sept. 14, 1911.

"DARWALL" ("YE HOLY ANGELS BRIGHT"), accompaniment for Orchestra.

"JERUSALEM," Parry: accompaniment for orchestra: (1922); *1st Perf.* Leeds Festival 1922.

"LET US LIFT UP OUR HEARTS," S. S. Wesley: accompaniment for orchestra: (1923); *1st Perf.* Worcester Festival, Sept. 6, 1923.

"OH LORD, LOOK DOWN FROM HEAVEN," Battishill: accompaniment for orchestra: (1923); *1st Perf.* Worcester Festival, Sept. 6, 1923.

"JEHOVAH QUAM MULTI SUNT HOSTES," Purcell: accompaniment for orchestra: (1929); *1st Perf.* Worcester Festival, Sept. 10, 1929.

LARGHETTO, Mozart
CAVATINA, Raff
ROMANCE, De Bériot   } as studies for violin: (1877); *Pub.* Schott;
ROMANCE, Vieuxtemps   arranged at the suggestion of Adolphe
GIGUE, Franz Ries   Pollitzer.

GOD SAVE THE KING: *Pub.* Novello, 1902.

BERCEUSE—PETITE REINE, Victor Berard: arr. for violin and pianoforte; *Pub.* Wilcocks (?), Ashdown, 1907.

OVERTURE IN D MINOR, CHANDOS ANTHEM II, Handel: *Pub.* Novello, 1923; *1st Perf.* Worcester Festival, Sept. 2, 1923.

FUNERAL MARCH FROM SONATA IN B FLAT MINOR, Chopin; *Pub.* Keith Prowse, 1933; *1st Perf.* Royal Phil. Soc. Memorial Concert, Feb. 25, 1934.

OP. 86, FUGUE IN C MINOR, Bach: (fin. April 24, 1921); *Pub.* Novello, 1921; *1st Perf.* Queen's Hall, Oct. 27, 1921.

FANTASIA IN C MINOR, Bach: *Pub.* Novello, 1922; *1st Perf.* Gloucester Festival, Sept. 7, 1922.

II. CHAMBER MUSIC

(a) *for solo instruments*

FUGUE IN G MINOR : for organ [?] : (*c.* 1870) ; incomplete.

CHANTANT : for pianoforte solo : (*c.* 1872).

FANTASIA : for violin and pianoforte : (1878) ; incomplete.

TWO POLONAISES : for violin and pianoforte : (March 7, 1879) ; "for J. K. with esteem " [E] ; incomplete.

FANTASIA ON IRISH AIRS : for violin and pianoforte : (1881) ; incomplete.

FUGUE IN F SHARP MINOR : (1881) ; incomplete—later re-copied for *The Spanish Lady.*

LIEBESAHNUNG : for violin and pianoforte : (August 16, 1889) ; *Ded.* " Alice "; companion piece to *Liebesgrüss.*

PIECE FOR ORGAN : (1906) ; "for Dot's nuns " [E].

STUDY FOR STRENGTHENING THE THIRD FINGER : (1877, re-copied 1920) ; *Ded.* Heifetz ; in possession of Mr. Hubert Marno.

. . . . .

GAVOTTE : for violin and pianoforte : *Pub.* Schott (1886 ?) ; *Ded.* Dr. C. W. Buck.

ALLEGRETTO ON G.E.D.G.E. : for violin and pianoforte : (*c.* 1888) ; *Pub.* Schott ; *Ded.* The Misses Gedge, Malvern Wells.

MINUET : for pianoforte ; *Pub.* The Dome, 1897 ; *Ded.* Paul Kilburn ; see Opus 21.

MAY SONG : for pianoforte : (fin. Mar. 2, 1901) ; *Pub.* W. H. Broome, 1901 ; Morrice Mus. Publ. Co., 1901 ; Elkin, 1928.

SKIZZE : for pianoforte : (1903) ; *Pub.* Musik-Beilag zur Neuen Musik-Zeitung, Stuttgart—Leipzig XXIV Jahrgang ; *Ded.* Prof. Julius Büths, Düsseldorf ; E. played it to Leonard Borwick at Ridgehurst, Jan. 17, 1903.

IN SMYRNA : for pianoforte : (Autumn, 1905) ; *Pub.* Queen's Xmas Carol Book, publ. *Daily Mail*, 1905.

OFFERTOIRE (ANDANTE RELIGIOSO) : for violin and pianoforte : *Pub.* Boosey (1903) ; *Ded.* Serge Derval, Antwerp ; attributed to " Gustav Francke."[1]

[1] See p. 231.

SONATINA : for pianoforte ; *Pub.* Keith Prowse (1932) ; *Ded.* May Grafton ; MS. in possession of May Grafton.

ADIEU : for pianoforte (transcribed for violin by Szigeti) ; *Pub.* Keith Prowse, 1932.

SERENADE : for pianoforte ; *Pub.* Keith Prowse, 1932 ; *Ded.* " John Austin, Friend and Editor for many years."

OP. 1, ROMANCE : for violin and pianoforte (arr. violin and orchestra) : (1878) ; *Pub.* Schott ; *Ded.* Oswin Grainger ; *1st Perf.* Worcester, Oct. 20, 1885.

OP. 4, No. 1, UNE IDYLLE : for violin and pianoforte : (*c.* 1883) ; *Pub.* Beare (?) Leonard (?), Ashdown, 1910 ; *Ded.* E. E. Inverness.

OP. 4, No. 2, PASTOURELLE : for violin and pianoforte ; *Pub.* Beare (?) Swan, 1906 ; Novello, 1912 ; *Ded.* Miss Hilda Fitton.

CP. 4, No. 3, VIRELAI : for violin and pianoforte ; *Pub.* Beare (?) Swan 1906, Novello 1912 ; *Ded.* Frank Webb.[1]

OP. 9, VIOLIN SONATA ; destroyed by E.

OP. 13, No. 1, MOT D'AMOUR : for violin and pianoforte ; *Pub.* Orsborn and Tuckwood, 1890 ?, Ascherberg, 1890.

OP. 13, No. 2, BIZARRERIE : for violin and pianoforte ; sent to Simrock, July 22, 1889 ; *Pub.* Orsborn and Tuckwood 1890, Ascherberg, 1890.

CP. 14, ELEVEN VESPER VOLUNTARIES FOR ORGAN : (1889–Jan. 1890) *Pub.* Orsborn and Tuckwood 1891, Ascherberg, 1891 ; *Ded.* Mrs. W. A. Raikes[2] ; No. 3 from unpublished string quartet.

OP. 15, No. 1, CHANSON DE MATIN : for violin and pianoforte ; *Pub.* Novello, 1899 ; *Ded.* F. Ehrke, M.D.[3]

OP. 15, No. 1, CHANSON DE MATIN : arr. for orchestra ; *Pub.* Novello, 1901 ; *1st Perf.* Queen's Hall, Sept. 14, 1901.

OP. 15, No. 2, CHANSON DE NUIT : for violin and pianoforte ; *Pub.* Novello, 1897.

OP. 15, No. 2, CHANSON DE NUIT : arr. for orchestra ; *Pub.* Novello, 1899 ; *1st Perf.* Queen's Hall, Sept. 14, 1901.

OP. 17, LA CAPRICIEUSE : for violin and pianoforte : (Dec. 24, 1891) ; *Pub.* Breitkopf and Härtel, 1893 ; *Ded.* Fred Ward.[4]

[1] Of Worcester, furniture dealer, friend and pupil of Elgar.
[2] m. to cousin of Lady Elgar.
[3] Of the Manor House, Kempsey, and 1st violin in Worcestershire Philharmonic Society Orchestra.
[4] Of Worcester, pupil of Elgar.

Op. 21, Minuet: for pianoforte; *Pub.* Joseph Williams, 1897; *Ded.* Paul Kilburn.

Op. 21, Minuet: arr. for orchestra; *Pub.* Joseph Williams, 1899; *1st Perf.* New Brighton, July 16, 1899.

Op. 22, Very Melodious Exercises in the First Position: (1892); *Pub.* Chanot 1892, Laudy 1927; *Ded.* May Grafton.

Op. 24, Etudes Caracteristiques Pour Violin Seul: (No. 4 comp. on April 30, 1882); *Pub.* Chanot, 1892; *Ded.* Adolphe Pollitzer.

Op. 28, Sonata in G: for organ: (fin. July 3, 1895); *Pub.* Breitkopf, 1896; *Ded.* C. Swinnerton Heap, Mus.D.; *1st Perf.* Worcester Cathedral, July 8, 1895.

Op. 46, Concert Allegro: for pianoforte: (fin. Nov. 21, 1901); *Ded.* For Fanny Davies; present whereabouts of MS. sketches uncertain.

Op. 82, Sonata in E Minor: for violin and pianoforte: (fin. Sept. 1918); *Pub.* Novello, 1918; *Ded.* Marie Joshua; *1st Perf.* Aeolian Hall, Mar. 21, 1919.

(b) *For Strings*

String Quartet in D Minor and Major: (1878); incomplete.

String Quartet in B Flat: (1878); incomplete.

String Trio in C: (Aug. 20, 1878); incomplete.

String Quartet in D: allegretto; adagio; intermezzo; finale; incomplete; intermezzo used in Op. 14 (c. 1888).

String Quartet: (1907); fragmentary.

Andantino: for violin, mandoline and guitar: (June 15, 1907); " For the Barbers " [E];[1] incomplete.

Op. 8, String Quartet: destroyed by E., but possibly to be identified with that in D, *c.* 1888.

. . .

Op. 83, String Quartet in E Minor: (Mar. 25–Dec. 24, 1918); *Pub.* Novello, 1918; *Ded.* Brodsky Quartet; *1st Perf.* Wigmore Hall, May 21, 1919.

[1] Discovering that Italian clients of a hairdresser at Capri diverted themselves with music while waiting their turn, Elgar composed this piece for the general benefit.

(c) *For Strings and Pianoforte*

TRIO : for 2 violins and pianoforte : (1878) ; incomplete.

TRIO : for violin, 'cello and pianoforte. " Sans " [1] : (Feb. 10, 1886) ; part of 1st movement only ; re-copied Sept. 21, 1920.

MARCH : for violin, 'cello and pianoforte[2] : (1924) ; for the Grafton family.

> •   •   •   •

OP. 84, QUINTET IN A MINOR : for strings and pianoforte : (Summer, 1918–April 1919) ; *Pub.* Novello, 1919 ; *Ded.* Ernest Newman ; *1st Perf.* Wigmore Hall, May 21, 1919.

(d) *For Wind*

PROMENADES:

I   MODERATO E MOLTO MAESTOSO : (1878).

II   MODERATO : (1878) ; " Madame T*au*ssaud's [E] [*sic*].

III   PRESTO : (Aug. 13, 1878).

IV   ANDANTE : (Aug. 26, 1878) ; " Somniferous " [E].

V   ALLEGRO MOLTO : (Sept. 26, 1878).

VI   ALLEGRO MAESTOSO : (1878) ; " Hell and Tommy." [E].

HARMONY MUSIC

I   ALLEGRO MOLTO : (1879).

II   ALLEGRO NON TANTO : (1879) ; *Ded.* W. B. Leicester.

III   ALLEGRO : (1879) ; incomplete.

IV   ALLEGRO MOLTO : (1879) ; " The Farmyard." [E].

V   ALLEGRO MODERATO ; MINUET ; ANDANTE ; ALLEGRO : (Mar. 24–Apr. 4, 1879) : 1st Movement " The Mission". 3rd Movement : " Noah's Ark." [E].

VI   ALLEGRO MOLTO ; ANDANTE ARIOSO : (May 7, 1879).

VII   ALLEGRO ; SCHERZO-ALLEGRO GIUSTO : (April 14, 1881).

[1] Possibly the trio mentioned in letter to Dr. Buck, 1887.
[2] Intended also for orchestra, according to the composer's markings in the MS.

INTERMEZZOS:

   I   Allegro Molto: (1879).

   II   Adagio: (1879).

   III   Allegretto: (1879); "Nancy" [E].

   IV   Andante Con Moto: (Apr. 28, 1879).

   V   Allegretto: (1879).

Menuetto—Allegretto: (1879).

Gavotte: (1879); "The Alphonsa" [E].

Sarabande—Largo: (1879); re-copied for *The Spanish Lady*.

Gigue—Allegro: (1879).

Andante Con Variazioni: (1879); *Ded.* "H. A. L." "Evesham andante." [E].

Adagio Cantabile: (1879); "Mrs. Winslow's soothing syrup". [E].

Op. 6, Wind Quintets: any of the above, but not specified by E.

(e) *For Strings and Wind*

Allegro: for oboe, violin, viola, 'cello: (Dec. 17, 1878); incomplete.

Fugue in D Minor: for oboe and violin: (May 6, 1883); "für Frank Elgar and Karl Bammert." [E]

III. DRAMATIC MUSIC

Rabelais Ballet: (1902–3); fragments.

Opera in 3 Acts: (Projected 1909).

King Arthur: (L. Binyon): incidental music; *1st Perf.* London, Old Vic., Mar. 12, 1923.

Beau Brummel: (Bertram P. Matthews): incidental music; *1st Perf.* Birmingham, Theatre Royal, Nov. 5, 1928.

. . . . .

Fringes of the Fleet: (Mar.–May 1917); *Pub.* Enoch, 1917; *1st Perf.* London Coliseum, June 11, 1917.

   1. The Lowestoft Boat; *Ded.* Admiral Lord Beresford. 2. Fate's Discourtesy. 3. Submarines. 4. The Sweepers (words by Rudyard Kipling). 5. Inside the Bar (words by Gilbert Parker); *Ded.* "The 4 Singers."

PAGEANT OF EMPIRE ; *Pub.* Enoch, 1924; *1st Perf.* Wembley Exhibition, 1924.

   (*a*) Empire March. (*b*) Songs—words by Alfred Noyes. 1. " Shakespeare's Kingdom." 2. " The Islands." 3. " The Blue Mountains." 4. " The Heart of Canada." 5. " Sailing Westward." 6. " Merchant Adventurers." 7. " The Immortal Legions." 8. "A Song of Union " S.A.T.B. (Nos. 5 and 7 arr. S.A.T.B.).

OP. 42, GRANIA AND DIARMID : (W. B. Yeats and George Moore) : (fin. Oct. 4, 1901) ; *Pub.* Novello, 1902 ; *1st Perf.* Gaiety Theatre, Dublin, Oct. 1901 (*Ded.* Henry J. Wood).

   (*a*) Incidental Music. (*b*) Funeral March. (*c*) There are seven that pull the thread (W. B. Yeats) song for Act. I.

OP. 66, CROWN OF INDIA : masque by Henry Hamilton : (Feb. 1912, sketches from 1902 to 1912) ; *Pub.* Enoch, 1912 ; *1st Perf.* London Coliseum, Mar. 11, 1912.

   1. (*a*) Introduction ; (*b*) Sacred Measure. 2. Dance of Nautch Girls. 3. Hail, Immortal Ind. 4. March of Mogul Emperors. 5. Entrance of John Company. 6. Rule of England. 7. Interlude. 8. Warriors' Dance. 9. Cities of India. 10. Crown of India March. 11. Crowning of Delhi. 12. Ave Imperator.

OP. 78, THE STARLIGHT EXPRESS : play by Violet Pearn based on book *The Prisoner in Fairyland* by Algernon Blackwood : (Nov.–Dec. 1915) but incorporating material from 1878 ; *1st Perf.* Kingsway Theatre, Dec. 29, 1915.

   To the Children : (Elkin, 1916) ; Little Winds Song and Wind Dance ; Curfew Song ; Laugher's Song ; The Blue-Eyes Fairy ; (Elkin, 1916) ; Tears and Laughter ; Sunrise Song ; My Old Tune ; (Elkin, 1916) ; Finale ; these movements were recorded by H.M.V.

OP. 81, THE SANGUINE FAN : ballet, based on a fan by Condor : (Feb.–Mar. 1917) ; *1st Perf.* Chelsea Palace, Mar. 20, 1917.

   Echo's Dance only : for pianoforte ; *Pub.* Elkin, 1917.

OP. 89 (1), THE SPANISH LADY : opera in two acts ; Libretto from *The Devil is an Ass* (Ben Jonson) by Elgar and Sir Barry Jackson ; (sketches date from 1878–1933) ; fragmentary.

   Songs from THE SPANISH LADY [1] : ed. Percy M. Young (Elkin, 1955), Modest and Fair ; Still to be Neat. Suite for str-orch. [2] : ed. Percy M. Young (Elkin 1956)

----

[1] Op. No. assigned by Elgar.
[2] Posthumous Works.

IV. ORCHESTRAL MUSIC

INTRODUCTORY OVERTURE FOR CHRISTY MINSTRELS : (1878); *1st Perf.* June 12, 1878, Worcester.

MENUETTO (SCHERZO) : (Oct. 1, 1878); part of symphony ?; re-copied Mar. 1930.

SYMPHONY IN G MINOR, AFTER MOZART : (1878); part of 1st movement extant.

MINUET—GRAZIOSO : (1879); *1st Perf.* Worcester, Jan. 22, 1879; lost.

AIR DE BALLET : (1882); *1st Perf.* Worcester, Aug. 11, 1882 ; lost.

AIR DE BALLET—PASTORALE : (1882); *1st Perf.* Worcester, Mar. 14, 1882 ; lost.

MARCH—PAS REDOUBLE : (1882); *1st Perf.* Worcester, Mar. 14, 1882 ; re-copied 1932–33 for *The Spanish Lady*.

" THE LAKES "—OVERTURE : (1885); lost.

SCOTCH OVERTURE : (1885); lost.

THREE PIECES FOR STRING ORCHESTRA ; (1888); lost.

    I Spring Song (Allegro).

    II Elegy (Adagio).

    III Finale (Presto); *1st Perf.* Worcestershire Musical Union, May 7, 1888.

VIOLIN CONCERTO : Destroyed Nov. 1890.

FESTIVAL MARCH IN C : *1st Perf.* Crystal Palace, Oct. 14, 1898 ; fragment.

OVERTURE—COCKAIGNE No. 2 : (1903); fragment.

FANTASIA FOR STRINGS : (*c.* 1903); *Ded.* " Hans "; fragment.

" IN MEMORIAM ": (June 2, 1908); " in memory of a Seer " (C. A. E.); part in short score only.

TUSCAN FANTASTICO IN A FLAT AND G : (1909); fragment.

SCHERZO FOR PIANOFORTE AND ORCHESTRA : (1909); fragment.

MARCH IN B FLAT : (Sept. 13, 1933); incomplete.

MUSIC COMPOSED FOR THE WORCESTER CITY AND COUNTY PAUPER LUNATIC ASYLUM and preserved in the archives of the Powick Hospital in the following part-books : Piccolo, Flute, Clarinet, 2 Cornets, Euphonium, 1st Violin (2 copies), 2nd Violin (2 copies),

Viola (incomplete), 'Cello and Bass (lacks No. 1), 'Cello and Bass (complete), Pianoforte.

LA BRUNETTE (5 QUADRILLES): *Ded*. Geo. Jenkins.[1]

DIE JUNGE KOKETTE (5 QUADRILLES OR CALEDONIANS): (May 19, 1879); *Ded*. Miss J. Holloway.[2]

L'ASSOMOIR (5 QUADRILLES): (Sept. 11, 1879); No. 5 is the same as Op. 1 B. No. VI.

MAUD (POLKA): (May 30, 1880).

PARIS (5 QUADRILLES): (Oct. 17, 1880); *Ded*. Miss J. Holloway; " introducing a French song—' La femme d'emballeur ' " [E].
(1) Chatelet. (2) L'Hippodrome. (3) Alcazar d'Eté (Champs Elysées). (4) La ! Suzanne ! (5) Café des Ambassadeurs : La femme de l'emballeur.

THE VALENTINE (5 LANCERS): (Feb. 2–15, 1880).

NELLY (POLKA): (Oct. 1881); attributed by E. to Fras. Thos. Elgar.

LA BLONDE (POLKA): (Oct. 15, 1882).

HELCIA (POLKA): (Oct. 1, 1883); " Composer in Ordinary to the W. C. and C. L. A." [E].

BLUMINE (POLKA): (May 22, 1884); on 1st violin part " von Eduard Wilhelm " [E].

SERENADE LYRIQUE: (June 1899); *Pub*. Chappell, 1899; *1st Perf*. London, St. James's Hall, Nov. 27, 1900 ; composed for Ivan Caryll's orchestra.

CARISSIMA: *Pub*. Elkin, 1914; *Ded*. Winifred Stephens[3]; *1st Perf*. London, Albert Hall, Feb. 15, 1914.

ROSEMARY (ALSO FOR PIANOFORTE SOLO): (Sept. 4, 1882, at Settle, Yorks); *Pub*. Elkin, 1915.

NURSERY SUITE: *Pub*. Keith Prowse, 1931 ; *Ded*. H.R.H. The Princesses Elizabeth and Margaret Rose; *1st Perf*. Recorded before T.R.H. The Duke and Duchess of York, Kingsway Hall, May 23, 1931; Promenade Concert, Aug. 20, 1931 : as ballet, (arr. Ninette de Valois) Old Vic, Mar. 21, 1932 ; " Aubade " incorporates hymn tune first composed in 1878.

[1] Clerk to the Asylum.
[2] Pianist and organist of the Asylum.
[3] Sister of Muriel Foster.

Aubade; The Serious Doll; Busy-ness; The Sad Doll; The Waggon (Passes); The Merry Doll; Dreaming; "Envoi."

NINA: *Pub.* Keith Prowse, 1934; *1st Perf.* Recorded H.M.V., Feb. 8, 1934 and Jan. 7, 1935.

OP. 1A, THE WAND OF YOUTH: music to a Child's Play: (Begun 1867, 1869 or 1871, revised 1879–81; revised again *c.* 1902; final versions 1906–7; *Pub.* Novello, 1907; *Ded.* C. Lee Williams; *1st Perf.* Queen's Hall, Dec. 14, 1907; as ballet, perf. by Lawnside Girls' School, Malvern, at Malvern Theatre, Oct. 7, 1930. (First Suite).

  I   Overture. (Extant sketch 1879).
  II   Serenade.
  III Minuet. (Extant sketch 1881).
  IV   Sun Dance. Used in " The Starlight Express."
  V   Fairy Pipers.
  VI   Slumber Scene.
  VII Fairies and Giants. (Copied by E. and noted as from 1867.)

OP. 1B, THE WAND OF YOUTH.
(Second Suite.) *Pub.* Novello, 1908; *Ded.* Hubert A. Leicester; *1st Perf.* Worcester Festival, Sept. 9, 1908.

  I   March.
  II   The Little Bells; quoted in *The Starlight Express.*
  III Moths and Butterflies; (Extant sketch, 1879); used in *The Starlight Express.*
  IV   Fountain Dance.
  V   The Tame Bear.
  VI   The Wild Bear; (Extant sketch 1879); used as a quadrille for Powick band.

OP. 3, CANTIQUE: (1879: revised and orch. Nov. 1912); *Pub.* Novello, 1913; *Ded.* Hugh Blair; *1st Perf.* Albert Hall, Dec. 15, 1912; formerly Adagio Solenne.

OP. 7, SEVILLANA: (at 4 Field Terrace, Worcester, 1884 (?), revised 1889); *Pub.* Tuckwood 1884, Ascherberg 1895; *Ded.* W. C. Stockley; *1st Perf.* Worcester, May 1, 1884.

OP. 10, THREE PIECES FOR SMALL ORCHESTRA: (1882-88, revised Jan. 23-24, 1899); *1st Perf.* Birmingham, Mar. 1, 1888.
  No. 1, MAZURKA: *Pub.* Novello, 1899; *Ded.* Lady Mary Lygon.
  No. 2, SERENADE (formerly INTERMEZZO), MAURESQUE: (1883); *1st Perf.* Birmingham, Feb. 23, 1883; originally " Pas redouble " March was part of the suite.

No. 3, CONTRASTS : THE GAVOTTE A.D.1700 and 1900.

OP. 11, SURSUM CORDA : (Apr. 1, 1894) ; *Pub.* Schott, 1901 (?) ; *Ded.* H. Dyke Acland ; *1st Perf.* Worcester Cathedral, Apr. 9, 1894.

OP. 12, SALUT D'AMOUR (LIEBESGRÜSS) [1] : arr. for orchestra : (1888) ; *Pub.* Schott, 1889 ; *Ded.* Carice [2] ; *1st Perf.* Crystal Palace, Nov. 11, 1889.

OP. 19, FROISSART : concert overture : (Apr. 6–July 1890 : at 51 Avonmore Road, W. Kensington) ; *Pub.* Novello, 1890 ; *1st Perf.* Worcester Festival, Sept. 9, 1890.

OP. 20, SERENADE FOR STRING ORCHESTRA : (May 1892) ; *Pub.* Breitkopf, 1893 ; *Ded.* W. H. Whinfield ; *1st Perf.* Complete Suite Bechstein Hall, Mar. 5, 1905 ; II only at St. Andrew's Hall, June 19, 1894 ; " Braut [3] helped a great deal to make these little tunes." [E].

   I.   ALLEGRO PIACEVOLE.

   II. LARGHETTO.

  III. ALLEGRETTO.

OP. 32, IMPERIAL MARCH : (fin. Feb. 6, 1897) ; *Pub.* Novello, 1902 ; *1st Perf.* Crystal Palace, April 19, 1897.

OP. 36, VARIATIONS FOR ORCHESTRA " ENIGMA ": (1898–99 Malvern) ; Score sent to N. Vert, Feb. 21, 1899) ; *Pub.* Novello, 1899 ; *Ded.* "My friends pictured within"; *1st Perf.* St. James's Hall, June 19, 1899.

OP. 39, POMP AND CIRCUMSTANCE. MILITARY MARCHES.

  I D. MAJOR : (Birchwood July 1901) ; *Pub.* Boosey, 1902 ; *Ded.* A. E. Rodewald and the members of the Liverpool Orchestra Society ; *1st Perf.* Liverpool, Oct. 19, 1901.

  II A MINOR : (fin. Aug. 13, 1901) ; *Pub.* Boosey, 1902 ; *Ded.* Granville Bantock ; *1st Perf.* Liverpool, Oct. 19, 1901.

  III C MINOR : (fin. Nov. 1904) ; *Pub.* Boosey, 1905 ; *Ded.* Ivor Atkins ; *1st Perf.* Queen's Hall, Mar. 8, 1905.

  IV G MAJOR : (fin. June 7, 1907) ; *Pub.* Boosey, 1907 ; *Ded.* G. R. Sinclair ; *1st Perf.* Queen's Hall, Aug. 24, 1907.

  V C MAJOR : *Pub.* Boosey, 1930 ; *Ded.* Percy C. Hull ; *1st Perf.* Queen's Hall, Sept. 20, 1930.

MILITARY MARCH IN B Flat : (1924) ; *Pub.* Boosey, 1956.[4] (Posthumous).

OP. 40, COCKAIGNE, (No. 1), " In London Town " : Concert Overture :

---

[1] In many forms.
[2] Caroline Alice (Elgar).
[3] i.e. C. A. E.
[4] This march has been edited and orchestrated by Percy M. Young from the MS.; remains in the possession of the Elgar Trustees.

(fin. Mar. 24, 1901); *Pub.* Boosey, 1901 ; *Ded.* " to my friends the members of British Orchestras "; *1st Perf.* Queen's Hall, June 20, 1901 ; End note—" Meteless and moneless on Malverne Hills " Piers the Plowman. [E]

Op. 43, DREAM CHILDREN : 2 pieces for pianoforte or small orchestra : (fin. Jan. 14, 1902); *Pub.* J. Williams, 1902, Schott 1913 ; *1st Perf.* Queen's Hall, Sept. 4, 1902.

Op. 47, INTRODUCTION AND ALLEGRO FOR STRINGS : (begun 1901 [1], fin. Feb. 13, 1905); *Pub.* Novello, 1905 ; *Ded.* Professor S. S. Sanford, Yale University, U.S.A. ; *1st Perf.* Queen's Hall, Mar. 8, 1905.

Op. 50, IN THE SOUTH (ALASSIO), Concert Overture : (Begun 1899 ; fin. Feb. 21, 1904); *Pub.* Novello, 1904; *Ded.* Leo F. Schuster; *1st Perf.* Covent Garden, Mar. 16, 1904; MS. score at R.A.M.

Op. 55, SYMPHONY IN A FLAT : (June 1907–Sept. 1908); *Pub.* Novello, 1908 ; *Ded.* Hans Richter, " true artist and friend "; *1st Perf.* Manchester, Dec. 3, 1908.

Op. 58, ELEGY FOR STRING ORCHESTRA : (fin. July 5, 1909); *Pub.* Novello, 1910; *Ded.* In mem. late Junior Warden of Musicians' Company—Rev. R. H. Hadden, M.A. ; *1st Perf.* Mansion House, July 13, 1909; played annually until 2nd World War, St. Paul's Cathedral, on St. Cecilia's Day, in memory of deceased members of the Company.

Op. 61, CONCERTO FOR VIOLIN AND ORCHESTRA : (*c.* Apr. 1909–Aug. 5, 1910); *Pub.* Novello, 1910; *Ded.* Fritz Kreisler ; *1st Perf.* Queen's Hall, Nov. 10, 1910.

Op. 62, ROMANCE FOR BASSOON AND ORCHESTRA : (Jan. 1910); *Pub.* Novello, 1910; *Ded.* Edwin F. James ; *1st Perf.* Hereford, Feb. 16, 1911.

Op. 63, SYMPHONY No. 2 IN E FLAT : (*c.* 1903–10); *Pub.* Novello, 1911 ; *Ded.* " His late Majesty King Edward VII "; *1st Perf.* London Music Festival, May 24, 1911.

Op. 65, CORONATION MARCH : (1902–May 1911); *Pub.* Novello, 1911 ; *1st Perf.* Westminster Abbey, June 22, 1911.

Op. 68, FALSTAFF : SYMPHONIC STUDY IN C. MINOR : (1902–13); *Pub.* Novello, 1913; *Ded.* Landon Ronald ; *1st Perf.* Leeds Festival, Oct. 1, 1913.

---

[1] Begun for full orchestra.

Op. 70, Sospiri (Seufzer); *Pub.* Breitkopf and Härtel, 1914; *Ded.* W. H. Reed; *1st Perf.* Queen's Hall, Aug. 15, 1914.

Op. 75. Carillon: With Recited Words of E. Cammaerts; (Nov. 1914). *Pub.* Elkin 1914; *1st Perf.* Queen's Hall, Dec., 1914.

Op. 76, Polonia: (fin. June 1, 1915); *Pub.* Elkin 1915; *Ded.* I. J. Paderewski; *1st Perf.* Queen's Hall, July 6, 1915.

Op. 77, Une Voix Dans Le Desert—with Recited Words of E. Cammaerts: (July 1915); *Pub.* Elkin, 1915; *1st Perf.* Shaftesbury Theatre, Jan. 29, 1916.

Op. 79, Le Drapeau Belge—with Recited Words of E. Cammaerts: *1st Perf.* Queen's Hall, Apr. 14, 1917.

Op. 85, Concerto for Violoncello and Orchestra in E Minor: (fin. Aug. 1919); *Ded.* Sidney and Francis Colvin; *1st Perf.* Queen's Hall, Oct. 26, 1919.

Op. 87, Severn Suite for Brass Band: (fin. Apr. 1930); *Pub.* R. Smith, 1930; *Ded.* G. Bernard Shaw; *1st Perf.* Crystal Palace Brass Band Festival, Sept. 1930.

Arr. for Orchestra: *Pub.* Keith Prowse, 1932; *1st Perf.* Worcester Festival, Sept. 7, 1932.

    1. Introduction (Worcester Castle). 2. Toccata (Tournament). 3. Fugue (Cathedral). 4. Minuet (Commandery)—(based on sketch of 1903). 5. Coda.

Op. 87A, The Above Arr. (Ivor Atkins) as Organ Sonata 2: *Pub.* Keith Prowse, 1933; *1st Perf.* Organ Music Society, 1933.

Op. 88 [1], Symphony III: (1933); Sketches only in possession of B.B.C., but on loan to British Museum.

Op. 90 [1], Concerto for Pianoforte and Orchestra: (Dating from 1909, 1914, 1917, 1926 and 1932); fragmentary.

V. VOCAL MUSIC

(a) *Cantatas, Oratorios and Odes*

Op. 25, The Black Knight: A Cantata: Poem by Uhland, trans. Longfellow: (May 18, 1890?–Sept. 1892); *Pub.* Novello, 1893; *Ded.* Hugh Blair, M.A., Mus.B.; *1st Perf.* Worcester, Apr. 18, 1893.

Op. 29, The Light of Life. (Lux Christi): words written and arr. by Rev. E. Capel-Cure, M.A.: (Jan.–June 1896); *Pub.* Novello, 1896;

[1] Op. No. assigned by Elgar.

Ded. C. Swinnerton Heap, Mus. D. : *1st Perf.* Worcester Festival, Sept. 10, 1896.

Op. 30, SCENES FROM THE SAGA OF KING OLAF : words by Longfellow and H. A. Acworth : (July 15, 1894–Aug. 1896) ; *Pub.* Novello ; for N. Staffs. Musical Festival ; *1st Perf.* Hanley, Oct. 30, 1896.

Op. 32, BANNER OF ST. GEORGE : a BALLAD : words by Shapcott Wensley : (Jan.–Mar. 1897) ; *Pub.* Novello, 1897 ; *1st Perf.* Kensington, May 18, 1897.

Op. 35, CARACTACUS : A CANTATA : words by H. A. Acworth, C.I.E. : (fin. Aug. 21, 1898) ; *Pub.* Novello, 1898 ; *Ded.* Queen Victoria ; *1st Perf.* Leeds Festival, Oct. 5, 1898.

Op. 38, THE DREAM OF GERONTIUS : words by Cardinal Newman : (fin. vocal score June 6, 1900 ; full score Aug. 3, 1900) ; *Pub.* Novello, 1900 ; *Ded.* A.M.D.G. ; *1st Perf.* Birmingham Festival, Oct. 3, 1900 ; MS. presented to Oratory, Birmingham, Aug. 9, 1902.

Op. 44, CORONATION ODE : words by A. C. Benson : (fin. Feb. 21, 1902) ; *Pub.* Boosey, 1902 ; Composed for the Grand Opera Syndicate for the State Performance at Covent Garden ; *1st Perf.* Sheffield Festival, Oct. 2, 1902.

Op. 49, THE APOSTLES : Libretto by Elgar : (fin. Aug. 17, 1903) ; *Pub.* Novello, 1903 ; *Ded.* A.M.D.G. ; *1st Perf.* Birmingham Festival, Oct. 14, 1903.

Op. 51, THE KINGDOM : Libretto by Elgar : (fin. Aug. 1906) ; *Pub.* Novello, 1906 ; *Ded.* A.M.D.G. ; *1st Perf.* Birmingham Festival, Oct. 3, 1906.

Op. 69, THE MUSIC MAKERS : words by Arthur O'Shaughnessy : (1902?–fin. July 18, 1912 ; orch. Aug. 21, 1912) ; *Pub.* Novello, 1912 ; *Ded.* Nicholas Kilburn ; *1st Perf.* Birmingham Festival, Oct. 1, 1912.

Op. 80, THE SPIRIT OF ENGLAND : words by L. Binyon : *1st Perf.* Albert Hall, Nov. 24, 1917.

No. 1. The Fourth of August : (fin. May 1917) ; *Pub.* Novello, 1917 ; *Ded.* To the memory of our glorious men, with a special thought for the Worcesters ; *1st Perf.* Birmingham, Oct. 4, 1916.

No. 2. To Women : (1915) ; *Pub.* Novello, 1916 ; *1st Perf.* Leeds, May 3, 1916.

No. 3. For the Fallen : (1915) ; *1st Perf.* Leeds, May 3, 1916.

(b) *Church Music*

[OP. 1]¹, SALVE REGINA : (1878) ; *1st Perf.* St. George's Church, Worcester, June 6, 1880 ; 50th anniversary of opening of church.

[OP. 2], TANTUM ERGO : (1878) ; *1st Perf.* St. George's Church, Worcester, June 29, 1879.

[OP. 3], No. 3, CREDO IN E MINOR : (*c.* 1879).

EASTER ANTHEM : " BROTHER FOR THEE HE DIED " : (1878).

HYMN TUNE IN G MAJOR : (1878).

HYMN TUNE IN F MAJOR : (1878) ; *Pub.* in Westminster Hymnal as " Drake's Broughton " ; quoted in *Nursery Suite*, I, 1931.

DOMINE SALVAM FAC REGINAM NOSTRAM VICTORIAM : (1879) ; *1st Perf.* St. George's Church, Worcester, Feast of SS. Peter and Paul, June 29, 1879.

TANTUM ERGO : *1st Perf.* St. George's Church, Worcester, Feast of SS. Peter and Paul, June 29, 1879.

O SALUTARIS HOSTIA : (for bass solo) : (April 17, 1882).

SO MANY TRUE PRINCESSES WHO HAVE GONE, John Masefield : for chorus ; for unveiling of memorial to Queen Alexandra, Marlborough House, June 9, 1932.

. . . .

4 LITANIES FOR B.V.M. : *Pub.* Cary, 1888 ; *Ded.* Fr. T. Knight, S.J.

O SALUTARIS HOSTIA : (*c.* 1880) ; *Pub.* Cary, 1888 ; MS. copied by M. Grafton.

ECCE SACERDOS MAGNUS : (1888) ; *Pub.* Cary, 1888 ; *Ded.* Hubert Leicester ; *1st Perf.* St. George's Church, Worcester, Oct. 9, 1888.

O SALUTARIS HOSTIA, Tozer's Benediction Manual, No. 47 : *Pub.* Cary, 1898.

OH MIGHTIEST OF THE MIGHTY : *Pub.* Novello, 1902 ; *Ded.* H.R.H. The Prince of Wales ; *1st Perf.* Coronation of Edward VII, Aug. 9, 1902.

LO ! CHRIST THE LORD IS BORN : Words by Shapcott Wensley ; *Pub.* Novello, 1909.

2 SINGLE CHANTS : (May 1907) ; *Pub.* New Cathedral Psalter.

¹ Op. Nos. originally given by Elgar.

E.   2D

2 DOUBLE CHANTS: (May 1907); *Pub.* Novello, 1909.

THEY ARE AT REST: Words by Cardinal Newman: *Pub.* Novello, 1910; *1st Perf.* Royal Mausoleum for anniversary of Queen Victoria's death, Jan. 22, 1910.

FEAR NOT, O LORD: Words from Joel II, 21–24, 26: (Jan. 1914); *Pub.* Novello, 1914; Harvest anthem.

I SING THE BIRTH: Words by Ben Jonson: *Pub.* Novello, 1928; *Ded.* Rev. Harcourt B. S. Fowler, Elmley Castle, Worcs.

GOOD MORROW: Words by George Gascoigne: *Pub.* Novello, 1929; *First Perf.* Windsor Castle, Dec. 9, 1929; "A simple carol for His Majesty's happy recovery."

OP. 2, NO. 1, AVE VERUM: (Jan. 27, 1887); *Pub.* Novello, 1902; *Ded.* " in mem. W. H." on MS. " very like ' Love Divine ' in Daughter of Jairus—Stainer " [E].

OP. 2, NO. 2, JESU, LORD OF LIFE AND GLORY, J. Cummins: arr. from " Ave Maria ": *Pub.* Novello, 1907; *Ded.* Mrs. H. A. Leicester.

OP. 2, NO. 3, AVE MARIS STELLA: *Pub.* Novello, 1907; *Ded.* Rev. Canon Dolman, O.S.B.; Hereford.

OP. 34, TE DEUM AND BENEDICTUS: (fin. July 31, 1897); *Pub.* Novello, 1897; *Ded.* G. R. Sinclair; *1st Perf.* Hereford Festival, Sept. 12, 1897. " Inter spem et metuum " [E].

OP. 64, CORONATION OFFERTORIUM: (Mar. 1911); *Pub.* Novello, 1911; *1st Perf.* Westminster Abbey, June 22, 1911.

OP. 67, GREAT IS THE LORD (Ps. XLVIII): (Aug. 24, 1910–Mar. 1912); *Pub.* Novello, 1912; *Ded.* Very Rev. J. Armitage Robinson, D.D., Dean of Wells; *1st Perf.* Westminster Abbey, July 16, 1912.

OP. 74, GIVE UNTO THE LORD (Ps. XXIX): (Jan.–Mar. 1914); *Pub.* Novello, 1914; *Ded.* Sir George Martin, M.V.O., Mus.D.; *1st Perf.* Sons of Clergy Festival, St. Paul's Cathedral, Apr., 30, 1914.

(c) *Part Songs—(accompanied)*

OP. 23, SPANISH SERENADE (Stars of the Summer Night): (Nov. 10, 1891; Scored June 12, 1892); *Pub.* Novello, 1892; *1st Perf.* Hereford, Apr. 7, 1893.

OP. 26, NO. 1, THE SNOW: (1894; orch. Dec. 19, 1903); *Pub.* Novello, 1895; *Ded.* Mrs. E. B. Fitton, Malvern; *1st Perf.* with orch., Queen's Hall, Mar. 12, 1904.

Op. 26, No. 2, FLY, SINGING BIRD, C. Alice Elgar: (1894; orch. Dec. 19, 1903); *Pub.* Novello, 1895; *Ded.* Mrs. E. B. Fitton, Malvern; *1st Perf.* with orch., Queen's Hall, Mar. 12, 1904.

Op. 27, FROM THE BAVARIAN HIGHLANDS, C. Alice Elgar: (1895; orch. Feb.–Mar. 1896); *Pub.* J. Williams, 1896; *Ded.* Mr. and Mrs. Henry Slingsby Bethell, Garmisch, Bavaria; *1st Perf.* Worcester, Apr. 21, 1896.
1. The Dance. 2. False Love. 3. Lullaby. 4. Aspiration. 5. On the Alm. 6. The Marksman (also arranged for orch. alone); *Pub.* Novello, 1907; *1st Perf.* Nos. 1, 3, 6, Crystal Palace, Oct. 23, 1897.

Op. 52, A CHRISTMAS GREETING, C. Alice Elgar: (fin. Dec. 8, 1907); *Pub.* Novello 1907; *Ded.* Dr. G. A. Sinclair and the choristers of Hereford Cathedral; *1st Perf.* Hereford, Jan. 1, 1908.

(d) *Part Songs (unaccompanied)*

" GRETE MALVERNE ON A ROCK ": (1897); *Pub.* privately, as a Christmas card, 1897.

CHORAL SUITE: (1909); Sketches only except for III which is complete.
1. Introduction. 2. In a Vineyard. 3. Op. 56, No. 1, Angelus; *Pub.* Novello. 4. Dance. 5. Vintage. 6. Envoi.
from Love Poems, Landor (1901).

MY LOVE DWELT IN A NORTHERN LAND, Andrew Lang: (Jan. 1890); (left at Novello's, Jan. 13); *Pub.* Novello, 1890; *Ded.* Rev. J. Hampton, M.A. Warden of St. Michael's College, Tenbury; *1st Perf.* Tenbury, Nov. 13, 1890.

TO HER BENEATH WHOSE STEADFAST STAR, Fred. W. H. Myers: (Feb. 7, 1899); *Pub.* Macmillan, 1899; *1st Perf.* Windsor Castle, May 24, 1899; one of a collection dedicated to Q. Victoria.

WEARY WIND OF THE WEST, T. E. Brown: (Nov. 1902); *Pub.* Novello, 1903; *Ded.* composed for Morecambe Musical Festival; *1st Perf.* Morecambe Festival, May 2, 1903.

EVENING SCENE, Coventry Patmore: (written at Rotherwas, fin. Aug. 25, 1905); *Pub.* Novello, 1906; *Ded.* in mem. R. G. H. Howson; *1st Perf.* Morecambe Festival, May 12, 1906.

HOW CALMLY THE EVENING, T. T. Lynch: *Pub.* Novello, 1907 in *Musical Times.*

THE BIRTHRIGHT, George A. Stocks: *Pub.* Novello, 1914.

MARCHING SONG, Capt. de Courcy Stretton, for S.A.T.B.: *1st Perf.* Albert Hall, May 24, 1908.

FOLLOW THE COLOURS: adapted for solo and *ad lib.* male voice chorus from *Marching Song*: *Pub.* Novello 1914; *1st Perf.* Albert Hall, Oct. 10, 1914.

THE WANDERER: (from Wit and Drollery, 1661) for T.T.B.B. *Pub.* Novello, 1923.

ZUT ZUT ZUT: (Richard Marden) for T.T.B.B.; *Pub.* Novello, 1923.

THE HERALD: (Alexander Smith); *Pub.* Novello, 1925.

THE PRINCE OF SLEEP: (Walter de la Mare); *Pub.* Elkin, 1925.

OP. 18, No. 1, O HAPPY EYES, C. Alice Elgar: (Jan. 1890?); *Pub.* Novello, 1896.

OP. 18, No. 2, LOVE, Arthur Maquarie: (Jan. 1890? revised June 2, 1907); *Pub.* Novello, 1907; *Ded.* C. A. E.

OP. 45, 5 PART SONGS FROM THE GREEK ANTHOLOGY: (fin. Nov. 11, 1902, Longdon Marsh); *Pub.* Novello, 1903; *Ded.* Sir Walter Parratt; *1st Perf.* Albert Hall, Apr. 25, 1904.
   1. Yea, Cast Me Down from the Heights of the Mountains (trans. Alma Strettell).
   2. Whether I find Thee (trans. Andrew Lang).
   3. After many a Dusty Mile (trans. E. Gosse).
   4. It's Oh to be a Wild Wind (trans. W. M. Hardinge).
   5. Feasting I Watch (trans. Richard Garnett).

OP. 53.
   1. There is Sweet Music, Tennyson: (Rome, Feb. 1907); *1st pub.* Novello, 1908; *Ded.* Canon Gorton.
   2. Deep in My Soul, Byron: (Rome, 1907); *Pub.* Novello, 1908; *Ded.* Julia H. Worthington.
   3. O Wild West Wind, Shelley: (Rome 1907); *Pub.* Novello, 1908; *Ded.* W. G. McNaught.
   4. Owls, E. E.: *Pub.* Novello, 1908; *Ded.* Pietro d'Alba (i.e. Peter Rabbit).

OP. 54, THE REVEILLE, Bret Harte: (fin. Dec. 26, 1907, Rome); *Pub.* Novello, 1908; *Ded.* Henry C. Embleton; *1st Perf.* Blackpool Festival, Oct. 17, 1908.

OP. 56 (1) ANGELUS (TUSCANY): words adapted from the dialect: *Pub.* Novello, 1909; *Ded.* Mrs. Charles Stuart-Wortley; *1st Perf.* Albert Hall, Dec. 8, 1910.

Op. 57, Go, Song of Mine, Guido Calvacanti, trans. D. G. Rossetti :
(Carreggi, May 1909); *Pub.* Novello, 1909; *Ded.* Alfred H. Littleton;
1st *Perf.* Hereford Festival, Sept. 9, 1909.

Op. 71 (1) The Shower, Henry Vaughan : at Mill Hill [1] : *Pub.* Novello,
1914; *Ded.* Miss Frances Smart, Malvern.
    (2) The Fountain, Henry Vaughan : at Totteridge [1] : *Pub.*
Novello, 1914; *Ded.* W. Mann Dyson, Worcester.

Op. 72, Death on the Hills, Maikov, trans. Rosa Newmarch : (Jan.
1914); *Pub.* Novello, 1914; *Ded.* Lady Colvin.

Op. 73 (1) Love's Tempest, Maikov, trans. Rosa Newmarch : (Jan.
1914); *Pub.* Novello, 1914; *Ded.* C. Sanford Terry.
    (2) Serenade, Maikov, trans. Rosa Newmarch : Hadley Green [2]
(Jan. 1914); *Pub.* Novello, 1914; *Ded.* Percy C. Hull.

(e) *Solo Songs*

The Language of Flowers : (May 29, 1872); *Ded.* " Lucy "; " poetry
by Percival " [E].

" If She Love Me" (Temple Bar Rondeau) : (Dec. 1878).

" Man " [*sic*] : (Jan. 1890).

" A Spear, A Sword " : (Aug. 25, 1892).

" Millwheel Song " I : (Dec. 6, 1892).

" Millwheel Song " II : (Dec. 9, 1892).

" The Wave ": (Jan. 4, 1894).

" Muleteer's Song ": (Jan. 4, 1894).

Rondel : The Little Eyes that never knew Light other than of Dawning
Skies, Swinburne : 1st *Perf.* Worcester Mus. Union, April 26, 1897;
sung by Miss Gertrude Walker, Worcester Mus. Union, acc. E. E.

Scena—" Callicles," M. Arnold : (Oct. 1913); intended for Muriel
Foster.

" Soldier's Song," Begbie : (Sept. 6, 1914); withdrawn.

Ozymandias, Shelley : (July 12, 1917).

Tarantella, Belloc : baritone and orchestra : (1933); incomplete.

.   .   .   .

As I Laye A-thinking, Thomas Ingoldsby : *Pub.* Beare, 1888.

---

[1] In the home counties, and accessible to Elgar from Hampstead.
[2] Near Worcester.

THE WIND AT DAWN, C. Alice Roberts: *Pub*. Magazine of Music, 1888 ; Boosey, 1907 ; *Ded*. Dr. Ludwig Wüllner ; first price of £5 in Magazine of Music competition.

LIKE TO THE DAMASK ROSE, Simon Wastell: (1892) ; *Pub*. Tuckwood, Ascherberg, 1893 ; *1st Perf*. St. James's Hall, Feb. 25, 1897.

QUEEN MARY'S SONG, Tennyson: (June 14–July 1, 1889) ; *Pub*. Orsborn and Tuckwood 1889, Ascherberg 1892 ; *Ded*. J. H. Meredith,[1] [pencil note by E. on MS.].

A SONG OF AUTUMN, A. Lindsay Gordon: (1892) ; *Pub*. Orsborn and Tuckwood, Ascherberg 1892 ; *Ded*. Miss Marshall.[2]

THE POET'S LIFE, Ellen Burroughs: (1892) ; *Ded*. Mrs. Fitton's name deleted in MS. ; *Pub*. with Op. 16, Nos. 1–3 as 7 lieder (1907).

LOVE ALONE WILL STAY. " LUTE SONG," C. Alice Elgar: (" written out " May 1898) ; *Pub*. The Dome, 1898 ; revised as Op. 37, No. 2.

DRY THOU FAIR, THOSE CRYSTAL EYES, Henry King: *Pub*. Souvenir of Charing Cross Hospital Bazaar, 1899 ; *1st Perf*. Albert Hall, June 21, 1899.

PIPES OF PAN, Adrian Ross: (before June 5, 1899) ; *Pub*. Boosey, 1900 ; *1st Perf*. Queen's Hall, May 12, 1900.

COME, GENTLE NIGHT, Clifton Bingham: *Pub*. Boosey, 1901.

ALWAYS AND EVERYWHERE, (F. E. Fortey from the Polish of Krasinsky) : *Pub*. Boosey, 1901.

LAND OF HOPE AND GLORY, A. C. Benson: arr. from Coronation Ode : *Pub*. Boosey, 1902.

SPEAK, MY HEART, A. C. Benson: (Aug. 26, 1902 ?) ; *Pub*. Boosey, 1903.

IS SHE NOT PASSING FAIR, Charles, Duke of Orleans, trans. Louisa Stuart Costello: (Oct. 28, 1886) ; *Pub*. Boosey, 1908.

THE KINGSWAY, C. Alice Elgar: (Dec. 25–7, 1909) ; *Pub*. Boosey, 1910 ; *1st Perf*. Alexandra Palace, Jan. 15, 1910.

A CHILD ASLEEP, Mrs. Browning: (Dec. 1909) ; *Pub*. Novello, 1910 ; *Ded*. Anthony Goetz.[3]

ARABIAN SERENADE, Margery Lawrence: *Pub*. Boosey, 1914.

[1] An honorary member of Worcester Amateur Instrumental Society.
[2] Mrs. Marshall and her daughter were friends of Lady Elgar.
[3] Son of Muriel Foster.

CHARIOTS OF THE LORD, Rev. John Brownlie : Jan. 1914 ; *Pub*. Boosey, 1914 ; *Ded*. Members of Fight for Right Movement ; *1st Perf*. Albert Hall, June 28, 1914.

FIGHT FOR THE RIGHT, William Morris : *Pub*. Elkin, 1916.

BIG STEAMERS, Rudyard Kipling : *Pub*. Teachers' World, June 19, 1918.

IT IS NAE ME, Sally Holmes : *Pub*. Keith Prowse, 1931 ; *Ded*. Miss Joan Elwes ; *1st Perf*. Dumfries, Oct. 1930.

THE RAPID STREAM, Charles Mackay : *Pub*. Keith Prowse, 1931.

WHEN SWALLOWS FLY, Charles Mackay : *Pub*. Keith Prowse, 1931.

THE WOODLAND STREAM, Charles Mackay : *Pub*. Keith Prowse, 1933 ; *Ded*. Stephen S. Moore ; *1st Perf*. Worcester Schools Music Festival, May 18, 1933.

OP. 5, A SOLDIER'S SONG, C. Flavell Hayward : renamed A WAR SONG : *Pub*. Magazine of Music, 1890 ; Boosey, 1903 ; *Ded*. F. G. P[edley], Worcester; *1st Perf*. Worcester, Mar. 17, 1884 ; Albert Hall, Oct. 1, 1903.

OP. 16 (1) SHEPHERD'S SONG, Barry Pain : (Aug. 22, 1892 ; *Pub*. Tuckwood 1895, Ascherberg 1896.

(2) THROUGH THE LONG DAYS, John Hay : (Aug. 31, 1885, at Settle, Yorkshire ; *Pub*. Stanley Lucas Weber 1887, Ascherberg 1890 ; *Ded*. Rev. E. Vine Hall ; *1st Perf*. St. James's Hall, Feb. 25, 1897.

(3) RONDEL, Longfellow from FROISSART : (Jan. 4, 1894) ; *1st Perf*. St. James's Hall, Feb. 25, 1897.

(All in 7 lieder) ; *Pub*. 1907.

OP. 31 (1) AFTER, Philip Bourke Marston : (June 21, 1895) ; *Pub*. Boosey, 1900 ; *1st Perf*. St. James's Hall, Mar. 2, 1900.

(2) A SONG OF FLIGHT, Christina Rossetti : *Pub*. Boosey, 1900 ; *1st Perf*. St. James's Hall, Mar. 2, 1900.

OP. 37, SEA PICTURES : (at Birchwood) : *Pub*. Boosey, 1900 ; *1st Perf*. Norwich Festival, Oct. 5, 1899.

I. Sea Slumber Song, Hon. Roden Noel : (July, 1899).
II. In Haven (Capri), C. Alice Elgar : (May 30, 1897) ; *Pub*. as " Love Alone " in The Dome, Jan. 1, 1898.
III. Sabbath Morning at Sea, Mrs. Browning : (July, 1899).
IV. Where Corals Lie, Richard Garnett : (July, 1899).
V. The Swimmer, Adam Lindsay Gordon : (July, 1899; norch., fin. Aug. 18, 1899).

OP. 41 (1) IN THE DAWN, A. C. Benson : *Pub*. Boosey, 1901 ; *1st Perf*. Queen's Hall, Oct. 26, 1901.

(2) SPEAK, MUSIC, A. C. Benson: *Pub.* Boosey, 1901; *Ded.* Mrs. E. Speyer, Ridgehurst.

OP. 48 (1) PLEADING, Arthur L. Salmon: (orch. Nov. 23, 1908); *Pub.* Novello, 1908; *Ded.* Lady Maud Warrender.

OP. 59 (3) OH! SOFT WAS THE SONG, Gilbert Parker: (Dec. 1909–Jan. 1910); *Pub.* Novello, 1910; *1st Perf.* Jaeger Memorial Concert, Queen's Hall, Jan 24, 1910.

(5) WAS IT SOME GOLDEN STAR, Gilbert Parker: (Dec. 1909–Jan. 1910); *Pub.* Novello, 1910; *1st Perf.* Jaeger Memorial Concert, Queen's Hall, Jan. 24, 1910.

(6) TWILIGHT, Gilbert Parker: (Dec. 1909–Jan. 1910); *Pub.* Novello, 1910; *1st Perf.* Jaeger Memorial Concert, Queen's Hall, Jan. 24, 1910.

OP. 60 (1) THE TORCH, Pietro d'Alba [E. E.]: from Eastern European Folk Song: (fin. Dec. 23, 1909, orch. July 26, 1912); *Pub.* Novello, 1910; *Ded.* Yvonne [1]; *1st Perf.* Hereford Festival, Sept. 11, 1912.

(2) THE RIVER, Pietro d'Alba: from Eastern European Folk Song: (Feb. 18, 1910, orch. July 1912); *Pub.* Novello, 1910; *1st Perf.* Hereford Festival, Sept. 11, 1912.

[1] Probably fictitious.

VI. MISCELLANEOUS

ORCHESTRATION OF EMMAUS, Herbert A. Brewer: *Pub.* Novello, 1901.

EDITION OF ST. MATTHEW PASSION, Bach: with Ivor Atkins: *Pub.* Novello, 1911.

MEMORIAL CHIMES FOR A CARILLON: for opening of Loughborough War Memorial Carillon: July 22, 1923 (MS.).

CIVIC FANFARE: for opening service of Hereford Festival: Sept. 4, 1923; *Ded.* to Percy C. Hull (MS.).

TOCCATA IN D MINOR: for organ (Bach), arr. Esser: additional parts by E. with original ending restored.

VII. LITERARY WORKS

PROGRAMME NOTES FOR WORCESTERSHIRE PHILHARMONIC SOCIETY, 1898–1904.

PREFACE TO THE SINGING OF THE FUTURE, David Ffrangcon-Davies, 1904.

LECTURES AS DELIVERED TO BIRMINGHAM UNIVERSITY, 1905–6. (In typescript at Broadheath).

FALSTAFF : MUSICAL TIMES, Sept. 1913. (Separately published in pamphlet form by Novello).

MY FRIENDS PICTURED WITHIN : Novello [1913].

GRAY, WALPOLE, WEST AND ASHTON—THE QUADRUPLE ALLIANCE : The Times Literary Supplement, Sept. 4, 1919.

NOTATION : Musical Times, 1920.

SCOTT AND SHAKESPEARE : The Times Literary Supplement, July 21, 1921.

FOREWORD TO FORGOTTEN WORCESTER, H. A. Leicester, 1930.

Bibliography

I. MAINLY BIOGRAPHICAL

ELGAR, Ernest Newman (London, 1904).

SIR EDWARD ELGAR, R. J. Buckley (London, 1905).

EDWARD ELGAR, A. J. Sheldon (London, 1932).

ELGAR: HIS LIFE AND WORKS, Basil Maine; 2 vols. (London, 1933).

ELGAR AS I KNEW HIM, W. H. Reed (London, 1936).

ELGAR, Thomas Dunhill (London, 1938).

ELGAR, W. H. Reed (London, 1939).

EDWARD ELGAR: MEMORIES OF A VARIATION, Mrs. Richard Powell (2nd ed.) (London, 1947).

EDWARD ELGAR, *Musical Times*, Oct. 1900.

EDWARD ELGAR'S HOBBIES, *Musical Standard*, Oct. 13, 1900.

DR. EDWARD ELGAR AT MALVERN, *The World*, Dec. 11, 1901.

ELGAR IN LONDON, *Pall Mall Gazette*, March 21, 1904.

DR. ELGAR: an interview by Rupert de Cordova, in *Strand Magazine*, May 1904.

SIR EDWARD ELGAR O.M., *The World*, Oct. 22, 1912.

II. MAINLY CRITICAL AND ANALYTICAL

ANALYTICAL NOTES, pub. by Novello and Co., Ltd.
  (1) *Scenes from the Legend of King Olaf*, Joseph Bennett [1896].
  (2) *Caractacus*, Herbert Thompson [1898].
  (3) *The Dream of Gerontius*, A. J. Jaeger [1900].
  (4) *The Apostles*, A. J. Jaeger [1903].
  (5) *The Kingdom*, A. J. Jaeger [1906].
  (6) *Falstaff*, Edward Elgar; first pub. in *Musical Times*, Sept. 1913.

EDWARD ELGAR (No. 2 in " The New School of British Music ")
Ernest Newman, *The Speaker*, Dec. 22, 1901.

UN MUSICISTA INGLESE, EDWARD ELGAR, R. A. Streatfeild, *Rivista d'Ialia*, Oct. 1912.

SIR EDWARD ELGAR, George Bernard Shaw, *Music and Letters*, Vol i, no. 1, 1920.

ELGAR, W. H. Reed; with additional notes by W. W. Cobbett, in *Cobbett's Cyclopedic Survey of Chamber Music*, 2 vols. (London, 1929).

ELGAR : INSTRUMENTAL WORKS, F. H. Shera (London, 1931).

ELGAR AND HIS MUSIC, J. F. Porte (London, 1933).

EDWARD ELGAR, Irving J. Stone, in *The Musical Record*, Vol. i, no. 4 (Philadelphia, 1933).

THE SIGNIFICANCE OF ELGAR, Everard Jose and Heath Cranston (London, 1934).

ELGAR'S ENIGMA, Richard C. Powell, Music and Letters, Vol. xv, no. 3, 1934.

Articles by Donald Tovey, H. J. Foss, R. Vaughan Williams, A. E. Brent Smith, and F. Howes in *Music and Letters*, Vol. xvi, no. 2, 1935.

ENIGMA VARIATIONS, C. Barber, *Music and Letters*, Vol. xvi, no. 2, 1935.

ELGAR'S THIRD SYMPHONY, W. H. Reed, *The Listener*, August 28, 1935.

ELGAR AND HIS ENIGMA, Ernest Newman, *Sunday Times*, Ap. 16, 23, 30, May 7, 1929.

ELGAR'S " SPANISH LADY," Sir Barry Jackson, *Music and Letters*, Vol. xxiv, no. 1, 1943.

ELGAR'S MUSIC FOR THE " STARLIGHT EXPRESS," A. E. Keeton, *Music and Letters*, Vol. xxvi, no. 1, 1945.

ELGAR, Daniel Gregory Mason, in *Contemporary Composers* (New York, 1918).

ESSAYS IN MUSICAL ANALYSIS, D. F. Tovey, vols. ii, iii, iv, vi (London, 1935–39).

III. GENERAL

CATHEDRAL ORGANISTS, John E. West (rev. ed. London, 1921).

DAVID FFRANGCON-DAVIES : HIS LIFE AND WORK, Marjorie Ffrangcon-Davies (London, 1938).

ECHOES, Compton Mackenzie (London, 1954).

EDWARD SPEYER : MY LIFE AND FRIENDS, with a foreword by H. C. Colles (London, 1937).

FAREWELL MY YOUTH, Arnold Bax (London, 1943).

FIFTY YEARS OF MUSIC IN BIRMINGHAM, 1850–1900, W. C. Stockley (Birmingham, 1913).

FIFTY YEARS OF CHORAL MUSIC : THE CITY OF STOKE-ON-TRENT CHORAL SCOIETY, 1901–1951 (Stoke-on-Trent, 1951).

JUST AS IT HAPPENED, Newman Flower (London, 1950).

MONARCHS AND MILLIONAIRES, Lalla Vandervelde (London, 1925).

MUSIC IN THE FIVE TOWNS, 1840–1914, R. Nettel (London, 1944).

MUSIC AND MUSICIANS, Edward A. Baughan (London, 1906).

MUSIC ON RECORD, Fred. W. Gaisberg (New York, 1943 ; London, 1946).

MY FRIENDS PICTURED WITHIN, Edward Elgar (London [1913]).

MY LIFE OF MUSIC, Henry J. Wood (London, 1938).

NORMAN O'NEILL : A LIFE OF MUSIC, Derek Hudson (London, 1945).

NOTES ON CATHOLIC WORCESTER, H. A. Leicester, K.C.S.G. (Worcester, 1928).

OVERTURE AND BEGINNERS, Eugene Goossens (London, 1951).

POST VICTORIAN MUSIC, C. L. Graves (London, 1911).

QUEEN'S HALL, Robert Elkin (London, 1944).

SAMUEL LANGFORD : MUSICAL CRITICISM, ed. Neville Cardus (London, 1928).

SIXTEEN SYMPHONIES, Bernard Shore (London, 1949).

TEN COMPOSERS, Neville Cardus (London, 1945).

THE FIRST SEVENTY YEARS : HISTORY OF WORCESTER COLLEGE FOR THE BLIND, Mary G. Thomas (London [1937]).

THE THREE CHOIRS FESTIVAL : THE OFFICIAL HISTORY OF THE MEETINGS OF THE THREE CHOIRS OF GLOUCESTER, HEREFORD, AND WORCESTER, c. 1713–1953, Watkins Shaw (Worcester, 1954).

WITH STRINGS ATTACHED, Joseph Szigeti (London, 1949).

SOURCES & ACKNOWLEDGMENTS

The main source for the biographical section of this work is the massive collection of archives preserved at Elgar's Birthplace at Broadheath, Worcester. I have to acknowledge the free access granted to this collection by Mrs. C. Elgar Blake and the Trustees of the Elgar will, who have also put at my disposal many other important documents. Among these are the diaries of Sir Edward and Lady Elgar from 1888 to 1920; the notes compiled by Sir Edward on his Bavarian holiday of 1893, and his Mediterranean cruise of 1905; some 300 letters written by him to A. Troyte Griffith and Leo Frank Schuster; the letter books from 1926 to 1930; the correspondence of Sir Barry Jackson, Canon Gorton, Richter, Bernard Shaw, and Stanford; the MS. notes on his friendship with Elgar compiled by A. Troyte Griffith; and many papers relating to earlier Elgars and Greenings.

A fuller record of documents will be given in the edition of Elgar's letters now in preparation.

Mrs. Elgar Blake has also permitted the long loan of many musical manuscripts of her father; among them are the six " Shed Books " and the ten volumes of sketches, in which are to be found the first drafts of most of his great works.

Mrs. Monica Greenwood submitted a long series of letters from Elgar to her father, Dr. C. W. Buck, as well as other material relative to Elgar's association with Yorkshire; Mr. Alan W. B. Webb letters and postcards to his father, Mr. Frank Webb; Mrs. Helen Walker letters and miscellaneous papers which were formerly the property of her father, Canon Gorton; Miss Herma Fiedler material concerning the Birmingham Professorship, originally in the possession of her father Professor Fiedler, and her grandfather Mr. Charles Harding; Mrs. Cicely Binyon the correspondence between Elgar and the late Mr. Laurence Binyon; Mr. G. Street Chignell a number of letters concerning the Worcestershire Philharmonic Society, and Elgar's early works; Mr. Harold Watkins Shaw, Hon. Librarian of St. Michael's College, Tenbury, the late Dr. G. R. Sinclair's " Visitors' Book," now in the keeping of St. Michael's College; Mr. Florian Williams excerpts from his manuscript *Forty years a music publisher*.

429

By the courtesy of the B.B.C. I have been able to see photo-prints of the third symphony; Mr. Robert Elkin has loaned MSS. scores of the *Starlight Express* and *Fan* ballet music; Miss Kathleen Boland the MSS. of various arrangements by Ernest Austin with annotations by Elgar. I have also consulted the sketches of *The Apostles* and of the projected last oratorio for the trilogy, which are in the British Museum Add. MSS. 47904 and 47905.

I am indebted for other material and information to the Town Clerks of Worcester and Hereford; Mr. T. Pope, Clerk of Powick Hospital, who spent some time guiding me through the Accounts and Minutes books of the Hospital, and also made it possible for me to see the MSS. in the possession of the Hospital; Sir Arthur Bliss, Master of the Queen's Music; Brigadier H. A. F. Crewdson, Clerk of the Worshipful Company of Musicians; Rev. G. R. Tamplin, Vicar of Elmore and Longney, Gloucestershire; Rev. F. B. Honey, of Claines; the Headmaster of the Worcester College for the Blind; Sir R. S. Thatcher, formerly Principal of the Royal Academy of Music; Rev. Father Arthur Kavanagh, S.J., of St. George's Church, Worcester; Mr. Hugh F. Bradburn, especially for his early recollections of Elgar in Worcester and Malvern; Mr. Harold Brooke of Novellos; Mrs. E. Hickman; Mrs. A. M. Hutchison; Mr. Stanley Godman; Mr. J. P. Little; Mr. Hubert Marno; Dr. Herbert Howells; and Mr. Raymond Tobin.

Miss May Grafton, niece of Sir Edward Elgar and one on whose kindness and efficiency he for so long depended, has put at my disposal such relics as are in the possession of her family. She has, additionally, been generous in her response to my requests.

The coat of arms of the City of Worcester is reproduced by permission of the Corporation. For other copyright material quoted I acknowledge the courtesy of the Executors of the estates of T. E. Lawrence, W. B. Yeats, Arnold Bennett, and George Bernard Shaw.

I further wish to acknowledge the courtesy of Elgar's publishers in lending me numerous scores. What I owe to my wife's help only I realise.

If, by inadvertence, there are omissions they are greatly regretted by the author, who is as sensible both of the inconvenience caused to many by the importunity of his requests, and of the general consideration and kindness shown by all those who have helped to swell his files.

GENERAL INDEX